# Stories of the South

# Stories
## of the South

*Race and the Reconstruction of
Southern Identity, 1865–1915*

K. STEPHEN PRINCE

The University of North Carolina Press  *Chapel Hill*

*This book was published with the assistance of the Fred W. Morrison Fund for Southern Studies of the University of North Carolina Press.*

Manufactured in the United States of America
Designed and set in Miller with Serifa display by Rebecca Evans

The paper in this book meets the guidelines for permanence and durability of the Committee on Production Guidelines for Book Longevity of the Council on Library Resources. The University of North Carolina Press has been a member of the Green Press Initiative since 2003.

Library of Congress Cataloging-in-Publication Data
Prince, K. Stephen.
Stories of the South : race and the reconstruction of southern identity, 1865–1915 / K. Stephen Prince.
    pages cm
Includes bibliographical references and index.
ISBN 978-1-4696-1418-2 (hardback)—ISBN 978-1-4696-1419-9 (ebook)
1. Reconstruction (U.S. history, 1865–1877) 2. Southern States—Race relations.
3. Southern States—History—1865–1951. 4. Group identity—Southern States.
5. Southern States—In literature. 6. National characteristics, American. I. Title.
E668.P94 2014
305.800975—dc23   2013038015

18  17  16  15  14   5  4  3  2  1

Portions of this book have been reprinted with permission in revised form from "A Rebel Yell for Yankee Doodle: Selling the New South at the 1881 Atlanta International Cotton Exposition," *Georgia Historical Quarterly* 92, no. 3 (Fall 2008): 340–71, courtesy of the Georgia Historical Society; "Legitimacy and Interventionism: Northern Republicans, the 'Terrible Carpetbagger,' and the Retreat from Reconstruction," *Journal of the Civil War Era* 2, no. 4 (December 2012): 538–63; and "Marse Chan, New Southerner; or, Taking Thomas Nelson Page Seriously," in *Storytelling, History, and the Postmodern South*, edited by Jason Phillips (Baton Rouge: Louisiana State University Press, 2013), 88–104.

FOR JULIA

# Contents

# Illustrations

# Stories of the South

# The Southern Question

This is a book about the reconstruction of southern identity in the five decades after the U.S. Civil War. At its core are the shifting and conflicting answers that Americans—northern and southern, black and white—offered to a single pressing question: *What is the South?* By any measure, the Civil War transformed the South. The war left hundreds of thousands of people dead, destroyed one of the most prolific slave-based agricultural regimes the world has ever known, and smashed the dream of a separate southern nation. In the process, it inaugurated the greatest social revolution in U.S. history, turning 4 million African American slaves into free people. However, the Civil War also had effects that were not quite so tangible. Antebellum notions of southern identity did not survive the nation's great conflagration. In the aftermath of the Civil War, the nature of the South—even its persistence as a culturally distinctive region of the United States—was very much an open issue. The South, as it had been, was no more. The question was what would take its place. Over the next fifty years, in cultural productions ranging from speeches to travel guides to novels to minstrel shows, northerners and southerners reimagined Dixie. Defining the character and identity of the South would be a central concern of the postwar era.

But this is not just a book about southern identity. As it analyzes the competing definitions of the South that vied for cultural predominance between 1865 and 1915, *Stories of the South* offers a new perspective on the rise and fall of racial democracy in the postbellum United States. More precisely, this book seeks to recover and map the intellectual and cultural context in which the era's political decisions were made, in which power was won, lost, and contested. Without appreciating the shifting place of the South in the nation's popular culture, we cannot fully understand the twisted path from Reconstruction to Jim Crow. If cultural productions did not, by themselves, cause the nation's turn from racial egalitarianism, I argue that the political retreat from Reconstruction could not have occurred without a contemporaneous cultural retreat from Reconstruction. This latter process is the focus of this book. The South was not just a place. It was also an idea. Stories of the South—interpretations of the region authored by northerners and southerners of both races and presented to the nation at large—allow us to re-create the imaginative landscape in which the all-too-real retreat from Reconstruction occurred.

"The North may have won the war," historian Samuel Eliot Morison wrote in 1965, "but the white South won the peace."[1] Although Morison's quip has become something of a historical truism, the mechanisms through which the South achieved this latter (and arguably more significant) victory remain imperfectly understood. How did a nation that fought a Civil War, emancipated the slaves, and reconstructed the South turn its back on race relations in the vanquished region so quickly and so completely? *Stories of the South* argues that by examining popular debates over the character of the South in the five decades after the Civil War, we can better make sense of the nation's abandonment of the egalitarian possibilities of Reconstruction. The South, simply put, was not the same place in 1915 as it had been in 1865. If the boundaries of the region had not changed, its place in U.S. culture most certainly had. A deeply troubling cultural distinctiveness had become the source of the South's literary popularity and economic appeal. A chronic inability to accept changes in race relations had been transformed into a widely accepted racial expertise. A dangerous enemy had become a staunch ally. When Americans looked south at the turn of the twentieth century, they saw—or thought they saw—a region transformed.

In making this case, *Stories of the South* mines the popular print culture of the postwar era, finding historical and political significance in texts, events, and conversations not usually privileged in discussions of Reconstruction and its aftermath. Postwar discussion of the South occurred in a cultural sphere that extended far beyond congressional debates and presidential proclamations. In newspapers, journal articles, travel guides, investment catalogs, photographs, cartoons, short stories, novels, plays, poems, songs, memoirs, histories, learned monographs, and lurid exposés, Americans grappled with the character of the South. At spectacular expositions and at the minstrel theater, in churches and at chautauquas, on southern tours and in northern living rooms, they described, discussed, and debated southern affairs. Indeed, references to "the Southern Question" were ever present in the postbellum period. In this crowded analytical marketplace, no single cultural form enjoyed a monopoly. Out of this cacophony of southern stories, Americans struggled to make sense of the region.

At all points, this reformation of southern identity was a national process. The character of the South was not, and could not be, an exclusively southern concern. Northerners played a central role, as both actors and audience. The traditional textbook understanding of the late nineteenth century, which implies an absolute break between Reconstruction (when northerners were deeply engaged with the South) and the Gilded Age (when they ceased paying attention to southern affairs), simply does not hold.[2] The reestablishment of white Democratic rule in the South did not put an end to northern interest in the Southern Question. Yankees kept an eye trained on the region well into the twentieth century. At the same time, black and white southerners were quick to recognize the power of northern popular opinion. Given vast regional disparities in political, economic, and cultural capital, northern consent was a vital prerequisite to control over the South. The close of Reconstruction did not alter this fact. Long after 1877, southerners of both races continued to make overtures to the North. For better or for worse, the South was the nation's problem.

A remarkable variety of storytellers involved themselves in debates over the Southern Question in the fifty years after the Civil War. The characters in this book are largely a self-selected group. They appear here because they consistently, self-consciously, and publicly worked to shape popular understandings of the South. Recognizing the social, economic, and political advantages that came with the ability to define the South, they sought to explain the region to audiences on both sides of the Mason-Dixon line. By definition, therefore, my source base is tilted toward those who had the time, education, and inclination to write themselves into the national debate over the nature of the South. Even so, they form quite a diverse group. My storytellers include not only politicians, reformers, clergy, and novelists but also minstrel performers, pamphleteers, and real estate hucksters. They are northern and southern, black and white, male and female. Some—such as Albion Tourgée, Frederick Douglass, Henry Grady, and Rebecca Latimer Felton—will be familiar to historians of the post–Civil War South. Others will not. What they shared was an understanding that words—stories—had the power to shape the future of the South and the nation.

Which brings us to the question of audience. I argue that postwar southern identity was, in large measure, constructed in the North. Thus, many of the era's most significant treatments of the South were crafted with a northern audience in mind. Of course, this audience was never monolithic. Diverse segments of the northern population engaged with the Southern Question in different ways, in different places, and at different times. Working-class Bostonians attending a minstrel show saw one depiction of the South; patrician New Yorkers reading plantation novels experienced another; Union veterans at a regimental reunion witnessed a third. Class, geography, and political affiliation shaped both the frequency with which northerners considered the South and the cultural forms in which they encountered it. In a larger sense, however, the regularity with which southern affairs appeared in the region's popular print culture made it all but impossible for any Yankee to avoid the South entirely. Anyone who picked up a book, opened a periodical, or attended a public event had a very good chance of running into the Southern Question.

Cultural production is seldom neat and tidy. Competing, even contradictory, depictions of the South could, and did, coexist in popular consciousness. For this reason, I do not posit a direct cause-and-effect relationship between cultural production and the legislative and judicial retreat from Reconstruction. Instead, I have attempted to re-create the intellectual landscape in which these political shifts took place. Admittedly, this was conflicted (and sometimes confusing) territory. Though it is clear that some discussions of the South reached a broader or more receptive audience than others, counternarratives and alternative approaches were always in evidence. Throughout, I have assumed that popular discussions of the Southern Question operated much like an artist's negative space, surrounding the era's more familiar political events and establishing the parameters within which the retreat from Reconstruction occurred. In order to fully understand the era's political developments, we must reconstruct the cultural and intellectual world in which they transpired.

Though I have tried to avoid oversimplification, a larger change-over-time argument structures my analysis. Across the five decades under consideration, a general movement from northern to white southern control of the Southern Question is discernible. In the immediate aftermath of Confederate defeat, northern Republicans assumed the power to redefine the South. Reconstruction was, in part, an attempt to create in the South a society more closely aligned with northern values and expectations. Over time, however, conservative white southerners came to recognize the value of a well-told story. In the years after 1877, the white South began to construct visions of their region expressly for northern consumption. White northerners, for their part, proved increasingly willing to defer to their southern brethren. By the 1890s, when the white South began to consider a Jim Crow solution to its race problem, the very terrain on which North and South met had been forever altered. Despite the best efforts of African American activists and white racial liberals, the early twentieth century saw an almost complete return to a sort of cultural home rule, as southern white supremacists claimed the exclusive right to explain their region to the nation.

Even as I tell this story about "the North" and "the South," I recognize that such regional identifiers are social and cultural constructions, collective fictions that are contrived and relational rather than fixed and absolute.[3] Like the more familiar historical triumvirate of race, class, and gender, regional identities are historically contingent and contextually defined. For this reason, I have taken care to avoid sweeping regional generalizations—the unvariegated "northerners" and "southerners" who populated an earlier generation of historiography.[4] I recognize and foreground the fact that other categories of experience and affiliation always complicated and supplemented regional identities. And yet to Americans who had just lived through the bloody Civil War, sectional identity certainly seemed solid, tangible, and permanent. Northerners and southerners alike were apt to insist on the innate characteristics of the sections and to adopt an intellectual position that amounted to regional determinism. Northerners acted a particular way because they were northern; southerners acted differently because they were southern. To postwar Americans, in other words, regional identities *were real.* As a result, conversations over the nature of the South and the character of its populations were endowed with a deep political significance. Region—like race, class, and gender—was a category of experience and identity that exerted a formative influence on the course of U.S. history.

To be clear: *Stories of the South* does not attempt to present a complete history of Reconstruction and its aftermath. A number of the period's best-known figures, events, and texts are not present in these pages or are mentioned only in passing. Nor does this book offer a wholesale revision of received historiographical wisdom. On the contrary, it builds on a rich historical literature about the retreat from Reconstruction. This book is best understood as an attempt to reshuffle the analytical deck. It is an interpretation of the past, a reconsideration of a familiar historical riddle, an alternative conceptualization of a transformative moment in U.S. history. Taken together, the close readings and historical analysis presented here provide fresh insights into the history of the postwar South and the nation's turn from Reconstruction. By tracing the ways definitions of the South shifted over time, I have re-created the cultural milieu in which postwar Americans flirted with, and ultimately abandoned, the promise of racial democracy. Between 1865 and 1915, northern and southern storytellers reimagined the South. This process—fraught, disputed, and contested—is the subject of this book, its own story of the South.

This book sits at the crossroads of two historiographies. On the one hand, it is indebted to an extensive literature that analyzes the nature of southern identity. On the other, it is tied to an equally well-developed body of scholarship that explores the late nineteenth-century abandonment of racial egalitarianism in the South. Although historians have not effectively tied them together, these two topics have much to say to one another. Almost by definition, works that address the retreat from Reconstruction grapple with the shifting definitions of the South in the national imagination; by the same token, studies of postwar southern identity cannot help but engage with issues of race relations and the relative power of the sections. Conversations over the nature of the South and the future of race relations in the region shared much interpretative ground. By self-consciously tying these two historiographies together, *Stories of the South* aims to shed light on both.

Throughout the twentieth century, the search for the "central theme" of southern history occupied many of the nation's preeminent historians. For Ulrich B. Phillips, the need to maintain white domination was at the heart of southern history and culture. David Potter claimed that a unique "culture of the folk," rooted in a deep and long-lasting connection to the land, set the region apart from the national mainstream. C. Vann Woodward ascribed the South's lingering peculiarities to the region's familiarity with the distinctly un-American experience of defeat. Carl Degler's attempt to rewrite U.S. history with the South at the center—casting it as the "thesis" to the North's "antithesis"—offered a helpful corrective but did little to displace larger notions of southern distinctiveness. Paul Conkin needed only three adjectives to describe the South: hot, humid, and sad.[5] To their credit, few of these historians were willing to cast the South as monolithic or unchanging. Even so, the overriding conviction of southern exceptionalism proved difficult to shake. David Smiley was not speaking in jest when he declared, "In the history of Southern history in America the central theme has been the quest for the central theme."[6]

A more recent generation of scholars has done much to complicate and enrich the study of southern identity. Contemporary scholarship tends to challenge notions of regional distinctiveness and exceptionalism, casting southern identity as a contested and contingent historical development rather than an objective sociological fact. A conscious attempt to treat the construction of southern identity in a national context has been a central concern of recent historical writing.[7] As Laura F. Edwards notes, "what made the South distinctive was always its comparison to somewhere else."[8] Much of the most innovative recent scholarship on southern identity has emphasized the role that nonsoutherners have played in constructing "the South." Susan-Mary Grant, for example, argues that antebellum southern distinctiveness was largely a northern construction, while Rebecca Cawood McIntyre explores the ways nineteenth-century tourism helped to fashion regional identity.[9] Moving into the twentieth century, Natalie J. Ring analyzes a group of reform-oriented individuals and institutions that imagined the South as a national (and international) "problem."[10] With an eye toward popular culture, Karen L. Cox considers depictions of Dixie in music, advertisement, fiction, and film.[11] Literary and media scholars have traversed similar ground. Jennifer Rae Greeson, Leigh Anne Duck, and Tara McPherson each insist on the central role that those outside the South have played in constructing popular ideas about the region.[12] The title of a collection edited by historians Matthew D. Lassiter and Joseph Crespino—*The Myth of Southern Exceptionalism*—nicely sums up the prevailing interpretive mood.[13]

*Stories of the South* takes its inspiration from both the older and newer schools of scholarship on southern identity. In line with more recent trends in the historiography, it views the postwar reconstruction of southern identity as a national affair. Because I argue that the meaning of the South was reconfigured in conversation between the sections, I have limited my focus to those stories of the South that reached an audience on both sides of the Mason-Dixon line. Northerners produced many of the period's most significant explorations of the South, while the political realities of the era meant that southerners consistently sought to shape northern popular opinion with regard to southern affairs. In this context, southern distinctiveness appears less a timeless truth than a product of historically specific political and cultural negotiations. At the same time, however, I believe that older notions of southern identity still have something to tell us. Though it must be recognized as a social construct, the idea of the distinctive South has served as a cornerstone of southern (and American) identity for much of the nation's history.[14] Southern exceptionalism was a lived reality for late nineteenth- and early twentieth-century Americans, with the fact of regional distinctiveness seldom questioned. The distinctive, exceptional South remains a relevant analytical category because it accurately reflects the way Americans, North and South, understood the region in the aftermath of the Civil War.

For all their insights into southern identity and exceptionalism, scholars have been slow to put these debates into conversation with work on the late nineteenth-century retreat from Reconstruction. In recent years, historians have offered a number of explanations for the nation's declining commitment to African American rights in the South after 1877. Charles W. Calhoun's *Conceiving a New Republic* locates the turn in the shifting priorities of the Republican Party.[15] Edward J. Blum's *Reforging the White Republic* argues that after a brief postwar flirtation with racial egalitarianism, northern whites increasingly came to embrace a set of values—specifically whiteness, Protestantism, and American nationalism—that they held in common with white southerners.[16] In *The Death of Reconstruction*, Heather Cox Richardson ties the retreat from racial democracy in the South to the changing relationship between labor and capital in the Gilded Age North.[17] Finally, scholars of Civil War memory have connected southern race relations to shifting understandings of the war and emancipation.[18] To date, however, historians have not explored how the waning of the nation's support for African American civil and political rights coincided with larger debates over the meaning and character of the South. The oversight seems curious. The sheer frequency with which Americans discussed the nature of the South in the postbellum decades presents the historian with an embarrassment of riches. Debate over the Southern Question was unceasing. When viewed over the span of five decades, the shifting answers that Americans offered to the question at the heart of this study—*What is the South?*—provide much needed context for understanding the failed promise of Reconstruction.

*Stories of the South* also advances a corrective to the literature's focus on "reunion" as the proper model for understanding the sectional relationship in the late nineteenth and early twentieth centuries.[19] Almost universally, the process by which northern and southern whites found political and cultural common ground in the aftermath of Reconstruction has been conceptualized in these terms. Though Nina Silber and David W. Blight, among others, have utilized the reunion framework to great effect, the historiography's overreliance on the language of reunion is problematic.[20] The reunion model flattens historical developments, implying that the post-Reconstruction era saw the reconnection of two static, unchanging regions. The contentious and complicated process by which southern identity was reformulated after the Civil War belies such a notion. The North did not find reunion with a fixed and timeless South. There was no such thing. The South was always a moving target. Between Reconstruction and the rise of Jim Crow, the character of the region was a matter of constant debate and discussion. Before reunion could occur, the story of the South needed to be rewritten. By the dawn of the twentieth century, this task was largely complete. The South that sought reintegration into the national mainstream was a distinctly new, postwar creation. In the popular imagination, the region had been transformed. The retreat from Reconstruction, therefore, was not a simple matter of "reunion." Together, turn-of-the-century northerners and southerners created a new South, a new sectional relationship, and a new nation.

*Stories of the South* is rooted in an exhaustive study of the print culture of the late nineteenth- and early twentieth-century United States. In researching this book, I have perused thousands of articles in newspapers and magazines, explored a variety of literary representations of the South, scanned a multitude of broadsides, playbills, small-run pamphlets, and political speeches, and examined scores of travelogues, industrial prospectuses, plays, songsters, poems, and scholarly treatises. I have also worked extensively in the personal papers of a number of historical figures—activists, politicians, boosters, authors, and performers—who loomed particularly large in postwar debates over the nature of the South. Through a selective discussion of historical texts, figures, and events, I have attempted to re-create the literary, cultural, and intellectual world of the postwar Southern Question.

*Stories of the South* is broken into three parts and six chapters. Each chapter can be read as a piece of stand-alone scholarship that introduces key characters and texts in an attempt to illuminate an aspect of the Southern Question. At the same time, a unified interpretative framework and a common set of questions tie the book together. Part 1, "Reconstruction, 1865–1880," reframes the early postwar period as an extended conversation over the nature of the South. Social and political methodologies still predominate in the historiography of Reconstruction, and with good reason.

The drama of emancipation and the electoral turmoil of the period justly reward these types of research. A cultural and intellectual approach to Reconstruction, however, helps to illuminate all that was at stake in the decade and a half after Appomattox. Chapter 1, "Imagining the South," describes the optimism with which the northern public treated the opening years of Reconstruction. Northerners had long dreamed of a South that more closely resembled their own society. In the wake of the war, they had a chance to make that dream a reality. Reconstruction, commentators insisted, must produce a northernized South. As Reconstruction dragged into the 1870s, however, many began to wonder what had gone wrong. This darkening outlook is the subject of chapter 2, "Of Carpetbags and Klans." The bloody Ku Klux Klan and the corrupt carpetbagger are two of the most familiar and lasting symbols of the Reconstruction period. This chapter uses the national conversation surrounding these two figures to track the turn from Reconstruction. Between 1868 and 1880, these symbols served as stand-ins in a larger debate over Reconstruction and its shortcomings. As imagined in popular culture, the Ku Klux Klan bespoke a murderous deviance at the heart of white southern society; the carpetbagger, meanwhile, came to stand for dangerous and improper northern involvement in the South. The growing consensus that the carpetbagger, not the Klansman, should be the primary object of public scorn (a conclusion, significantly, that extended to northern Republican and African American circles) echoed the nation's increasing discomfort with an interventionist Reconstruction.

Part 2, "Construction, 1880–1895," is made up of three chapters that collectively form the analytical heart of the book. Often treated as a political interregnum, the years between the close of Reconstruction and the onset of Jim Crow represent a crucial moment in the evolution of the sectional relationship. In these years, conservative southern whites increasingly asserted control over the Southern Question. As they did, they fundamentally altered the nature of the debate. Chapters 3, 4, and 5 explore three different arenas in which the character of the South was discussed and reformulated between 1880 and 1895: New South boosterism, plantation fiction, and southern-themed performance culture.

Chapter 3, "New South, New North," offers a fresh take on the New South program of the 1880s and 1890s. Led by Henry W. Grady, New South boosters perfected a language of capitalist growth and economic development, trumpeting a complete revolution in southern sentiment and finding a highly receptive audience north of the Mason-Dixon line. As they promised northerners tidy profits, however, New South spokesmen made it known that northern involvement in southern racial practices would no longer be tolerated. Chapter 4, "The Pen and the Sword," analyzes the wave of southern literature that swept the nation in the 1880s and 1890s. In their romantic portraits of dashing cavaliers and faithful slaves, southern authors such as Thomas Nelson Page and Joel Chandler Harris performed important cultural work, insisting on the exclusive right of white southerners to tell the South's story to the nation. Despite the protests of southern dissidents George Washington Cable and Charles W. Chesnutt, enraptured northern readers willingly ceded narrative control in exchange for a continued dose of "moonlight and magnolias." Chapter 5, "Performing Race, Staging Slavery" turns to the concert halls and minstrel theaters of the North to analyze depictions of the South in Gilded Age performance culture. The period's popular theater specialized in outmoded and wholly unrealistic depictions of the antebellum plantation. Though groups such as the Fisk Jubilee Singers attempted to offer a more authentic vision of the southern African American experience, the buffoonery and spectacle of late nineteenth-century minstrelsy idealized slavery and naturalized white supremacy.

Part 3, "Destruction, 1890–1915," is made up of a single chapter and an epilogue. Chapter 6, "Jim Crow Nation," uses political, literary, and scientific writings on the "Negro Problem" to explore the place of the South in the national imagination at the turn of the twentieth century. In particular, it highlights the remarkable transparency with which the structures of segregation and disfranchisement were put in place. The systematic destruction of African American rights occurred in full view of the nation. In the face of mounting racial violence and political manipulation, African American activists struggled against conservative white southerners for the hearts and minds of the white northern mainstream. In the end, a string of white supremacist stories—including D. W. Griffith's 1915 film *The Birth of a Nation*, the subject of the book's epilogue—proved too compelling for northern audiences to resist. Jim Crow may have been born in the South, but the nation watched at every step. As southern African Americans struggled against a concerted campaign of terrorism and political oppression, northern whites looked on with equanimity. If we are to fully understand this willful inaction—the culmination of the nation's fifty-year retreat from racial democracy—we must listen to the stories that Americans told about the South.

# PART I

# Reconstruction, 1865–1880

# CHAPTER ONE

# Imagining the South

When the leaders of the Confederate government fled Richmond in early April 1865, Alexander Gardner packed his cameras and headed south. The Scottish-born Gardner had arrived in New York City in the late 1850s, becoming a protégé and associate of the legendary photographer Mathew Brady. Gardner worked with Brady through the first years of the war before establishing his own studio in Washington, DC, in 1863. When Richmond fell, Gardner rushed to the Confederate capital, eager to provide an inside view of the city that was, according to a contemporary journalist, "the epitome of the whole contest" and yet still "a mystery" to northerners.[1] In all, Gardner would take more than fifty photographs in Richmond. Though he shot a number of notable landmarks, including the capitol building and the notorious Libby Prison, Gardner's most lasting images were the ones he took in the city's warehouse district. Retreating Confederates had torched a number of buildings as they left the city on the night of April 2, and the fire quickly spread. By the time Union troops were able to control the blaze the next morning, a quarter-mile stretch along the James River lay in ruin. The area was quickly dubbed "the Burnt District."[2]

Gardner's images of the Burnt District provide a stunning catalog of the effects of war. They depict a barren, almost alien landscape. Hulking skeletons of once proud buildings loom over ash-lined streets. Empty windows stare blindly on massive piles of rubble. A haphazard assortment of chimneys and wall fragments point skyward. One shell of a building is almost indistinguishable from the next, denying the viewer any sense of their shape or function before the fire. Human ingenuity and engineering seem no match for the ravages of fire and war. Few of Gardner's pictures of the Burnt District contain people. Those who do appear merely emphasize the otherworldly desolation of their surroundings. More than anything

The "Burnt District" in Richmond, Virginia, photographed by Alexander Gardner (1865). Library of Congress.

else, the Burnt District resembled an ancient ruin, a scene almost regal in its absolute desolation.[3]

It was not just Richmond. A couple of months earlier, George Barnard, a contemporary of Gardner's traveling with the army of General William Tecumseh Sherman, took a similar series of photographs some 400 miles to the south. In South Carolina, Barnard found destruction and disarray that surpassed even the wreck of Richmond's Burnt District. In Columbia, the state capital, he took a number of photographs that captured the results of a fire that had destroyed much of the city. A view from the second floor of the South Carolina capitol building offers an awesome vista of devastation and destruction. A central road runs to the distant horizon, with stark reminders of the conflagration that destroyed Columbia written on every scorched tree, empty block, and dilapidated building. In Charleston, which northern journalist Sidney Andrews would describe as a "city of ruins, of desolation, of vacant houses, of widowed women, of rotting wharves,

Ruins in Columbia, South Carolina, photographed by George Barnard (1865).
Library of Congress.

of deserted warehouses, of weed-wild gardens, of miles of grass-grown
streets, of acres of pitiful and voiceful barrenness," Barnard found more
of the same.[4] Here, Barnard photographed the shell of the rail depot, the
blasted facade of the Pinckney mansion, and what remained of Secession
Hall and Fort Sumter. Barnard's pictures of Charleston read like a morality
tale. The seedbed of southern extremism, the cultural and political center
of the Old South, had been reduced to rubble. Where there had once been
a thriving city, Barnard's camera now found emptiness.[5]

In photographic views of southern desolation and nothingness, the
nation caught a glimpse of the challenge—and opportunity—of Reconstruction. These photographs bespoke a single, hard truth: the South, as
it had been, was dead. What remained was a ruin, an empty shell. Most
Yankees had little trouble defining the South as it had been before the war:
backward, barbaric, traitorous, dominated by a slaveholding aristocracy
and peopled by a degraded majority.[6] The war, however, had done away
with this South as surely as it had done away with Richmond's warehouse
district. Lordly plantation owners now presided over empty mansions
and emptier fields. Southern fire-eaters had been forced to eat their own
words while the southern majority struggled to find anything to eat at all.

War damage in Charleston, South Carolina, photographed by
George Barnard (1865). Library of Congress.

Haughty southern belles heaped their scorn on Yankee soldiers, but they
did so while wearing tattered dresses and coarse homespun. Most significant of all, the overthrow of slavery removed the economic, political, and
social backbone of antebellum southern life and transformed 4 million
slaves into 4 million freedpeople. All of this was captured in photographic
images of the desolate South. The South, as Americans had long understood it, was no more. The question was what would take its place.

Having won the war, saved the Union, and ended slavery, members of
the northern Republican majority now took it upon themselves to re-create
the South. Throughout 1865 and 1866, as President Andrew Johnson battled with congressional Radicals and southerners of both races attempted
to reestablish their lives in the aftermath of slavery, northern writers and
thinkers took part in a different sort of Reconstruction. As soon as the guns
of battle stilled, Yankees looked to the South. They pondered the region's

past, analyzed its present, and planned its future. This cultural and intellectual work was at the core of the Reconstruction process. Reconstruction would realign the South's political structures, rebuild its economic base, and recalibrate the region's social order, but this was only a start. The South—defined as a place—would be Reconstructed, but so would the South *as an idea*. Reconstruction was never an exclusively political affair. At its heart lay a single burning question: *What is the South?* In winning the war, northerners claimed the right to formulate an answer. They would rewrite the story of the South.

The first years of Reconstruction provide a unique platform from which to reconsider the meaning and possibilities of the era. What is most striking is the sense of optimism with which northern Republicans approached the rebuilding of the South. Victory in a long and bloody war seemed to prove the righteousness of the northern cause. At the same time, the relative impotence of northern Democratic opposition in the immediate postwar years created an artificial, if fleeting, sense of cohesion and entitlement.[7] For a brief moment, northerners imagined that they could re-create the South. The region had long been a problem in American life. Reconstruction would provide a solution. The results would be breathtaking. Events, of course, proved much of this optimism misplaced. Internal division, a half-hearted commitment to racial egalitarianism, and concerted opposition from southern white supremacists combined to make a mockery of northern Republican dreams. In 1865 and 1866, however, anything seemed possible.

## The South as It Is

In July 1865, a Canadian-born, Massachusetts-raised Harvard graduate named John Dennett boarded the steamer *Creole*, bound for Richmond, Virginia. Dennett headed south at the behest of *The Nation*, a newly founded newsmagazine, whose editors sought "trustworthy information as to the condition and prospects of the Southern States" in the immediate postwar period.[8] During his eight months in Dixie, Dennett journeyed through Virginia, the Carolinas, Georgia, Alabama, Mississippi, and Louisiana. He traveled by boat, train, horse, and foot, visiting cities, backwoods farms, battlefields, and freedpeople's schools. Along the way, Dennett interviewed anyone he happened to stumble on: unrepentant rebels, emancipated slaves, backcountry Unionists, transplanted Yankees. Serving as the eyes and ears for a northern population desperate for reliable information on the South, Dennett intended to provide an unbiased, unvarnished vision of "The South as It Is"—the title of his column in *The Nation*.

John Dennett was not alone. Northern travel writers and correspondents descended on the South in droves in 1865 and 1866. Dennett's columns vied with Sidney Andrews's dispatches to the *Boston Daily Advertiser* and the *Chicago Tribune*. Whitelaw Reid of the *Cincinnati Gazette*, novelist John Trowbridge, and essayist Gail Hamilton produced book-length travelogues following extended southern tours. Carl Schurz, a German expatriate reformer and major-general in the Union army, spent three months in the South, sending a series of letters to the *Boston Daily Advertiser* and an official report to the U.S. Congress. Benjamin Truman, a journalist and long-time associate of President Andrew Johnson, used his post as *New York Times* correspondent to promote the policies of his friend and benefactor. Both before and after the surrender at Appomattox, Henry McNeal Turner, chaplain for a regiment of the United States Colored Troops, sent dispatches to the *Christian Recorder*, an African American newspaper based in Philadelphia. Armed with their notebooks and pencils, these travel writers were Reconstruction's advance guard, charged with collecting and disseminating data on the state of the defeated region.

Once in the South, travel writers investigated widely and wrote voluminously. Travelers took note of the South's peculiar plant life, describing the sight of a cotton field at harvest time or a grove of live oaks draped in Spanish moss. They complained about the region's war-ravaged railroad system and subpar hotel accommodations. They noted, with a mixture of pride and regret, the effects that Yankee shells had had on southern cities like Charleston and Vicksburg. They also addressed less tangible issues: parsing the difference between Unionism in North and South Carolina, commenting on the bitter rebelliousness of many southern women, offering damning indictments of the ignorance and immorality of southern poor whites, and describing the African American transition from slavery to freedom. Most of all, they worked to capture the region's state of mind in the immediate postwar period, to determine its attitude toward Reconstruction, and to begin to imagine its place in a reunited nation.

In all of this, the travelers claimed a posture of strict objectivity. *The Nation* assured its readers that John Dennett would maintain total impartiality, "simply reporting what he sees and hears, leaving the public as far as possible to draw its own inferences."[9] New Englander John Trowbridge insisted that his massive *The South: A Tour of Its Battlefields and Ruined Cities* was a "record of actual observations and conversations, free from fictitious coloring." Trowbridge claimed to offer "plain facts" without "any political or sectional bias."[10] Carl Schurz prefaced his report to Congress with a promise that he headed south with an entirely open mind and no political agenda. "I would not have accepted the mission," Schurz wrote, "had I not felt that whatever preconceived opinions I might carry with me to the south, I should be ready to abandon or modify, as my perception of facts and circumstances might command their abandonment or modification."[11] These southern tours were to be simple fact-finding endeavors. The nation did not need theories about the South, it needed solid information: the South as it is.

Once on the ground, however, this posture of objectivity proved impossible to maintain. With the exception of Henry McNeal Turner (born and raised in the South, but serving in the Union army) and Carl Schurz (who had moved to the United States following Germany's 1848 revolution), the travel writers were all of northern extraction. In addition, the presumed audience for their writing was located entirely above the Mason-Dixon line. By definition, therefore, postwar travel writing was largely a genre *by* northerners and *for* northerners. By 1865, Yankees had amassed a voluminous and often contradictory literature devoted to the nature of the South and its place in the nation. If antebellum northerners could never agree on the precise nature of the South, there was, by the late antebellum period, little argument regarding the overarching, ever present fact of southern distinctiveness. As postwar travel writers headed south, they carried this cultural and intellectual baggage with them. Promises of objectivity notwithstanding, the travelers' depictions of the South always reflected northern presuppositions and prejudices.

But there was an even more fundamental issue. In the wake of a war that destroyed southern identity as thoroughly as it devastated the region's fields and cities, travel writers would not—could not—find the true nature of the South written on the faces of Confederate soldiers or etched into the houses of New Orleans. They would not discover it on the back roads of Virginia or scattered in the scorched remains of Columbia, South Carolina. The questions that most interested travel writers and their northern readers—questions of attitude, emotion, and worldview—were largely invisible to the naked eye. Try as they might to cast their project as one of simple research and discovery, postwar travel writers were actually engaged in a process of creation. The travelers' words did not reflect a preexistent reality; they helped to shape that reality, to create the "South" of the postwar world. Travel writers were not simply reporting. They were establishing a new language and a new set of expectations with which to engage the South. Collectively, the travel writers drafted a new story of the region. This cultural work served as an important precondition to the political work of Reconstruction.

Travel writing, needless to say, begins with travel. Northerners used to the comforts and conveniences of their own region were ill prepared for the rigors and aggravations of life in the war-torn South, and the travel writers freely expressed their displeasure with the region's transportation infrastructure. Once Whitelaw Reid left the confines of the *Northerner*, the aptly named steamer that carried him to Virginia, he was subjected to a variety of nightmarish conveyances. Seats and windows seemed a luxury that southern railroads could no longer afford. The same might be said of speed and efficiency: Reid calculated that his train from Lynchburg, Virginia, to the Tennessee border averaged a speed of "a trifle over nine miles an hour."[12] Gail Hamilton commented that a southbound train from Louisville looked "suspiciously like the cast-off clothing of some Northern railway," while John Dennett complained of a "dirty and exceedingly uncomfortable" train that traveled no faster than a person might walk.[13] The alternatives were little better. Sidney Andrews rode on the roof of a carriage near Sparta, Georgia, an experience that he would have considered pleasant, were it not for the constant fear of decapitation by low-hanging branches.[14] Such experiences prompted Andrews to offer his readers a warning regarding the travails of southern travel: "Let no man come into the Carolinas this fall or winter for a so-called pleasure-trip. . . . I have travelled over most of the stage and railway routes in the two states; and I assure you that, though I may have found some profit, I have not found very much pleasure."[15]

Finding suitable lodging proved equally challenging. *New York Times* correspondent Benjamin Truman fumed at the state of hotels in Atlanta. "Those things that are running under the name of hotels at present are most abominable," he wrote. "Only think of paying $4 for a piece of jerked beef three times a day, and then [being] huddled into a dirty room with half a dozen men, one wash-bowl, and no towel."[16] After a night spent at the Snagsby House in Meridian, Mississippi, Whitelaw Reid felt comfortable recommending any of the town's *other* hotels to subsequent visitors, reasoning that "they cannot fare any worse" than he had.[17] Though all travelers dealt with problematic accommodations, none seemed to take it as personally as Sidney Andrews. Andrews devoted the better part of a

Frontispiece of John Trowbridge's travelogue, *The South: A Tour of Its Battlefields and Ruined Cities* (1866). The image depicts a tropical and exotic South. Library of Congress.

September 1865 column to the indignities he suffered during a short stay at the only hotel in Orangeburg, South Carolina. His room was dirty and barely furnished. What it lacked in creature comforts, however, it more than made up for in creatures. Andrews was forced to share the space with spiders, bed bugs, "several very social and handsome mice, and a healthy and lively swarm of uncommonly large mosquitoes."[18] The food was even worse. "The table is wretched," Andrews wrote. "The tea, eggs, and waffles are the only articles even passably good. Bread and biscuits are alike sour and leaden, and all the meats are swimming in strong fat."[19]

More significant was what the travelers found when they left their hotels. The vista that Whitelaw Reid encountered in northern Florida offered him ample proof that he was no longer in Ohio. "Beneath the few spreading live-oaks, were superb oleanders, as large as Northern apple-trees, and in full bloom," Reid wrote. Reid also saw palmetto, cactus, and "a score of Southern flowering shrubs, to which our Northern amateur florists could give no names."[20] John Trowbridge offered a similarly enraptured description of the plant life in and around Savannah's Bonaventure cemetery:

"Whichever way you look, colonnades of huge live-oak trunks open before you, solemn, still, and hoary. The great limbs meeting above are draped and festooned with long fine moss. Over all is a thick canopy of living green, shutting out the glare of day."[21] On paper, such descriptions merely reflected the natural environment as northern travelers found it. In practice, however, they subtly distanced northern readers from the South, making it appear both alluring and alien.[22] The frontispiece of Trowbridge's travelogue depicted the author conducting an interview while seated under a palmetto tree, in the midst of a cotton field worked by black field hands. As a visual introduction to Trowbridge's text, the frontispiece reinforced the notion of regional difference that underlay postwar travel writing. Relying on a number of familiar visual cues (tropical plants, cotton, black laborers) the image immediately established the divide between North and South. The specific location depicted remained a mystery, though this did not seem to matter. The image presented a generic, but undeniably exotic, South.

While descriptions of the South's natural environment invoked distance but not necessarily inferiority, discussions of the region's built environment tended to be more pointedly negative. Travel writers found southern architecture to be singularly disappointing. From the humblest shack to the loftiest mansion, southern structures failed to stack up to their northern counterparts. In Meridian, Mississippi, Whitelaw Reid noted that the town's residences seemed equally divided between "disconsolate looking negro huts" and "shabby" white residences that were equally disconsolate, if a bit larger.[23] The region's showier buildings also came in for their share of criticism. Carl Schurz arrived in Beaufort, South Carolina, eager to see the "elegant mansions" about which he had heard so much. Instead, he found a conglomeration of "clumsy, sober-looking, square structures, with nothing of that ornamental elegance which we are accustomed to find in the country houses of the North."[24] Travelers found the South's towns and cities to be equally unimpressive. "Savannah, Charleston, Wilmington, Richmond, have always seemed important names," Whitelaw Reid wrote. "While never unconscious that none of them were New York, or Boston, or even Baltimore," northerners had "always associated with them the idea of large population, fine architecture and general metropolitan appearance." The briefest stay in the South would disabuse any visitor of such notions. Reid found Savannah, the self-appointed "metropolis of the South Atlantic Coast" to be a "scattered, tolerably well-built town" and little more. He even managed to raise the ire of a local shopkeeper when he noted that Savannah was roughly the same size as Lynn, Massachusetts.[25]

More generally, travelers marveled at how much of the South remained unimproved and unoccupied. While on a train in South Carolina, Sidney Andrews saw little sign of "either work or existence" beyond Charleston. He passed only two towns in a seventy-seven-mile journey, "and even these," he scoffed, "are small and unimportant places."[26] In Virginia, John Trowbridge found the same "desolate scenes" everywhere: "old fields and undergrowths, with signs of human life so feeble and so few, that one began to wonder where the country population of the Old Dominion was to be found." Trowbridge marveled that "large and fertile Virginia, with eight times the area of Massachusetts, scarcely equals in population that barren little State."[27] Near Lynchburg, Virginia, John Dennett spent the better part of a week on horseback looking for—and failing to find—signs of human civilization.[28] Despite the South's natural wonder and agricultural bounty, the region remained woefully underdeveloped. Northerners, such commentary suggested, would have used nature's gifts more wisely.

Of greater significance than the surface appearance of things was the character of the South's people. A central component of the travel writers' work was an attempt to categorize and classify the populations of the South, a process that might best be described as a sociological mapping of Dixie. Travelers probed and labeled the South's constituent parts, flattening complexities and systematically turning real people into stock characters. Such categorization allowed northern writers to render the South understandable to themselves and to their readership, making this intellectual work an important first step toward the reconstruction of the South. The collection of knowledge by observation, classification, and differentiation was a prerequisite to reforming the region.[29]

The feelings of the white South toward the North and the federal government were matters of great interest in the immediate postwar period. Had the war exhausted the South's spirit of rebellion, or did hatred still smolder in southern hearts and minds? Though specifics varied from state to state and from correspondent to correspondent, the postwar travel writers agreed on a few points. They insisted, first of all, that the white South had largely given up the dream of separate nationhood and had come to regard secession as a mistake. As Sidney Andrews put it, "They want peace and quiet, and seem not badly disposed toward the general government." Individuals might "rant and rave and feed on fire," but "another war is a thing beyond the possibilities of time."[30] Travel writers were quick to note, however, that an abdication of open warfare did not mean that southern whites had abandoned the ideas that led to secession in the first place. "They are all Rebels here, — all Rebels," a northern man living in Virginia told John Trowbridge. "We have for breakfast salt-fish, fried potatoes, and treason. Fried potatoes, treason, and salt-fish for dinner. At supper the fare is slightly varied, and we have treason, salt-fish, fried potatoes, and a little more treason."[31] Benjamin Truman noted that the whites of southern Alabama were loyal, "if loyalty means a perfect willingness to submit to the decree of the sword." "But," he quickly added, "patriotic they are not."[32]

The true keepers of rebel sentiment in the South, travelers declared, were the region's white women. White southern women quickly developed a reputation for their fury, their unswerving faith in the Confederacy, and the lengths to which they would go to avoid walking under a U.S. flag or making physical contact with a Union soldier.[33] Carl Schurz saw a soldier scolded for attempting to pass a dish of pickles to a southern woman, while Sidney Andrews was reproached for attempting to start a conversation on a train.[34] As Whitelaw Reid put it: "The men of North Carolina may be subjugated, but who will subjugate the women?"[35] Henry McNeal Turner, chaplain for a black Union regiment stationed in North Carolina, took special delight in lampooning southern womanhood. In Smithville, Turner reported, rebel women hung some of the "ugliest faces" he had ever seen out of their windows for the sole purpose of turning away in disgust when a northern soldier approached. Turner claimed to have narrowly escaped serious injury when a woman with a bitter countenance and an extraordinarily long nose wheeled around right in front of him.[36] A few months later, the chaplain mischievously noted that the women of Goldsboro, North Carolina, were extraordinarily slow to avert their eyes when Union troops got undressed in order to cross a river. "I was much amused to see the secesh women watching with the utmost intensity, thousands of our soldiers, in a state of nudity," Turner reported. "I suppose they desired to see whether these audacious Yankees were really men, made like other men."[37]

Travelers frequently turned their attention to a class of people they collectively denominated "poor whites," a population whose material, mental, and moral condition prompted much criticism and more than a little ridicule. In Spotsylvania, Virginia, John Trowbridge encountered a teenager named Richard H. Hicks ("H stands for Hicks: Richard H. Hicks; dat's what dey tell me"). Trowbridge quizzed the illiterate Virginian on issues of high culture, asking him if he had ever heard of Sir Walter Scott, Long-fellow, or Lord Byron. In each case, Hicks "never knowed dar was such a man." Trowbridge marveled at his companion's ignorance: "What a gulf betwixt his mind and mine! Sitting side by side there, we were yet as far apart as the great globe's poles."[38] Gail Hamilton was both moved and repulsed by the conditions in which Tennessee's rural whites lived their lives. She found poor whites to be downright "pitiable," possessing "a gray, earthy look, as if the Lord God had formed them of the dust of the ground" but had neglected to add the "breath of life." Hamilton went so far as to declare this class "dirty white"—as much a comment on their uncertain racial status as their bathing habits.[39] The South's poor whites were cast as an exotic population, a debauched and debased white peasantry without a northern counterpart. As Whitelaw Reid put it: "For dirt, and for utter ignorance of all the decencies of civilized life, no people in America, of any color, can compare with them."[40]

Northern travel writers naturally spent a great deal of their time discussing the South's newly emancipated African American population. Postwar travel writing tended to take a bifurcated approach to the freed-people. On the one hand, white northerners were deeply influenced by mid-nineteenth-century racial ideology, and carried a set of racialized expectations that would not have been out of place in the minstrel theater. Travel writers universally quoted black speakers in thick dialect. One of the first black men Sidney Andrews encountered was a porter who called out, "Luf dis yer nig tote yer plun'er, Mass'r."[41] Even when relating more signifi-cant conversations, travel writers relied on a patronizing representation of black patterns of speech. Whitelaw Reid's use of dialect subtly infantilized a Charleston black man who made an important point on the economics of Reconstruction: "Gib us our own land and we take care ourselves; but widout land, de ole massas can hire us or starve us, as dey please."[42] Reid's description of a classroom full of black children was similarly rife with con-temporary racial presumptions. Even as he complimented the freedpeople for their eagerness to learn, Reid noted that "such masses of little wooly heads, such rows of shining ivories, and flat noses and blubber lips, I had never seen collected before."[43] Such language established a particular set of expectations of southern African Americans. When filtered through prevailing racial orthodoxy and rendered in demeaning dialect, black de-mands for land or education were rendered frivolous and vaguely comical. Even Henry McNeal Turner, a black southerner writing for a northern African American newspaper, subtly distanced himself and his readership from the mass of southern black people when he noted the "rhapsodical paroxysms" and "heaving genuflections" with which North Carolina freedpeople greeted both political speeches and religious sermons.[44]

On the other hand, beyond the dialect and the echoes of minstrelsy, northerners recognized the South's black population as an important ally in the Reconstruction process. Carl Schurz told Congress that "in all questions concerning the Union, the national debt, and the future social organization of the south, the feelings of the colored man are naturally in sympathy with the views and aims of the national government."[45] Travelers also found the freedpeople to be singularly free of the vices that they saw as endemic to southern civilization. In the midst of a conversation obsessed with white southern discontent, malaise, filth, and disorder, the travelers' depictions of black homes and neighborhoods stand out. John Trowbridge described Hampton, Virginia, as a "thrifty village, occupied chiefly by freedmen." Trowbridge found "an air of neatness and comfort" in the black homes, with "no idleness anywhere."[46] Gail Hamilton spent an afternoon at the home of a black Union veteran and his wife. Though the structure was small, it was "whitewashed and well kept." The yard was "clean-swept," with a portion devoted to a garden; the house's interior was "the perfection of neatness."[47] As they emphasized the thrift, cleanliness, intelligence, self-sufficiency, and industry of southern African Americans, travel writers relied on an implied comparison with southern whites. Rather than cultivating grudges and demanding government handouts, the freedpeople were well on their way to making a life in freedom.

In these discussions, the question of labor was never far from travelers' minds. As landowners and laborers attempted to adjust to the new order of things in a postslavery South, northern travelers provided a running commentary.[48] For their part, southern whites seemed to speak with one voice regarding the potential of African Americans as free laborers. "In at least nineteen cases of twenty," Carl Schurz wrote in his congressional report, southern whites believed that "you cannot make the negro work, without physical compulsion." Schurz continued: "I heard this hundreds of times, heard it wherever I went, heard it in nearly the same words from so many different persons, that at last I came to the conclusion that this is the prevailing sentiment among the southern people."[49] Other travelers affirmed the truth of Schurz's statement. A white Georgian told Whitelaw Reid that "there was no use talking about it, the niggers wouldn't work unless you had the power to compel them to it."[50] A South Carolinian was "good enough" to school Sidney Andrews on race relations in the South: "You Northern people are utterly mistaken in supposing anything can be done with these negroes in a free condition. They can't be governed except with the whip."[51]

Northern travelers offered another explanation. The problem, they concluded, was not the South's black population but its white population. John Trowbridge reported that "it seemed impossible for the people of Mississippi—and the same may be said of the Southern people generally—to understand the first principle of the free-labor system." White southerners "could not conceive of a man devoting himself voluntarily to hard manual toil, such as they had never seen performed except under the lash."[52] John Dennett met a Mississippi planter who was unclear what type of "compulsion" he was supposed to use to make his black laborers work, now that he was denied the whip. When asked whether "all Negro labor must be compulsory," the planter responded abruptly: "Why, of course it must."[53] Another planter, this one a Virginian, complained to Dennett that he was having a hard time keeping black laborers on his plantation. When pressed, the planter admitted that he refused, on principle, to pay his employees anything for their work. "Having tried the new labor system, with the essential feature of it left out," Dennett wrote, he "finds it a failure."[54] Such evidence did not bode well for the future of free labor in the South. African Americans seemed to take naturally to the free labor system, but northern travelers expressed significant doubts regarding the willingness—even the capability—of southern whites to adapt. "The real question," Sidney Andrews concluded, "is not 'What shall be done with the negro?,' but 'What shall be done with the white?'"[55]

After writing his last southern communication from Mississippi, John Dennett turned north, heading back to Boston. While traveling by train through Connecticut, he gazed out his window and "contrasted the pretty villages and busy, prosperous towns which we were passing, the trim fences, the neat dwellings, the frequent school-houses and churches, the carefully cultivated farms, and all the other evidences of intelligence and industrious thrift," with what he had seen in the South: a "dreary region," "thinly peopled, full of uncleared forests and undrained swamps and sandy levels, the wretched railways and worse roads, the slovenly plantations with their mean houses, the hovels of the laborers with their degraded population, and the disorderly towns."[56] Though the effects of road-weariness should not be discounted, Dennett's comparison of the prosperous and intelligent North with the unkempt and backward South offers an important clue to the sectional assumptions at work in postwar travel writing.

Though they were ostensibly writing about the South, travel writers could not help but do so largely with reference to the North. John Trowbridge reminded himself and his readers that, for the sake of objectivity and fairness, "one must forget the thriving and energetic North when he enters a country stamped with the dark seal of slavery."[57] This advice, however, was often troublesome in practice. Travel writers proved incapable of taking the South on its own merits. Instead, their approach to the region was always comparative. The North was a constant presence, the figure hanging over all discussions of Reconstruction and the South. When the travel writers discussed southern architecture, or transportation, or agricultural practices, the North was the inevitable point of comparison. The same went for the individual southerners they encountered. Rebels, Unionists, poor whites, and freedpeople alike were held up to a northern standard and, in most cases, found wanting.

As a genre, then, the postwar travel narratives assumed and reinforced notions of fundamental and inalienable difference between North and South. If the North was orderly, industrious, and dynamic, the South must be untidy, lazy, and static. Since the South was violent, ignorant, and backward, it stood to reason that the North represented enlightenment, education, and progress. An idealized North was the ever present point of comparison, the standard against which the South was judged. For northern travel writers, the postwar South was always defined as much by what it was *not*—northern—as by what it *was*. This arrangement, needless to say, sent a powerful message about Reconstruction. In the space between the South they found and the North they idealized, travel writers discerned a path for change in the region.

### Yankeefying Dixie

While postwar travel writers set out to capture "The South as It Is," a much larger body of northern orators, authors, and journalists were engaged in a related project, imagining and describing the contours of the future South—the South as it would be. As northern Republicans began to pivot from war to Reconstruction in the first months of 1865, they faced a political crisis of startling magnitude. How should the nation reintegrate a section of the country that had seceded and made war on the remainder?

The revolution of emancipation raised challenges no less daunting, including the transition to free labor, the protection of African American civil rights, and the cultivation of a biracial political sphere in the South. Beyond these specific policy issues, however, a larger cultural and intellectual problem loomed. The war had destroyed the South. Reconstruction must build it anew, and northerners would lead the way. But what would the reconstructed South look like? What would "the South" mean in a postwar world? Before they could build a new South, northerners needed to imagine it.

More often than not, the future South that they envisioned bore a striking resemblance to their home region. Yankeefication—the conviction that a successful Reconstruction would be one that resulted in a South effectively indistinguishable from the North—was a dominant ideal during the early years of Reconstruction.[58] Whether explicitly or implicitly, northern commentators imagined the South of the future largely with reference to their own society. Reasoning that victory in the war proved both the supremacy of northern arms and northern culture, proponents of Yankeefication called for a bit of curative sectional homogenization in the postwar era. Reconstruction must mold the people and institutions of the South into a form that more closely resembled the North. Reconstruction would not just reform the South. It would Yankeefy it.

Insisting, as Union veteran Albion W. Tourgée did, that the South would be "saved when desouthernized and thoroughly nationalized" was one thing.[59] Actually desouthernizing the South was quite another matter. Regional boosterism aside, would-be Yankeefiers faced a variety of daunting questions as they set about exporting northern culture to the South. Their project presupposed a consistent and stable "North" as a model against which to judge the reconstruction of the South. Northern identity, however, had long existed as a part of a great dualism, cognitively inseparable from the southern identity that was its polar opposite.[60] The Civil War marked a vital turning point in conceptions of northern identity.[61] Even as it validated the North, proving its cultural superiority over the South (to northerners, anyway), the war robbed the region of the standard against which it had always defined itself. It was not merely the nature of the South that was in flux in the early years of Reconstruction. Yankeefication also raised vital questions about northern identity. In calling for a Yankeefied Dixie, northern Republicans would also need to define themselves.

Northerners encouraged Yankeefication on a number of fronts. Postwar commentators expressed an abiding faith in the ability of the North's free labor system to revolutionize southern society in the aftermath of the Civil War. Never merely an economic system, the free labor ideology—which stressed the inherent dignity of work, the desirability of economic independence, and the real possibility of individual advancement through zealous labor—was central to northern identity in the mid-nineteenth century. It was also at the heart of the Yankeefiers' plans for the Reconstruction of the South.[62] Northerners frequently complained of the antebellum South's problematic relationship with labor. "Labor in the South was the peculiar badge of the servile class, and was deemed disparaging to a freeman," the *New York Times* wrote. "Southerners generally made it a matter of pride to do as little of it as possible."[63] The *Chicago Tribune* similarly noted that southerners of both races "have been taught to believe that freedom consists in having somebody else to work for you."[64] There could be no hope for true reform in the region until southerners learned the value of a hard day's labor. Northern commentators insisted that the advent of free labor in the South promised social and moral benefits in addition to economic ones. The love of work would turn the South's poor whites into a prosperous yeomanry, its freed slaves into valuable laborers, and its waste places into paradise. As Carl Schurz put it, "The immense resources of the soil will, as by enchantment, spring to light under the magic touch of free labor, and her riches will be enjoyed by a free, happy, and—who doubts it?—*loyal* people."[65] Though the actual implementation of a postslavery labor regime in the South would prove to be one of the most pressing challenges of the era, many northerners began the period with an unfettered optimism in free labor's almost magical transformative powers.[66]

Literature produced for the instruction of the freedpeople offers an important window into the mentality of the postwar North. Moralistic and didactic, these books provided a roadmap for the transition to northern free labor values. Abolitionist Lydia Maria Child's *The Freedmen's Book* featured reading material designed to encourage literacy and to provide instruction in proper conduct and values. In an essay titled "Advice from an Old Friend," Child took it upon herself to lecture the freedpeople in acceptable patterns of behavior. Her list of desirable attributes (cleanliness, thrift, hard work, honesty, temperance, self-help) reads like a primer in northern self-understanding.[67] Similarly, *The Freedmen's Spelling Book* offered a thorough dose of Yankeefication along with its lessons in spelling. Lesson 17 instructed that "it is a sin to sip rum" and "a la-zy man can not get a job."[68] Lesson 184 taught that "La-bor is a u-ni-ver-sal du-ty, and ben-e-fi-cial to all. Some la-bor with the hands, and others with the mind, but all must work."[69] "John Freeman and His Family," a short story written for use in southern black schools, offered up an idealized depiction of the freedman-turned-free laborer as northern culture imagined him. The text opens with the dawning of freedom on the Lenox plantation in Hilton Head, South Carolina. Immediately after learning of his emancipation, John Freeman lectures his family on their new duties. Freedom, he explains, "is not to be let loose like the wild hogs in the woods, to root along in the bogs." No, he says, "every freeman, black and white, works for a living . . . in some 'spectable profession."[70] John Freeman and his family immediately embrace the dictates of northern free labor morality, offering a model for the South's actual freedpeople and highlighting the centrality of these values to the Reconstruction endeavor.

Religion offered another important arena in which northerners hoped to recast the South in their own image. The American Missionary Association (AMA), founded in 1846 as an organization of evangelical Christians dedicated to abolitionism and the spread of the Gospel at home and abroad, explicitly encouraged the northernization of southern religious structures during Reconstruction.[71] In its 1865 annual report, the AMA insisted that the South's "people, white and black, must be born again, not of war, nor of blood, nor of legislation, but of truth and the Spirit of God—not merely into a religion of emotion or form, or sectarian or sectional bigotry, but into an enlightened, practical, and philanthropic piety."[72] In establishing a dichotomy between southern religion (emotional, sectarian, sectional) and northern religion (enlightened, practical, pious), the report laid bare the assumptions that underlay the AMA's work in the postwar South. In October 1865, Congregationalist minister William T. Eustis Jr. delivered an address titled "Religious Reconstruction of the South" before a meeting of the American Home Missionary Society. Eustis flatly denied that the South possessed any religious institutions worthy of northern consideration. Southern white preachers were the handmaidens of slavery and secession, while southern black religion lacked structure and organization. Eustis considered the establishment of "the true christian church" to be "essential to the reconstruction of Southern society." Such a church—modeled, of course, on Eustis's own northern Congregationalism—would "do much to avert the perils of the hour, by staying demoralization, and rendering reconstruction a regeneration, by substituting intelligence for ignorance, and virtue for barbarism."[73] As this language suggests, Eustis's religious reconstruction was largely a matter of northernization.

Yankeefiers were similarly eager to establish proper (that is, northern) gender roles in the postwar South.[74] Union veteran John De Forest's novel *Miss Ravenel's Conversion from Secession to Loyalty*, published in 1867 but written during the first part of 1865, provides an important example of this gendered Yankeefication.[75] Despite the novel's title, Miss Lillie Ravenel, southerner and secessionist, actually undergoes two "conversions" in the text. Both, significantly, are brought about through marriage. The first, from secession to loyalty, happens near the novel's midpoint, when Miss Ravenel marries John Carter, a Virginian serving in the Union army. With a husband in blue, Miss Ravenel embraces the Union cause. Carter's sudden death, however, allows another Union soldier to win Miss Ravenel's affections. Edward Colburne provides a stark contrast to Miss Ravenel's first husband. While Carter was brave, boisterous, adventurous, and exciting, Colburne is reserved, scrupulously honest, morally upright, and temperate. But there is a larger difference. Carter was a southern gentleman; Colburne is a Connecticut Yankee. By the novel's end, Miss Ravenel, the metaphorical embodiment of southern womanhood, has come to embrace the superior culture of her second husband's native land. The Yankeefication of Lillie Ravenel culminates when Colburne asks if she would like to return to her native New Orleans. Her response—"Oh, never . . . always at the North! I like it so much better!"—encapsulates the deepest meaning of the novel, and northern culture's fondest hopes for Reconstruction.[76]

Though one can discern a number of specific variants of the Yankeefication platform—economics, education, religion, gender—what is truly remarkable is the extent to which northern commentators felt comfortable *not* explaining themselves. To many, "Yankeefying Dixie" was a complete sentence, one that conveyed everything to be accomplished in reconstructing the South. Such confidence was a particular product of its time and place. The knowledge of what Reconstruction would become—one of the bloodiest, most hotly contested eras in the nation's political and social history—can make it difficult to see the buoyant optimism with which many northerners greeted the first years of the period. It was this optimism that led the *Chicago Tribune* to insist that "the work of transition to the ordinary paths of peace will be accomplished in a marvelously short time," while the *New York Times* anticipated that "Reconstruction when once fairly begun, there is every reason to believe, will be accomplished very speedily."[77] Even as they recognized the lingering hostility of the South's antebellum leadership class, northern Republicans depicted the spread of northern institutions and ideas as a natural, almost organic, process. Having cleared away the wreckage of the past, northerners expected to sit back

**THE RETURN HOME.**

COLUMBIA. "Tell me, Soldier, did you not pass a Wayward Sister of mine on the road?"
RETURNING SOLDIER. "I did. I fetched her a good part of the way myself; but she says she don't require my services any more now; and here she comes over the hill."

"The Return Home," *Harper's Weekly*, May 20, 1865. This engraving captures the optimism central to the postwar Yankeefication project. Special Collections Department, Tampa Library, University of South Florida.

and watch their civilization take root. Given time, space, and guidance, they assumed, the South would naturally come to emulate the superior civilization of the North. This was not a plan, it was an inevitability.

In formulating the Yankeefication platform, commentators relied on a compelling, if simplistic, political framework forged in the fire of antebellum sectional conflict and the Civil War. If southern distinctiveness had brought about the war, it stood to reason that the goal of Reconstruction must be ending that distinctiveness. Reconstruction would produce one homogenous nation out of two distinct sections. It went without saying, of course, that the victorious North would never willingly embrace southern culture. The South must come to the North. "The Return Home," a May 1865 *Harper's Weekly* illustration, nicely captures the logic of postwar Yankeefication. The sketch features a worried Columbia, symbol of the United States, speaking with a Union soldier on a country road. Columbia asks the soldier whether he has seen her "Wayward Sister"—the South—on his travels. The soldier affirms that he had "fetched her a good part of the way myself," but "she says she don't require my services any more now."[78] She was now walking northward on her own. It might be necessary to carry the region, but only temporarily. Once the South found her feet, there was only one direction she would head. Unified in their embrace of northern principles, the North and the northernized South would overcome past antagonism and make their way to a bright national future.

Yankeefication was a dominant ideology, but it was not uncontested. African Americans in the North divided on the wisdom of Yankeefication. In early 1864, with the outcome of the Civil War still very much in doubt, Frederick Douglass, the nation's most influential African American author and orator, made a circuit of northern lecture halls delivering a speech titled "The Mission of the War." In it, Douglass explicitly called for the northernization of the South. Douglass insisted that the nation's great tragedy must result in something more than the mere maintenance of the Union. The war represented a "national opportunity, which may be improved to national salvation, or neglected to national ruin."[79] Southern treason, secession, and slaveholding had brought war on the nation. Reconstruction must replace the debauched and debased society of the antebellum South with something brighter, higher, and better. The South, Douglass affirmed, must be reborn in the image of the victorious North. "We are, in fact, and from absolute necessity," Douglass said, "transplanting the whole South with the higher Civilization of the North."[80] When "the New-England schoolhouse" dominated the national landscape and the "Southern whipping post" had disappeared forever, the transformative work of the war would be complete. This, Douglass insisted, was the mission of the war. It must also be the goal of Reconstruction.

Other black commentators expressed more hesitancy regarding the wholesale export of northern culture to the postwar South. The Reconstruction-era North was, to put it mildly, no egalitarian paradise.[81] If slavery had largely disappeared in the North by midcentury, white supremacy and a rigidly enforced caste system remained. African American voting rights were still severely curtailed in most northern states, substandard living conditions were a fact of life for many people of color, job opportunities were often scarce or nonexistent, and segregation in public accommodations remained the de facto law in many large northern cities. In 1865, voters in Connecticut, Minnesota, and Wisconsin failed to approve black suffrage in their states.[82] The horrific 1863 New York Draft Riots, meanwhile, still burned in the public memory, offering a chilling reminder that racial violence could thrive north of the Mason-Dixon line.[83] In this context, many African Americans responded with considerable skepticism to calls for the Yankeefication of Dixie.

In October 1864, many of the nation's leading African American thinkers and activists, including Frederick Douglass, John S. Rock, William Wells Brown, Henry Highland Garnet, and John Mercer Langston, met in Syracuse, New York, for a National Convention of Colored Men, the first such convention held since the outbreak of the war. Over four days of meetings, the predominantly northern delegates passed a series of bold resolutions, organized a National Equal Rights League (which would meet in Cleveland, Ohio, the following year), and prepared a "Declaration of Wrongs and Rights" that challenged white America to live up to the principles embodied in the nation's founding documents. Significantly, the convention operated under the assumption that racism and oppression were national, not sectional, issues. Other than a plank offering "the right hand of fellowship" to southern freedpeople, the convention largely refrained from singling out the plight of southern African Americans.[84] Instead, delegates insisted that southern slavery was merely one manifestation of a systematic national denial of black rights. Both North and South, African Americans had suffered "well-nigh every cruelty and indignity possible to be heaped upon human beings." For the National Convention of Colored Men, racism transcended region. On the basis of African Americans' status as "natives of American soil" and "citizens of the Republic," the convention called for a Reconstruction that would re-create the North as it rebuilt the South.[85] In the aftermath of war, they declared, the entire nation must be reborn in freedom, justice, and righteousness.

Other African American commentators expressed similar feelings. Simply put, the notion of Yankeefication held little value for those in the North who found themselves discriminated against on a daily basis. In February 1865, Henry Highland Garnet, a Presbyterian minister and former slave, became the first African American to address the U.S. Congress. Less than two weeks after Congress passed the Thirteenth Amendment, Garnet offered an eloquent denunciation of the slave system and the politicians who supported it. In an echo of the 1864 National Convention of Colored Men, however, Garnet never uttered the word *South* during his address, preferring to cast slavery as a national sin. The nation, not just the South, must take steps to secure justice and equality for all. Garnet called for "all unjust and heavy burdens" to be "removed from every man in the land," asked that "all invidious and proscriptive distinctions" be "blotted out from our laws," and demanded "no more trouble concerning the black man and his rights than there is in regard to other American citizens."[86] Garnet refused to partake in facile comparisons between northern righteousness and southern tyranny. Even as he recognized the imminent demise of slavery, he emphasized the work that remained to be done.

A memorial speech for Abraham Lincoln provided a platform for William Howard Day, an African American author and educator, to express nearly identical sentiments. Speaking on July 4, 1865, in Washington, DC, Day demanded an end to inequality, in the North and South. Insisting that the shadow of the martyred president's coffin lay across the nation, Day urged his audience to complete the great work that Lincoln had begun. Northerners must "pledge our untiring resistance" to "tyranny," whether it appeared in the guise of "the iron manacles of the slave, or in the unjust written manacles for the free."[87] Racial discord and inequality, Day reminded his listeners, had had a long life, in the North and South. Since the first Europeans and Africans arrived on the nation's shores, the ideology of "THINGHOOD" had been the blight that threatened to ruin the American experiment.[88] "North and South alike were inoculated with its virus," Day intoned. "It has lain like a gangrene upon the national life."[89] The demise of slavery and the Confederacy had removed a particularly objectionable symptom of this disease, but the underlying malady remained. In this context, northern conceit and celebration seemed dangerously out of place.

Perhaps the most damning critique of Yankeefication came from Frances Ellen Watkins Harper, a black novelist and activist. Speaking before the National Women's Rights Convention in New York in May 1866, Harper urged northerners to recognize the shortcomings of their own society before attempting to re-create it in the South. Racial oppression was not a southern phenomenon, Harper reminded her listeners. It was alive and well in New York and Philadelphia. "You white women speak of rights," Harper said, but "let me go to-morrow morning and take my seat in one of your street cars . . . and the conductor will put up his hand and stop the car rather than let me ride." As they imagined a reformed and revivified South, Yankees blithely ignored the inequality that surrounded them. Northern

African Americans did not have this luxury. Like Garnet and Day, Harper called for a truly national Reconstruction, one that would stamp out inequality wherever it existed. The "grand and glorious revolution which has commenced," Harper said, "will fail to reach its climax of success, until throughout the length and brea[d]th of this American Republic, the nation shall be so color-blind, as to know no man by the color of his skin or the curl of his hair."[90] The goal of Reconstruction must be something greater than the replication of a racist and antiegalitarian northern culture in the South. A true Reconstruction would attack inequality wherever it surfaced.

African American critiques of the Yankeefication project point to a deep historical irony. By definition, Reconstruction had to occur at a time when white northerners were least prepared to grapple with it. Having triumphed in a war of unparalleled savagery, Yankeefiers were in no mood to look critically at their own society, even as they sought to re-create it in the South. Rather than dispassionate engagement with the concrete needs of the South, the Yankeefication platform encouraged unthinking regional chauvinism and bred a popular understanding of Reconstruction that was little more than a collective affirmation of the superiority of northern culture. Yankeefication may have been popular among large segments of the northern population precisely because, ideologically speaking, it required so little of its adherents. It was a discourse, a set of linguistic tropes, that northerners consistently mistook for a plan of action. In the heady glow of their postwar optimism, most failed to discern the difference. At their worst, advocates of a northernized South displayed a remarkable naiveté and a wholesale disregard for both the challenges of Reconstruction and the depth of white southern hostility and opposition. The central questions of Reconstruction—how to help a race move from slavery to freedom, how to promulgate reunion between formerly bitter adversaries, and how to make one nation out of two sections—appeared simplistic and unproblematic when filtered through the distorting lens of Yankeefication. Blinded by their own optimism, many northern Republicans failed to recognize that the times required something more than lofty rhetoric and self-satisfaction.

## Go South, Young Man!

The advocates of Yankeefication put enormous faith in the transformative power of northern migration to the South. Indeed, the figure of the migrant allowed Yankeefiers to overlook many of their program's obvious intellectual shortcomings. Migrants, not yet tarnished by the associations with "carpetbagger" politics they would accrue after the Reconstruction Acts of 1867, were to serve as missionaries of the northern way of life, with a bit of the North carried in every carpetbag. The May 3, 1865, issue of the *Boston Herald* commented that "a southward movement of our population has been going on for the last four years, but the emigrants have carried muskets and cannons." The close of hostilities and the advent of Reconstruction had not stemmed the tide of bodies heading south, but it had changed its purpose. "The next southward movement will be of a different character," the *Herald* wrote. "The emigrants will carry the arts and machinery of peaceful industry, and will go to make homes in the fertile regions restored to the Union and to law, and to invigorate the slip shod society of the South with the spirit of free and educated labor."[91] This stream of migrants carried more than their own hopes for a better life. They brought with them the northern dream of a Yankeefied South. As the *National Freedman*, the organ of the New York–based National Freedman's Relief Association, put it, "If the mountain would not come to Mohamed, he was resolved to go to the mountain; and so if the South will not come to Northern views, Northerners are resolved to go to the South and plant their views there, to germinate and ripen into a harvest of Yankee notions and institutions."[92]

Throughout the first years of Reconstruction, thousands of eager northerners went to the mountain. Some migrants tried their hand at cotton planting.[93] Others thought that the reestablishment of southern industry would provide an excellent livelihood for ambitious northerners knowledgeable in the ways of business. The Connecticut man with whom John Dennett spoke on his way to Richmond was probably typical in that he "wasn't particular what sort of business he engaged in," but he thought he would prefer the southern climate and optimistically figured he could "bring down a good lot of goods and sell them."[94] Any northerner with skill, ambition, or an imagination could build a new life in Dixie. For northerners in the early Reconstruction period, the region held a singular attraction. It represented a new frontier, a fabulous speculating opportunity, the proving ground for the North's free labor ideology, and perhaps even a fallen comrade in need of redemption.

All migrants, of course, were not created equal. In stark contrast to the would-be venture capitalists who accompanied John Dennett on the steamer *Creole* were the hundreds of northern men and women who went south in the early years of Reconstruction to act as schoolteachers, preachers, and missionaries under the auspices of organizations such as the American Missionary Association and the National Freedmen's Relief Association.[95] Congregationalist minister Henry Ward Beecher, arguably the most important northern churchman of the postwar period, saw an "immense field throughout all the Southern States for men that know how to teach school, and men that know how to preach the Gospel," and insisted that "there never was such a time for young men, there never was such a time for maidens, there never was such a time for Christian beneficence and self-denying labor, as is coming upon us now."[96] Missionary teachers responded to Beecher's call in droves.

The migrant teachers of the American Missionary Association did their part to bring about the northernization of the South in the years after Appomattox.[97] According to the AMA, God had ordained the Civil War in order to clear a path toward emancipation, and Union victory represented a divine affirmation of the superiority of the northern cause. Though both sides had suffered terribly, the outcome of the war amounted to a divine mandate.[98] For this reason, a failure to fully reform the South—to finish the work of the war—would be an affront to God. "Divine justice has been awfully displayed in the punishment of the whole nation," the *American Missionary*, the association's official organ, wrote in July 1865, "and its sword is apparently still suspended awaiting our future conduct."[99] In the cosmology of the American Missionary Association, postwar northernization was a religious imperative. In Yankeefying Dixie, the AMA was simply fulfilling its divine obligations. Along with the gospel, migrant teachers and preachers would work to spread the gospel of the North.

The National Freedmen's Relief Association, founded in 1862, was similarly explicit regarding its desire to inculcate northern ideas and practices in its freedpeople's schools. Northern missionary teachers were not simply educating. They were also Yankeefying. Teachers "carry more than their education," the organization stated in its journal, the *National Freedman*. "They carry their race, their moral training, their faculty, their character, the influence of civilization, the ideas, sentiments, principles, that characterize Northern society, and which we hope will one day characterize Southern." Education was valuable in and of itself, but a *northern* education would aid the freedpeople much more. "We want, not schools merely, but Northern schools, Northern men and women down South, teaching, mingling with the people, and instituting the North there among the old populations. In this way we civilize all at once, by communicating simultaneously all the chief intellectual elements of civilization."[100]

On the ground, teachers worked to meet both their regional and their religious mandates. Missionary teachers made continual reference to the North in evaluating the successes or failures of their endeavors. Josiah Beardsley was initially skeptical about the abilities of his African American students in Baton Rouge, Louisiana. After nine months of work, however, Beardsley boasted that the first class in his school would "compare favorably with any of our best white schools at the north."[101] A teacher visiting Savannah, Georgia, was delighted to note that a black school had begun to operate out of one of the city's old slave markets. "These halls in which the poor slave mother has often groaned in the anguish of her soul," he wrote, "are now resounding with the merry shouts of happy school children."[102] Another Georgia teacher reported that "we have our meeting and sabbath school in the old cotton house of Tom Butler King. Strange transition from the rattle of the cotton gin to the sweet songs of Zion, but this is a day of great changes, when God is overturning old systems, old practices, to give place to new, and I trust better."[103] In the transition from slave market to classroom and from plantation cotton gin to Sabbath school, teachers saw the outlines of a reformed and Yankeefied South.

Significantly, however, northern culture reserved an important place for migrants with motives less explicitly altruistic than those of the missionaries and teachers of the American Missionary Association and the National Freedman's Relief Association. In January 1866, the *Hartford Daily Courant* wrote that "those pioneers who carry into the South, thus early in the progress of restoration, the habits of energy, of thrift and of industry acquired by a Northern education, will be doing a service to the country."[104] Since a central tenet of the Yankeefication program was the idea of the natural, inevitable spread of northern-style institutions and ideas in the Reconstruction South, it followed that all that was required to initiate this process was the arrival of these ideas in Dixie. This would be the function of the northern migrant. By their very presence, these pioneers would perform an invaluable cultural work. "The spirit of an active and industrious people will electrify the sluggishness of feudalism," *Harper's Weekly* wrote in July 1865. "The country will be covered with small estates—the safety of a nation; school-houses will spring up at the four corners of cross-roads; churches of a purer doctrine will bless a happier people; and all this will be done naturally, simply, and without violent shocks, if the people of this country wisely use the present golden moment."[105] Nothing in particular was required of the migrant, other than remaining true to his or her northern heritage. The undeniable appeal of the northern worldview would take care of the rest, leading southerners of both races to adopt northern habits, and yielding, in time, a Yankeefied South.

A wave of inducements to migration swept the newspapers, magazines, and books of the North in 1865 and 1866. Albert T. Morgan, a Union army veteran who migrated after the war to plant cotton, recalled in his 1884 autobiography that "the influential newspapers North had contained glowing descriptions of parts of the South, and editorials encouraging immigration into that region." He commented that "the former cry, 'Go West, young man,' had undergone just enough variation by the substitution of 'South' for 'West,' to effect a change . . . in the purposes of those of the North who were seeking new homes."[106] Postwar northern newspapers encouraged migration to the South with breathless hyperbole. "In all the known world, there is not another field for the employment alike of Capital and Labor so promising as is afforded throughout the length and breadth of the late Slave States of our union," the *New York Tribune* crowed in June 1865. In August, the *New York Times* declared that "in the history of America, never has there been promised such speedy returns to energy and enterprise as are now proffered in the Southern half of the Union."[107] Six months later, the same paper promised that "the Southern States want capital and labor. Under their propitious skies, there are leagues of fruitful lands, of which we may say . . . 'Tickle them with a hoe, and they will laugh with a harvest.'"[108]

Journalist Thomas Wallace Knox presented a wry commentary on the Yankee obsession with migration in his 1865 memoir. "Every one has heard the statement, circulated in Ireland many years since, that America abounded in roasted pigs that ran about the streets, carrying knives and forks in their mouths, and making vocal requests to be devoured," Knox wrote. "Those who desire to seek their homes in the South," he warned, "will do well to remember that baked pigs are not likely to exist in abundance in the regions traversed by the National armies."[109] A few pages later, however, he noted that "a few hundred dollars will do far more toward securing a home for the settler in the South than in the West." Although migrants could not be assured of preroasted pigs, most everything else in the South was primed and ready for their arrival. "Labor is abundant, and the laborers can be easily controlled by Northern brains," Knox explained. "The land is already broken, and its capabilities are fully known. Capital, if judiciously invested and under proper direction, whether in large or moderate amounts, will be reasonably certain of an ample return."[110]

Recognizing the widespread migratory impulse among its northern readers, *Harper's Weekly* printed a series of detailed maps of the southern states in early 1866. Many northerners envisioned a brighter future in the South, and *Harper's Weekly* sought to aid them in their planning. To this end, the column accompanying each map provided readers with information regarding the state's average temperature, latitude and longitude, area, total farmland, soil quality, waterways, manufacturing potential, and schools. In a small chart, each state was further broken down into its constituent counties, with the racial makeup and average cotton yield provided for each. A northerner intent on moving south could use these southern maps to find the spot best suited to resettlement, down to the county level. The maps, *Harper's* explained, were designed to provide "knowledge, knowledge, knowledge" of the South, "the key with which the golden treasure of the Future is to be unlocked."[111] Migrants hoping for a bit more guidance could turn to a group of organizations dedicated to moving committed northerners to the southern states, including the American Land Company and Agency, run by Massachusetts governor John A. Andrew, the General Southern Land Agency, established by Kemp P. Battle of North Carolina, and the New England Emigrant Aid Company, which had been chartered in 1854 to move Free Soil New Englanders to Kansas, but shifted its sights to the South as early as 1862.[112]

Throughout the early part of 1865, the *Christian Recorder*, an African American newspaper, was similarly filled with promigratory rhetoric. The South, the paper wrote in January 1865, would greatly benefit from "an infusion of the intellectual development of the Northern colored men and women." Northern teachers were uniquely equipped to help the freed-people learn a vital lesson in the transition to freedom: that "though they be black, they are as good as any other class whose skin is whiter than theirs."[113] Black businessmen and craftsmen were also assured of their ability to do great work in the South. "The sunny South only awaits the twitch of Northern enterprise, the vivacity and life of New England; to lift her from the night of barbarism, reinvigorate and redeem her," a *Christian Recorder* correspondent declared in March 1865. The South "now presents the greatest field of labor which has ever opened for the colored people of the North. There needs to be a migration of those in the large cities, diffusing their knowledge and enterprise into those of the South."[114] A month later, Henry McNeal Turner took a break from his travel writing duties to encourage black migration to North Carolina. Under the heading "Colored Men of Enterprise Read This," Turner reported that black "men of money, men of art, men of enterprise, and men of learning" would find a "most favorable opportunity" in Wilmington.[115] In these calls for migration, philanthropy and opportunism were tightly linked. African American migration to the South would prove a double blessing. As northern migrants instructed the freedpeople, shared their expertise, and rebuilt the South, they would also serve as the nucleus of an educated, successful, and northernized African American community in the South.

Yankeefication, then, was not merely an ideological project. It was, on a certain level, literal. The South could not be redeemed until it had actually been northernized, by an influx of northern blood and expertise. Individual migrants might respond to the knock of opportunity or the call of adventure. In moving south, however, they would perform a great service for the country. At some point, commentators expected, northern culture would naturally take root in the South, turning native southerners of both races into Yankees, in spirit if not in fact. This second species of Yankeefication presupposed the first. If the central premise of the work—that exposure to northern methods would induce an organic transformation in southerners—remained maddeningly vague, few northerners seemed to mind. The plan required faith that somehow, at some point, the South would simply (and almost magically) become northernized. At the height of their postwar optimism, many northerners found this expectation reasonable. With the help of Yankee migrants, the South stood poised to become, in the words of Albion W. Tourgée, "just the pleasantest part of the country."[116]

The reality of life in the Reconstruction South, however, often fell short of the rhetoric that had drawn Yankees to Dixie in the first place. By mid-1866, the luster of migration had already begun to fade. The vast majority of northerners who sojourned south in 1865 to make their fortune in cotton planting had returned to the North by 1867.[117] Bad harvests and bad luck played a part, but so did southern white hostility and violence. Similarly, the 1865–66 school year marked a peak for northern missionary schoolteachers in the South. Their numbers steadily declined thereafter.[118] Northerners who remained in the South did so with eyes open. In the afterglow of Civil War victory, northern Yankeefiers thought anything was possible. As time passed, so did this confidence.

Time spent in the South caused many of representatives of the American Missionary Association to feel a palpable disenchantment. As early as July 1865, a teacher in Mississippi expressed his dissatisfaction with missionary life. "If you do return to Natchez," he wrote a colleague, "you will not leave it with the same feelings you left with last April. The longer

I stay the less is my confidence in the 'Freedmen.'" He complained in the same letter of the "strong animosity harbored in the bosom of the Southern people against Yankees."[119] George Whipple, secretary of the American Missionary Association, received a number of letters testifying to the difficulties encountered in the South. William Fiske, a teacher stationed in Louisiana, wrote Whipple of his plight in January 1866. Finding himself temporarily without a position, Fiske had considered a move to Alabama but was warned that "the spirit of the people is still unreconciled to the new order, + there is much violence + confusion." He inquired about conditions elsewhere in Louisiana, but received "universal testimony of both black + white, that I should not be safe there from personal violence." This sort of "aimless lawlessness," he added, "begins to produce some right reflection."[120] In September 1866, an AMA affiliate in New Orleans wrote Whipple complaining that the city's school board had "dismissed from the Public School nearly one hundred white teachers, for the sole reason that they . . . reflected . . . northern ideas." Though the author urged the AMA to hire these "earnest Christian women" immediately, the letter spoke volumes about the progress (or lack thereof) of northern ideas in New Orleans.[121]

Northerners in the South working under the auspices of the Freedmen's Bureau offered more of the same. The Bureau of Refugees, Freedmen, and Abandoned Lands was a federal organization charged with assisting southern African Americans in their transition to freedom. Despite their connection to the federal government, Freedmen's Bureau agents often found themselves woefully understaffed, underfunded, and unprepared for the lengths to which southern whites would go to maintain white supremacy.[122] In his 1866 annual report, Davis Tillson, assistant bureau commissioner for the state of Georgia, testified to a litany of abuses against the freedpeople: false imprisonment, contracts signed under threat of violence, unjust dismissal to avoid payments due, whipping, robbing, and murder. Tillson recommended military intervention to stop the violence. "Although the appeal to force, even in this case, is objectionable," he wrote, "experience has shown it to be unavoidable."[123] Reports of armed white men gathering outside freedpeople's schools prompted Mortimer A. Warren, bureau superintendent in New Orleans, to arrive at a similar conclusion.[124] In a letter to an associate in the American Missionary Association, Warren wrote that it would take an "army" of missionary teachers to work real change in the South. "We must raise them, enlist, equip, drill, and lead them to the battle. The rebellion is over, but we soldiers of the cross have a greater battle on our hands. We must stop our skirmishing, concentrate our forces, fortify our base, and fight."[125] Such militaristic language, of course, entirely undercut the logic of Yankeefication. White southerners did not seem to be embracing northern methods. Far from it. The notion of Reconstruction through migration might have seemed reasonable to those safely ensconced in New York or Ohio, but things looked a bit different on the ground in Louisiana and Georgia.

Army chaplain and travel writer Henry McNeal Turner had likewise turned an important corner by the middle of 1866. From his post in Georgia, Turner watched conditions in the South worsen. He began to seriously consider black emigration to Africa.[126] Back in March 1865, while the war still raged and Turner still furnished the *Christian Recorder* with his missives from the Carolinas, he had suggested "the propriety to the colored politicians north, of investigating that momentous subject, EMIGRATION, very thoroughly." At that point, he had insisted that "it is not my intention" to stake a stand on the issue, "pro or con."[127] By July 1866, however, Turner had made up his mind. In a letter to William Coppinger, secretary of the American Colonization Society, Turner expressed his amenability to emigrationism, and asked whether Coppinger would be willing to employ him as a lecturer in the South. "By that means," Turner reasoned, "thousands of our people . . . would hear of this thing who can't read, and know nothing of it, nor are likely to hear."[128] In a November 1866 article in the *Christian Recorder*, Turner noted the recent exodus of a group of Georgia African Americans to Liberia. "I have been a stern opposer of that scheme for many years," Turner wrote. "But at present, I am willing to congratulate every man that will go."[129] Though he would continue to work for the betterment of black people in the United States, Turner had begun to look abroad for a future for the race.

By the middle of 1866, conditions in the South made it clear to all but the most willfully blind observer that the expected Yankeefication had failed to materialize. The tide of northern migration to the South had risen, crested, and reversed itself, without any discernible change in the region's feelings toward the North. Southern whites spent the latter part of 1865 implementing Black Codes designed to limit African American rights and to ensure a captive and quiescent labor force. The senators and congressmen who arrived in Washington, DC, in December 1865 to claim their seats under the terms of Andrew Johnson's lenient Reconstruction policy included ten Confederate generals and Alexander Stephens, former vice president of the Confederacy.[130] Brutal racial massacres in New Orleans and Memphis in the spring and summer of 1866 offered bloody proof of the white South's resolve. Such events did not bode well for advocates of a northernized South. The dream of a Yankeefied Dixie still shone brightly, but its supporters had been chastened. Robbed of much of their naive optimism, northerners settled in for the long haul.

### Radical Yankeefication

Yankeefication also provides a helpful analytical lens through which to view the political platform of that class of congressional leaders known to themselves, to their enemies, and to history as the Radical Republicans.[131] When the Republicans of the Thirty-ninth Congress assembled in December 1865, enticing visions of a new and northernized South were common currency. Unlike most northerners, however, congressional Republicans faced the challenge of formulating actual policies designed to bring about this transformation. While most northerners could rely on vague generalizations and the panacea of migration in their calls to revolutionize the South, congressional Radicals were both empowered and required to take immediate steps in the political and legislative arenas. In so doing, they were forced to tackle a set of questions that most advocates of Yankeefication elided: What was the true nature of northern society? What specific elements made up this culture, and what pieces of legislation could Congress rely on to transplant them? How would northerners know when the process was complete? Was it even possible to impose an alien culture on a reconstructing South?

Radicals were a highly self-conscious group, aware that their views placed them ahead of the mainstream but certain that history would validate and reward them. Although the Reconstruction of the South presented a number of unique challenges, it provided opportunities in equal measure. If managed correctly, Reconstruction would mark the birth of a new nation, clothed in righteousness and democracy. Such opportunities did not come around often, and the Radicals did not intend to let this one pass by. As Ohio representative James Ashley noted, "This Congress is writing a new chapter in American history. Let every man whose great privilege it is to record his name where it will stand forever, so record it as to secure the triumph of justice, and his name and memory shall have a life coequal with the Republic."[132] Or as Massachusetts senator Charles Sumner put it, "Congress must dare to be brave; it must dare to be just."[133]

The Radical program offered a curious amalgam of optimism and realism. While their long-term vision—of a reunited nation fulfilling its destiny as a bastion of peace, freedom, and equality the world over—was vaguely utopian, the Radicals had little faith in the organic growth of northern sentiment in the South. As long as defeated but unrepentant Confederates retained political control, as long as colossal estates disfigured the landscape of the region, as long as the federal government failed to make the civil and political rights of the freedmen permanent and nonnegotiable, there could be no true revolution in southern sentiment. Reconstruction by migration, northernization by example—these notions held little appeal for the Radical Republicans. Radicals insisted that the Yankeefication of Dixie was absolutely vital to the future health of the nation, but they assumed that it could only be brought about through direct action on the part of the North and the federal government. With this in mind, congressional Republicans produced a body of legislation designed, at least in part, to spur the influx of northern values and ideas into the defeated Confederacy.

When Congress convened in December 1865, Pennsylvania representative and arch-Radical Thaddeus Stevens summarized the plight of the South as follows: "Dead men cannot raise themselves. Dead States cannot restore their own existence."[134] The states of the South had left the Union and made war on the nation, Stevens insisted. In the process, they had voided their right to congressional representation, to a say in their future, and even to statehood. Politically speaking, there was no South. Stevens was concerned, however, about the persistence of the social structures that had distinguished the antebellum South, particularly the dominance of a small cadre of landowning oligarchs. Reconstructing the South, Stevens argued, necessitated the complete obliteration of the antebellum way of life. "The whole fabric of southern society *must* be changed," he insisted in September 1865, "and never can it be done if this opportunity is lost."[135] Confiscation of rebel lands, the cornerstone of Stevens's plan for Reconstruction, was rooted in precisely this impulse. In breaking up the South's largest estates and establishing a free labor workforce of African Americans and yeoman whites, Stevens aimed to "humble the proud traitors" responsible for the war.[136] More than this, however, he hoped to wipe the slate clean. To expect the South to spontaneously assimilate to northern patterns of thought without first removing the structural remnants of the old ways appeared to Stevens the height of folly. Yankeefication would require a little salutary destruction.

Radicals consistently advocated northernization by force, or what Senator Henry Wilson referred to as a "vigorous prosecution of peace."[137]

Ohio Radical Benjamin Wade warned his colleagues in early 1866 that Reconstruction was simply war by other means: "Do you suppose that in a moment the temper and disposition of men who breathed fire and wrath against you for four long years, and murdered three hundred thousand of your bravest sons . . . have been so changed that they will ask to be taken back into that Government which they had invoked foreign despotisms to overthrow?" Predictably, Wade answered in the negative: "He is a most unreasonable man who expects that in the twinkling of an eye you can make a people cordially cooperate in this free Government who the day before were endeavoring to overthrow it."[138] An end to open hostilities, Wade argued, was only the beginning. The South had yet to repent, so the North could not relax. Despite the confidence of many Yankeefiers outside of Congress, Radicals were convinced that northern sentiment would not grow in the South unless the federal government forcefully created a more conducive atmosphere. In an 1867 speech, Indiana representative George W. Julian insisted that "what these regions need, above all things, is not an easy and quick return to their forfeited rights in the Union, but *government*, the strong arm of power, outstretched from the central authority here in Washington." An extended period of federal oversight would encourage the desired northernization by making it "safe for northern capital and labor, northern energy and enterprise, and northern ideas to set up their habitation in peace, and thus found a Christian civilization and a living democracy amid the ruins of the past."[139]

It is important to note that congressional Radicals did not propose to transplant northern society as it was. Instead, they fashioned an idealized vision of northern culture and set about placing *this* at the heart of the Reconstruction effort. As they worked toward a renewed and reconstructed South, therefore, Radicals simultaneously reimagined the North. In a December 1866 speech, New York congressman and self-described "radical" Hamilton Ward offered a millennial vision of the nation's future, making abundantly clear both his understanding of northern culture as a force for righteousness and his debt to the doctrine of Yankeefication:

> The South shall cease to be a section and become a part of the
> nation; her sons and daughters shall build altars to freedom in her
> waste places; the wilderness shall vanish, the church and school-
> house will appear, and light and knowledge will illumine her dark
> corners; freedom of speech, of opinion, and of the press will be
> as much secured in South Carolina as in Maine; all men shall be

citizens, and high and clear in the fundamental law will that charter of citizenship be found guiding the nation like a pillar of flame; the whole land will revive under the magic touch of free labor, and we shall arise from the ashes of the rebellion to a purer life and a higher destiny, illustrating the grand truth of man's capacity for self-government.

Through the agency of Yankee customs, laws, and institutions—the school-house, the church, free labor, and, significantly, universal citizenship—a new South would be born, and with it would arise a new nation. Finally free from sectional conflict, the United States would take its place as a global force for good, spreading its message of "justice and equality" to the far corners of the world. This vision of the United States as "the terror of tyrants and the hope of slaves" was simply the Radicals' North, writ large.[140]

The Radical Yankeefiers presided over some of the most significant legislative achievements in American history. The Fourteenth Amendment, which went to the states for ratification midway through 1866, expanded the bounds of U.S. citizenship and defined the federal government's obligations to the people. The Reconstruction Acts, passed in 1867, dismantled the white supremacist governments erected under Andrew Johnson, reestablished military control over the South, and provided the franchise to the African Americans of the South, constructing (for the moment, at least) a genuine biracial democracy in Dixie. The Radicals' revolution, however, wound to a grinding halt by mid-1867, with many of its central components, including land confiscation and redistribution, left undone. Even so, Radical Yankeefication was significant not only for its legislative achievements but also for its attempt to redefine the North, the South, and the nation along explicitly egalitarian, democratic lines. Although the effort fell short, the attempt to enshrine racial democracy at the ideological and imaginative center of the nation was, perhaps, their most "radical" step.

CHAPTER TWO

# Of Carpetbags and Klans

By 1868, Reconstruction had transformed the nation. As the year opened, biracial conventions across the South were at work drafting new state constitutions under guidelines established in the Reconstruction Acts of 1867. In July, the Fourteenth Amendment, the crown jewel of the Republican Party's attempt to redefine American citizenship, was formally enshrined in the Constitution. In November, newly enfranchised African American freedpeople cast their first votes in a national election, helping to secure a Republican-dominated South and to elect Republican Ulysses S. Grant, the hero of the Union war effort, to the presidency. Late in the year, the U.S. Congress began debates on the Fifteenth Amendment. Approved by Congress in February 1869 and ratified by the states a year later, the third and final Reconstruction amendment nationalized black suffrage and formalized the nation's commitment to an expanded—if not yet universal—electorate.

And yet in the midst of these unprecedented changes, discordant notes could be heard. With the legal and political apparatus of Radical Reconstruction in place across the South by 1868, the challenges associated with building Reconstruction gave way to the problems of maintaining and solidifying it. Were they to judge on the basis of large-scale structural shifts, Northern Republicans might have concluded that Reconstruction was on its way to a glorious conclusion in the not-too-distant future. There was, however, a different yardstick to be applied, one rooted in the stickier question of southern sentiment. From this viewpoint, matters appeared less encouraging. For all the revolutionary changes that had taken place across Dixie, much remained the same. White southerners refused to play the role that the northern prophets of a Yankeefied South had assigned them in 1865. Two and a half years of Reconstruction had done little to appease southern hostility. If anything, northerners fretted, the South seemed more resistant to change, more set in its ways, than it had been immediately after the war.

The year 1868 also saw the first sustained northern discussion of two groups that would loom large for the remainder of Reconstruction: the carpetbaggers and the Ku Klux Klan.[1] The Ku Klux Klan was a southern organization of night-riding terrorists committed to the overthrow of Reconstruction and the maintenance of white supremacy.[2] The carpetbaggers were northern transplants to the South who found in Republican Party politics a calling and a livelihood.[3] As flesh-and-blood historical figures, the carpetbagger and the Klansman waged an extended war for control of the South. As symbols, they took part in a battle of a different sort. From the late 1860s to the late 1870s, the carpetbagger and the Klansman served as the imaginative anchors in a prolonged northern discussion of Reconstruction's shortcomings. Though other figures, including the scalawag, the Yankee schoolmarm, and the southern black legislator, would play important roles in shaping the debate after 1868, the corrupt carpetbagger and the bloody Klansman were constants in northern print sources. In the context of a Reconstruction threatening to spin wildly out of control, the carpetbagger and the Klansman became convenient signifiers, with each standing in for a larger set of presumptions, explanations, and prescriptions. When northern commentators talked about carpetbaggers or the Klan, therefore, they were seldom *just* talking about carpetbaggers or the Klan.

To mobilize either figure was to take a stand on a vitally important question: Who has the right to rule in the South? To highlight the rascally carpetbagger was to suggest that the chaos of Reconstruction was due to northern failures of imagination, planning, and implementation. From this viewpoint, Reconstruction, led by a band of hopelessly corrupt northern interlopers, appeared to be little more than a cynical plot to rob and pillage the impoverished South. To focus instead on the bloody deeds of the Ku Klux Klan (or, after 1872, on related organizations like the White League, the White Line, and the Red Shirts) was to argue that the white South was innately depraved, unreasonably resistant to change, and eager to resort to violence. By extension, it was to insist that the North's involvement in the South was necessary and righteous. These competing explanations of southern affairs—along with their most visible symbols—structured much of the national debate over the meaning and course of Reconstruction after 1868.

Discussions of the carpetbagger and the Klansman present a convenient means by which to track shifting northern sentiments regarding the Reconstruction project. Though both figures occupied a central position in northern culture throughout the period, a clear shift in emphasis is apparent. In 1868, the Ku Klux Klan stood as the predominant symbol of Reconstruction run amok for most northern Republicans. Northern Democrats, meanwhile, were far more likely to focus on the frauds and peculations of the carpetbaggers. By the mid-1870s, however, the majority of northern Republicans had shifted their gaze to the carpetbagger, concluding that northern interventionism, not white supremacist violence, was to blame for continued southern unrest. The Ku Klux Klan and its affiliated organizations had not dropped from sight completely, but the trend is undeniable. In identifying the carpetbagger, rather than the Klansman, as the primary villain of the era, northern Republicans affirmed their unwillingness to preside over the further Reconstruction of the South.

## The Birth of Two Symbols, 1866–1868

Technically, a carpetbagger was simply a northerner who went south in the wake of the Civil War and took part in Republican Party politics. From the beginning, however, the moniker carried more negative connotations. In late 1867, an Alabama newspaper editor coined the term in an attempt to discredit the South's new political order and those who supported it. "Carpetbagger" was meant to describe a class of lowly northern opportunists who preyed on the defeated South, perverted sectional peace, and rose to power by deceiving African American voters. The fact that this class was largely a figment of the white southern imagination did little to dampen the term's appeal. From Alabama, it spread quickly among like-minded southerners and northern Democrats.[4] By the time a Confederate veteran named Dick Bascom published a book-length treatment of the topic, carpetbag excoriation had become a veritable art form. In *The Carpetbagger in Tennessee*, Bascom offered the following general definition of his subject: the carpetbagger was "a place hunter, a miserable adventurer spewed out from the offal of the North,—a vile barbarian unfit for human society, a pest, a thieving, plundering vagabond at large to scourge and curse the world and poison its peace." He continued: "The genus 'Carpetbagger' is a man with a lank head of dry hair; a lank stomach and long legs; club knees and splay feet; dried legs and lank jaws, with eyes like a fish and a mouth like a shark." "Add to this," he concluded, "a habit of sneaking and dodging about in unknown places,—habiting with negroes in dark dens and back streets,—a look like a hound, and a smell like a pole cat."[5] The figure of the carpetbagger—the thieving outsider, the rakish adventurer, the bookish Puritan hopelessly out of place below the Mason-Dixon—gave opponents of Reconstruction a common language with which to critique northern-led racial democracy.

In response to the rising chorus of carpetbag bashing, northern Republicans launched a rhetorical counteroffensive. The Republican architects of Reconstruction insisted that northern migrants carried with them the moral attributes and the material wealth that the South desperately needed. In an October 1868 speech, Massachusetts senator Charles Sumner argued that carpetbaggers were "American citizens, who, in the exercise of the rights of citizenship, carry to the South the blood, the capital, and the ideas of the North." They were missionaries carrying northern Republican values to the South and had made the selfless and patriotic choice to devote their northern skills and fortunes to the reworking of southern society. "The carpet-bag," Sumner concluded, "is the symbol of our whole population."[6] Writing in the *Independent*, abolitionist William Lloyd Garrison agreed, insisting that "northern enterprise, industry, invention, skill" would redeem the South. These would be forthcoming, he said, "just as soon as the possession of a carpet-bag is no crime in that section."[7]

The conviction that the carpetbaggers were the dregs of northern society—those without wealth, family, or community standing to tie them to the North—was central to the emergent carpetbagger critique. It is only logical, therefore, that northern Republicans spent a great deal of time constructing more reputable antecedents for northern migrants. Most frequently, commentators insisted that those northerners resident in the South in 1867 and 1868 were the logical successors of the Union soldiers who had traversed the region between 1861 and 1865. As Massachusetts senator Henry Wilson told a Philadelphia audience, "The men who rode to Gettysburg and broke the advancing columns of Lee, have a right to live where they please. They may take their knapsack or their carpet-bag with them."[8] The *Independent* approvingly quoted a Texas freedman who stated that "it was the carpet-baggers who freed us; they carried their carpetbags on their backs and guns on their shoulders."[9] A *New York Tribune* editorial explained that a northerner in the South could gain acceptance as soon as "he damns Congress" and "hurrahs" for the Democratic Party. But, it added, "those who went down with 'U.S.' printed on their carpet-bags, and these swung over their shoulders, don't like to talk that way."[10] Union general

Benjamin Butler offered an alternative nomenclature for those tradition-
ally denominated "carpetbaggers." Butler preferred the term "*Knapsack-
ers*," he said, because "most of them, when first entering upon Southern soil,
took all they had with them, save bullets, in that soldierly convenience."[11]

Other commentators looked a bit further afield. By taking the most
general definition of the term—a person from one place who settled in
another—it was possible to turn almost anyone into a carpetbagger. In October 1868, Union general Daniel E. Sickles recast U.S. history as a tale of
carpetbaggers. "The whole West is peopled by a race of our carpet-baggers.
William Penn was a carpet-bagger of the right sort. Daniel Boone of Kentucky, Lewis Cass of Michigan, Stephen A. Douglas of Illinois—these were
all 'carpet-baggers,'" Sickles said. "The *May Flower* brought a colony of
carpet-baggers." In each instance, "our carpet-baggers carry intelligence
and civilization and enterprise wherever they go."[12] A *Chicago Tribune*
article added a few more honorary carpetbaggers to the mix, including
such figures as Andrew Jackson, James K. Polk, Abraham Lincoln, Daniel
Webster, Henry Clay, and Ulysses S. Grant. Each of these, "with carpet or
saddle-bags, left their native States, and migrating to others, filled State
offices of every grade."[13] If these were carpetbaggers, the term could hardly
be taken as one of reproach. *Zion's Herald*, a New England Methodist
paper, went so far as to compare the carpetbaggers to the apostles of Jesus
Christ, who had left their homes to spread the gospel. Future generations,
the paper predicted, would regard these latter-day apostles, like their pre-
decessors, as "saints."[14]

Southern attacks on the carpetbagger could prompt outbursts of unin-
hibited political and regional chauvinism. In an installment of the come-
dic Petroleum V. Nasby letters, the protagonist makes trouble for himself
when he leads the residents of his adopted Kentucky home, "Confederit X
Roads," in drafting an anticarpetbagger statute. Nasby is undone when he
remembers that "I wuz not a native uv Kentucky; that I wuz a northerner,
and that I had come to Kentucky an advencherer!"[15] Humorist Orpheus
Kerr picked up on a similar theme in his 1868 book *Smoked Glass*. After
Kerr's narrator behaves peculiarly on a southern train—he pays his fare
and is dressed in clothes without holes—he is marked as a "scorpion
carpet-bagger from the plebeian North" and shunned accordingly.[16] An
1868 cartoon in *Harper's Weekly* played on familiar stereotypes of the ignorant and uncultured white South, depicting two southerners castigating
a "D——d Carpet-Bagger" for engaging in a "Yankee trick" they had never
before witnessed: painting a picture.[17]

APPRECIATION OF ART IN NORTH CAROLINA.

FIRST NATIVE. "Who's 'im, Bill?"
SECOND NATIVE. "D——d Carpet-Bagger!"
FIRST NATIVE. "What kind of a Yankee trick is that he's up to?"
SECOND NATIVE. "Be dad-drat if I know. Shall I split his gizzard!"

"Appreciation of Art in North Carolina," *Harper's Weekly*, October 31, 1868.
As this image suggests, northern defenses of carpetbaggers were frequently
tinged with antisouthern sentiment. Special Collections Department,
Tampa Library, University of South Florida.

Humor aside, there were larger issues at stake in this conversation. When northern Republicans cast the carpetbaggers as trailblazers and missionaries, they insisted on the necessity and righteousness of a northern-led Reconstruction effort. Since the white South had effectively forfeited its right to self-governance, the Reconstruction of the region must proceed under the leadership of the only class of "southerners" worthy of the national trust: those who were not actually from the South. At least early on, therefore, northern Republicans tended to respond to southern carpetbag critiques with what we might call a "positive good" defense of the carpetbaggers. By this logic, the carpetbaggers were the ambassadors of a superior civilization and the harbingers of salutary change. The chorus of complaints emanating from the South was not evidence of carpetbagger corruption or malfeasance. It was proof of the white South's lingering rebel sentiment and unreasonable resistance to change. Carpetbaggers were not vultures destroying the South; they were patriots playing a vital part in the Reconstruction effort.

In stark contrast to the "terrible carpetbagger," an image that southern partisans had pulled out of thin air, there was nothing contrived or constructed about the Ku Klux Klan.[18] When it burst onto the northern cultural landscape in early 1868, the Klan was already a full-fledged white supremacist militia, a terrorist organization well-schooled in the art of political violence. The Klan had been in existence since 1866. According to the recollections of a founding member, six former Confederate soldiers were gathered one night in a law office in Pulaski, Tennessee, when one of the number had an inspired notion: "Boys," he exclaimed, "let us get up a club or society of some description."[19] For the most part, the early Klan contented itself with holding meetings, parading through Pulaski in full regalia, and staging elaborate initiation rituals in a grove outside town. The political and social upheaval of Reconstruction-era Tennessee, however, brought about a shift in the character of the organization. While the new Klan maintained the oaths, costumes, and initiation rituals established in Pulaski, diversion took a backseat to intimidation. The Klan soon spread beyond Tennessee, boasting chapters in every ex-Confederate state by April 1868. African Americans and white loyalists lived in constant fear in many localities, as the nightly rides of the Klan made a mockery of justice and democracy. Northerners, meanwhile, could not help but take notice.[20]

Northern engagement with the Klan began as a series of scattered reports on violence throughout the South, as commentators struggled to make sense of the string of outrages tied to the group with the peculiar name. The readers of the *New York Times* were first made aware of the Ku Klux Klan in a February 1868 article describing the brutal beating of a white Republican and two African Americans near Lynnville, Tennessee. The newspaper offered a brief history of the Klan, noting that "for something like six months past, perhaps longer, there has existed in the counties of Giles and Maury, a rebel organization under the euphonious soubriquet of the 'Kuklux Klan.'" Although "the organization was represented to outsiders as a harmless conclave of congenial and convivial spirits to encourage tournaments, masquerades, &c.," the *Times* insisted that real object of the organization was to "drive Union men out of the country, or at least keep them in constant alarm, and to overawe the negroes and prevent them from exercising their rights at the ballot box."[21] Soon thereafter, a Tennessee correspondent from the *Chicago Tribune* reported a series of "outrages perpetrated in this State, of late, by a secret society of villainous, venomous, and cowardly rebels, united together under the name of Kuklux Klan."[22] The Klan murder of Georgia Unionist George Ashburn on March 31, 1868, received broad coverage in the northern press. A party of masked men, furious over Ashburn's Radical stand at the Georgia constitutional convention, smashed in the door of his boardinghouse in Columbus and shot him multiple times. Initial reports were vague as to the perpetrators of the deed, but attention soon turned to the Ku Klux Klan, whose "cabalistic placards" had been "posted throughout the city the week previous to the murder."[23]

In the face of these reports, northern Democrats vociferously contested the very existence of the Ku Klux Klan. In April 1868, as northern Republicans were beginning their engagement with the organization, the Democratic *New York World* noted that "the Radicals have discovered a hideous new monster. They allege that a secret organization, bearing the odd name of the 'Ku-Klux-Klan,' or 'Kuk-Klux-Klan' (for we find variation in the spelling), has spread a vast net-work of affiliated societies all over the South." Although the Radicals had not yet decided precisely what the Klan was all about, the newspaper was confident that they would use their new monster to advance a nefarious agenda.[24] Three days later, the *World* reported that a number of congressional Radicals, including Benjamin Wade and Benjamin Butler, had received threatening letters bearing the marks and symbols of the Ku Klux Klan. The paper noted, however, that "these pleasant epistles were received about the 1st inst. The inference therefore is that they were merely prepared as 'April fool' jokes by some wag who is now enjoying the fun hugely."[25]

An 1868 short story called "The Masked Lady of the White House; or, the Ku-Klux-Klan" nicely encapsulates the prevailing Democratic line of argumentation. The story posits that the Ku Klux Klan was, in fact, founded by a secret conclave of ten Radical Republican congressmen in Washington, DC. Worried that a too-hasty conclusion to Reconstruction would render them irrelevant, the Radicals wager that a handful of "outrages in the Southern States upon Union men and Northern immigrants" would stir up "the proper feelings of indignation and anger" in the North.[26] And so the Ku Klux Klan is born. To fan northern curiosity, the Radicals dress up their creation with an assortment of "oaths[,] ceremonies, and initiation mysteries" of "the most weird, bloody, and terrific character."[27] A mysterious masked lady (hence the title) is the only witness to the Radicals' treachery. In this story, as in most Democratic treatments of the Klan, the violence of the on-the-ground Ku Klux Klan is rendered inconsequential, as attention shifts completely to the actions of unscrupulous Washington Republicans.

Even among Republicans, however, some doubt persisted as to the true nature of the organization. Did the Ku Klux Klan represent a concerted attempt to overthrow Reconstruction, or should the organization be understood as a simple social club whose taste for mischief sometimes led to violence? A frequently repeated story from the South pointed toward the latter interpretation. The masks and robes of the Klan, commentators agreed, made Klansmen appear ghostlike, a fact that came in handy when the organization made house calls. "Not long since one of these midnight bands went to some darkey quarters and one of them asked for a drink of water," reported a *New York Times* correspondent. The terrified resident brought the apparition a bucket of water, "which the man in white drank down without trouble and immediately called for more. The negro, confirmed in his wildest fears by this unnatural demonstration of capacity, dropped his bucket and fled in great terror." The Klansman had simply directed the flow of water into a receptacle hidden inside his robes. The freedman, however, believed the apparition when it averred that it had not had a drop of water to drink since Manassas. Incidents such as this, the correspondent reported, which occurred all across Tennessee, had caused great alarm among the "superstitious and weaker-minded of the blacks."[28]

By the middle of 1868, however, the sheer preponderance of evidence and the constant chorus of outrage stories had convinced most Republicans that the Ku Klux Klan was something more than a good-natured secret society with a taste for pranks. Every day, it seemed, northern newspapers had a crime to report from some corner of the South—a beating, a shooting, a rape, a hanging. As early as September 1868, the *Chicago Tribune* commented on this trend: "Day after day, now from Texas, now from Tennessee, came reports of its doings. Now it was a negro whom the Ku Klux Klan hung without a trial, now a loyal white man, whom it butchered in cold blood or forced into exile."[29] As the reports came in from various southern correspondents, northern Republicans could not help but recognize the truth. The violence of the Ku Klux Klan served notice that the white South understood Reconstruction to be war by other means.

Thus, by mid-1868, the carpetbagger and the Klansman were both familiar figures on the nation's political and cultural landscape. As mobilized in popular discussion, they advanced two distinct views of the South and Reconstruction. To focus on the alleged malfeasance of the carpetbaggers was to depict the South as a land unlawfully invaded and defiled, and to paint Reconstruction as an orgy of plunder and oppression. Discussions of the Ku Klux Klan, for their part, tended to cast southern whites as dangerous barbarians incapable of accepting defeat and desperately in need of political, social, and moral regeneration. Though they had their roots in a shared recognition that all was not right in Dixie by 1868, the discourses surrounding the carpetbagger and the Ku Klux Klan offered diametrically opposed approaches to remedying the South's problems. A focus on the Ku Klux Klan seemed to mandate continued northern oversight of the region; an emphasis on the carpetbagger gestured toward a hasty conclusion to Reconstruction. The course and fate of Reconstruction rested, in large measure, on where northerners chose to place the blame.

## The Bloody South: The Ku Klux Klan in Northern Culture, 1868–1872

In 1868, E. C. Buell had an encounter with the Ku Klux Klan. While sitting in a tavern in New York, Buell was accosted by a strange-looking man, thrown into a carriage, and carried to a "shanty" on the outskirts of town. Inside, Buell spied newspaperman Horace Greeley's white hat being used as a bucket to transport blood. A number of Klansmen were busily chopping Secretary of the Navy Gideon Welles into strips, while their comrades beat on Secretary of War Edwin Stanton like a drum. President Andrew Johnson was there as well. He had, it seems, "opened a new tailor shop," where he made designer jackets out of hangman's nooses. Buell was overwhelmed by the horrible pageantry and the sinister choreography of the Klan's den. The noise was deafening, the bloodshed nauseating, and the chaos enough to make a more sober man's head spin. Said Buell: "What I saw, I'll remember forever, / The thought of it causes a shiver, / The dread three K's, the awful three K's, / the horrible Ku-Klux-Klan." And then Buell woke up. In the midst of the bloody chaos of the Klan's den, he felt a sharp blow to the back of his head, and found himself face-to-face with "old Dan" the bartender, who castigated his patron for passing out on the bar: "Then he called me a dunce and a fool, sir, / Said I'd been asleep on a stool, sir, /

You can be sure I was glad to find that I had, / And had not seen the horrible Klan."[30]

In reality, E. C. Buell was a "celebrated comedian and comic singer" based in New York, and the Klan encounter was the first entry in a small collection of his minstrel and comic songs published in 1868. Although the book contained the lyrics to many of Buell's most popular songs, including such favorites as "The Wild Young Irish Girl," "You Talk Too Much with Your Mouth," "Think of Your Head in the Morning," and "Teutonic Troubles," the Ku Klux Klan song was popular enough to warrant titling the collection *E. C. Buell's Ku Klux Klan Songster.* Buell's song was a simple comic ditty, designed to incite drunken laughter rather than deep contemplation. Even so, the song speaks volumes about how the northern public engaged with the Reconstruction-era Klan. Though he may have been the only one to describe the experience in rhymed couplets, E. C. Buell was not the only Yankee to suffer an extended Ku Klux Klan nightmare.

Simply put, northerners had never seen anything quite like the Ku Klux Klan. Although the association of the South with violence was certainly nothing new, the scale of the Ku Klux Klan combined with its air of dark mystery to make the organization irresistible to northerners. Even as they castigated the Klan and the region that had spawned it, northerners found themselves strangely attracted to the organization. They investigated, interviewed, hypothesized, debated, orated, and sometimes fictionalized, all in an attempt to make sense of the mysterious (and mysteriously compelling) organization terrorizing the South. Reports of Klan "outrages" filled newspapers, while editorial pages sagged under the weight of their own rhetoric. Careful explorations of the meaning, membership, and character of the Klan vied for readership with a series of sensationalist descriptions of lurid activities and bizarre rituals. The night riders of the Reconstruction Ku Klux Klan never crossed the Mason-Dixon line, but this did not prevent a full-fledged Klan mania from overtaking the print culture of the North.

The outrage story, a matter-of-fact newspaper account of Klan violence in the South, remained the most common means by which northern readers engaged with the Ku Klux Klan. From their first appearance early in 1868, such stories were a constant in northern media sources, offering a running commentary on the worrisome state of affairs in the South. On any particular day, a northern reader might open his or her newspaper to find that three black men had been hanged in South Carolina, or that a Unionist had been chased out of Tennessee, or that the Republicans of Georgia feared for their lives. Individually, the articles simply recounted personal suffering in the South. As a unit, however, they testified to the violent land of nightmares and broken promises that was the Ku Klux Klan's South.

A spate of Klan "exposés" that appeared on the northern literary marketplace between 1868 and 1872 covered much the same ground. If the daily updates provided in northern newspapers proved insufficient, Yankee readers could find in these pamphlets a condensed catalog of Klan atrocities, with descriptions frequently bordering on the grotesque. The anonymous author of *The Nation's Peril*, for instance, described the murder of Edward Thompson, a Georgia black man whom the Klan had "literally beaten to a jelly," and the case of Henry Lowther, who was "castrated in a most rude and brutal manner, begging piteously and writhing under the pains inflicted by his tormentors."[31] Another pamphlet, *Horrible Disclosures: A Full and Authentic Exposé of the Ku-Klux Klan*, narrated the fate of Holofornes Snow, a former slave who was hanged in front of his own cabin and then shot fifty-six times.[32] The same pamphlet capitalized on the propagandistic value of the Klan's crimes against women, inviting northern readers to imagine the agony of a Tennessee father forced to watch the rape of his wife and daughter by an entire band of Klansmen and narrating the attack on "Miss Phoebe Blanchfield, a beautiful New England girl of twenty-two," who was raped, mutilated, and left for dead in the woods, all for the crime of teaching at a freedmen's school in Alabama.[33]

These outrages, and hundreds like them, offered a vision of a violent and dangerous region: the Bloody South. A *New York Tribune* correspondent reporting from Raleigh, North Carolina, declared himself "utterly unable to present any adequate picture of the horrible tales that have come to my ears in one short day of my stay here." The correspondent had arrived in North Carolina "prepared to find that the stories of outrage which have reached the North were greatly exaggerated; but the reality seems to be that the one-tenth part has not been told." Despite the constant stream of outrage stories, northerners could barely comprehend the scale and ferocity of Klan violence. "Take your idea of Ku-Klux outrages," the correspondent instructed. "Whip your man or woman half to death, string up your victim to a tree and let him hang for days, bring to mind the worst case of rape you have ever heard of." Then, "multiply these instances by a hundred and throw in every form of torture and cruelty which ingenuity can suggest, with a few thousand lesser whippings which separately count for little, and you will get some idea of the state of affairs in North Carolina. The truth," he concluded, "has not been told in the North."[34]

At its heart, a Klan attack was a moment of starkly individualized terror. Generally taking place at or near one's home, the attack represented an intentional violation of one's privacy and self-sovereignty. Though the Klan responded to large-scale political occurrences, its attacks were intensely personal. In dragging African Americans and white Republicans from their homes and beating them (or worse) the Klan served notice that such groups could expect no quarter in the postwar South. This aspect of Klan terror is given eloquent voice in Frank Bellew's 1872 *Harper's Weekly* sketch, "Visit of the Ku-Klux." The drawing depicts the inside of an African American cabin somewhere in the South. A family of five occupies the foreground, but three masked and armed Klansmen loom in the shadows. The image casts the night visits of the Ku Klux Klan in deeply personal terms. Bellew has placed the viewer inside the cabin, thereby focusing attention on the victims of the Klan attack, rather than on their assailants. The Klansmen appear on the periphery, their costumes and masks rather nondescript and their numbers not particularly overwhelming. The power of the image is rooted in its ability to reduce the Klan to its very essence: individualized, face-to-face violence, fear, and death.[35]

Despite the image's intensity and familiarity, Bellew's sketch is not, in fact, representative of the larger body of northern thought and commentary on the KKK. The very things that make the image so evocative—the focus on the victims, the invasion of the domestic sphere, the starkly individualized nature of political terrorism—also make it somewhat atypical. Klan coverage almost always had more to say about the perpetrators of Klan violence than about its victims. Northerners encountered Klan victims almost exclusively as an aggregate, a collective entity. Because the next attack (and, therefore, the next outrage story) was always just around the corner, northerners never had a chance to focus on an individual attack for long. Whether over a series of days in a newspaper or a series of pages in one of the aforementioned pamphlets on the Klan, victims existed as part of a continuum tying one outrage to those that came before and to those that would follow. As such, the individual victims of the Klan were rendered curiously silent and effectively invisible.

The very nature of northern Klan reporting, therefore, encouraged Yankees to view the organization macroscopically. Rather than focusing

Frank Bellew, "Visit of the Ku-Klux," *Harper's Weekly*, February 24, 1872. Bellew's focus on the victims of the Ku Klux Klan makes this image somewhat atypical in the period's Klan discourse. Library of Congress.

on individual victims, northern Republicans almost unconsciously trained their collective gaze on the society that allowed such violence to take root and flourish. The Ku Klux Klan, in other words, came to represent more than the sum of its outrages. It served as a synecdoche, a part of the South that explained the whole. The constant, predictable appearance of Klan outrage stories in major northern newspapers and small-run pamphlets spoke to the essential deviance of southern white society. Klan attacks became the raw materials out of which northerners fashioned an image of a backward, bloody, and dangerous South.

Northern Republican commentators tended to assume that the activities of the Ku Klux Klan provided an accurate measure of the state of political feeling among the majority of white southerners. According to Charles Stearns, an abolitionist and Kansas Free-Soiler who had migrated to Georgia after the war, the Klan was "rather the exponent of the average Southern sentiment, than an exceptional class of any nature whatsoever."[36] The organization was no aberration, Stearns insisted. It was a natural outgrowth of the region's experiences and worldview. In an 1870 pamphlet, another northern-born Georgia resident argued that "the 'skull and bones,' the insignia of the Ku-Klux Klan and not the stars and stripes, represent the dominant power in that region."[37] Somewhat more imaginative was the northern-born author of an 1868 pamphlet, who claimed to have been initiated into the Klan in a ceremony that prominently featured the following lines: "Every Southron belongs to us, by birth, by education, by the love of liberty inhaled with the balmy breezes of the sunny South, by the hatred of the northern clans imbibed with his mother's milk."[38] Though the initiation story was somewhat far-fetched, the notion that "every Southron" belonged to the Ku Klux Klan was evident in much northern discussion of the organization.

In their attempt to understand the KKK, northern Republicans frequently turned to the past, putting the Klan at the tail end of an extended genealogy of southern malfeasance. *Harper's Weekly* opened a December 1868 article on "Ku-Kluxism" with a description of the 1856 caning of Charles Sumner, before offering a greatest hits of southern atrocities during the Civil War: the scalping of dead Union soldiers at Pea Ridge, the massacre of African American soldiers at Fort Pillow, the hellish condition of the Confederate prisons. "All this we should willingly leave to the historian," the journal claimed, "but for the unfortunate development of the same barbarism since the close of the war."[39] In a similar vein, the *Independent* offered a Klan-inspired reworking of William Seward's "Irrepressible Conflict" between the sections, casting American history as a timeless struggle between northern "Civilization" and southern "Barbarism." For nearly a century, the article explained, "a highly civilized people, educated and formed by the blessed influences of freedom and education, have been contending, in various fields and under different banners, with a semi-barbarous race, springing from the same stock as ourselves, but depraved, debauched, and demoralized by the influences of slavery."[40] In light of this larger history, the journal found the activities of the Klan distressing but not entirely surprising.

Most often, the Klan served as evidence that the white South was still fighting the Civil War. In editorials written for his newspaper, the *New National Era*, Frederick Douglass consistently employed the word *rebel*, forcing his readers to acknowledge a continuity between southern past and southern present.[41] In February 1870, he noted that "the whole rebel population, with only just enough exceptions to prove the rule, seem to have been transformed either into assassins or the most brutal and ruffianly tyrants."[42] A few months later, Douglass had not changed his tune. "When are these outrages to end?" he asked. "Probably not until the present generation has died out. They are still rebels at heart, and hate the colored man as bitterly as ever, and the Union even more bitterly, if possible."[43] Still later, he characterized the Klan as "the new rebellion, so long threatened by southern traitors."[44] In Douglass's hands, the Klan was simply the logical extension of the South's bloody past, a "huge, misshapen reptile spawned from the foul decay of slavery and rebellion."[45] Official hostilities may have ended with the surrender at Appomattox, but the sentiments that caused the rebellion were alive and well.

Union veteran and North Carolina resident Albion Tourgée likewise feared that the white South was again at war. "I could stand it very well to fight for Uncle Sam," Tourgée reflected, "but this lying down, tied hand and foot with the shackles of the law, to be killed by the very dregs of the rebellion," was another matter entirely. Tourgée called on congressional Republicans to recognize the true condition of affairs in the South and to act accordingly.[46] Massachusetts congressman Benjamin Butler, a former Union general and one of the most consistently Radical voices in Washington, warned that if the Klan and its allies persisted in making war on the Union, the loyal North was more than willing to act in kind. "When our bugle sounds 'boots and saddles,'" Butler promised, "every Republican will mount ready for the fray, and each squadron will gallop into column eager to meet their old foes." Recalling his wartime glory days, Butler vowed that "when our trumpet rings out 'Charge!' we shall dash forward as one man, to the music of the good old tune of 'John Brown's body lies mouldering in the ground, But his soul is marching on.' And the dismayed and discomfited allied army of the Democracy, rebels, and Ku-Klux Klans will again go down before us."[47] Much of Butler's bluster can be dismissed as political theater, but his conflation of "rebels" and "Ku-Klux Klans" was no accident. Klan masks had replaced rebel gray, but Butler found that little else had changed.

Tales of the Ku Klux Klan's Bloody South tapped into a pair of conflicting impulses at the heart of Republican Reconstruction. On the one hand, discussion of the Klan buttressed the case for a thorough—and thoroughly northern—Reconstruction of the region. The Civil War, it was clear, had not eradicated the last vestiges of a society defiled by slaveholding. The region was still backward, still rebellious, still violent. It was incumbent on northern Republicans to replace these attributes with more wholesome ones, by any means necessary. On the other hand, the Klan raised uncomfortable questions about the entire Reconstruction enterprise. What if white southerners *were* still fighting the Civil War? What if the South was *too* bloody? What if the region proved unreconstructable? The Ku Klux Klan served as a vessel into which northern Republicans poured their deepest fears about the South. Nothing less than the fate of Reconstruction and the future of the nation hung in the balance.

In constructing a picture of a deviant white South, northerners did not rely solely on acts of violence. Although they paid copious attention to the constant stream of Klan outrages occurring across the South, Yankees never lost sight of the peculiar theatricality with which the Klan went about its bloody business, nor could they entirely shake the notion that there was something vaguely otherworldly about the Ku Klux Klan. As they debated the political meaning of the Klan and the effect of southern violence on the Reconstruction process, northerners also engaged with the more theatrical aspects of the Klan, pondering the meaning of the group's name, cataloging the secret codes and passwords with which it communicated, and exploring the dark secrets of its initiation ceremonies.[48] Northerners' consistent use of the Klan as a synecdoche for the larger South—the Klan's deviance was the South's deviance, and vice versa—turned the group's costuming, ceremony, and symbols into evidence every bit as significant as its violence. Even something so seemingly innocuous as a secret hand signal or password could offer the engaged northerner abundant proof of the essential, timeless aberrance of white southern society. In making a case against the Bloody South, then, the cloak was as important as the dagger.

Republican commentators eager to provide their readers with unfettered access to the internal workings of the KKK offered a dizzying array of distinctive (and often contradictory) accounts of various aspects of Klan ceremony and practice. Curious northern readers would have found, for instance, that the name "Ku Klux Klan" might have been rooted in the Greek word for circle, Kuklo, or it might have been related to the sound a gun made when being cocked ("ku klux") and fired ("klan!"), or, perhaps, it might have meant nothing at all.[49] Less discriminating readers might have even believed that the organization drew its moniker from the infamous Texas bandit Nal K. Xulkuk—"Ku Klux Klan" spelled backward.[50] An attempt to decode the secret signals, passwords, and handshakes of the KKK would have yielded a mind-boggling sequence of doffed caps, pulled ears, pocketed hands, and snapped fingers, along with a variety of nonsensical verbal cues and riddles.[51]

Innumerable Klan notices reprinted in northern media sources, meanwhile, provided a glossary of ghoulish terms and nightmarish figures.

Some Klan notices consisted of straightforward threats addressed to a single individual or family. Many, however, lacked this specificity and immediacy. Quite a few, in fact, said nothing at all about black suffrage, Radical Republicans, Yankee aggression, or Reconstruction. Early in 1868, the *Chicago Tribune* printed the following notice, without any editorial comment:

DEN OF SKULLS, DAY OF RETRIBUTION
    Spirits of the dead arise! Your Chief commands—To-day the 7th of the mortals' month of March you will scatter the clouds of the grave and be ready for THE MYSTERIOUS MISSION. The guilty we free to commit dark deeds that mortal eyes do not see. We disown them and must be the avengers. BE READY. "*In hoc signo.*"
    THE SUPREME CYCLOPS[52]

What Chicago readers were supposed to make of this bizarre pronouncement remains an open question. In 1871, in the midst of a debate over enforcement legislation in the South, Republican congressman Job Stevenson of Ohio saw fit to read seven Klan notices into the *Congressional Record*. As part of a discussion relating to the right of the federal government to take steps against political violence in the South, Stevenson thought it pertinent that "twice hath the sacred serpent hissed," that "the Grand Cyclops never sleeps," and that "his bony fingers have pointed to the 'Bleeding Band.'"[53] Such ghoulish characters were common enough in Republican writings to become an object of Democratic mockery. "At the call of the Cyclops," teased the *New York World* in 1871, "Gnome, Dragon, Night Hawk, and all sally forth, bearing a black isosceles triangle shaped banner bordering with yellow, and having thereon as a terror to the negroes the image of a ramping hippogriff spouting Latin like any heraldic lion, wolf, or bear."[54]

When northerners sought the most fantastic and phantasmagorical aspects of the Klan, they turned to the organization's initiation ceremonies. In April 1868, northern papers reported that Memphis police had raided a Klan hideout, arresting twenty men and seizing "a lot of masks and a skull" as well as "a document purporting to be a constitution of the Order."[55] The constitution offered curious northerners a tantalizing glimpse inside the Ku Klux Klan. Among other secrets, the document described a Klan initiation, an elaborate affair that included hooded Klansmen brandishing daggers and an oath of eternal fealty sworn on a human skull.[56] Such reporting allowed northerners to vicariously and somewhat voyeuristically

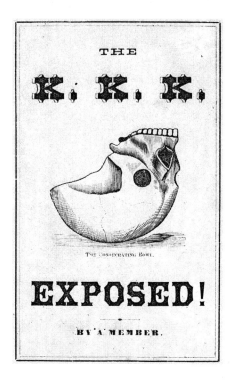

Frontispiece of *The Oaths, Signs, Ceremonies, and Objects of the Ku-Klux-Klan*, an 1868 Klan pamphlet, depicting the "Consecrating Bowl" allegedly used in Klan initiations. The image highlights the centrality of the mysterious and the grotesque in popular discussions of the Ku Klux Klan. Hargrett Rare Book and Manuscript Library, University of Georgia Libraries.

engage with the dark rites of the KKK. Most descriptions of Klan initiations followed the general outlines of the Memphis constitution, but many offered new twists or rituals, most of them tending toward the grotesque. The author of one exposé insisted that Klan initiates were forced to seal their oaths with the "consecrating drink": human blood, served in a human skull.[57] Another described a ceremony culminating in the execution of a traitor to the Klan. Usually a lifelike wax effigy was used, but sometimes, the pamphlet suggested, the initiation ended with a real sacrifice.[58]

Given the consistently fantastic nature of Klan discourse, it is hardly surprising that commentators occasionally stretched the limits of believability. Two documents, in particular—the strange tale of W. P. Norman and a novella called *The Terrible Mysteries of the Ku Klux Klan*—highlight the ease with which Klan fact could slide into Klan fiction. Even in the midst of a conversation dominated by the surreal and the barely believable, these texts stand out, their dark spectacle and obvious fictionalization setting them off from the main body of Klan commentary. Not tied to fact or evidence, these flights of fancy offered readers an unmediated vision of the Bloody South at its most monstrous, diabolical, and imaginative.

The narrative of W. P. Norman, which appears in the middle of a relatively realistic 1868 Klan pamphlet called *Horrible Disclosures*, speaks to the monster at the heart of the South—literally. While in Mobile, Alabama, on business, an Ohio native named William Pembroke Norman is plucked off the street and hauled before a meeting of the Ku Klux Klan. After a brief "trial," he is sentenced to death, for the crimes of "sympathy with the radicals, and advocacy of negro suffrage."[59] To this point, the story appears plausible, if a bit far-fetched. When Norman is shuttled to the dark bowels of the Klan's building, however, the tale quickly takes a turn. In a subbasement, Norman comes face to face with the "very embodiment of hideousness," a monster known as the Black Death. Norman describes the creature as follows: "It represented a huge blackamoor, with white wool, tusks like a polar bear, eyes like twin *ignis-fatui*, and a gaunt body that denoted great strength and activity. From head to foot this strange being was bedecked with bones, that rattled as he moved, and seemed to afford him the utmost delight. From his neck [descended] a chain to which was attached an infant's skull, eyeless, toothless, and loathsome; but he kissed it, and fondled it, and mumbled over it, and grinned at me like the incarnation of the king of hell."[60] The monster attacks Norman, tossing him around like a ragdoll and torturing him for several hours with a "murderous looking bowie-knife."[61] Barely clinging to life, Norman finally manages to scramble through a small window, escaping the clutches of the Black Death. To his shock, he finds himself back in the business district of Mobile, where passersby go about their business as usual, seemingly unaware of the Black Death and his chamber of horrors.

For sheer fantasy, even W. P. Norman's ordeal pales in comparison with the events described in *The Terrible Mysteries of the Ku Klux Klan*. The text, allegedly the dying confession of a Klansman as transcribed by his doctor, is fifty-six pages of perverse nightmare-scape. The tale opens with the arrival of a northern traveler in a small southern town. Witnessing a number of bizarre visions, culminating in an epic battle in the sky between a "jet black monster" and a "splendid majestic figure" in white, the traveler is inspired to undertake a journey to the "Den of the Red Death" in order to join the Ku Klux Klan.[62] His passage across a surreal southern landscape leads him up a mountain, past two giant monsters, over a cliff, through a Civil War battlefield (complete with ghostly cavalry), across a river of blood, and finally into the Den of the Red Death. The initiation, which takes up almost half of the text, features burning swords, sentient skeletons, magical mirrors, and human sacrifices, all presided over by the beautiful and horrible "Red Death." Overwhelmed by what he is forced to recall, the initiate dies before completing his narration, the last terrible mysteries of the Ku Klux Klan unspoken.[63]

On one level, such texts are so ridiculous as to appear almost useless to historians. At the same time, however, the very extremity of these stories renders them significant. In the unnamed traveler's journey across a twisted and blood-soaked southern landscape, in W. P. Norman's encounter with the gruesome Black Death in the dungeon of a building in Mobile's business district, northerners found metaphorical confirmation of everything they had come to suspect about the Ku Klux Klan's South. The region is depicted as a violent wasteland and a hallucinogenic dystopia. The KKK is only a reflection of a deeper, more generalized, southern malfeasance. Even if such texts were not factually on point regarding the KKK, they tapped into a deeper sort of truth, a shared understanding that lay deep within northern Republican culture during Reconstruction. If there were not literally monsters in southern basements, there was still plenty about the Bloody South that northerners found monstrous.

By early 1871, congressional Republicans had resolved to take affirmative steps against the Ku Klux Klan. The Ku Klux Klan Act, passed in April, was the third in a series of Enforcement Acts designed to provide the federal government with the legal means to attack the organization. The Ku Klux Klan Act put certain crimes under federal jurisdiction and gave the president the power to suspend the writ of habeas corpus in response to organized political violence. Recognizing that they had to understand the Klan in order to defeat it, congressional Republicans also convened a bipartisan committee to undertake a series of hearings into southern violence. Beginning with sessions in North Carolina, the committee soon sent representatives across the South. The subcommittees interviewed a broad swath of the southern population, including Klan members and Klan victims. After almost a year of work, the Joint Select Committee to Inquire into the Condition of Affairs in the Late Insurrectionary States presented their findings—twelve volumes' worth—to Congress.[64]

The hearings offered an unprecedented opening for average southerners to present their understanding of the Ku Klux Klan to the nation. The Klan's predominantly African American victims eagerly seized the opportunity. Though congressional Democrats subjected witnesses to rigorous and frequently hostile cross-examination, the subjectivities and understandings of the witnesses still ring through the testimony. In the midst of the almost deafening chorus of Klan commentary that swept the nation between 1868 and 1872, the words of individual victims offer a distinct and moving testimony to the true nature of the Reconstruction Klan.[65]

As a general rule, Klan victims expressed little interest in the more phantasmagorical aspects of Klan practice. When Elias Hill testified before the subcommittee in Yorkville, South Carolina, he described his beating by the Klan in excruciating detail. It was only after a direct question, however, that he felt compelled to mention the disguises worn by his attackers.[66] Essic Harris of North Carolina noted that one of his attackers wore "a false face with horns on it," but only to explain his failure to identify any of his assailants.[67] In Mississippi, William Coleman testified that his attackers wore masks and claimed to have ridden directly from the battlefield at Shiloh. When asked if the Klansman identified themselves as dead Confederate soldiers, however, Coleman was dismissive: "They didn't tell me nothing about spirits."[68] Having encountered the night riders of the Klan face-to-face, Klan victims cared little for the spectacle and pageantry that so captivated northern commentators.

Similarly, Klan victims were quick to note the baldly political purposes of the organization. When asked to explain how they came to be Klan targets, victims consistently turned to one explanation: their Republican politics. When Klansmen visited Samuel Bonner of Spartanburg, South Carolina, they asked whether he had voted for Robert K. Scott, the Republican candidate for governor. When Bonner admitted that he had, one of the Klansmen hissed, "Yes, I can smell you now, you are a d——d radical." Bonner, along with his mother and sister, were dragged from the house and beaten.[69] Daniel Lipscomb was beaten because he was "a good old rattler"—Democratic slang for "Radical."[70] Clem Bowden testified that after the Klan attacked him for his Republicanism, they moved on to his wife, reasoning that "she might have taught me better than to be a radical."[71] White Republican officials confirmed the essentially political nature of Klan violence. J. B. Eaves, a white Republican in North Carolina, testified that he knew of only one Klan attack on a Democrat in the state. He identified the unlucky outlier as a Cleveland County man named Rourke, who had been "going after bad women."[72] This, however, was the exception that proved the rule. Unlike northern commentators, who spent years debating the true meaning of the Ku Klux Klan, the organization's victims held few illusions as to the Klan's true import. In victim testimony, the Klan was depicted as a band of political terrorists who aimed to destroy the Republican Party in the South and overturn the rights inscribed in the Fourteenth and Fifteenth Amendments.

In their testimony, Klan victims frequently offered their own scarred and broken bodies as evidence of the Klan's ferocity. White Republican legislator James Justice (a Klan victim himself) reported that such physical evidence of Klan violence was quite common in North Carolina. "I have seen a great many persons in Raleigh," he testified, "who have come there and exhibited their persons to anyone who might wish to see them, with their backs lashed, and with wounds from gun and pistol-shots."[73] Joseph Beckwith reported that after the Klan attempted to hang him outside his Mississippi home, "I was suffering for three months so that I couldn't see hardly, and I did no work for two or three weeks. My eyes were bloodshot for three months."[74] In Alabama, John Childers told the committee that his assailants had struck him from behind with a shotgun, adding that "the scars are here on my skull to show for themselves."[75] James H. Alston would always carry a reminder of the Klan with him: "I have now in me buck and ball that injures me a good deal, and I think it will be for life."[76] Such corporeal evidence of the Klan's reign of terror became a common sight in much of the South.

Victims also offered eloquent testimony to the emotional and psychological effects of a Klan attack. Charlotte Fowler of South Carolina described the horror of a child forced to watch the murder of her grandfather in the doorway of his house. "The little child followed its grandfather to the door," Fowler recalled. "I heard the report of a pistol, and they shot him down; and this little child ran back to me before I could get out and says, 'Oh, grandma, they have killed my poor grandpappy.'"[77] After Klansmen seized his son Billy, Augustus Blair of Huntsville, Alabama, followed the group to a woods, where he listened as the eighteen-year-old was stabbed to death. The distraught father testified that "I was not further from them than twenty yards. I crept right around behind the patch of briars and laid there. He never hollered but once, but I could hear him."[78] Such experiences necessarily produced deep alienation and fear, emotions that Klan victims frequently described in their testimony. Jane Surratt told the South Carolina committee that she worried that her children might never recover from the emotional scars inflicted by the Klan. "They whipped my son miserably bad; they whipped my daughter very bad; she has not been able to do much since; I don't believe she will ever get over it."[79]

In the midst of a national conversation about the Ku Klux Klan that only infrequently found the time to engage with the lived experience of Klan victims, the testimony collected by the Joint Select Committee offers a remarkable glimpse at how southern African Americans understood the

KKK. Klan victims used the hearings to tell *their* story of the South. In the process, they constructed an important counternarrative to prevailing notions of the Ku Klux Klan. Eschewing fantasy, costuming, and spectacle, their testimony consistently emphasized the callous disregard with which black lives and rights were treated in much of the South and the lasting effects of Klan violence on African American families and communities. Speaking with a power and an immediacy conspicuously lacking in most of the era's Klan reporting, victim testimony offered a damning indictment of southern racial violence and a poignant plea for federal protection.

## Tigers and Lambs: The Joint Select Committee Report and the Election of 1872

The year 1872 offered Americans two opportunities to grapple with the Klan/carpetbagger binary. In February, Republican and Democratic committee members produced two distinct reports to accompany the findings of the Joint Select Committee to Inquire into the Condition of Affairs in the Late Insurrectionary States. While the Republicans emphasized Klan violence and political terrorism, the Democrats turned their minority report into a critique of oppressive Reconstruction policy and unnecessary northern interventionism, with the carpetbagger playing a starring role. Nine months later, the election of 1872 replayed the same debate. Horace Greeley's campaign to unseat the incumbent, U. S. Grant, turned the election into a referendum on Reconstruction. Throughout the campaign, Greeley's supporters strove mightily to tie Grant to dastardly carpetbaggers, while Grant's advocates all but declared their opponent to be a member of the Ku Klux Klan. In both cases, discussion of the carpetbaggers and the Ku Klux Klan served as a proxy for larger debates about the progress of Reconstruction, the state of the South, and the future of the nation.

If the Joint Select Committee's hearings presented an opening for those closest to the Klan—its members and victims—to explain themselves to the nation, the Republican majority report and the Democratic minority report published in February 1872 offered a sterling opportunity for the major political parties to shape Klan discourse. By most reasonable estimations, such an exhaustive survey should have been sufficient to establish the truth about the Ku Klux Klan, or at least to set out an agreed-upon body of facts. But this was not to be. The committee's majority and minority reports failed to find much common ground in their depictions of the South. They seemed, in fact, to be talking about two entirely different regions. As *Frank Leslie's Illustrated Newspaper* put it, "The committee to whom this matter was confided have made not one, but two reports—a majority and a minority report. These two reports directly contradict each other—the first affirming one state of things at the South, the other insisting on directly the reverse." *Leslie's* marveled that "one declares the South to be a ravening tiger; the other, a persecuted lamb. One believes in the existence of a Ku-Klux organization," while "the other roundly declares that the existence of any such organization is a myth, a falsehood and a fable."[80]

The Republican majority report offered a forthright appraisal of the Ku Klux Klan and its meaning for the Reconstruction effort. The committee's Republicans insisted that the Klan was a "widespread and dangerous conspiracy" made up of "cowardly midnight prowlers and assassins who scourge and kill the poor and defenseless."[81] Spread across the South and supported by a broad coalition of southern whites, the Klan was unified in its opposition to Reconstruction, Republicanism, and black suffrage. Committee Republicans recognized that "reluctant obedience" might be all the nation could hope for from the South, but they warned that this obedience would be secured, even if it "require[d] the strong arm of the Government to protect its citizens in the enjoyment of their rights, to keep the peace[,]" and to prevent a "war of races."[82] Though they were, given the circumstances, remarkably sympathetic to the position of white southerners—urging an end to limitations on ex-Confederate office holding and asking northerners to display "forbearance and conciliation" toward the South—the Joint Select Committee's majority found in the testimony clear confirmation of the prevailing Republican understanding of the Ku Klux Klan.[83]

The Democrats did not concur. The Democratic view of the Ku Klux Klan had changed little since 1868. Alternately denying the Klan's existence and condoning its activities (a tactic that prompted Republican congressman George C. McKee of Mississippi to opine, "Oh, consistency, thou art too rare and costly a jewel to be spared to Ku Klux and Democrats!"), Democrats argued that the purported Klan conspiracy was largely a function of fevered Republican imaginations.[84] The real story was not the Klan, Democrats insisted, but "the atrocious measures by which millions of white people have been put at the mercy of the semi-barbarous negroes of the South" and Republicans' persistence in "defaming the people upon whom this unspeakable outrage had been committed."[85] The twelve volumes of testimony, Democrats insisted, proved not the existence of the Ku

Klux Klan but the lengths to which Republicans would go to besmirch the good name of the South.

When Democrats engaged with the Ku Klux Klan, the carpetbaggers could never be far behind. Discussion of northern oppression obscured and abetted by tall tales of Ku Klux terror seemed to flow naturally into commentary on the South's most visible and egregious oppressors. In response to the majority's portrayal of a peaceful Reconstruction under siege, the minority depicted a beleaguered South staggering under the weight of a dictatorial president and a dangerous occupying force. "Before even breathing-time was allowed them," the Democratic minority wrote of the white South, "a set of harpies, most of whom had shirked the dangers of the battle-field, camp-followers, horse-holders, 'cow-boys,' plunderers from both sides during all the years of strife, rushed down singly and in squads on that people, thus prostrate and defenseless, and for their own private gain seized and carried off whatever could be found worth seizing in that country."[86] The minority insisted that the "genus carpet-bagger has been mainly the cause of the present deplorable condition of affairs" in the South. This "demon of discord and anarchy" provided all the explanation necessary for the rise of the Ku Klux Klan.[87] The Klan "was the legitimate offspring of misrule; it follows and disappears with its parent."[88] The peculiar force destroying the South was not the Ku Klux, but the carpetbagger. Ridding the South of the former, the Democrats insisted, simply required ridding it of the latter.

Seven years of Reconstruction and twelve volumes of testimony had convinced the Joint Select Committee—Republican and Democrat alike—that the South remained in serious turmoil. The underlying cause of this condition, however, was an open question. The presidential election of 1872 would put it to a vote. The election pitted Ulysses S. Grant, seeking a second term, against Horace Greeley, the long-time editor of the *New York Tribune* and the nominee of the Liberal Republicans, a group of disaffected Republicans and reform Democrats unhappy with the conduct of Reconstruction and fed up with the corruption and cronyism of the Grant administration.[89] The Liberals found in the "terrible carpetbagger" an ideal symbol of all that was wrong with Grant's Reconstruction policy.

An 1871 trip across the Deep South had turned Horace Greeley against the carpetbaggers with a vengeance.[90] Upon his return to New York, Greeley treated a packed house at Lincoln Hall to a lengthy harangue against corrupt northern officeholders and parsimonious swindlers, ending with the suggestion that carpetbaggers had taken the "apostolic injunction to 'pray without ceasing'" as an invitation to "prey" without ceasing.[91] Greeley had sounded the call. For northerners weary of Reconstruction and uncomfortable with the conduct of the Grant administration, the carpetbagger made a handy scapegoat. Liberal and reform-leaning newspapers spent most of 1872 vying with each other to see who could offer the most scathing indictment of the carpetbaggers. "What a spectacle of scoundrels," Greeley's *New York Tribune* howled in August, "whole festoons of leeches swelling with the public life-blood, until satiated they drop off and sink into their original obscurity!"[92] The *Springfield Republican* adopted an identical metaphor, writing that the carpetbaggers' cries of "more"— "more debt, more taxes, more stealings"—made them seem like "so many daughters of the horse-leech."[93] From Louisiana, a *Chicago Tribune* correspondent added: "The carcass brings the vultures; the booty brings the robbers."[94] Writing in the *Cincinnati Commercial*, former Oberlin College president Asa Mahan cast the carpetbaggers as "clouds of vampires, lighting upon and sucking the blood of the body politic."[95]

At the heart of the Liberal critique was a conviction that the carpetbagger's control of southern politics was fundamentally illegitimate and undemocratic. Continuously connecting carpetbaggers to Grant, their patron and benefactor, Liberals warned that the president's patronage power had allowed him to amass an army of faithful appointees in the South, making him the "unseen force" that controlled southern state governments.[96] The carpetbaggers, the *Chicago Tribune* insisted, were Grant's "household troops" in Congress. "They owe to him their positions in their States, and he owes to their votes his majority in Congress."[97] It was Grant, the paper reiterated later that month, who had "fastened the carpet-bag *regime* upon the Southern States."[98] Aided and abetted by undue federal involvement in the South, the carpetbaggers invaded the region and sucked the state treasuries dry. In so doing, they subverted the meaning of democracy, rendering the voters of the South powerless in the face of the unholy alliance connecting Washington, DC, and the southern state capitols.

Grant's supporters could not help but notice that "an infinite deal of rant and slander" regarding the carpetbaggers seemed to be emanating from the Liberal camp.[99] Abolitionist Gerrit Smith wondered why Greeley had "ten words against the Carpet baggers where he had one against the Ku Klux," while the *Independent* declared Greeley's carpetbagger fixation to be "simply stupid."[100] When they were not defending the carpetbaggers, Grant Republicans sought to tie Greeley to the Ku Klux Klan. A southern correspondent for the *New York Times* informed readers that "the whole Order of the Kuklux is for Mr. Greeley and against Gen. Grant."[101] In September, the editorial page of the same paper darkly warned that "Mr. Greeley's constant talk about carpet-baggers is meant for Southern ears, and to them it conveys hints easily understood of the latitude which Greeley as President would allow to the vindictive passions of the Kuklux."[102] The *Boston Daily Globe* agreed, offering the following summation of the candidate's Reconstruction plans: "by letting loose the Ku-Klux clans, he proposes to rescue the Southern States from the hands of the so-called carpet-bag governments."[103] Though they were largely unwilling to offer a forthright defense of the carpetbaggers—a notable shift from the "positive good" rhetoric of 1868—Grant Republicans clearly considered them to be the lesser of two evils. Greeley's myopic focus on the carpetbaggers, they insisted, suggested a dangerous ignorance of the true state of affairs in the South.

The election of 1872 offered voters a choice, therefore, not just between Greeley and Grant but between two alternative visions of Reconstruction, characterized by the carpetbagger and the Ku Klux Klan. In November, Grant won handily, taking 55 percent of the popular vote. While Grant's victory might be chalked up to a number of sources—the president's continuing popularity, the nation's unreadiness for Greeley's message of reconciliation, the vagaries of the Liberal platform—it also suggests that, as of November 1872, the nation found the Ku Klux Klan to be more troubling than the carpetbaggers. The majority of Americans had, for the time being, united behind Reconstruction, Grant, and fear of the KKK. This consensus, however, would not last.

### The South Besieged: The Carpetbagger and the Turn from Interventionism, 1872–1877

When John Russell Bartlett, a linguist and Rhode Island politician, set about preparing the fourth edition of his *Dictionary of Americanisms* in 1877, he found the philological terrain of the United States a far different place than he had left it in his 1859 third edition. Four years of war and a decade of Reconstruction had changed the language as much as it had the nation. On page 100 of Bartlett's updated *Dictionary*, which offered readers "a glossary of words and phrases usually regarded as peculiar to the United States," one finds the entry for the term "Carpet-bagger," nestled between "Carolina Potato" and "Carpet-Weed." The *Dictionary* does not offer a single definition of the term, instead providing a number of passages drawn from a variety of published sources. Collectively, they shed light on how the term was mobilized and understood in U.S. culture. South Carolina's redeemer, Governor Wade Hampton, offers his take ("and when I say *carpet-baggers* I mean by that thief"), as does President Rutherford B. Hayes ("those who went South for the purpose of holding office as a matter of business should be stigmatized as a *carpet-bagger*"). A notice that carpetbag governors in nine states had amassed a collective debt nearing $200 million stands next to a humorous aside describing a precipitous decline in carpetbag sales, owing to the luggage's infamous handlers. The lengthiest passage, drawn from a particularly vicious *North American Review* article by Jeremiah S. Black, longtime Democratic politician and inveterate opponent of Reconstruction, offers a veritable catalog of carpetbagger insults and stereotypes: "unprincipled adventurers," "camp followers," "thieves," pillaging "hordes" who moved south "to feed on the substance of a prostrate and defen[s]eless people."[104]

The treatment of the carpetbagger in the *Dictionary of Americanisms* points to a pair of important truths. First, the sheer heft of the entry suggests the centrality of the carpetbagger to popular discussion of Reconstruction. "Ku Klux Klan," by way of comparison, merits only a brief definition ("originally a secret political organization in some of the Southern States, but which subsequently laid aside all connection with politics, and resorted to murder to carry out their purposes") and a single popular example, drawn from an 1868 campaign tune.[105] More significant, however, is the obvious fact that the definitions of carpetbagger are universally, undeniably, and unequivocally negative. Though Bartlett offered seven distinct usages, drawn from both sides of the Mason-Dixon and all across the political spectrum, the term is uniformly cast as an epithet and an insult. As a rough measure of the place of the carpetbagger in the American imagination by 1877, the *Dictionary of Americanisms* speaks volumes.

Bartlett was not alone. The steadily increasing visibility of the carpetbagger and the nearly universal disdain with which the figure came to be treated, even by northern Republicans, reflected important trends in Reconstruction politics in the years following the election of 1872. These shifts were neither immediate nor complete. In many cases, they were not even conscious. Even so, their existence and import are undeniable. Between 1872 and 1877, the popular view of northern politicians in the South underwent a profound transformation. Writings from both sides of the Mason-Dixon line began to depict carpetbaggers as scheming vagabonds and impecunious swindlers. Rather than victims of Klan attacks, northern politicians in the South were increasingly likely to be excoriated as the assassins of proper governance south of the Mason-Dixon. In a mere handful of years, the carpetbagger became terrible.

The outlines of this shift are made readily apparent in Edward King's popular travelogue *The Great South*, published as a series of articles in 1874 and as a book a year later. For the most part, King had very little to say about Reconstruction. One could argue, in fact, that King could call the South "Great" precisely because he ignored contemporary politics almost entirely, focusing instead on character sketches, environmental description, and historical narration. As a result, King's text is remarkably even-handed, possessing none of the vitriol of its better-known contemporary, James S. Pike's *The Prostrate State*.[106] When he ever so briefly took up the question of the carpetbagger, however, King did something interesting: he wrote in caricature. Describing a visit to the Louisiana legislature in New Orleans, King noted that the body's African American members "constantly [submit] to corrections and suggestions from some lean white man, dressed in new clothes, who smiles contemptuously, as, from a carpet-bag point of view, he superintends this legislative farce."[107] Such a characterization is entirely out of keeping with the majority of King's text. This over-drawn, rather unbelievable image—the puppet-master carpetbagger, smiling cruelly as he directs his black legislative minions in a cynical mockery of proper governance—is culled straight from the southern conservative anticarpetbagger playbook, and yet there it sits, presented as the gospel truth for millions of curious Yankees to read.

King's wholehearted embrace of this stereotype is indicative of the way northern culture at large came to view the carpetbaggers between 1872 and 1877. Northern Republicans began to mimic not only the tone but the very language of the South's anticarpetbagger propaganda. Thomas Wentworth Higginson, a Union officer and commander of an African American regiment during the Civil War, declared that any Yankee politician who remained in the South by 1874 was, more likely than not, a "mean man," a "scoundrel," and "like Shakespeare's Shylock."[108] The *Christian Union*, meanwhile, "denounced the peculations and frauds of the 'carpet-baggers,' by which two or three of the Southern States have been reduced to the direst extremity of poverty and degradation."[109] As even Radical-leaning Republican publications began to pepper their articles on Reconstruction with matter-of-fact references to the "wholesale plundering of carpetbagging adventurers," they subtly undermined the case for continued northern involvement in southern affairs.[110]

Perhaps recognizing the prevailing winds, a number of African American commentators sought to rhetorically distance the southern freedpeople from the carpetbaggers. In 1873, J. Sella Martin, a minister and former slave, bemoaned the fact that the violence of southern whites had driven the region's black population into the arms of the carpetbaggers. "It ought to have been seen long ago," Martin wrote, "that if the Southern whites left the negro in his ignorance, the rapacious and unscrupulous Northern adventurer would find him."[111] A year later, the editors of the *Christian Recorder* complained that "we colored people are charged with encouraging and affiliating with thieving carpet baggers who are ruining the South." In fact, the newspaper insisted, the South's black population was eager to "help rid the South of these corrupt political vampires who rob and cheat and prey upon the prejudices of our people" and "feed upon the political carcass of a prostrate state."[112]

Those commentators who tried to remain charitable toward the carpetbaggers were forced to recognize the change that had taken place. "There is among the republicans of the north general dissatisfaction with the corruption and bad government which have prevailed in these states," reported the *Hartford Daily Courant* in 1876. "A feeling has been gaining ground that the reconstruction measures have been a failure, and have resulted in placing the states too often at the mercy of mere adventurers."[113] In a speech to the Union League Club of New York, William Craft, an escaped slave and coauthor (with his wife, Ellen) of the narrative *Running a Thousand Miles for Freedom*, worried about the growing consensus that cast the carpetbaggers as "the greatest rogues in the land," a characterization that Craft considered "a great mistake."[114] The *Chicago Inter-Ocean*, which retained a thoroughgoing Radicalism throughout Reconstruction, noted that "the opinion seems to have obtained to some extent in the North that of all things despicable, the 'carpet-bagger' is most to be despised."[115]

*Carpetbagger* even became a convenient shorthand, a slang synonym for "uninvited" and "unwanted." "The First of the Carpetbaggers," a short story that appeared in the *Christian Union* in 1875, opens with the arrival of a Yankee widow named Mrs. Peterson at an estate near Richmond, Virginia, sometime in the 1850s. The family of the house takes the stranger in while she looks for her brother-in-law, who, she claims, works as an overseer in the area. As the search extends across an entire summer, the family begins to suspect the truth: there is no brother-in-law, Mrs. Peterson is a fraud, and they have been duped. When the family finally succeeds in evicting the "carpetbagger," the slave charged with carting her back to Richmond confirms these suspicions and adds a surprising twist. Based on her obvious familiarity with the city, the stranger was not even a northerner, but a native of Richmond, "po' white trash" who made a decent livelihood abusing the kindnesses of others.[116] An 1876 issue of *Harper's Bazaar* offered a similar usage. A short article predicted that Philadelphia's upcoming Centennial Exposition would bring a host of unwashed and uncouth out-of-towners to the city. Although the article had nothing to do with Reconstruction or southern politics, it referred to these unwelcome visitors as "carpetbaggers."[117] In both cases, the term was used as a generalized description, meant to evoke a set of characteristics rather than an occupation or a particular life trajectory. The context, be it the Centennial Exposition or the Reconstruction South, mattered less than these timeless personality traits. To be a carpetbagger was to be in the wrong place, at the wrong time, for the wrong reasons; it was to be out of one's element, one's very presence rendered obnoxious, invalid, and illogical.

But what does the northern Republican turn on the carpetbaggers reveal about the fate of Reconstruction? During Ulysses S. Grant's second term, an ever increasing proportion of the northern Republican population came to believe that the interests of the South would be best served by a policy of noninterventionism or, in the words of a *Springfield Daily Republican* correspondent, by "a little vigorous letting alone."[118] In the context of a southern political scene that seemed to be spinning wildly out of control, northerners were forced to confront the unpleasant fact that northern involvement in southern affairs did not seem to be remedying what ailed the region. Almost a decade of military, political, and cultural interventionism had not made the South more like the North. Quite the contrary, the region now seemed more distinct, more violent, more *southern*. Reconstruction, in other words, had become a problem, not a solution. Rather than attempting to re-create the South, northerners wondered how to fix Reconstruction or, failing that, how to extricate themselves from it.

As a symbol of problematic northern interventionism in the South, the figure of the "terrible carpetbagger" stood at the center of this shift. The carpetbaggers' unique social and political position—literally the embodiment of northern control over the South—made the debate over their qualifications and capabilities a matter of surpassing importance. The contest over the carpetbagger was really a debate over the meaning and value of northern involvement in the South. As the image of the corrupt and terrible carpetbagger became ever more common after 1872, the logical underpinnings of northern interventionism in the South were brought into question. Reconstruction itself, like the carpetbagger who had become its most visible symbol, began to appear somehow corrupt, contrived, and improper. The northern Republican turn on the carpetbagger, therefore, was actually a reflection of a larger retreat from northern interventionism, generally construed. In accepting the general outlines of a southern-authored vision of the terrible carpetbagger by the mid-1870s, northern Republicans affirmed their unwillingness to preside over the further Reconstruction of the South.

During Grant's second term, politics as usual quite simply ceased to exist in many states across the South. The contested 1872 gubernatorial election in Louisiana led to the creation of two separate legislatures in New Orleans, a state of affairs that culminated in the horrific Colfax Massacre. In 1874, Arkansas's "Brooks-Baxter War" saw armed bands encamped in the streets of Little Rock as two governors tried to make good on their competing claims to power. The same year, Louisiana was under siege again, as the White League seized and held the State House for a week before withdrawing. Early in 1875, the Louisiana legislature's Democrats fraudulently purged enough Republican members to secure themselves a majority, which they enjoyed until U.S. forces intervened. Mississippi was little better. After a bloody practice run in a local Vicksburg election in 1874, the state's white supremacist conservatives went for a bigger prize, using a systematic campaign of racial violence to secure the election of a Democratic governor a year later. In 1876, the "Mississippi Plan" became a model for South Carolina's white supremacist Red Shirts, who used violence and terror to elect former Confederate general Wade Hampton.[119] As these occurrences—"annual, autumnal outbreaks," in Grant's telling phrase—piled up, it began to appear that a state of barely suppressed chaos was the political default in the Deep South.[120]

Given the prominent role that white terrorist violence played in many of these events, northern commentators could have been forgiven for relying on the familiar Ku Klux Klan framework to make sense of the goings-on below the Mason-Dixon. Though the Klan itself had dissipated in response to enforcement legislation and federal prosecution, white southerners continued their frontal assault on Reconstruction and black rights throughout Grant's second term. Under a variety of new monikers—the White League, the White Line, the Red Shirts—southern white supremacists kept the Klan alive, in spirit if not in name. As events in Louisiana, Arkansas, Mississippi, and South Carolina suggested, politics and violence remained inextricably linked across the South.[121]

In fact, a few northern Republicans did seek to fan the flames of interventionism and to rally their comrades for a continued struggle against southern white supremacy. In an 1874 speech, Indiana senator Oliver P. Morton fumed that "Louisiana has been a vast slaughterhouse. Murder has been committed on nearly every plantation. The streets, the woods, and the by-ways have been slippery with blood."[122] In language almost identical to that used to describe the outrages of the KKK a few years before, Morton insisted that the Bloody South was alive and well. In a series of columns written for *Harper's Weekly* between 1872 and 1876, journalist Eugene Lawrence continuously beat the drum of southern deviance, lambasting the violence of white southerners and their Democratic allies. Significantly, Lawrence continued to use the term *Ku Klux Klan* to describe southern white supremacist terrorism, insisting that the Klan needed to be treated in the present tense, not the past. "The white man's party has revived," he wrote in 1874. "The Ku-Klux outrages are renewed; but they are no longer hidden under the shades of night, with masks and secret pass-words."[123] As late as 1876, Lawrence published articles in *Harper's Weekly* titled "The Ku-Klux and the Colored Voters," "Northern Settlers and the Ku-Klux," and "The Ku-Klux Democracy."[124]

It is perhaps unsurprising that African Americans, who bore the brunt of white southern violence throughout Reconstruction, were least willing to let go of the bloody memory of the Ku Klux Klan. In "The Conflict for Civil Rights," an 1874 poem, Henry McNeal Turner gave voice to the continuing reality of white supremacist violence in the South: "We can see their lines gleaming like rebel array, The Klans and the Leaguers all eager for prey." Turner vowed, however, that the South's black population "will not yield, not in fear of the grave, the rights that belong to the free and the brave."[125] In 1875, a correspondent for the *Christian Recorder* calling himself "Veni Vidi" (Latin for "I came, I saw") described a white mob's attack on a peaceful political meeting in Vicksburg, Mississippi, calling it "one of the most outrageous and sickening affairs it has ever been my lot to witness, even in this blood thirsty section of our country." Working from a carefully planned script, armed whites entered the meeting, began a scuffle, and then shot at and beat dozens of black Republicans who tried to escape. More armed white men blocked the windows, while dozens more waited outside the main doors. "Cry peace, peace," the correspondent wrote, but "there is no peace."[126]

Despite the abundant evidence of white southern barbarity, however, this Klan-focused interpretation of the troubles in the South increasingly became a minority viewpoint. Instead, northern Republican commentators tended to emphasize two other themes that united the southern political fiascoes enumerated above. In each case, northern-born politicians played a starring role. The victorious candidate in Louisiana's 1872 election was Illinois native William Pitt Kellogg, while former governor Henry Clay Warmoth was an active member of the opposition. As governor, Kellogg was the primary target in Louisiana's 1874 military coup and a victim of the state's 1875 legislative hijinks. Joseph Brooks, an Ohioan, attempted to unseat scalawag Elisha Baxter in Arkansas, sparking that state's "war." And Adelbert Ames and Daniel Chamberlain—both New Englanders—found themselves out of work following the brutal campaigns in Mississippi and South Carolina. These "autumnal outbreaks" quickly became the central drama of Reconstruction, and, without fail, a carpetbag could be found amid the wreckage.

Beyond this, northern commentators were quick to notice the increasingly central role that an interventionist federal government seemed to be playing in southern political affairs. Largely against his will, President Grant waded knee deep into southern politics in the mid-1870s, with presidential proclamations required to end the electoral standoffs in Louisiana and Arkansas. The question of military interventionism proved even more fraught. White supremacist terror and systematic vote suppression made southern Republican pleas for federal military support a regular occurrence. Grant responded to such calls on a case-by-case basis, but even when he declined to send troops, the possibility (or the threat) of intervention was constant.[127] Such appeals to Washington established the Grant administration as a mediator in state and local politics, producing a calculus of power unique to the Reconstruction South, and making the military bayonet a key player in southern political affairs. To many northerners, then, the federal government began to appear the biggest carpetbagger of all.

Few made the connection between carpetbagger rule and federal intervention as stridently as journalist Charles Nordhoff, who went south in 1875 at the behest of *New York Herald* editor James Gordon Bennett. A Republican and former abolitionist, Nordhoff had soured on Reconstruction by the mid-1870s. He supported Greeley in the election of 1872 and was, it seems, predisposed to strike a negative tone in his handling of Reconstruction, his protestations of objectivity to the contrary.[128] In his dispatches from Arkansas, Louisiana, Mississippi, and Alabama, Nordhoff seized on the carpetbagger as a sower of discord and dissension. He bemoaned the "great misgovernment" that had run rampant across the South, perpetuated "mostly by men who called themselves Republicans, but who were for the great part adventurers, camp followers, soldiers of fortune."[129] He denounced the corruption and excess of the carpetbagger "ring" in Arkansas, accused the carpetbag rulers of Louisiana of seeking to "debauch and demoralize" the state as they robbed it blind, and complained that Mississippi's Adelbert Ames and his allies had "used the ignorance and greed of the negroes to help them in their political schemes."[130] Carpetbag rule, according to Nordhoff, was cynical, fraudulent, untenable, and dangerous.

In his dispatches, Nordhoff consistently argued that it was the military and political interventionism of the Grant administration that allowed the adventurers to maintain their stranglehold on power. "There are no wrongs now in the South which the interference of the Federal Government" could remedy, he insisted flatly. "This interference is purely and only mischievous. It has disabled and demoralized the Republican State governments, whose members, sure that they would be maintained by the Federal arm everywhere, abandoned their duties, and took to stealing and maladministration."[131] Carpetbaggers "encouraged disorder, so that they might the more effectually appeal to the Federal power and to the Northern people for help to maintain them in the places they so grossly and shamelessly abused."[132] Together, the twin evils of federal interference and carpetbag rule had produced a state of chronic upheaval and pitted the federal government against the expressed will of the southern majority. Without Grant's meddling, Nordhoff argued, southern politics could reestablish itself on a healthier (and carpetbag-free) footing.

By 1874 and 1875, mainstream Republican papers—those that had supported Grant in 1872—began to join their Liberal counterparts in using the carpetbagger to express a generalized discomfort with northern interventionism. In many cases, mainstream Republican organs offered critiques that were almost indistinguishable from those of their Liberal counterparts, linking the political fortunes of rascally carpetbaggers to the question of federal interference in the South. During the Louisiana White League coup of 1874, the *Christian Union* complained that the "cowardice and unscrupulousness" of carpetbag governor William Pitt Kellogg "seem to exceed those of the most illustrious carpet-baggers with whom the South has been cursed" and reminded its readers that it was only with the "assistance of the army and navy of the United States" that Kellogg was able to claim the governor's office in the first place.[133] In November

1874, the *Independent's* Washington, DC, correspondent described a "set of 'carpet-baggers' here from Arkansas doing their best to coax and bully the President into the support of their schemes." The correspondent expressed his hope that Grant would ignore them, and that the nation had witnessed "the last case of improper Federal interference inside a state."[134] Early in 1875, after federal troops entered the Louisiana State House to forcibly reconstitute the legislature, the *New York Times* reflected on the problematic relationship between northern Republicans and carpetbaggers in the South. "The carpetbaggers have often been great scamps, and the Federal authorities have sometimes interfered where they ought not to have done," the *Times* wrote. "The relation, too, of such communities to the Federal Government is an unnatural one, and ought to come to an end as soon as possible."[135] Continued federal involvement with southern affairs had fostered an unhealthy dependency on the part of the South's carpetbagging class. It was time to cut the tie.

Significantly, the plight of African Americans and the effective nullification of the Fourteenth and Fifteenth Amendments—the very occurrences that justified military intervention—often took a backseat in these conversations. At the Republican nominating convention in June 1876, Frederick Douglass defended continuing northern intervention in the Reconstruction South and reminded the nation of its duty to African Americans. Douglass asked for an "assurance, that if it be necessary, the black man shall walk to the ballot-box in safety, even if we have to bring a bayonet behind us," and insisted that "the government of the United States and the moral feeling of the country" must "surround the black voter as by a wall of fire."[136] While Douglass's speech undoubtedly drew cheers at the convention, the sentiment that lay behind it was increasingly unpopular. Yankees had come to eschew further interventionism by word and by deed, a position that had as much to do with the carpetbaggers as it did with the freedpeople.

Popular revulsion toward the carpetbaggers posed a serious problem for those worried about the maintenance of African American voting rights in the South. Any northern action on behalf of the South's black population threatened to be a de facto boon to the carpetbaggers. A *New York Times* correspondent writing from Shreveport, Louisiana, regretfully noted that "the policy of the Federal Government in viewing the bad element of Louisiana white men through a magnifying glass, and the frauds and corruptions of the carpet-baggers through a diminishing glass, is so exasperating to just men that it goes far to make them forget the real danger to the colored man."[137] Or, as a contributor to the *Independent* put it, "There is a most artful mixing up of the wrongs of colored voters with the privileges of a corrupt set of carpet-baggers."[138] Whether or not northern Republicans were willing to intervene in southern affairs on behalf of the freedpeople by 1874 and 1875, they were most certainly unwilling to do so on behalf of the carpetbaggers. The "artful mixing up" resolved itself in a northern disavowal of interventionism, generally construed.

The figure of the corrupt carpetbagger aided northern Republicans immeasurably in navigating the retreat from an activist Reconstruction in the mid-1870s. To focus on the carpetbagger's dangerous and disruptive presence in the South was to admit that Reconstruction itself had become dangerous and disruptive. The problem was no longer the brutality and illiberality of southern white supremacy, but the forcible maintenance of a fundamentally illegitimate order in the South. Attacks on the carpetbaggers set Reconstruction apart, concretizing an understanding of the period as somehow removed from the mainstream of American political history. The power of the terrible carpetbagger trope lay in its ability to delegitimize Reconstruction, casting it as arbitrary, unnatural, and above all, temporary. Eventually, it assured Americans, proper order would be restored and control of the South returned to the native white southerners who were its rightful leaders. The solution was as appealing as it was simplistic. Remove the carpetbag interlopers and the federal apparatus that supported them, and the nightmare of Reconstruction would be finished.

When newly inaugurated president Rutherford B. Hayes recalled the remaining federal troops from Louisiana and South Carolina in April 1877, he steadfastly maintained that his actions did not constitute a retreat from Reconstruction. Few commentators, however, harbored any illusions as to the lasting import of his actions.[139] The *Boston Globe* matter-of-factly noted that "the withdrawal of the military power of the United States" from the South "will close up the long period of reconstruction."[140] The *Chicago Tribune* lauded the removal of the "Military Nurses" from South Carolina, calling it "the final act in the drama of Reconstruction."[141] Even those organs that disagreed with President Hayes's southern policy could not help but recognize the inevitable. The *Christian Recorder* grimly noted that African Americans "can expect nothing from President Hayes" except "utter abandonment by him and the Republican Party."[142] After twelve long years, the events of April 1877 were hailed as a distinct stopping point, the closing of an epoch, the end of Reconstruction.

. THE NEW POLICY TRAIN.

CONDUCTOR HAYES—"*All aboard, Mr. Packard! We want to take all you Carpetbaggers in one trip!*"

"The New Policy Train," *Frank Leslie's Illustrated Newspaper*, April 21, 1877.
Rutherford B. Hayes's new southern policy figured as a turn against the carpetbaggers.
Yale University Library.

The month also witnessed another end, one that bore no less significance for contemporary Americans: the close of the carpetbagger era. The advent of Democratic regimes in Florida, South Carolina, and Louisiana meant the ouster of the only carpetbag governors that remained in the South. Commentators joined together in bidding "adieu"—more often "good riddance"—to the carpetbagger, and to northern interventionism more generally. The *New York Tribune*, long a bastion of northern Republican carpetbagger bashing, considered itself vindicated. "The Republican party has been running a political poorhouse quite too long," the *Tribune* opined. "It gave opportunity for adventurers, who were utterly without standing or consideration in any Northern community, and who if not propped up by United States bayonets could not have been elected to any office by colored men of the South, to fasten themselves upon the party and the country as the representative Republicans of reconstructed States."[143] In voicing support for Hayes's southern policy, *Harper's Weekly* expressed satisfaction that the federal government was out of the business of "forcibly sustaining governments of adventurers."[144] John Mercer Langston, an African American educator, lawyer, and politician, added his voice to the chorus, criticizing "the unhandsome and obnoxious conduct of political adventurers" and finding hope for the future in the carpetbagger's long overdue demise.[145] *Frank Leslie's Illustrated Newspaper*, meanwhile, printed a cartoon that depicted "Conductor Hayes" escorting Stephen B. Packard, the loser in Louisiana, to a northbound train already containing Daniel Chamberlain, his South Carolina counterpart. A sign suspended from the train reads: "All aboard for the North. Carpetbaggers are especially requested to avail themselves of this rare opportunity."[146]

The *Chicago Tribune* went so far as to run a lengthy obituary for "The Carpet-Bagger," detailing his move to the South, his peculiar theories of representative governance, and his long-overdue demise. The carpetbagger, the *Tribune* gravely noted, "had been more or less in the army, especially less." After his move south, he bravely tried—but totally failed—to ingratiate himself with his new neighbors: "It may be said of him, in his connection with the Southern people, 'He was poor, yet for their sakes he became rich.'" His true downfall, though, was his unfaltering belief in an outmoded sectional relationship. To his last days, the carpetbagger expressed a belief that "the true mode of bringing the South to a hearty allegiance to the Union was by sitting down on them forever and forever." Few mourned his passing.[147]

## Fools, Klansmen, and Carpetbaggers: Albion W. Tourgée and the Memory of Reconstruction, 1879–1880

At least one American refused to accept the terms of the carpetbagger compromise that ended Reconstruction. By 1879, northern migrant and Republican appointee Albion W. Tourgée was ruined, vilified, and heartbroken. More than this, however, he was angry. Angry at the white South for its bad faith, angry at the North for its betrayals, angry at himself for having failed to turn the tide of history. Locked in his house in Greensboro, North Carolina, Tourgée picked up his pen and scratched out a satirical novel that would make him a literary celebrity while serving as the opening shot in an extended cultural battle over the memory of Reconstruction.[148] As depicted in *A Fool's Errand*, Reconstruction was a tug-of-war between the Klansman (the embodiment of white southern malfeasance and hatred) and the carpetbagger (the representative of northern ideals and aspirations). Like Tourgée himself, the novel's protagonist, Comfort Servosse, is a Union veteran who heads south with high hopes in the aftermath of Appomattox, only to discover that he has been on a "fool's errand." By the end of the novel, the violence of the Ku Klux Klan has destroyed the carpetbagger and his dreams for a rejuvenated and reformed South.

Tourgée, of course, had experienced firsthand the precipitous decline in the popular opinion of the carpetbagger, giving his defenses of carpetbaggers a tenor both personal and political. In a series of articles published in the *Northampton Journal* under the pen name Henry Churton, Tourgée complained that the "unfortunate 'carpet-bagger'" had become the North's preferred scapegoat for the failures of Reconstruction. "We are told over and over again," he continued, "that the 'carpet-baggers' ruined, plundered, stole, corrupted and overthrew the reconstructed State governments of the South, and therewith fell the Republican party, the innocent victim of these political buccaneers."[149] Such fantasies, Tourgée insisted, only obscured the true lessons of Reconstruction, insulating from blame those who truly deserved it: bloody white southerners and weak-willed northern Republicans. In *A Fool's Errand*, Tourgée made a similar point, marveling at the seeming ease with which northern Republicans had turned against the carpetbagger. "Perhaps there is no other instance in history," he wrote, "in which the conquering power has discredited its own agents, denounced those of its own blood and faith, espoused the prejudices of its conquered foes, and poured the vials of its wrath and contempt upon the only class in the conquered territory who defended its acts, supported its policy, promoted its aim, or desired its preservation and continuance."[150]

As he defended the carpetbaggers, Tourgée tried to redirect attention to the bloody deeds of the Ku Klux Klan. In 1880, Tourgée published *The Invisible Empire*, a supplement to *A Fool's Errand* that aimed to provide northern readers with "a better understanding of the opinions, feelings, and modes of thought among the Southern people."[151] In fact, *The Invisible Empire* was a thinly veiled attempt to use the bloody history of the Ku Klux Klan to urge a renewed commitment to an interventionist southern policy. Combing the 1872 Ku Klux Klan report, Tourgée unearthed outrage after outrage, murder after murder, casting his searchlight on the dark history that the nation seemed determined to forget. Tourgée believed that the window for a true reconstruction of the South, based on equal rights and racial justice, had not yet closed. In order to seize the opportunity, however, northern Republicans would need to divorce themselves of their recently acquired taste for self-flagellation, embracing the single shining fact that Tourgée placed at the center of his work: Reconstruction had not been subverted by dastardly northern carpetbaggers, it had been murdered by bloody southern Klansmen.

The zeal with which Albion Tourgée attempted to reverse the relative fortunes of the Klansman and the carpetbagger is, perhaps, the best evidence of the newly forged national consensus on the meaning of Reconstruction. Between 1868 and 1877, a remarkable shift occurred. American culture would never entirely shake its fascination with the mysteries of the Ku Klux Klan, but the larger lessons learned from Reconstruction pointed in another direction.[152] It would be not the Klansman but the carpetbagger who would stand as the central cautionary figure in the story of Reconstruction. The Southern Question, in all its permutations, would not soon be relegated to the political and cultural periphery. Whatever the character of the sectional relationship in the years to come, however, the specter of the carpetbagger would continue to haunt any discussion of northern interventionism in the affairs of the South.

## PART II

# Construction, 1880–1895

# CHAPTER THREE

# New South, New North

In December 1889, the *New York Ledger* printed an American epic. It was a tale of loss and redemption, the literary record of a people's journey from the heights of success to the pits of degradation and back again. The author promised to show how a population "reduced to poverty by a war" had again made their "honorable way to wealth and prosperity," finding salvation in "unaccustomed work." After a period of enforced darkness, they had undertaken a "march of restoration and development" unrivaled in human history. "We shall see how the warhorses went to the furrow," the author wrote. "How the waste places were closed. How the earth smiled at their rude and questioning touch. How the mountains opened and disclosed treasures not dreamed of before. How, from chaos and desolation, the currents of trade trickled and swelled and took orderly way. How rivers were spanned and the wildernesses pierced with iron rail." The unprecedented changes in the natural landscape were matched only by shifts in the hearts and minds of the people themselves. Guided by an "All-wise hand," a once desolate civilization had been reborn.[1] This remarkable story, this unique tale of strength and hope, progress and possibility, offered a shining example to the world.

The protagonist in this unusual tale was the white population of the South. Having suffered a catastrophic defeat in war and borne unbearable indignities during Reconstruction, the white South had found its feet and its voice, and stood poised to reclaim its once enviable position in the nation. Or so insisted the fable's author, Henry W. Grady. The managing editor of the *Atlanta Constitution* was something of a journalistic celebrity on both sides of the Mason-Dixon. Having made a name for himself in New York on the basis of his December 1886 speech to the New England Society at Delmonico's restaurant, Grady was commissioned to author a series of six articles for the *Ledger* in late 1889. His subject was a figure that sprang to national prominence in the 1880s, a cultural construction with a contemporary appeal impossible to deny and a historical significance easy to overlook: the New South.[2]

The New South was, on its most basic level, a story. It was a new definition of Dixie, dreamed up by Henry Grady and his allies—"boosters" in the traditional historiographical parlance—and offered to the nation at large. Relying on alluring visions of industrial growth, urban development, economic regeneration, mineral wealth, and sectional reunion, boosters spent the 1880s and 1890s spinning yarns about the South and its place in the nation. After decades of conflict, the storytellers insisted, the South had ceased to be a problem. It had become, instead, a land of opportunity. The traumas of slavery, war, emancipation, and Reconstruction were behind it. Its future would not be measured in heartache, bloodshed, or harsh words but in factories built, enterprises started, and dollars earned.

The New South's appeal did not stop at the Mason-Dixon line. It was, at all points, an essentially intersectional affair, a story of the South formulated and disseminated with the express intent of reconfiguring and recasting the North/South relationship for a post-Reconstruction age. To state the matter simply: northerners did not stop looking south in 1877. Understanding this all-important fact, New South storytellers began, in a conscious and concerted manner, to construct images of their society expressly for northern consumption. In the wake of decades of sectional conflict, a bloody Civil War, and an excruciating Reconstruction effort, the appeal of a reformed, revitalized, contented, patriotic, and hardworking South was undeniable. The New South offered a welcome vision of stability, progress, and technological innovation, rooted in the pacifying and patriotic influences of hard work and the almighty dollar. In newspapers and speeches, tourist pamphlets and tables of manufactures, at spectacular expositions and in cities such as Nashville, Atlanta, and boomtown Birmingham, New South boosters invited northerners to marvel at the unprecedented and awe-inspiring changes that had already occurred, and to imagine those changes yet to come. The goal of the New South program, therefore, was not just a New South. It was also a new sectional relationship.

For all their talk, the New South boosters failed to deliver the economic and industrial revolution they had prophesied. The New South program brought its share of changes to the region, increasing its industrial base, enlarging its cities, lengthening its railroads, and tying it to the larger capitalist marketplace. Measured against the dreams of the boosters, however, the program fell well short of its mark. But this fact does not diminish the larger historical significance of the New South program. Even if southern reality never matched New South rhetoric, the story augured a vital shift in the sectional relationship. The New South offered Yankees an ally, an investment opportunity, a stabilized sectional relationship, a reunited nation, and an end to sectional conflict and the ever vexing Southern Question. The key point, however, was not just *what* was said about the New South but *who* said it. Rather than fending off charges of backwardness, treason, and barbarism, white southerners had begun to explain themselves to the nation. The white South had found its voice, and was talking back. Whether the South ever became the paradise it claimed to be was somewhat immaterial. The story was enough.

## The New Spirit

Early in 1883, the Euzelian literary society at Wake Forest University selected a nineteen-year-old student named Thomas Dixon Jr. to deliver its anniversary address. Though Dixon would, in later years, become famous for his Reconstruction novels *The Leopard's Spots* and *The Clansman*, his topic, on this occasion, was the New South. "What is the first indication of a new South?" young Dixon asked. His answer: "A new spirit is abroad. You see it in the quickened step of the business men, in the straightened fence-row, and new cultivator of the farmer; the press pulsates with it; you hear it from the platform, see it in the smiling face and hear it in the cheerful tones of our citizens; you feel it in the very atmosphere we breathe — it buoys us up, invigorates and nerves us for action." The essence of the New South, Dixon insisted, was something that could not be measured or counted. It was, instead, a "spirit," a feeling that manifested itself in every arena of southern life. Though it could not be defined, it was there, quietly animating and enlivening. Dixon himself had felt the new spirit, under whose influence "the world looks brighter, the flowers fresher, the birds sing more sweetly and the pulse beats quicker and stronger."[3]

In his musings on the South's new spirit, Dixon was not alone. In order to shape southern behavior and, as significant, blunt northern criticism, New South boosters needed to create a new story for the region, a vision of a South untainted by slavery, secession, and Reconstruction. Their first step was to create "the New Southerner." The shift from old to new was often depicted as a generational affair. "The new and young blood of the south," an editorialist wrote in 1882, "are rising up as rulers and law-givers.

These men have no revenges to nurse, no disappointments to enrage, and no ambitions which cannot receive within the union and under the old flag a broader and brighter glory than could ever be won in the restricted field of a miniature republic."[4] Henry Watterson, editor of the *Louisville Courier-Journal* and New South booster extraordinaire, offered a similar explanation. "The men who led the secession movement no longer appear upon the scene," Watterson wrote in 1885. "A fresh crop of ideas has sprung up in the South. A new body of public men has come to the front. They were not responsible for the mistakes of their fathers, and, except to be loyal to their fathers' memory and motives, are nowise concerned to defend that which they have no mind to repeat."[5] In his 1881 musings on an "Old Southern Borough," meanwhile, North Carolinian Walter Hines Page found no distinction as stark as that separating the new generation— bustling, active, enterprising—from the old. They were, Page wrote, quite literally products of "two distinct civilizations."[6]

More often, however, boosters viewed these changes as a progression that took place within individuals, rather than across generations. Though the new spirit was, by its very nature, inchoate and hard to define, a few ideas were fairly constant. Of these, none was more central than the embrace of hard work. As Henry Grady put it, in perhaps the most famous line of his 1886 Delmonico's speech, "We have fallen in love with work."[7] Across the South, a large segment of the white population seemed to have simultaneously discovered the joys of an honest day's labor. In theory, at least, the value system of the Old South had put a premium on relaxation, casting hard work as a peculiar (and distasteful) Yankee habit, one that was utterly beneath the white population of the South. In the altered circumstances of the postwar period, however, white southerners changed their tune, paying lip service to the basic premises of a northern-style free labor ideology. In 1887, Vanderbilt professor Wilbur Fisk Tillett summarized this shift. "The white man of the New South is preeminently a worker," Tillett wrote, "as compared with the white man of the Old South, who, if not an idler, was at least a man of multitudinous leisure."[8] In the movement from "multitudinous leisure" to "we have fallen in love with work," the outlines of the new spirit were plainly visible.

This new appreciation of labor fed naturally into an increased engagement with the capitalist marketplace and a new attention to moneymaking pursuits. The "best assurance" of the South's reformation, the *St. Louis Globe-Democrat* declared, was to be found in "the steadily increasing importance attached to trade and industry."[9] Moneymaking was to be valued in its own right, of course, but it also provided evidence of larger changes deep within the southern psyche. In embracing the tenets of the market-place, the South took a step away from its troubled past, moving itself firmly into the Gilded Age mainstream. These facts were not lost on north-erners: a New Englander visiting Atlanta in 1881 expressed his delight that "the only balm of relief for a shattered people, money-making pursuits and commercial developments, has found a way to every household."[10] Each dollar made in the New South, therefore, served something of a dual purpose. On the one hand, increased capital would aid immeasurably in southern recovery. On the other, the South's newfound commitment to acquisitive capitalism possessed a significant symbolic resonance. The pur-suit of wealth would unify the country, eradicating any lingering southern distinctiveness in the post-Reconstruction era.

This embrace of business was often paired with a rather stylized retreat from the political realm. As numerous references to "bourbonism" and "the blighting rule of braying politicians" suggest, the New South claimed to have little use for the squabbles and demagoguery of electoral politics.[11] Hoke Smith, a Georgian and the secretary of the interior under President Grover Cleveland, noted that "if you wish to interest the people of the South to-day, talk to them of the resources and development of their section. Once they enjoyed more the eloquent words of the political orator, but now the plain business presentation of questions connected with material growth finds the most attentive listeners."[12] Where the politician would divide, New South storytellers argued, the businessman sought to unite. In their collective embrace of work, business, and the dollar, boosters suggested, the North and the New South might find their long delayed reunion.

More than this, it may have been the simple desire to be *new* that most fully set off the New Southerner from what had come before. The New Southerner avowed a willingness to break from the traditions of the past and a desire to approach future change with an open mind. Businessman and farmer, city dweller and black belt planter, New Southerners would unite under the banner of novelty. As A. J. Lafargue, a newspaper edi-tor from Louisiana, put the matter at a national editorial convention in 1887, the South was "new in brains, new in business enterprises, new in diversified industries and varied commercial pursuits, new in a reawak-ened agriculture, and an activity, push, thrift and a growth that is almost marvelous."[13] In the context of a region long depicted as constitutionally incapable of change and innovation, a willingness to embrace the new could seem the most important development of all.

"Montgomery Ave., Sheffield, Ala., 1884." This image from a promotional pamphlet designed to attract northern capital depicts the southern landscape before the advent of the "new spirit." Warshaw Collection of Business Americana—Alabama, Archives Center, National Museum of American History, Smithsonian Institution.

It was not just the people of the South who were imbued with the new spirit. The landscape of the region seemed to have fallen under its influence as well. If untapped riches and unused potential epitomized the southern past, boosters heralded a future marked by construction, growth, and development. Train lines now ran next to the South's agricultural fields, buildings raced for the southern sky, and the rich earth suddenly seemed capable of producing bustling cities along with cotton, tobacco, and rice. In 1882, Henry Grady envisioned "a better and grander Georgia—a Georgia that has filled the destiny God intended her for." Her "towns and cities" would be "hives of industry, and her country-side the exhaustless fields from which their stores are drawn." The state's rivers would echo with "the music of spindles," as its forests filled with "the roar of the passing train."[14] Implicitly contrasting the impenetrable woods and poorly managed plantations of the Old South with the wonder of the New South's built environment and newfound mastery of nature, boosters found a deep beauty in examples of the region's industrial might. The city fathers of Dayton, Tennessee, hoped to attract settlers by describing "huge blast furnaces, enormous coal mines, long rows of coke ovens, mills, factories,

MONTGOMERY AVENUE, SHEFFIELD, ALA., IN 1887.

"Montgomery Avenue, Sheffield, Ala., in 1887." In only three short years, boosters claimed, a rural path had become a bustling New South thoroughfare. Warshaw Collection of Business Americana—Alabama, Archives Center, National Museum of American History, Smithsonian Institution.

water power, rolling-mills, pipe-works."[15] A "bewildering scene" awaited travelers to the city of Lynchburg, according to a Virginia guidebook. "Such a medley of railways and water courses is rarely ever seen outside, and still less inside, of a city," it marveled. "Factories, mills, foundries, railway shops, lumber and coal yards, saw and planing mills, are all piled together in a narrow area under the southern bluffs." Taken together, these evidences of industrial development produced "truly a stirring scene."[16]

Most impressive, perhaps, was the rapidity with which these developments seemed to be taking place. A Florida-based real estate firm noted that the city of Orlando, "which four years ago was but a hamlet in the woods," now offered "more than forty stores, six churches, a seminary, opera house, four first class hotel edifices, several smaller ones, machine shops, three livery stables, two large carriage repositories, an ice factory" as well as "drug stores, a bakery, confectioner, etc. etc., affording all the comforts and even luxuries of first class towns in the older States."[17] The authors of a guide to Sheffield, Alabama, made an identical point. "Until lately Nature furnished all that was to be seen. Where wide streets are being formed, solid structures are growing up on every hand, where workmen are as busy as bees, and stores, offices and dwellings are clustered, were only a woodland tract and cultivated lands. The transformation is wonderful."[18] A pair of images accompanying the text—depicting the transformation of Sheffield's Montgomery Avenue from a forest path to an urban thoroughfare—offered visual confirmation of the area's remarkable development.[19] In less than a decade, the new spirit had carved thriving southern metropolises out of the backwoods of central Florida and northern Alabama. It stood poised to work a similar revolution in southern society at large.

In order to truly rewrite the place of the South in the nation's consciousness, boosters required a new myth of the South, a single storyline capable of unifying the South and winning over the rest of the nation. They found it, in the idea of *progress*. In the hands of the New South storytellers, the South became a land of inevitable growth. Defined, at its very core, by prosperity and abundance, the New South refused to stand still. Constant forward motion was its default setting. Economic development was not a goal to be pursued; it was a predictable, almost involuntary, part of everyday life. Progress was the New South's status quo, growth its sole occupation, breathtaking expansion par for the course. More factories, more trains, more money; new industries, new cities, new prosperity. Progress was more than a word for the New South. It was a state of being.

The New South's most accomplished apostle of progress was Richard Hathaway Edmonds, the long-time editor of the Baltimore-based *Manufacturers' Record*. If Henry Grady was the New South's most visible spokesman, Edmonds was undoubtedly its most ebullient. On its face, Edmonds's *Manufacturers' Record* appeared to be a simple trade publication dedicated to southern industry. In practice, however, it was much more than this. From its inception in 1882, the *Manufacturers' Record* beat the drum of southern prosperity with a tenacity unmatched by any other organ of the New South. No evidence of industrial progress was too insignificant to investigate, no display of agricultural initiative too small to report. The *Record's* weekly updates offered a running commentary on the New South's remarkable industrial progress, while Edmonds's calls for diligence, thrift, creativity, and investment marked out a roadmap for its future.

Though Edmonds claimed to recognize "the importance of due care in avoiding all exaggerations about the advantages or growth" of the South— "the truth itself," he was quick to add, "is wonderful enough"—his weekly editorials offered a parade of superlatives regarding the current condition of the South, frequently paired with an assurance that in a week, a month, a year, things would look even brighter.[20] His views on the New South are nicely encapsulated in an 1888 editorial, fittingly titled "The South's Brilliant Future." "Who can picture the vast, the illimitable future of this glorious sunny South?" Edmonds enthused. "The more we contemplate these advantages and contrast them with those of all other countries, the more deeply will we be impressed with the unquestionable truth that here in this glorious land, 'Creation's Garden Spot,' is to be the richest and the greatest country upon which the sun ever shone."[21] Edmonds would find his life's work in attempting to make this dream a reality.

The core of the *Manufacturers' Record*—its key contribution to the New South's myth of inevitable progress—was not to be found in Edmonds's lofty editorial rhetoric, or in his paper's city-boosting articles, or in its paeans to technological innovation and agricultural diversification. Its intellectual center was its weekly Construction Department, whose purpose, as the introductory note explained, was to "publish every week, a list of every new factory, of whatever kind, projected anywhere in the South; every railroad undertaken, and every mining company organized."[22] The matter-of-fact prose belies the remarkable presumption at work. Edmonds and the *Manufacturers' Record* sought to note every expansion, construction, or incorporation that took place across the entire South. Every time a venture organized, expanded, or was sold—each time a factory was built, rebuilt, or updated—each time the manufacturing, industrial, business, or agricultural landscape of the New South changed one iota—every time progress reared its head or development made a peep—Richard Hathaway Edmonds and the *Manufacturers' Record* would record it and broadcast it to the world.

The week of March 8, 1884, readers perusing the columns of the Construction Department would have found that "a Furniture factory will probably be started at Claremont, Va.," that "E. A. Snow & Co., High Point, N.C. will prepare to manufacture boxes," and that "the Phillips & Huttorff Manf. Co., of Nashville will build a foundry at Elyton, Ala., for moulding stove castings, mantels, &c., to consume 50 tons of pig iron a day."[23] In May of the same year, the *Record* reported that "the Americus, Preston & Lumpkin Railroad, to run from Americus to Lumpkin, Ga. has been organized" and that "the Mississippi Manufacturing Co., Vicksburg, Miss., have secured ground for building a spoke and hub factory."[24] The August 15, 1885, installment of the Construction Department noted that "electric lights are to be established in Helena, Ark.," that "a brick yard has been established in Sanford, Fla. by Mr. Weiskoff," and that "B. Baer,

Owensboro, Ky., states that he will erect in that city a 12-ton ice factory."[25] March 1886 brought the incorporation of the Swearingen Manufacturing Company in Louisville, the opening of a carriage factory in Memphis, and talk of a waterworks in Thomasville, Georgia; June 12, 1886, saw a planing mill in Tennessee, a hotel in Maryland, and the expansion of a creamery in Mississippi.[26]

The list, of course, could go on and on. This was precisely the point. Each installment of the Construction Department filled at least one newspaper page, and sometimes occupied as many as three. Taken individually, the improvements, openings, and expansions noted were relatively insignificant. Yet as a collective, they offered an inspired testimony to the remarkable growth of the New South. Featuring dozens of examples drawn from every southern state, the Construction Department was intended to be overbearing, unwieldy, and awe inspiring, with the stark, unavoidable fact of *progress* jumping off every page. The department's predictable weekly appearance—the fact that each list carried with it the memory of those past and the promise of those to come—only added to this larger meaning. Growth, expansion, movement, progress. These, Edmonds insisted, were the essence of the New South.

Edmonds was not alone. Though most boosters were, understandably, disinclined to follow him in actually listing each and every business that opened across the South, much the same point could be made through other means. Hence the New South's inordinate fondness for numbers. "The industrial growth of the South in the past ten years has been without precedent or parallel," Henry Grady wrote in 1889. "How, from poverty, such progress has been wrought can be told only in figures! Words cannot compass it."[27] Figures—data, statistics, tables, charts—were indeed the lingua franca of New South boosting. When language fell flat, when rhetoric rang hollow, storytellers could turn to the universal language of numbers to flush out their fable of progress. The *New Orleans Daily Picayune*, for instance, offered the following tally of southern businesses opened in 1887:

Agricultural implement factories 22, breweries 5, bridge works 8, car works 23, cotton and woolen mills 147, electric light works 98, flour and grist mills 177, foundries and machine shops 184, blast furnaces 73, gas companies 57, glass works 17, ice factories 80, mines and quarries 504, natural gas companies 115, oil mills 45, pipe works 4, potteries 12, railroad companies 232, rolling mills 23, stamp mills and smelters 43, steel plants 10, street railways 152, water works 135, woodworking establishments 640, miscellaneous 804.[28]

Again, the exact number of grist mills and steel plants was not really the point. New South boosters imbued the statistics of southern progress with an almost mystical power. These numbers possessed a deeper, symbolic meaning. They were progress embodied, made real. An increase in cotton growth, therefore, was not just an increase in cotton growth. More iron produced did not just mean that the South had increased its capacity to produce iron. In the hands of white southern storytellers, such gains implied a change on the grandest scale and carried with them the promise of deeper shifts in the worldview, morality, and psyche of the South. Statistics of industrial growth became, in the final summation, irrefutable proof of the very existence of the New South.

There was always a Janus-faced aspect to the New South's romance with progress, leading boosters to develop a corollary to their fable of inevitable growth. Present-day expansion was wonderful, but it was the ever present, unyielding promise of future growth that anchored the story of the New South. If progress was the New South's foundational myth, therefore, *potential* was its sustaining force. Potential served as the intellectual bridge that tied together the present and the future. Potential, in the language of the ever optimistic New South boosters, was merely growth that had not happened yet.

It is in this context that one must approach the New South's peculiar obsession with its own material resources.[29] Many New South texts read like tedious laundry lists, perhaps none more so than M. B. Hillyard's *The New South*. Described as the author's "offering of love to the South," Hillyard's text is some 400 pages of dense description, covering every aspect of the South's copious mineral potential.[30] The general introduction contains entries for "Agriculture," "Iron Interests," "Coal," "Cotton Manufacturing," "Milling," "Timber," and "Rosin, Pitch, and Turpentine." The state-by-state chapters that follow hew to a similar pattern, with regional specialties added as necessary: oysters for Virginia and Maryland, precious stones for North Carolina, fish for Florida.[31] Though it presents itself as a general account of the New South, the text is, in fact, a primer on the region's material possibilities, with hardly a person to be found.

When viewed through the twin lenses of progress and potential, however, the book takes on an entirely different aspect. What had appeared to be a dry perusal of mineral deposits becomes a glorious celebration of the

New South. Though many of these resources remained untapped at the time of Hillyard's writing, the myth of inevitable progress left little doubt as to the New South's eventual mastery of them. The mines, factories, and mills necessary to fully harness the South's material possibilities had not, technically, been built yet. However, the very existence of these resources constituted something of a promise. The fact that the South *could* build an industrial, agricultural, and manufacturing empire necessarily implied that it *would*. According to the New South's myth of inevitable growth, potential noted was only a short step from progress achieved.

A similar vision pervades the New South's city-boosting literature. In the New South, there were only two types of cities: boom towns and towns that were about to boom. Atlanta was, of course, the New South city par excellence, but it had plenty of competition.[32] Fully formed cities and towns came to seem a natural product of the South's rich soil, appearing with the same abundance and regularity as cotton bolls and tobacco leaves. The *Manufacturers' Record*, in particular, was committed to publicizing the South's next "coming town," wherever it might be.[33] During the 1880s, innumerable cities, towns, hamlets, and crossroads, ranging from Fayetteville, North Carolina ("it may be predicted with absolute certainty that the many and great advantages of Fayetteville, N.C., will soon double the population"), to Greenville, South Carolina ("it combines to a singular degree the advantages of both factories and agriculture"), to Clanton, Alabama ("moving onward and upward with astonishing strides"), came in for the *Record*'s special brand of boosting.[34] In each case, the *Record*'s account was equal parts propaganda and prophecy, recounting the astounding progress already made by the would-be boom town and guaranteeing greater things to come. As if by magic, nascent metropolises had taken root in every corner of the New South.

Thanks to the conflation of progress and potential, the New South's present and its future were virtually indistinguishable. Though one could visit (or read about) the South in the here-and-now, touring its cities and visiting its farms, this present-tense South was already on the move, ready to become obsolete. Attempt to map the New South, and four new cities would appear before you could conclude your survey. Count the iron manufactories or cotton mills, and you would be out of date before you had gotten started. The New South was outside of time, somewhere between present and future. The only constants were growth and development. Past progress, present-day potential, and future glory melded together in a seamless whole, a mystic land of ever expanding prosperity and inevitable growth. This was the story of the New South.

## Dixiefying the Yankee

A new South was born at twenty-three minutes to three o'clock on October 5, 1881, to the strains of Handel's "Hallelujah Chorus" and the hum of a gigantic Corliss engine whirring to life. A little more than one year after a leading cotton expert first raised the idea of a national exhibition of cotton manufacturers and growers, a military band playing "Hail Columbia" led a procession of speakers and distinguished visitors through Atlanta's Oglethorpe Park to the opening ceremonies of the 1881 International Cotton Exposition. The ceremony, like the fair that it opened, was a finely orchestrated affair, loaded with pomp and circumstance and imbued with "the symbolism of a resuscitated fraternity of feeling, and the promise of a grand and noble future for the South, and wholehearted recognition and co-operation on the part of the North."[35] Although the designers of the 1881 exposition had initially envisioned little more than a meeting of the nation's cotton growers and manufacturers, the sparkling fairgrounds, imposing architecture, and dramatic opening ceremonies (complete with fireworks, a chorus of 800 Georgians singing the "Hallelujah Chorus," and a purportedly spontaneous rendition of "Yankee Doodle" on the part of the gathered multitude) heralded the rebirth of the South and announced a final cessation to the sectional hostilities that had plagued the nation for as long as anyone could remember.[36]

When they made their way each morning to the corner of Peachtree and Wall Streets in downtown Atlanta and boarded first-class "exposition coaches" for the short trip to the city's northwestern outskirts, northern visitors entered into a staged spectacular of extravagant proportions, a three-dimensional representation of "the South." This South was defined by free labor, not slavery. It was a South of science, not superstition; capitalists, not the Klan; the future, not the past. Every aspect of the fair, from the American flags to the Corliss engine to the well-tended fields of cotton, upheld and furthered this image. Visitors to the fair heard nothing about crop liens, the Mississippi Plan, or the Lost Cause. Instead, it was uniformed railroad conductors, beautifully manicured grounds, orderly rows of cotton, and the most innovative agricultural and industrial technology as far as the eye could see. The South might have remained a problem in

American cultural and political life, but the New South—its reconstructed, modernizing, progressive, patriotic, and enlightened attributes on prominent display at the fair—promised a solution. A northern newspaper correspondent, who declared that he was "ashamed" of the suspicion he had long harbored toward the South, perfectly captured the spirit of the event: "I have attended brilliant receptions and have been made to feel at home—made to feel as if I was one of you and not a stranger." "I have," he concluded, "become a southern man in sentiment and in sympathy."[37]

He was not alone. The charms of the New South made "southern men" out of a great many northerners in the last two decades of the nineteenth century. Throughout the 1880s and 1890s, thousands of Yankees ventured south. As a *Frank Leslie's* correspondent noted in 1890, "There is no portion of our great country which now claims greater attention from all classes (from the capitalist with his millions to the artisan or farmer with his modest savings) than the 'South'—the 'New South,' as it is called."[38] Some went south for business, some for pleasure. Some went for a short jaunt, some for the long haul. Some did not go south at all, but their investments in southern industry and agriculture made a perfectly acceptable proxy. In a remarkable reversal of the "terrible carpetbagger" language that had taken such a toll during Reconstruction, white southerners now actively cultivated a northern presence in the South, publishing a spate of tourist guides, rhapsodizing over investment opportunities, and imploring the immigration of skilled laborers and farmers. The figure of the Yankee in Dixie would play an important role in the post-Reconstruction South. By their very presence, northerners in the South spoke to the changed state of affairs in the region. Wined and dined, feted and fawned over, these Yankees added their own chapter to the story of the New South.

Although the Gilded Age saw a nationwide boom in railroad construction, this growth was most pronounced in the South, with the region laying track at a faster pace than any other part of the country between 1880 and 1900.[39] This construction affected every aspect of life in the South, making communication and transportation more efficient, bringing a burgeoning capitalist marketplace to the southern backcountry, and forever altering the regional landscape. The railroad boom also fostered a sharp rise in northern tourism to the South. The sectional détente of the post-Reconstruction era led well-to-do northerners to take a new interest in "the southern tour." Railroad companies seized on this impulse, offering package deals and reduced rates to the South, and publishing promotional literature aimed at northern audiences. By definition, the tourist experience was bounded by the main lines and branches of the southern railway system. Clutching their guidebooks as they departed New York, Philadelphia, or Cincinnati, northern tourists were prepared to experience "the New South." They would, but that experience would be indelibly shaped by the track—both literal and literary—laid out by the boosters and their railroad allies.[40]

For the most part, tourist guides followed a predictable formula. Opening in a northern railroad hub, the guides led their readers on an imagined tour of the Southland, paying attention to both natural wonders and bustling cities, while offering detailed descriptions of train schedules, excursion opportunities, and hotel accommodations. *Summer Resorts and Points of Interest in Virginia, Western North Carolina, and North Georgia,* produced by the Virginia Midland Railways in 1884, led would-be voyagers from Washington, DC, through Culpepper and Charlottesville, to Lynchburg and Danville, and to a number of health springs and summer resorts, before turning to the hunting and sporting possibilities of western North Carolina and north Georgia.[41] Another tourist book, promising a guide to the "Scenic Attractions and Summer Resorts" of the South, opened in Hagerstown, Maryland, and took travelers through Virginia (Antietam, Luray, Roanoke, Norfolk), Georgia (Macon, Atlanta, Rome), and Tennessee (Memphis, Knoxville, Johnson City), as well as parts of Alabama, Mississippi, and Florida.[42] In an attempt to boost travel on its southern lines, the Pennsylvania Lines West published *A Handbook of the South,* a beautifully produced guide that exposed travelers to the "glamour of the past, the beauty of the present and the promise of the future."[43]

New South tourist guides needed to walk a fine line. On the one hand, visitors to the South thirsted for an experience that was authentically "southern." New or not, northern tourists entered the South carrying a set of expectations and presuppositions. As they emphasized the region's distinctive history, therefore, New South guidebooks also incorporated a number of visual cues that reinforced the southernness, and therefore the interest, of the areas being discussed. Images of southern flora and fauna were commonplace. Sketches of palm trees and magnolia blossoms dotted New South guidebooks, offering a constant reminder that Yankee tourists were sojourning in a tropical and exotic landscape. Guidebooks also turned to stylized and caricatured depictions of southern African Americans in an attempt to construct a vision of a distinctive and romantic South.[44] A guide to Richmond, Virginia, featured sketches of a black fisherman dressed in rags and a grinning black child labeled "the ward of the nation."[45] A tourist book produced by the Plant Railway system of Florida supplemented its sketches of plants and flowers with pictures of black children enjoying watermelon and sugarcane.[46] Such sketches helped to reproduce the picturesque and exotic South that northerners demanded, offering visual confirmation that travelers were not in New England any more.

At the same time, however, the very existence of the guides was predicated on a single idea, which was reproduced and reinforced on every page. The New South was open to northerners. Though travelers would be introduced to exotic sights, sounds, and cities, the travel books insisted that the South was no longer a foreign country or an impenetrable backwater. Railroads crisscrossed the region, making travel a breeze. Northerners could expect to sojourn in comfortable, well-appointed coaches, and to stay in clean hotels in modern and bustling cities. Though it remained distinctly southern, the South had lost its rough edges. The inclusion of train schedules, lists of boardinghouses, and elaborate maps—all the information that a northern reader would need to make his or her southern tour a reality—furthered this larger message. Travel in the South was simple, safe, and enjoyable. The routes and attractions were all laid out, the work already done. One only needed to get on the train.

In order to drive home this point, a number of tourist guides used the invented travels of fictional northerners to orient their readers and structure their narratives. *The Dream of "Ellen N,"* an 1886 production of the Louisville and Nashville railroad, followed the travels of a brother/sister pair from Cincinnati along the winding course of the L & N (or "Ellen N," in the narrator's affectionate shorthand).[47] *To the Shenandoah and Beyond,* an 1885 travel book, featured the scholarly narrator, Theodore, and his alarmingly dim-witted wife, Prue, with some help from an elusive friend named Baily.[48] Georgia journalist John Temple Graves, meanwhile, put the fictitious Reveres—a father, daughter, and two male cousins—at the center of his travel book, written for the Savannah, Florida, and Western Railway Company.[49] Such narratives served a dual purpose. They managed to impart the same essential travel information as their nonfiction counterparts (at times rather awkwardly: the characters' propensity to spout out random facts regarding railway schedules, tourist sites, and sleeping cars can be rather distracting), but their use of northern narrators lent an immediacy conspicuously lacking in the more traditional tourist guides. If Theodore, Prue, and the Reveres could enjoy the New South, their readers might, too.

New Southerners also eagerly courted those northerners considering a longer stay in Dixie. As the *Manufacturers' Record* put it in 1888, "the South has the immigration fever. It is well that it is so. Here is a vast country capable of supporting many times the entire population of the United States. It is a country that needs a larger population for its highest development and prosperity."[50] Boosters claimed that the New South was too prosperous, too successful, and growing too fast for its current population to manage. The wide-open spaces of the South offered an abundance of room, while its booming cities and bustling factories afforded plenty of work and promised great rewards for migrants. Boosters also served notice that the South's days of Yankee-hating and Republican-bashing were over. The New South had no time for such counterproductive pursuits. A convention of southern governors, meeting in Richmond in 1893, declared themselves "anxious to have immigrants settle among them" and insisted that "to the worthy immigrant they extend the hand of welcome, with the assurance that he will find an educated, warm-hearted, hospitable, progressive people, among whom he can live in amity and peace without regard to his religion, his politics, or his nativity."[51] The *Louisville Courier-Journal* agreed, noting that "we want all the Northern capital and energy we can get. Men who bring such commodities will be made welcome, and become a part of us in social, political, and patriotic life."[52]

Localities across the New South competed for the favor of would-be northern migrants. Residents of Richmond produced a 100-page tome designed to promote migration to their city, chock full of information relating to Richmond's history, landscape, infrastructure, agricultural possibilities, and manufacturing potential.[53] Iberia Parish, Louisiana, the self-professed "Garden Spot and Paradise of the United States," had the following message for the "thrifty home seeker" of the North: "We say come to the Gulf parishes of Louisiana and build up a home for yourself and family, where agriculture is not an untried experiment, but a demonstrated fact; where a competence surely awaits well directed effort and industry; where failure is not in the catalogue of possibilities."[54] Tallapoosa, Georgia, offered "almost unlimited" natural resources, "284 days of sunshine," and a money-back guarantee on an exploratory trip to Georgia.[55] A plucky northerner named James Foss sang the praises of Florida's Marion and Orange Counties in a pamphlet called *Florida Facts* and then offered to sell would-be migrants some of the hundreds of acres he owned in the area.[56] Northerners looking to relocate faced an embarrassment of rich alternatives.

Having decided to go south, Yankee migrants faced the question of what to do when they got there. A pair of northern-authored books, William H. Harrison Jr.'s *How to Get Rich in the South* and Eugene Cook Robertson's *The Road to Wealth Leads through the South*, offered guides for the northerner inclined to get the most money out of the New South with the least possible effort.[57] As Harrison noted, "To the man who will use his brains and his energy, the South certainly presents greater opportunities for gaining wealth and enjoying it than any other portion of the country." In the South, he added, "land is cheap, and the lazy man can live easier and the energetic man can get rich faster than in any other country."[58] Opening with some commentary on the region's wonderful climate, its need for settlers, and the inevitability of a glorious and prosperous future for the New South, both texts quickly turned into familiar lists of the various agricultural pursuits and industries in which the savvy northerner might strike it rich. From goats to peanuts, from timber to cotton, the paths to wealth in the South were endless. Riches were there for the taking, a southbound train ticket away.

Though the New South was open to the idea of northerners coming to Dixie to make their fortune, it much preferred those who brought a fortune with them. In an 1883 speech to northern bankers, Henry Watterson made a rather bald plea for outside investment: "You can see for yourselves here in Louisville what the south has done—what the south can do. If all this has been achieved without credit and without your powerful aid[,] . . . what might not be achieved if the vast aggregations of specie in fiscal centers should add this land of wine, milk and honey to the fields of investment[?]"[59] No New South storyteller worked as hard to secure northern investment as Richard Hathaway Edmonds. Edmonds understood that the progress of the New South mattered little if outside capital remained unaware of it. "The advantages of the south must be constantly placed before the whole country," he wrote in 1887. "It is not enough that some great effort be made for a week or a month to attract public attention, expecting this to do for all time, but week after week and month after month the work must be vigorously pushed."[60] Edmonds took his own advice, shilling for the New South in every issue of his paper. Among its myriad other purposes, the *Manufacturers' Record* served as a clearinghouse for southern investment opportunities, or, as Edmonds put it, a "medium of communication between the North and West, and the South through which the people of the former sections can learn of the openings for industrial enterprises in the latter, and through which the Southern people can make known the opportunities for profitable investments in their section."[61]

Northern investment in the South was not just good business; it was also patriotic. New South boosters and their northern allies imbued northern capital with almost magical restorative powers. Economics would succeed where politics had failed. Investors would quite literally purchase a reunion. As Henry Grady put it in an 1887 speech in Augusta, Georgia: "In her industrial growth the South is daily making new friends. Every dollar of Northern money invested in the South gives us a new friend in that section," Grady said. "We shall secure from the North more friendliness and sympathy, more champions and friends, through the influence of our industrial growth, than through political aspiration or achievement."[62] Union veteran and Harvard professor Nathaniel Southgate Shaler echoed Grady in an 1890 issue of the *Arena*, giving eloquent voice to the peacemaking power of the dollar: "Left to the influence of politics alone, the subjugated South and the victorious North would have remained long apart: without some common ground of sympathetic contact it is difficult to see how the division could ever have been healed. This common ground of relations has been found in business interests. Northern capital has invaded the South more swiftly and more effectively than the northern armies managed to do, and on the old battle-fields, victors and vanquished have forgotten their ancient strife in the friendly converse of men who are winning wealth each for the other."[63]

Commentators on both sides of the Mason-Dixon line saw in the New South's interest in northern tourism, migration, and investment evidence of a complete revolution in southern sentiment. In the face of the sheer volume of promigratory rhetoric, however, it is easy to overlook important differences between the New South's approach to migration and the calls for resettlement published in the first months after Appomattox. The New South extended its welcome to northerners on particular (and particularly *southern*) terms. If the 1865 migrants rallied under the banner of a Yankeefied Dixie, their counterparts in the 1880s might more aptly be described as Dixiefied Yankees.

One of the more obvious manifestations of this shift was the New South's consistent, almost petulant, insistence that the mere fact of a northern presence in the South did not constitute a northernized South. Even as the New South beckoned migrants and investors, it hotly denied that it needed northern assistance. Henry Watterson's *Louisville Courier-Journal* charitably offered "the Northern people full credit for what they have done here" but remained unwilling to "invest them with the credit of lifting the South from the ruin into which civil war threw her." The region's miraculous economic growth was a testament to southern skills and determination. "Northern capital has helped in this," the newspaper argued, "but it has been only a drop in the ocean."[64] Even as they eagerly sought northern migration and investment, therefore, New South storytellers downplayed the significance of both. In his *New York Ledger* articles, Henry Grady insisted that "the South has been re-built by the Southern people" and by "Southern brains and energy."[65] The New South would not be a northernized South. Northerners were welcome, but southerners must remain in control.

As they worked to shape the national conversation surrounding the New South, boosters also carefully circumscribed northern visitors' experience within it. In 1889, an iconoclastic white Virginian named Lewis Harvie Blair commented on the peculiar manner in which northern visitors managed to see the New South without seeing the South. Northern visitors "occupy pretty much the position of kings who, surrounded by ministers and courtiers whose interest it is to keep them in darkness, rarely if ever know the true state of affairs," Blair wrote. They are "usually taken in charge and coached by interested parties, who carry them to a few selected spots like Birmingham and Chattanooga, where there is much life, activity and growth, and are told exultingly, 'There! Look! Does not this remind you of Pennsylvania?'"[66] The visitors "have not seen the hundreds and hundreds of miles of poor country passed through, with its fenceless plantations, its unpainted and dilapidated homesteads, its small proportion of cultivated fields and its large proportion of lands returning and returned to state of nature." Such visitors, Blair concluded, "lose sight of the real South."[67]

Though Blair made this process sound a bit more conspiratorial than it actually was, he was not that far off base. By its very nature, the "New South" that northern tourists and would-be migrants experienced was an artificial construction. Northern tourists followed carefully planned itineraries. Northern migrants and investors had their attention directed to particular sites of economic opportunity or to particular lines of work. The degree of guidance and oversight clearly varied from case to case, but the New South's controlling hand was ever present. Northern journalist Charles Dudley Warner admitted—bragged, actually—that because of his busy schedule his 1887 southern itinerary "could only include representatives of the industrial and educational development of the New South."[68] Warner, however, could not hold a candle to Presbyterian clergyman Henry M. Field, who toured the South in a glass-enclosed railway car.[69] Northerners did not see the South as it really was. Through the ingenuity of boosters and publicists (not to mention the complicity of northern travelers themselves), northerners saw the South as the South wanted to be seen.

When President Grover Cleveland accepted an invitation to attend the Piedmont Exposition in Atlanta in 1887, Henry Grady personally organized the trip. In a letter to a Cleveland staff member, Grady painstakingly laid out his proposed agenda for the visit. Grady would dispatch three first-class carriages, "the handsomest ever sent out on a road," from Atlanta to Washington to pick up the president and Mrs. Cleveland. As the train rumbled south, the governors of Virginia, North Carolina, South Carolina, and Georgia would join the presidential party. Once in Atlanta, Cleveland's time was to be carefully regimented. Monday he was to "get a good night's rest"; Tuesday he would tour the exposition and witness a fireworks display that "will equal anything seen at Coney Island"; Wednesday he would deliver a speech and attend a public reception on the exhibition grounds; Thursday the president was to see Atlanta and its environs. Grady promised that "the president will leave Atlanta convince[d] that his visit to the exposition has been the pleasantest and most significant event of his administration." He warned, however, that "the president will find it wise not to accept invitations to other points in the South." Should Cleveland deviate from the proposed schedule, "the significance and importance of his visit to Atlanta will be dissipated." In closing, Grady made a promise: "If the president will only adhere to his programme as announced by us, and leave the matter in my hands, I will be responsible for the overwhelming success of the southern tour."[70]

Henry Grady's transparent attempt to shape President Cleveland's introduction to the New South is deeply significant. Grady's careful choreography and gentle scolding highlight just how much was at stake. By tying Cleveland to a carefully constructed itinerary made up of the best railway coaches, the best hotels, the best homes, and the best of the exposition, Grady could ensure that the president experienced the best of the New South. If Cleveland accepted other invitations, however, the purity of the New South's message would be compromised. It was therefore imperative that the president stay the course, taking in Grady's artfully packaged version of "the South." Though few Yankee tourists warranted Henry Grady's personal attention, the difference was one of degree rather than kind.

For the most part, northern visitors were happy to accept this arrangement, evincing no awareness that they had been handled and manipulated, and no suspicions that the New South might not be the true South.[71] Indeed, the awakening of previously hostile or indifferent Yankees is a predominant theme in the literature of the New South. Like the northern newspaper correspondent who had become "a southern man in sentiment and in sympathy" in the wake of the 1881 exposition, northern visitors were eager to declare their newfound affinity and respect for the South. After his sojourn in Dixie, Henry Field insisted that "never again can we feel that we are strangers here. Kindred in blood, we are brothers in heart."[72] A *Christian Union* correspondent was convinced that "what one has heard about the resistance which a Northern man will encounter in the South in getting his rights, solely on account of his being a Northern man, is certainly untrue."[73] On the basis of an 1888 tour, former Cornell University president Andrew D. White noted that, "I like the character of the people I met. A good feeling everywhere prevails toward the union. The south is heartily and thoroughly reconstructed. A great awakening in business is evidenced."[74] I. Register Layton, who toured the New South in 1885, declared that he had "met face to face with the people of the South, and received from our Brethren there the warm grip of friendship." In the process, he found "hearts that were tender and true, hospitable and kind, generous and good, and throbbing with the impulse of brotherly love, that thrilled our own with a hearty response."[75] Finally, a visit to the World Cotton Centennial Exposition, held in New Orleans, prompted a contributor to the humor magazine *Puck* to write, with deadly seriousness: "Instead of the South we have been taught to know—the lazy, dissatisfied, turbulent, quarrelsome South, there is a new South, that is only anxious to rival the North in works of usefulness." "Sectional feeling," the enthusiastic New South acolyte concluded, was now "an Extinct Satan."[76]

Northern author Rebecca Harding Davis's "Here and There in the South," a work of short fiction serialized in *Harper's New Monthly Magazine* in 1887, reflects on the charms of the New South and powerfully evokes the character of the Dixiefied Yankee. Part travelogue, part guidebook, part light romance, Davis's story is all New South. The story opens with a train full of northerners en route to Virginia. Arriving in Charlottesville, James and Sarah Ely, a northern clergyman and his wife, are shocked to run into an old acquaintance, a Virginian bearing the unlikely name of Wollaston Pogue. After catching up on the last two decades, Pogue insists that the Elys join him in traveling to his new home in Atlanta. He readily admits his ulterior motives. "You northern people know little about the New South," Pogue complains, before promising to remedy that lack of information.[77] The brief visit soon turns into a full-fledged southern tour. Over the story's final four installments, Wollaston Pogue and his daughter Lola lead the Elys from Atlanta to Mobile, Biloxi, and New Orleans. Along the way, they visit the New Orleans exposition, journey though the Louisiana bayous, and even stop at Jefferson Davis's house. As the tour continues, the party picks up a planter-turned-small farmer named Dupre Mocquard (a character of special interest for Lola Pogue), as well as the mysterious Madame de Parras and her granddaughter Betty.

The story is an enthusiastic reinterpretation of a central New South trope: the awakening of the skeptical northerner. Entering the South with a host of misperceptions and preconceptions, the Elys—through the instrumentality of their assorted southern guides—soon come to understand and embrace the New South. Initially, the northerners rebel at the very novelty of the New South. James Ely is "bewildered and annoyed" by the region's "busy, commonplace stir, this sudden plunge of the defeated South into the world's marketplace."[78] It was, to be certain, a far cry from the lethargy and grandeur of the antebellum South. Eventually, however, the Elys see the light. "I wish all Northerners could come down and see these people as they are," James Ely exclaims in Mobile. "Great heavens! what injustice we do them."[79] Sarah Ely proves a bit more resistant to the charms of the New South, but she too succumbs after experiencing the New Orleans exposition. "The closer you come to them," she explains in a letter to her sister, "the more you find they are very much like ourselves at heart."[80] When their journey must, at last, draw to a close, the Elys are loath to bid goodbye to their friends and to the New South. When they arrived in the South, they were just Yankees. By the story's end, the Elys have been Dixiefied.[81]

## The New North

Reaching those northerners who ventured south was only half the battle. The New South also needed to change minds in the North. If outsiders continued to approach the South with jaundiced eyes—smelling fraud at every election and wondering about the Klan affiliation of every white southerner encountered—all the new spirit in the world would be for naught. From the earliest days of the New South project, therefore, northern opinion was the mirror that the South held up to itself. Reprints of northern-authored articles on the New South were commonplace in southern newspapers, as was attention to the words and deeds of influential northerners. It was no exercise in shallow self-congratulation when the *New Orleans Daily Picayune* reprinted the *New York Herald*'s suggestion that "the south is not putting on any airs, but she is making barrels of money."[82] Nor was it a convulsion of regional narcissism when the *Atlanta Constitution* reprinted a *Philadelphia Press* piece lauding "the growing liberalism" of the South.[83] Likewise, there was more than egotism at work when Richard Hathaway Edmonds reported that banker Jay Gould thought the South had made "such progress since the war as was never made by New England, even in her palmiest days" and that Andrew Carnegie considered the New South to be "Pennsylvania's most formidable industrial enemy."[84] Such engagement was a matter of paramount importance. The very idea of a New South was predicated on a shift in the thoughts, presumptions, and behavior of the North. A New South that existed only in the mind of the South was no New South at all.

The New South, in other words, required a New North. The term itself appeared with some regularity in New South literature, and the concept was ever present. The idea of the New North was, in fact, as central to the ideology of the New South as the new spirit or the myth of inevitable progress. The New North would accept the New South on its own terms. It would abandon divisive partisan politics and the bloody shirt, focusing instead on the sectional reunion being forged by the almighty dollar. The New North would look for areas of unity and commonality, rather than cultivating difference and sowing discord. In matters relating to the South and to the sectional relationship, the New North would defer to the New South. In return, New South storytellers held out a prize almost impossible to turn down: an end to the sectional conflict and, at long last, a solution to the Southern Question.

The New North was an ingenious bit of rhetorical sleight-of-hand. Subtly reversing a long-standing set of assumptions, New South boosters insisted that the force perpetuating the sectional conflict resided north of the Mason-Dixon, not south of it. The South's reformation was complete, they insisted. It had, therefore, become incumbent on the North to show its own growth and development. Would the North accept the New South, thereby proving its broad-mindedness and patriotism, or would it reject southern overtures and forestall sectional reunion? The notion of the New North possessed a subtext that was subtly but undeniably accusatory; the Southern Question had been replaced with a Northern Question. The South was no longer a national problem, New South storytellers insisted. It remained to be seen whether the North had become one.

For the most part, such ideas were couched in the sweetest language the New South could muster. Henry E. Bowen, a southern contributor to the *Independent*, argued that "the people are awakening, and the *old* South with its hatred of the North and its hot-blooded infatuation, is giving place to the *new*." Bowen appealed to the better angels of northern nature, urging his Yankee readers to "let the doubter see for himself and heed not the vain mouthings of politicians. Give the people of the South a fair chance and treat them like brothers, and they are ready to meet you more than half way."[85] The *Atlanta Constitution* chastised one of its own correspondents for putting too much stock in the pernicious scribblings of a small number of northern holdouts, explaining that "a few newspapers and a few politicians up north are trying to revive the old war feelings, but the thoughtful and patriotic citizens of the republic, the majority of the people, have no ill feeling, no enmity against the south, and they are watching our progress and prosperity with pride and pleasure."[86]

At times, however, boosters traded their honey for vinegar, calling for a New North in language that was decidedly acerbic. In an article in the *North American Review*, Henry Watterson insisted that a carefully cultivated myth of white southern deviance was the glue that held together the Republican coalition in the North. In certain circles, he wrote, "no occasion is missed for establishing and enforcing the assumptions on which the native white people of the South are to be subverted: that they are lawless in practice and disloyal at heart; that they hate the blacks and seek to disfranchise them; that they actually do suppress all liberty of speech and action."[87] In 1885, a Mississippi newspaper lambasted certain northern Republicans for their willful blindness regarding the progress of the South. "When there is universal peace and fraternity; when the South is vastly more successful and harmonious with its labor than is Ohio; when the industry of the South presents increased products up in the hundreds of millions," these northern "Bourbons" studiously ignored the facts, "declaring that there is only lawlessness and anarchy in the whole South."[88] The *Nashville American* made the point even more caustically: "While we are listening to so much rant and cant about the 'new South' by all means let us have a new North. What this country really needs is a new North—a North

"The Four Rips; or, Twenty Years behind the Age," *Puck*, September 16, 1885.
In the New North, concern for African American civil rights seemed hopelessly
behind the times. Library of Congress.

that will have less of Puritan bigotry, intolerance, arrogance and less of the
Puritan disposition to deprecate others and boast its own virtues."[89]

However they framed it, New South boosters had subtly shifted the
conversation. An 1885 *Puck* cartoon dramatized this changed state of affairs. The cartoon depicts a reunion, of a sort, between North and South, as
figures labeled "northern capital" and "southern goods" sign a truce under
the beaming gaze of Uncle Sam. A bustling New South fairly sparkles in
the background, while a contented—if minstrelesque—black labor force
harvests an abundant cotton crop. Four bearded and bedraggled northern Republican politicians are the only outliers. Dressed in their habitual
bloody shirts and spoiling for a fight over such "old issues" as the "intimidation of the negro" in the South, the quartet quickly finds that times
have changed. Uncle Sam calls them up short, offering a rejoinder that
perfectly encapsulates the New South's challenge to the North: "My Fossil
Friends, the War ended twenty years ago. Have you been sleeping ever
since?" Rather than war heroes and dedicated politicians, these northern
Republicans had become "the Four Rips," real-life Van Winkles who were

"twenty years behind the age."[90] The war was over, the South New. The bloody shirt and the Bloody South were equally passé. Northerners needed to accept these facts or risk irrelevance.

White supremacy was built into the very foundation of the New South program. It would also play a central role in discussions of the New North. White southern boosters almost universally swore to uphold those rights that African Americans had already gained, but they were in no hurry to extend the novelty of the New South to its racial arrangements.[91] Though boosters preferred to talk about factories, diversified agriculture, and New South progress, they would stand firm for white supremacy when it counted. As Henry Grady unapologetically insisted in an 1887 speech, "The supremacy of the white race of the South must be maintained forever, and the domination of the negro race resisted at all points and at all hazards— because the white race is the superior race."[92]

The ghost of Reconstruction haunted the New South at every turn, a constant reminder of the dangers of northern interference and interventionism. The New South's compulsion for self-explanation—its need to tell its own story—was a direct result of the Reconstruction experience. Boosters made it clear that the New South could not accept northern attempts to control, define, legislate, or even narrate activities south of the Mason-Dixon line. This logic was applicable to the awe-inspiring stories of southern growth and to the overarching fable of southern progress, but it was no less applicable to the darker, bloodier ground of the race question. There would be no repeats of Reconstruction. The New North must defer to the South on the race issue.

In July 1884, Robert Bingham, a North Carolina educator, appeared before a Washington, DC, audience, and proceeded to tell the assembled Yankees precisely how little they knew about southern race relations. "Ladies and gentlemen, a very large proportion of you are from the North. I came here to conciliate, not to offend you; but I tell you that the great mass of your people, however much you think you know about it, are profoundly ignorant of the conditions in the South and of the relations between the races."[93] Even as he pleaded for federal aid to southern education, Bingham held fast to a central New South mantra: when it came to southern affairs, particularly racial ones, the North was uninformed, unequipped, and unprepared. It should, therefore, be uninvolved. "I think that I know the Southern white man better than it is possible for any one who has not lived in the South all his life to know him. I think that I know the

Southern negro better than it is possible for any one who has not lived in the South all his life to know him," Bingham offered. "I am sure that I know the Southern white man and the Southern negro better than any person whatsoever, who has never been in the South at all, however well such a one may imagine that he understands the whole subject and I tell you that social relations must be left to take care of themselves in the South."[94] Control of southern race relations must rest with those who understood the issues involved. This was the New South's charge to the New North.

In an open letter to Richard Hathaway Edmonds, Senator George Graham Vest, a Democrat from Missouri, mocked northerners for their idiotic credulity in believing scurrilous reports on southern race relations. "If the charges made by the partisan press of the North be true—that the Southern people are systematically engaged in oppressing the negro, and that they spend their days in scheming for that purpose, and their nights in murder and intimidation—then they are beyond question the most remarkable race of people who have existed upon the face of the earth," Vest wrote. "It is simply impossible that a people addicted to the practices portrayed by the Northern press and re-hashed in the halls of Congress could use the oppressed and sullen labor of the negro to bring about the amazing results contained in the special copy of the *Manufacturers' Record* which you have been kind enough to send me."[95] In this letter, Vest performed an impressive argumentative pirouette. The New South was thriving economically, he said, so it obviously treated its black residents equitably. Vest's logic collapses like a house of cards with the slightest prodding—A did not necessarily lead to B—and yet it was precisely this logic that underlay the New South's engagement with the North and the race question. The New South was an economic dynamo, New South storytellers argued, so it must be allowed to settle its own racial affairs.

Boosters insisted, however, that northerners did not need to worry. Relations between the South's white population and its black population were warm and cordial. It was when outside agitators got involved that things took to a turn for the worse. Richard Hathaway Edmonds preferred the poetry of progress to the work of white supremacy, but when he addressed the race question his arguments were familiar. "If the South is left to itself, if no inimical legislation interferes with the existing status," Edmonds wrote in a *Manufacturers' Record* editorial, "the troublesome race question will be consigned to oblivion."[96] Yankees knew nothing about race relations in the South. When they had meddled with southern affairs during Reconstruction, the results had been horrific. They must, under the new dispensation, leave such matters to those equipped to handle them. Hoke Smith offered the same conclusion: "The negro race had lived for several generations in slavery. During that time great confidence, as a rule, existed between the negro and his master. Many instances could be given of the strong affection felt by the one for the other." The two races in the South had a long-established working relationship, marked by trust and affection. It was only during Reconstruction, when the North had gotten involved, that the relationship had soured. "As the hold of the carpet-bagger began to lessen," Smith was pleased to report, "friction rapidly ceased between the white man and the colored man in the South."[97] Without carpetbaggers, Smith argued, there was no race problem.

The New South presented the North with something of a quid pro quo. White boosters offered a new vision of the South, defined by mineral wealth, profitable investment, and economic reunion. Beyond this, they held out the promise of a mutually acceptable end to the sectional conflict. In exchange, the New North must abdicate its controlling stake in southern affairs, including racial ones. It would be a mistake to reduce the entire New South program to a cover for a white supremacist agenda. Such a reading unfairly simplifies a complicated historical moment and flattens a multifaceted cultural program. If the New South program was not to blame for the rise of Jim Crow segregation in the 1890s, however, it was certainly a precondition for it. Without the establishment of an alternative characterization of the South—a "good" South to counteract visions of the bloody, traitorous, and backward South—northern equanimity in the southern racial politics of the 1890s and 1900s is harder to fathom. In accepting the New South's bargain, the New North willingly ceded the reins of the race question. If this did not, in and of itself, guarantee the destruction of those civil rights remaining to southern African Americans, it did mark a singular shift in the sectional relationship and a step on the road to Jim Crow.

The "New North" was not just a clever turn of phrase or a New South buzzword. It was real, a factor in the cultural history of the nineteenth century and the retreat from Reconstruction every bit as significant as its southern counterpart. Yankees tired of an interminable sectional conflict and the ever present Southern Question saw in the New South an opportunity to turn the page, and they eagerly seized it. Boston businessman Edward Atkinson, the brains behind the 1881 Atlanta International Cotton Exposition, was ecstatic to find that "the old 'Solid South' is dead, and that a new South is rising from the ashes, eager to keep step with the North in the onward march of the Solid Nation."[98] Northern organs reveled in the growth of southern industry and the changes in southern temperament with a zeal that could often equal that of Grady or Edmonds. Internalizing the words of the New South boosters, northern commentators repackaged and recycled them in their own calls for a change in the sectional relationship. The fact that the alluring story of the New South might require a concession or two did not seem to cross many northern minds; when it did, it ruffled few feathers. The New South was simply too appealing, its message too resonant, the North's desire for a reprieve from its southern worries too strong.[99]

New Northerners began by bidding a formal goodbye to the largely derogatory images of the South that had been their constant companions for at least two decades. After making a trip through the South, a Philadelphia resident was contrite: "We have misunderstood the South in more ways than one," he wrote. "We have not appreciated her industries or shown the good fellowship we should have shown."[100] The New York–based *Christian Union* complained that some people in the North seemed unaware of the fact that "a quarter of a century has passed away, and that it has wrought changes as radical in public sentiment in the Southern States as it has in the organic laws and civic institutions." Blinkered by lingering hostilities and accustomed to sectional ill will, these Yankees "know that the South was subjugated; they suppose that it lies still in sullen subjugation. They know it fought for secession and resisted emancipation; and they imagine that it would dissolve the Union to-day if it dared, and would re-enslave the blacks if it could."[101] Such views were folly. The days of the Bloody South were long gone. It was time for northerners to wake up to this fact.

Carl Schurz's tour of the New South produced a picture entirely different from the one he had offered in his 1865 report to the U.S. Congress. In 1885, Schurz concluded that the South, if not perfect, was no worse than the rest of the nation. "I think it is safe to affirm that to-day, twenty years after the close of the war, the Southern people are as loyal to the Union as the people of any part of the country," he wrote.[102] Edward Atkinson implored his fellow northerners to forget the dead issues of the past, focusing instead on the possibilities and potentialities of the future. "The day of the Ku-Klux, general abuse, or even general intimidation or undue influence in respect to act or vote, has nearly gone by," Atkinson wrote in a letter to a friend.[103] Alexander McClure, a Pennsylvania newspaperman, agreed, insisting in his 1886 book *The South: Its Industrial, Financial, and*

*Political Condition* that "there is a New South, with new teachings, new opportunities, new energies."[104] What the nation lacked, these New North boosters argued, was not a New South—evidence of its existence was undeniable—but a North ready to recognize the changed circumstances and act accordingly.

In the North as well as the South, business and money were at the heart of the New South's appeal. It was no coincidence that when Pennsylvania congressman William D. Kelley searched for a metaphor to describe the New South, he settled on a legendary city of gold. "Wealth and honor are in the pathway of the New South," Kelley wrote. "She is the coming El Dorado of American adventure. May the Almighty speed and guide her onward progress."[105] Kelley, for one, was fully onboard. Echoing southern boosters, northern commentators found in the movement from politics to business abundant proof of the South's reformation. "It is like the discovery of a new world," journalist and travel writer Charles Dudley Warner marveled. "Instead of a South devoted to agriculture and politics, we find a South wide-awake to business, excited and even astonished at the development of its own immense resources in metals, marbles, coal, timber, fertilizers, eagerly laying lines of communication, rapidly opening mines, building furnaces, foundries, and all sorts of shops for utilizing the native riches."[106] The North had been willfully blind for far too long. The South had changed; it was new. This fact was emblazoned on every factory, every improved farm, every railroad tie, every urban center, every smiling face across Dixie. The *Los Angeles Times* was more concise. The state of Alabama, it quipped, "raises about 50 per cent. more cotton than she did ten years ago. And less hell."[107]

Visual culture also registered these changes. Throughout Reconstruction, depictions of white southerners in *Harper's Weekly* cartoons were, to say the least, uncharitable. White southerners generally appeared as unrepentant rebels in chin whiskers and floppy hats, their scowling countenances and angular features perfectly capturing the bile and malice that flowed within. What a surprise, then, was "The Queen of Industry; or, the New South," an 1882 Thomas Nast image. In stark contrast to the traditional angry rebel iconography (an example of which conveniently adorns the upper left corner, bearing the moniker "King Cotton"), Nast depicts the New South as a beautiful young woman, quietly minding a loom.[108] Her face is placid and serene, her work unhurried but steady. Above the Queen's head, Nast places a small illustration of a bustling New South city, complete with train, steamship, and smokestacks. The presence of a half

Thomas Nast, "The Queen of Industry; or, the New South," *Harper's Weekly*, January 14, 1882. Nast's sketch presents an alternative personification of the South for a new, post-Reconstruction age. Library of Congress.

dozen African Americans picking cotton is a stark reminder of the significant continuities in southern history. Unlike their antebellum counterpart, however, who finds himself stuck under King Cotton's foot, these latter day black laborers seem to be in firm control of the product of the southern soil. "The Queen of Industry" offers a testament the transformative power of the New South's story.

For the most part, northern supporters of the New South contented themselves with ignoring the racial implications of the New South program. As mentioned above, this silence suited white southerners just fine. Some northerners, however, went further. "The prejudice of race is five-fold stronger in the North than in the South," Alexander McClure wrote. "While the North maintains its deep prejudice of race, the people of the South have a general and strong sympathy for the negro."[109] Playing a pitch-perfect New Northerner, McClure offered the following conclusions: "The intelligent and dispassionate Northerner who closely observes the relations of the two races North and South, is forced to confess that with all our boasted superior devotion to the black race, and with all our assaults upon the South for the oppression of the blacks, the negro is better treated by the South than by the North."[110] The race problem, according to Charles Dudley Warner, was the South's particular burden. "The North can not relieve her of it, and it can not interfere." Warner insisted that "there is generally in the South a feeling of good-will toward the negroes, a desire that they should develop into true manhood and womanhood." Besides, he added, "we who live in States where hotelkeepers exclude Hebrews can not say much about the exclusion of negroes from Southern hotels."[111] After visiting the 1881 Atlanta exposition, a Chicagoan named Lauren Dunlap offered the following statement, which appeared in the *International Review*: "The negro question or problem is not incapable of satisfactory solution. Its agitation will be brought to an end, its settlement will come, with the vigorous treatment of southern questions . . . by Southern states-men, and from a Southern standpoint."[112] No southern booster could have said it better.

## New South Dissenters

The appeal of the New South was never universal. Dissenters from both sides of the Mason-Dixon and both sides of the color line leveled a series of critiques throughout the 1880s and early 1890s. New South dissenters shared a conviction that the story of the South should be told with refer-ence to what had stayed the same rather than what had changed. Where boosters saw progress, dissenters saw stasis. The New South, they insisted, was not a real place. It was a mirage, a literary construction, a clever piece of regional advertising. Most often, such critiques centered on the region's race politics. For all its boomtowns and railroad track, critics argued, the New South still refused to accept the outcome of the Civil War and the dictates of Reconstruction. Until it did, it would be "new" in name alone.

George Washington Cable, a Louisiana-born Confederate veteran equally well-known for his "local-color" fiction and his racial liberalism, had little patience for the rhetoric of the New South boosters. In an 1885 *Century* magazine article titled "The Freedmen's Case in Equity," Cable insisted that while the race question—"the greatest social problem be-fore the American people to-day"—loomed, southern self-congratulation seemed premature and inappropriate.[113] Cable systematically aired the New South's dirty laundry, calling national attention to those issues (no-tably segregation and the convict lease system) that boosters preferred to keep hidden from view. Until the South learned to deal with its African

American population on the basis of fairness, morality, and political equality, Cable insisted, any change would be merely skin deep. "For more than a hundred years," he wrote, legal, political, and cultural notions of black inferiority had been "the absolute essentials to our self-respect."[114] Southern whiteness, Cable argued, was rooted in the oppression of southern African Americans. While this flawed worldview remained central to regional and racial identity, the claims of New South boosters would ring hollow.

Cable had the temerity to look the boosters' New South in the face and declare it wanting. But he went further than this, lashing out at one of the New South's foundational principles. The race question, Cable argued, did not belong to the South alone. It was, he said, a national issue. As such, Cable implored his northern readership to play an active role in southern racial affairs. "There rests," he wrote, "a moral responsibility on the whole nation never to lose sight of the results of African American slavery until they cease to work mischief and injustice. It is true these responsibilities may not fall everywhere with the same weight; but they are nowhere entirely removed." The status of the South's black population was not a purely southern concern; it was a national one. The North, he feared, had largely "retreated" on the issue and had "thrown the whole matter over to the States of the South," to the detriment of both regions and both races.[115] In the face of booster propaganda, Cable urged readers on both sides of the Mason-Dixon line to imagine a new South that was *truly* new, one that would pair economic progress with a deeper moral and political growth.

Henry Grady would not allow such poisonous sentiments to stand. In a response to Cable published in *Century* three months later, Grady cast doubt on Cable's very southernness (his Louisiana birth and Confederate credentials notwithstanding) and reiterated the prevailing racial credo of the New South: "The South must be allowed to settle the social relations of the races according to her own views of what is right and best."[116] A short rejoinder by Cable published later in the year served as the closing volley in the Cable/Grady *Century* debate, but Cable continued to demand more of the New South and its most prominent spokesman than promises and propaganda. Speaking before a Connecticut African American club, Cable tried his hand at poetry:

You've probably heard of one Grady.
A speech to New Englanders made he.
They thought it delightful
Becuz he wa'n't spiteful

And they're what they call 'tickled' with Grady.
He was eloquent, also, was Grady;
Patriotic! and bright as a lady.
But on Men's Equal Rights
The darkest of nights
Compared with him wouldn't seem shady.[117]

Cable would not let the New South claim novelty while harboring old resentments; he would not allow the New North to wash its hands of the nation's African Americans for the sake of convenience and ease. Only when action replaced words, when moral growth overtook pleasant propaganda, he argued, would the South truly become "new."

Most African Americans likewise responded coldly to the appeals of the New South boosters. Recognizing the emptiness of the New South's promises, black newspapers heaped scorn on the boosters and the wares they peddled. At the heart of these critiques lay a conviction that nothing had changed in the South. Racism, violence, hatred, and bloodshed were as much a part of day-to-day life in the 1880s as they had been in the 1860s. The South might be new, in others words, but it was still the South. "They say it is a new South," the *Richmond Planet* opined in 1890. "If so it has certainly inherited many of the Old South's principles."[118] The *New York Freeman* was a lonely dissenting voice following Henry Grady's triumphant 1886 speech at Delmonico's. "The white men of the South, — in legislatures, in courts of justice, in convict camps, in churches, in hotels and theatres, in railroad and steamship accommodation — do not do justice to their colored fellow-citizens," the *Freeman* argued, "and when a man like Grady stands up and lies about these matters, we are here to strike the lie on the head."[119] New South or not, prejudice and second-class citizenship were still a fact of life for southern black people. Grady's lofty rhetoric could not change this essential fact. The *Washington Bee* expressed a similar skepticism. Though they welcomed the dawning of a truly new era in the South, the newspaper's editors recognized how much remained to be overcome: "When the Southern black laws are repealed; when colored ladies and gentlemen are allowed to ride in first class coaches; when educational institution[s] are regarded free to all; when ku-kluxism is abandoned; when the midnight assassins are brought to justice and when religion is not regarded as a mockery, we shall proclaim the 'New South.'"[120]

Henry McNeal Turner, now serving as a bishop in the African Methodist Episcopal Church, was similarly scornful of the claims of the New South prophets. For Turner, southern history since the Civil War appeared to be one continuous tale of white brutality and barbarism. "There is not a night, or a day either, the year round, that our people are not most brutally being murdered," Turner wrote in 1883. "The reign of blood and slaughter is but little less than ten years ago, if any. True, we do not hear so much of the Ku Klux and White Leaguers as formerly, but it is because the vampires have changed their tactics and not because there has been any material reformation in the condition of things." Turner took issue with a North that willfully closed its eyes to the true condition of the South. White "banditti" continued to brutalize black people while the nation looked the other way. "The half has never been told," Turner wrote, because "neither North or South wants it told." In the interests of reunion and investment, northerners "close up the great dailies of the country to all communications which essay to recite the deeds of death and horror perpetrated upon our people."[121] As North and South celebrated their reunion, Turner worried, "the ballot of the black man," had become "a parody, his citizenship a nullity and his freedom a burlesque."[122]

In his 1884 book *Black and White: Land, Labor, and Politics in the South*, T. Thomas Fortune, a southern-born, New York–based black journalist and activist, delivered a stinging rebuke to the New South program. Fortune's text is a landmark in the black radical tradition, offering a full-throated critique of economic oppression and political violence in the South. Significantly, Fortune never mentions the New South by name. Because Reconstruction had not altered the underlying economic structures of the South—"the giant form of the slave-master, the tyrant, still rises superior to law, to awe and oppress the unorganized proletariat," Fortune wrote—African Americans remained at the mercy of the southern white elite.[123] The war and Reconstruction had done little to chasten this class, Fortune insisted. "They cared nothing for the Union *then*; they care less for the Union *now*."[124] If anything, things had gotten worse for African Americans under the enlightened watch of the New South boosters. Southern blacks "are more absolutely under the control of the Southern whites; they are more systematically robbed of their labor; they are more poorly housed, clothed and fed, than under the slave régime; and they enjoy, practically, less of the protection of the laws of the State or the Federal government."[125] In T. Thomas Fortune's New South, traditional southern racial antipathy had been tethered to a nascent industrial capitalism. Beyond this, there was nothing novel about the New South. The oppression, the injustice, and the brutality remained.

Booker T. Washington, principal of the Tuskegee Institute in Alabama and one of the most significant black leaders at the turn of the century, took a different approach to the question of African Americans and the New South. In stark contrast to Turner and Fortune, Washington affirmed many of the claims of white boosters. In fact, Washington often sounded like a New South booster himself. His speech at the 1895 Cotton States and International Exposition in Atlanta, which established Washington as a recognized leader of the race, is rife with New South rhetoric and symbolism.[126] Washington welcomed the South's "new era of industrial progress."[127] He lauded the value of hard work and disavowed political agitation.[128] He reminded his white listeners that the South's black laborers had "tilled your fields, cleared your forests, builded your railroads and cities, and brought forth treasures from the bowels of the earth," all "without strikes and labour wars."[129] Washington's conclusion—that sectional reunion, racial compromise, and "material prosperity" would combine to "bring into our beloved South a new heaven and a new earth"—was a perfect distillation of New South thought.[130] The echoes of Henry Grady and Richard Hathaway Edmonds were not coincidental. Booker T. Washington was speaking a language that the New South and the New North could understand. Rather than denying the existence of the New South (as Turner and Fortune did), Washington sought to carve out a place for African Americans within it. Washington did not simply parrot the rhetoric of the New South. In an attempt to secure a share of the region's newfound prosperity, Washington claimed that rhetoric for his own. If the New South was as bustling, modern, and cosmopolitan as the boosters claimed, both races should benefit. By embracing the logic of the New South, Washington challenged southern whites to live up to their own stories.

Even in the face of such critiques, the appeal of the New South was too strong for many Yankees to ignore. White southerners had seized the right to tell their story to the nation for the first time since the war. The tale they offered—a fable of regional rebirth, intersectional harmony, and a revolution in morality as complete as the revolution in industry—was a compelling one. In exchange for a revived South and a reunited nation, New South boosters asked only that white northerners leave the settling of the race question to those best equipped to handle it. Yankees could embrace the New South or choose to prolong the sectional conflict in the interest of black rights in the South. One path seemed to lead to a new era of sectional harmony, promising a New North, a New South, and a new nation. The other led to more of the same: same old squabbles, same old distrust, same old South.

The New South's message of progress may not have cornered the market on northern visions of the South, but it did not have to. Even if its hold was never complete, the story of the New South forever altered the landscape on which the Southern Question was addressed. Where Yankees had once seen the South only as a problem, the New South held out a solution. Rather than focusing on electoral chicanery, a solidly Democratic South, and the abridgement of civil rights, northern commentators engaged with the tonnages of iron produced, the growth of boom towns, and the sprouting of factories across the South. They delighted in the opportunities open to the migrant, the adventures open to the tourist, and the extravagant expositions open to all. The New South did not necessarily eradicate northern visions of the Bloody South, but it certainly made such visions easier to forget.

# CHAPTER FOUR

# The Pen and the Sword

In July 1880, John B. Wardlaw Jr., a southern-born Princeton graduate and professor of English language and literature at a small women's college in Virginia, delivered an address on a subject—southern literature—that many of his contemporaries would have considered a contradiction in terms. As it then stood, Wardlaw admitted, "our southern literature is meager and insufficient," capturing "neither the finest genius nor the most earnest and deliberate efforts of the southern mind."[1] Although the South had "furnished a majority of the leading minds that have figured in the history of this country," its lack of literary attainment was a source of consternation and embarrassment.[2] The lifestyle of the Old South and the "general cast and tendency of the Southern mind," Wardlaw explained, had not been conducive to sustained literary production. Changing circumstances in Dixie and across the nation, however, were conspiring to work a change. The very eccentricities of southern life that had long barred the region from the American literary mainstream now augured success in the same field. The South's unique worldview and heroic past promised a literature that could appeal to the nation at large while maintaining its distinctively regional cast. "The time is ripe for the growth of our southern literature, and large results await the willing and capable pen," Wardlaw claimed.[3] The 1880s, he promised, would be the decade of southern fiction.

At the time he spoke, Wardlaw had little basis for this confidence. A year earlier, Louisiana native George Washington Cable had garnered praise for a collection of short stories called *Old Creole Days*, but otherwise the South's postwar literary fields remained rather barren. Shortly after Wardlaw's speech, however, an Atlanta journalist named Joel Chandler Harris published *Uncle Remus: His Songs and His Sayings* to massive acclaim, both North and South. The book's success spurred scores of imitators and encouraged northern publishers to take a chance on other southern literary productions. Southern-authored and southern-themed fiction, often dubbed "local color," inundated the nation's literary marketplace for the remainder of the decade. Though this work ranged from the undeniably masterful to the imminently forgettable, the South quickly carved out an important place in the nation's literary consciousness.

By 1890, Richard Watson Gilder, editor of *Century* magazine, could marvel that southern literature "has blossomed so suddenly, so exquisitely, so profusely, that I for one have hardly been able to keep track of it."[4] The quantity and the quality of southern fiction produced in the preceding decade, Gilder claimed, had completely upended the nation's literary tastes, prompting at least one desperate northern-born author to ask, "When are you going to give the North a chance?" For Gilder, this development seemed to herald a new era in the sectional relationship. If the literary shortcomings of the antebellum South were rooted in that society's distinctive and aberrant culture, the region's newfound fictional productivity provided evidence of a move back into the national mainstream. "Artistically speaking, the South is a 'long-lost sister,' but happily returned in our day with mutual greetings of affection," Gilder wrote. "It is well for the North, it is well for the nation, to hear in poem and story all that the South burns to tell of her romance, her heroes, her landscape."[5] Rather than a remnant of southern distinctiveness, Gilder insisted, the new southern literature was a harbinger of reunion. Even as it maintained its southern flavor, this literature promised an end to sectionalism.

Albion Tourgée was not so sure. In an article published in the *Forum*, the author expressed wonder at the recent revolution in American literary sentiment. "A foreigner studying our current literature," Tourgée wrote, "and judging our civilization by our fiction, would undoubtedly conclude that the South was the seat of intellectual empire in America."[6] Like Gilder, Tourgée saw in the sudden rise of southern fiction the beginnings of a larger shift in the sectional relationship. For Tourgée, however, this was a cause not for celebration but concern. Lured by the romance and passion of southern stories, each one "full of life and fire and real feeling," northerners seemed determined to ignore the presence of sentiments that Tourgée found "not only Southern in type, but distinctly Confederate in sympathy."[7] While southerners systematically rewrote the nation's recent history and their region's place in it, northerners looked on passively. Literature, Tourgée warned, had a distinct political and cultural power.

Southern writers stood poised to win with the pen what they had lost with the sword.

For good or for ill, the literary explosion of the 1880s and 1890s opened a new front in the battle over the Southern Question. Like Brer Rabbit, who used the fact that he had been "bred en bawn in a brier-patch" to great effect in one of Uncle Remus's most famous stories, a new generation of southern authors used their familiarity with the "brier-patch" of the South to rewrite the region's place in the national imagination.[8] This southern-authored, southern-themed literature bore an implicit regional message. Since those who had never lived in a brier-patch could never truly understand it—Brer Fox had learned this lesson the hard way—they would do well to defer to those who had been "bred en bawn" there. By this logic, a southern upbringing imparted authenticity, while northern parentage denied an individual the right to speak authoritatively about southern affairs. Southerners understood the South; they would tell its story to the nation. In light of the continuing struggles over the meaning of the South in the post-Reconstruction era, this was truly a momentous development.

The lives and works of a quartet of southern authors—Joel Chandler Harris, Thomas Nelson Page, George Washington Cable, and Charles W. Chesnutt—capture the power of southern literature in the late nineteenth century. Though it is important to recognize that these four authors were part of a larger literary conversation that also included the likes of Albion Tourgée, Frances Ellen Watkins Harper, and Paul Laurence Dunbar, among others, I have focused on Harris, Page, Cable, and Chesnutt for three related reasons. First, they all had deep southern roots. Of the four, only Chesnutt was not born in the South, though he spent his childhood and young adult years there. Second, each enjoyed wide readership and popularity north of the Mason-Dixon line. All four were widely and positively reviewed in the nation's major journals and literary magazines. Finally, in their speeches, analytical writings, and personal correspondence, all of them were outspoken on the political potency of southern fiction. These similarities provide a base of comparison from which to better judge their stylistic and intellectual differences.

In the stories of Joel Chandler Harris and Thomas Nelson Page, northern readers were transported to an idyllic southern past peopled with dashing cavaliers and dutiful slaves. While Harris's Uncle Remus quickly became the archetypal "faithful slave" in American culture, it was Page who more self-consciously used fiction in the service of white supremacy.

In stark contrast to Harris and Page, George Washington Cable and Charles Chesnutt hoped to use literature to advance an egalitarian and democratic agenda. Relying on their own southern bona fides, the Confederate veteran-turned-racial liberal and the African American author from North Carolina offered important and insightful critiques of southern race relations, past and present. Cable and Chesnutt, however, were fighting an uphill battle. In the wake of Reconstruction, the prevailing literary tastes in the North ran more toward moonlight and magnolias than race and revisionism. Having surrendered the right to narrate the southern past, northern readers worried little about the political consequences. They were more than happy to settle for a good story.

## Joel Chandler Harris:
## Fact and Fiction in Uncle Remus's Cabin

Uncle Remus burst onto the northern cultural landscape in 1880 and stuck there with the tenacity of a tar baby. The fictional creation of an Atlanta journalist named Joel Chandler Harris, Remus was an elderly ex-slave who spent his nights regaling his former master's son (and the American reading public) with tales of wonder and mystery. Each night, Remus called forth Brer Rabbit, Brer Fox, Brer Tarrypin, and Brer Wolf from a time and place when "de beastesses kyar'd on marters same ez fokes."[9] As northern readers settled themselves around the small cabin fire, however, it was Uncle Remus who truly came alive. In Harris's fictional slave, northerners found a guide to black life in the South.

Raised in a small Georgia town, Joel Chandler Harris was too young to serve in the Civil War, spending the war years apprenticing at a small plantation newspaper published at Turnwold plantation, near Eatonton. Nights spent with the plantation slaves formed the basis for the Uncle Remus tales that Harris would publish in later life. After the war, Harris worked in the newspaper business all across Georgia, building a reputation as a reporter and a humorist, before landing a job with the *Atlanta Constitution* in 1876.[10] Harris proved to be a competent and engaging journalist, but it was his Uncle Remus sketches that would make him a legend. Remus first appeared in the fall of 1876, depicted as a rather crotchety ex-slave who stumbled into the *Constitution*'s office from the streets of Atlanta. In this guise, he appeared periodically in the newspaper for the next three years. In 1879, however, Harris recast the character as a plantation slave, using him as a mouthpiece for the animal stories he had first heard on Turnwold plantation. The response was immediate. Remus tales began to appear every Sunday in the *Constitution*, newspapers around the country reprinted Harris's sketches, and Harris, much to his own chagrin, became a minor celebrity. In late 1880, the New York–based publisher Appleton's collected thirty-four animal tales narrated by Uncle Remus, a number of plantation proverbs and songs (all in dialect), a longer Harris original titled "A Story of the War," and twenty-one of the older character sketches featuring Remus in conversation with the staff of the *Atlanta Constitution*. The result, *Uncle Remus: His Songs and His Sayings*, remains a milestone in American cultural history.

*Uncle Remus* is an enormously complex book. It defies simple categorization, presenting a peculiar amalgam of fact and fiction, history and literature.[11] The thirty-four animal tales, featuring the hijinks of Brer Rabbit and company, are the centerpiece of the text. These stories, Harris insisted in his introduction, were presented just as he heard them from the black storytellers of Turnwold, "without embellishment and without exaggeration."[12] The tales themselves are the genuine article, the collective construction of generations of storytellers, authentic folklore by any measure.[13] Animal tales had a long history in Africa and in American slave communities. The basic relationship embedded within them—in which the smaller, weaker animal (Brer Rabbit, sometimes Brer Tarrypin) triumphs over the larger, stronger animal (Brer Wolf, Brer Fox, Brer Bear) using wit, guile, and imagination—had an obvious and undeniable appeal to an enslaved population.[14] In these tales, the traditional rules of slavery ceased to apply. The victory did not always go to the strongest.

Of course, Harris did not simply repeat the tales as they had been told to him. His key contribution to the text was the character of Uncle Remus. Although he was true to the animal tales themselves, and in this sense was only partially their author, the character of Uncle Remus was all Harris's. The animal tales had existed in black oral culture for hundreds of years; Remus, the faithful slave, lived only in the mind of the white South.[15] Remus is deferent toward white people, seemingly pleased with his lot in life, including the portion spent in slavery, and wholly ambivalent about freedom. He works when he feels like it and seldom seems concerned about payment, beyond the occasional slice of mince pie. Indeed, his sole responsibility on the plantation is to recount tales from the good old days for the entertainment of the little boy. Needless to say, there is no racial

Image of Uncle Remus from the
1881 edition of Joel Chandler Harris's
*Uncle Remus: His Songs and His Sayings.*
Special Collections Department, Tampa
Library, University of South Florida.

violence, no sharecropping debt, and no Reconstruction in Remus's world. There is only the loving relationship of a white southern boy and an elderly black man.[16]

Since the animal tales are sequential in only the most general sense, it is the character of Remus that provides the connective tissue and structures the internal logic of the text. In the first dozen or so tales, Uncle Remus plays a distinctly subsidiary role, existing more as a vessel than as a character. He is allowed no existence outside of his nightly storytelling sessions with the little boy. As the series continues, however, Remus moves to the center of the narrative, gaining a personality and a character apart from the tales he imparts. In later stories, Remus begins to editorialize, to monologue, and to converse with the little boy on a range of topics. He even begins to tailor his stories to suit the needs of the moment, embedding morals within them—do not meddle in other people's business, do not get a "swell-head"—for the boy's benefit.[17] The animal tales are a constant, but by the end of the cycle, Remus has stepped out of their shadow, using and shaping the tales, rather than existing only as a reflection of them. Uncle Remus was a figment of Joel Chandler Harris's imagination, but over the course of the text he comes to seem almost as real as the yarns he spins.

As written, therefore, *Uncle Remus* is an unusual mixture of folkloric preservation and literary creation. The reader is left to parse through the strands of history and fiction that coexist in the text, deciding where to draw the line between the two. For his part, Harris offered little instruction or assistance. He insisted that the animal tales were reproduced faithfully; beyond this, he left matters to the reader's discretion. At no point in the text does Harris state outright that Remus is his own fictional creation. His references to "Uncle Remus's story" and "the story . . . as Uncle Remus tells it" further confuse the issue, implying a basis in reality.[18] Neither entirely fact nor entirely fiction, neither history nor literature, *Uncle Remus* occupies a liminal space between genres. This in-between status was the source of much of its cultural power.

If the text as it existed on paper was a complicated amalgam of genres and styles, however, the text as northerners read it was significantly simpler. Northern readers consistently flattened many of the ambiguities that define *Uncle Remus*, gleefully accepting Harris's book as a true statement regarding southern African Americans. In the process, they elevated Uncle Remus to the status of archetypal freedman. The relationship between the little boy and Remus, by extension, came to stand in more generally for black-white relations in the South. Readers empowered the text to speak authoritatively, not just about the oral culture of the black past but about the fundamental character of African Americans and about race relations in the postwar South. In the words of one reviewer, northern readers saw in Uncle Remus (both the character and the text) "truth in the garb of fiction."[19]

A key to this slippage is found in Harris's introduction to the 1880 Remus volume. Harris was concerned that Appleton's planned to place the text in its humorous collection, so he authored an introduction that emphasized the factual portions of the text—the faithful recreations of the animal tales and the supposedly authentic black dialect—at the expense of its fictional components. "However humorous it may be in effect, its intention is perfectly serious," Harris insisted.[20] In an attempt to authenticate his tales, Harris cited the work of a number of contemporary folklore scholars, giving the introduction something of a scientific air. By placing *Uncle Remus* in conversation with the findings of "Professor J. W. Powell," "Herbert H. Smith, author of 'Brazil and the Amazons,'" and "Professor Hartt," Harris established the folkloric value of the text, and, from its first page, focused attention on the text's value as a work of social science, rather than as a work of fiction.[21] In so doing, he subtly shaped his readership's engagement with *Uncle Remus*.

Northern reviewers followed Harris's lead. An article in the *New York Herald*, for instance, almost failed to mention that Uncle Remus contained elements of fiction. The reviewer parroted many of Harris's claims, repeating some of his comparisons to Amazonian and Native American folktales, as well as offering some of his own, to the fables of Aesop and La Fontaine.

The text's greatest importance, this reviewer suggested, was to be found in the timeless appeal of a folk tradition that "carries us back to the cradles of the human race in Asia and Africa." In the animal tales, the reviewer claimed, "we may be sure that we have fallen on an indigenous product of the human mind at a certain stage of its primitive simplicity and unculture."[22] The *New York Times* took a similar approach. The most significant aspects of the book, the review insisted, were "the strange myths which are still kept alive by the negroes in Southern plantations, and the dialects, which curious subjects Mr. Harris has cleverly arranged and presented to us with a great deal of skill and judgment."[23] The *Times* reviewer spent the vast majority of a lengthy review discussing the nature of folklore, the importance of the rabbit in African and African American animal tales, and the intricacies of black southern dialect as captured by Joel Chandler Harris. In both cases, reviewers intent on casting the book as a serious text in the field of folklore largely ignored the character whose name appeared on the front cover. In the hands of these reviewers, *Uncle Remus* became an unvarnished, unadulterated collection of African American folk tales.

A *New York Evening Post* reviewer took a different approach. After opening with praise for Harris's "attempt to gather and preserve the highly significant folklore of the plantation," the reviewer subtly shifted gears, moving from a discussion of *Uncle Remus* (the book) to Uncle Remus (the character). Because Harris had treated the tales with such respect and care, the reviewer seems to have assumed that he exercised the same due diligence in his presentation of African Americans more generally. The *Evening Post* reviewer insisted that Harris's depiction of Remus "is not burlesque, but painstaking portraiture," made all the more important by "the fact that changed surroundings and new life conditions are working the rapid disappearance of the type of character here depicted."[24] The move is subtle, but significant. Consciously or not, the reviewer transferred the historical creditability that Harris accrued in handling the folktales to his depiction of Remus. Because the folktales were real, the fictional character giving them voice must be real as well.

In a few instances, misinformed reviewers seem to have actually thought that Uncle Remus was a real person. One used the fact that "Mr. Harris disclaims any originality in the conception of Uncle Remus's fables" to deduce that the same relationship applied to Uncle Remus himself. Since Harris had not written the folktales, the reviewer assumed that he had not created Uncle Remus either. The tales had a life beyond and outside of the text, so Remus must have one as well. Even if Harris "is not the maker of his hero," the reviewer insisted, "he is that hero's revealer, and in that revelation of the characteristic contents of a typical freedman he tells a momentous truth to [those] that have ears to hear."[25] Even more outrageous was a wildly inaccurate review that labeled Harris "a Northern man," and pictured him sitting, brow furrowed, in front of a real, live Uncle Remus, busily attempting to catch the former slave's syntax and diction. Uncle Remus, the reviewer insisted, "is an old negro man who has lived all his life in one family, after the war settling down in Atlanta on the plantation of Mr. Huntingdon, who had married his 'Miss Sally,' and he tells the stories or 'Folk Lore of the Old Plantation' to their little boy of seven years old, who goes nightly from the 'big house' to his cabin to hear them."[26] Evidently entirely unaware of the text's fictional components, this reviewer offered Remus's imagined biography as the life story of a real man.

Most reviewers, of course, did not believe that Uncle Remus was actually alive. Even so, better-informed readers still tended to blur the line between fact and fiction when talking about Remus. If he was not literally real, most insisted that he was something other than pure fiction. Readers turned Remus into an archetype, the symbolic embodiment of his race. One reviewer admitted that Uncle Remus was "unfortunately more than half a creature of the imagination" but nonetheless insisted that "he is the ideal negro, he represents the homely common-sense and the poetic feeling which is covered by black skin all over the world."[27] Another paper labeled him "a typical plantation negro, one of the sort of old men who have been old as far back as any one can remember, and who are looked upon as oracles by their own race and loved for their genial nature and homely wit by their white brethren."[28] *Appleton's Journal* suggested that Harris's "portrait of Uncle Remus" was "as faithful and realistic as a photograph, but with touches that no mere photographer could hope to achieve."[29] The *New York Times* may have put the matter best, however: "The fine old fellow is alive and so is the little boy who listens."[30] It was precisely Remus's in-between status—not quite fact, not quite fiction—that made him such an ideal symbol.

The matter of "negro character" was at the heart of the American reading public's response to *Uncle Remus*. This phrase appeared over and over again in commentary on the text. The *Boston Commonwealth* declared that "these sketches embody the best imitation of the negro character and customs yet attempted."[31] The *Hartford Times Commercial* noted that "these unique chapters of Negro life and character" are "valuable not alone for their quaint humor, but as an original study of Negro character."[32] A Chicago newspaper, meanwhile, said the book "presents a new and attractive phase of negro character, giving hints of his really poetic imagination and embodying the quaint and homely humor, which is his most prominent characteristic."[33] On one level, it is hard to disagree with the claim that *Uncle Remus* added a new chapter to white America's knowledge of "negro character." Harris did bring forth a collection of slave stories and animal trickster tales previously hidden from northern white readers. Even as they appreciated the "quaint and homely humor" of the trickster tales, however, reviewers proved incapable of separating the message from the medium. The animal tales, true inheritances of an oral slave culture, were permanently fused to a white-authored stereotype of the plantation slave. In the end, it may be that readers were not so much looking for the essence of "negro character," as they were looking for *a* "negro character." This they found in Uncle Remus.

Uncle Remus was frequently compared to Uncle Tom, the enslaved hero of *Uncle Tom's Cabin*, Harriet Beecher Stowe's 1852 antislavery classic. The *Eclectic*, a northern newsmagazine, preferred Uncle Remus to his fictional forbearer. The magazine argued that Stowe's creation was pure fiction. Uncle Tom had been "evolved from the depths of [Stowe's] consciousness, and represents nothing but the creative power of a realistic imagination suffused with intense feeling." Uncle Remus, in contrast, was "the actual, living plantation negro, whose personality gave (and still gives, we hope) a flavor and picturesqueness of its own to plantation life in the South."[34] The *New York Commercial Advertiser* came to a similar conclusion regarding the two texts: "'Uncle Tom's Cabin' presented the negro in his external aspects. The book could do little more than that. It was a story told by a spectator. In 'Uncle Remus,' we see the mind of the black laid bare, can almost see the coursing of the blood through his veins, can feel his heart beat."[35] This strident insistence that Uncle Remus was real (or at least more real than Uncle Tom) offers a striking testament to the power of Harris's work. Readers seemed determined to accept Remus at face value. As a result, Uncle Remus came to replace Uncle Tom as the archetypal plantation slave in the northern imagination.

This move was not culturally neutral. Both characters, of course, were white-authored stereotypes, and neither was truly capable of speaking for the nation's African American population. On paper, Uncle Remus is a more interesting, engaging, and believable character than Uncle Tom. The former has thoughts, relationships, and emotions, while the latter is largely a two-dimensional prop. Context, however, must not be discounted. Uncle

Tom appears in an explicitly antislavery work, while Uncle Remus effectively refuses his emancipation by staying on his old master's plantation. A white man kills Uncle Tom; Uncle Remus tells stories for the amusement of a white boy. *Uncle Tom's Cabin* was, according to Abraham Lincoln, the book that started the Civil War; in "A Story of the War," Uncle Remus fights for the Confederates. With regard to race relations in the South, the nature of slavery, and the meaning of the Civil War, the shift from Uncle Tom to Uncle Remus was a vitally important one, indeed.

But there was also a larger regional dynamic embedded in the transition from Uncle Tom to Uncle Remus. Notwithstanding the outlier review that described Harris as a Yankee, the author's southern extraction lent an important air of authenticity to the text and proved central to the book's appeal. The *Hartford Times-Commercial* encouraged its readers to trust white southern representations of black dialect, and, by extension, their depictions of the South more generally: "It may not perhaps seem to some northern people, who get their ideas of southern life and character from Mrs. Stowe, that this style of talk is quite so true to the reality, but no southerner can for a moment doubt its much more faithful reflection of the genuine article."[36] An Iowa reviewer considered the popularity of *Uncle Remus* in the South to be implicit proof of the text's factuality. "Southern people, they who were cradled in the innermost circle of American-Ethiopian character, and who were hushed to sleep by the lullabys of the plantation dialect," the reviewer reasoned, "are not likely to be won to approval of any mere imitation of the genuine article. Hence, Uncle Remus appears before the general public with *prima [facie]* evidence of character and work."[37] These reviews pointed in a single direction: regarding black life in the South, white southerners simply knew better. Northerners would do well to defer to them.

## Thomas Nelson Page:
## Insiders, Outsiders, and the Power of Fiction

In the pantheon of late nineteenth-century authors of southern local-color fiction, only Thomas Nelson Page matched the popularity and critical acclaim of Joel Chandler Harris. During the last two decades of the nineteenth century, Page was a darling of the American literary world. He published a string of successful books, placed his short stories in every major literary magazine in the country, and won praise from northerners and southerners alike for his fictional depictions of a genteel and harmonious

Old South. Enthusiastic accolades were commonplace. Reviewers called Page "the brightest star in our Southern literature" and lauded his "beautiful and faithful pictures of a society now become a portion and parcel of the irrevocable past."[38] Joel Chandler Harris once said of two of Page's stories, "Marse Chan" and "Unc' Edinburg's Drowndin'," "I would rather have written these two sketches than everything that has appeared since the war, or before the war, for that matter."[39]

Even so, it is relatively easy for modern readers to dismiss Thomas Nelson Page as a talentless scribbler whose predictable fantasies happened to strike a chord with a reading public afraid of modernity and desperate for an escape. Page made his career extolling the beauty and grace of southern society before the Civil War. The Old South, he wrote, was a "civilization so pure, so noble, that the world to-day holds nothing equal to it."[40] Marked by a "singular sweetness and freedom from vice," it was a land of purity, honor, and wonderment, peopled with dashing gentlemen, blushing ladies, and faithful slaves.[41] Every day in Page's Old South was marked by a fishing expedition for the children, a fox hunt for the gentlemen, and, judging by the frequency with which the holiday occurs in Page's writing, a Christmas celebration for all. On the basis of his stories, one might conclude that Page's entire literary and political worldview rested on his conviction that "even the moonlight was richer and mellower 'before the war' than it is now."[42]

A more complicated picture emerges, however, when Page is viewed as a thinker as well as a writer. During his literary career, Page published dozens of essays and delivered hundreds of speeches on southern historical and literary themes. Although he admitted in his unpublished memoir that his initial move into writing was rooted in simple "vanity" and a "desire to see myself in print," Page quickly styled himself a leading expert on southern literature.[43] In the process, he developed an intricate reading of the southern past and the sectional conflict and presented a surprisingly modern take on the power of culture and public opinion. Page's literary philosophy rested on three central premises. First, Page argued that the manner in which the public at large understood the South—as a location, a people, and a civilization—carried great social, cultural, and political weight. Second, he believed that for the vast majority of U.S. history, southern disinterest and extenuating circumstances had allowed northerners to exercise almost exclusive control over the images of the South at play in American culture. Third, Page insisted that the white South must learn from its mistakes. The region must tell its own story to the nation in the post-Reconstruction era. Thomas Nelson Page was not just writing stories. He was rewriting the past, present, and future of the South so that the region could reclaim its place at the forefront of American life.

"Marse Chan," Page's first widely read story, offers a commentary on the nature of storytelling as Page understood it. The tale opens with an unnamed white traveler's unexpected meeting with Sam, an elderly former slave, on a horse path in Virginia. While Sam looks for his old master's dog, the visitor questions him about their surroundings. Sam embarks on a lengthy recitation of the history of the plantation on which they stand, beginning with the birth of Master Channing—"Marse Chan"—and ending with his death on a Civil War battlefield. The story-within-a-story, written in dialect, is the essence of the tale. The framing narration by the traveler exists only to provide Page with a mechanism for switching into dialect. "Unc' Edinburg's Drowndin'" and "Meh Lady," the next two stories Page published, are structured in the same fashion. In each case, a white inter-loper enters into an ex-slave's sphere of influence, where he is regaled with stories of the past.[44]

While the racial difference between the faithful slave and the white traveler is ever present in the stories, it is important to note that the two characters share another relationship: storyteller and audience. This as-sociation is stable, predictable, and defined by the fact that information travels in only one direction. Through stories, an insider guides an outsider to a knowledge of their surroundings. A place is rendered understandable through tales of its past, as narrated by one who is in a position to know that past intimately. For Page, this arrangement was so natural and logical as to require little comment. The connection between insider/storyteller and outsider/listener reappears again and again in Page's writing, and provides a central explanatory metaphor for his views of southern history and literature.

When Page turned his attention to the history of the United States, he was struck by the extent to which the sectional relationship failed to cleave to the expected storyteller/listener pattern. For Page, the central theme of American history from settlement to the Civil War was the consistent failure of the South to explain itself to the world. Studiously ignoring a well-developed tradition of southern apologia, Page claimed that the South had never successfully told the nation its story.[45] The antebellum southerner, Page wrote, "was eminently self-contained, and his own self-respect satisfied, he cared not for the world's applause. He was content to live according to his own will" and found "no human tribunal to which he wished to submit his acts."[46] Secure in its righteousness, the Old South felt no need to justify itself.

This self-assurance, Page argued, was to blame for the antebellum South's failure to produce a regional literature. In an 1888 speech, Page argued that "though life is brief, art is perpetual. And of all art, the widest reaching and most enduring is literature."[47] The truths and values of a society, he insisted, were not made real and lasting until they had been encapsulated in fiction. Turning to the Old South, however, Page was forced to admit that the "discussion of Southern literature during the period which preceded the late war naturally resolves itself into a consideration of the causes which retarded its growth."[48] The true story, in other words, was not the literature of the antebellum South but its absence. Though fiction might have provided a storehouse for the collected truths of the civilization, the Old South's disdain for self-representation suffocated the southern literary impulse. The South's conspicuous lack of a regional literature rendered its political, social, and cultural theories evanescent and impermanent. While northern outsiders misconstrued and misrepresented the nature of southern society, southern insiders kept mum.

This argument was not merely academic. The tragic fate of the Old South, according to Page, was directly related to its literary shortcomings and its failure to explain itself to those outside its borders. "Only study the course of the contest against the South," Page wrote, "and you cannot fail to see how she was conquered by the pen rather than by the sword."[49] Despite the genius of Robert E. Lee, the bravery of Stonewall Jackson, and the strength of the women on the home front, larger cultural forces ensured the defeat of the Confederacy. The North's inability to understand the nature of southern society brought the nation to war, and the same failure by the European nations denied the Confederacy the global support that would have brought it victory. "Owing to the want of a literature at the South and to the ignorance and misapprehension of the South on the part of the world," Page wrote, the region "found itself forced into a position where it was confronted by the entire world and stood at the bar of Christendom without an advocate and without a defen[s]e."[50] Although every southern boy knew precisely what he was fighting for, the world at large had not the foggiest idea. The South, too self-assured to account for itself in a literature, did not attempt to explain its cause until it had already been lost. "It is almost incredible," Page concluded, "that a race so proud of its position, so assertive of its rights, so jealous of its reputation, should have been so indifferent to all transmission of their memorial."[51]

In his study of the past, Page found guidance and direction for the future. Having tied the defeat of the Old South to that society's literary shortcomings, Page set out to ensure that the region would not make the same mistakes again. From his vantage point in the 1880s and 1890s, Page found much that had changed since Reconstruction, but he sensed that much remained the same. The overthrow of the Reconstruction governments left the white South free to manage its own affairs for the first time since Appomattox. Even so, Page sensed that white southerners had yet to fully learn their lesson. The region had begun to rule itself again, but it had not yet taken steps to write its own story. Until it did so, the failures of the Old South would continue to haunt the New.

In his speeches and essays, Page urged like-minded southerners to embrace the political power of fiction, using the medium to mold popular ideas about the South. White southerners, he insisted, must learn the power of public opinion. For the first time in their region's history, they must take active steps to shape the way outsiders perceived the region. They would lean hard on the written word, casting aside the outmoded, derogatory definitions that northerners unthinkingly accepted as the truth about the South. Northerners who did not know a magnolia from a dogwood would no longer define Dixie. Southerners would write their own story. This imagined construction—a vision of the true South as authored by white southerners and offered to the world at large—was at the heart of Thomas Nelson Page's literary program.

In this project, Page found inspiration in the unlikeliest of places. Page pointed to the long-term effects of Harriet Beecher Stowe's *Uncle Tom's Cabin*, a novel he admired for its impact as much as he loathed it for its content. In Page's estimation, *Uncle Tom's Cabin* "did more, perhaps, than any one thing that ever occurred to precipitate the war." The novel "blackened the fame of the Southern people in the eyes of the North and fixed in the mind of the North a concept not only of the institution of slavery, but of the Southern people, which lasted for more than a generation, and has only begun of late, in the light of a fuller knowledge, to be dislodged."[52] The text unified northern sentiment, creating an image that quickly became the commonsense understanding of the South and of slavery. In spite of its misrepresentations, Stowe's South was *the South* as northerners understood it. The lesson of *Uncle Tom's Cabin* was clear: fiction, if properly mobilized, could become truth. Taking a cue from Harriet Beecher Stowe, Page sought to harness this power.

Page's first task would be the reconstruction of southern history. In

Page's analytical writings as well as his fiction, historical considerations loom large. This focus, however, does not suggest a knee-jerk antimodernism. Page's turn to the past was rooted in a deep belief in the tangible importance of historical understanding to the health of a society. Page tended to view southern history holistically, making little distinction between southern past and southern present. Although the Civil War marked a cataclysmic shift in the course of that history, it did not fundamentally disrupt the larger continuities. Slavery was gone, but the essence of the Old South lived on. Proximity to the glorious civilization of the antebellum South set the southern people apart from the rest of the nation and formed a core component of regional identity. In this context, an engagement with the past was a mark not of disdain for the present but of concern for it.

Page worried, however, that recent history was "being recorded by writers organically disabled to comprehend the action of the South."[53] Because postwar southerners continued to display insufficient interest in reclaiming their past, northern writers dominated the historical landscape, just as they had before the war. The result, Page wrote, was a "strange and wondrous record" that "goes by the name of history," but "is no more like history than I to Hercules."[54] In the popular (i.e., northern) understanding of the past, southerners stood "charged with the crime of attempting to perpetuate human slavery, and for this purpose with conspiracy to destroy the best government the world has ever seen," while "nearly everything that has counted for much in the history of this country, either sprung from or took its color from New England."[55] Such aspersions on the Old South, of course, bore directly upon the New. With such an ignominious past hanging over their heads, how could postwar southerners be expected to thrive? "We are paraded as still exhibiting unconquered the same qualities untempered by misfortune," Page wrote. In the popular imagination, southerners were still "nullifying the Constitution, falsifying the ballot, trampling down a weaker race in an extravagance of cruelty, and with shameless arrogance imperiling the nation as much now as when we went to war."[56] The pressing threat of a misinformed but suffocating public opinion convinced Page that unless white southerners immediately reclaimed their past (and, by extension, their present), "in a few years there will be no South to demand a history."[57]

It is important to note that Page did not blame northerners for the negative images of the South that prevailed in American culture. "It is not their fault that our history has not been written," Page told a meeting of Confederate veterans in 1892. "Gentlemen, it is our fault."[58] Lacking any self-accounting from the South, the North "has recorded of us in the main only what it honestly believes."[59] Yankee defamations were rooted not in spite or hostility but in ignorance. The issue was one of capability, not intent. The North simply had no business attempting to tell the story of the South. In Page's estimation, "no mind will be able to produce the delicate and subtle phases of that civilization but one that has received its spirit into the warp and woof of its thought."[60] Only a born southerner, Page argued, was capable of painting the history of the region in all its true glory, for only a born southerner could comprehend it. Page urged his fellow white southerners to recognize the enormous stakes, to wake from their slumber and tell their own story to the world. "If we are willing to be handed down to coming time as a race of slave-drivers and traitors, it is as well to continue in our state of lethargy and acquiescence," Page wrote, but "if we retain the instincts of men, and desire to transmit to our children the untarnished name and spotless fame which our forefathers bequeathed to us, we must awake to the exigencies of the matter."[61]

Page did not consider historical and fictional writing to be opposing disciplines. At times, Page even implied that literature was to be valued for its ability to paint a truer picture of the past than history, as when he offered the startling claim that since "no histographer [sic] has yet recorded the beautiful story of the Southern Civilization[,] . . . it may be left for some writer styling himself a novelist to tell the story and perpetuate the life that is gliding so rapidly into the irrevocable past."[62] In the hands of an expert armed with the requisite insider knowledge, literature could get at the colors of life much more effectively than history. When Page called for a history of the South, therefore, he did not mean a mere recitation of the facts. He sought, instead, to elevate the more ethereal and abstract facets of southern society, those things that southerners intuitively grasped and northerners consistently failed to comprehend: the spirit of the region, its inner workings, its mindset, its worldview, its soul.

For Page, the significance of the southern literary resurgence of the 1880s and 1890s was clear. Southerners had finally begun to present "the South" to a national audience, and northerners appeared willing to let them shape popular understandings of Dixie. No longer would the natural relationship between storyteller and audience—between insider and outsider—be violated. Southerners would tell their story, northerners would listen. Each time Page wrote about a faithful slave or a foxhunt, each time he put the South at the center of the nation's "discovery" or the American Revolution, each time he praised the southern moonlight or defended the

Lost Cause, he engaged in a process that was as much political as it was literary. By a kind of cultural alchemy, Page assumed, these assorted images and snapshots of southern life would become—for the South, the North, and the world—the accepted truth.

## George Washington Cable:
## Race Politics and Local Color

Though George Washington Cable was one of the most celebrated authors in the late nineteenth-century United States, his personal journey from white supremacy to racial liberalism was arguably more implausible than any fiction he wrote. As a teenager in New Orleans at the height of the antebellum sectional conflict, Cable was a staunch southern partisan, "reeking with patriotism of the strongest pro-slavery type."[63] Though he opposed secession, the youthful Cable threw his support behind the Confederacy with the outbreak of war. When the Union army occupied New Orleans in 1862, Cable's family fled to Mississippi. Soon after, the eighteen-year-old Cable joined the Confederate cavalry, serving for two years and surviving a bullet wound to the chest. After the war, he returned to New Orleans, working a variety of jobs through the 1870s. To this point, Cable's views on race largely accorded with the majority of his white contemporaries. However, motivated by a staunch Presbyterianism and a fiercely logical mind, Cable quietly undertook a study of religious, legal, political, and historical texts. He soon concluded that the South's racial caste system was unjust and immoral. By the early 1880s, he had become an impassioned advocate for racial egalitarianism.[64] Ignoring the prevailing orthodoxy that deemed southern race relations an exclusively southern concern, Cable stood before audiences on both sides of the Mason-Dixon line and demanded civil and political equality for African Americans. Cable spoke out against segregation in transportation, attacked the South's convict lease system, and called for comprehensive prison reform. Though he paid a steep price for his apostasy—by the late 1880s, Cable was largely a persona non grata among white southerners—his forthright calls for democracy and justice made him one of the postwar era's most significant white southern racial liberals.[65]

At first glance, Cable's fiction seems curiously disconnected from this reform agenda. If Cable's politics were distinctly atypical for his time and place, his fiction hewed more closely to the expected patterns of late nineteenth-century local-color fiction. On the surface, Cable's work does not appear substantively different from that of Joel Chandler Harris and Thomas Nelson Page. In Cable's fiction, as in Page's and Harris's, readers found the curtain drawn back on a long-lost place and time. In Cable's case, the setting was New Orleans at the dawn of the nineteenth century. His works, notably the short story collection *Old Creole Days* (1879), the novel *The Grandissimes* (1880), and the novella *Madame Delphine* (1881), are saturated with the sights, sounds, and scents of old Louisiana. Cable wraps his readers in the sweet smell of orange blossoms, the melody of the cake seller's songs, the feel of a tropical breeze, and the swirling excitement of a carnival ball. His extensive use of dialect—capturing the varied cadences of French-speaking aristocrats, Caribbean street vendors, and Creole conmen, among others—paints a stunning auditory portrait, while his frequent references to street names and cardinal directions ground his stories in the real-life geography of the city. In Cable's work, New Orleans is never simply a setting. It is an integral part of the story. As much as a storyteller, therefore, Cable saw himself as a literary tour guide, an escort to a place at once foreign and fantastic.[66]

One would not expect to find a challenge to southern racial politics embedded in such a stylized and romantic vision of the region's past. As a result, it can seem as if there were two different George Washington Cables: one a writer of standard-issue regionalist fiction, the other a committed critic of southern race relations. Such a dichotomy, however, fails to align with Cable's own self-understanding. Cable did not draw a hard and fast distinction between his political and literary writings. Indeed, he was outspoken in his embrace of fiction as a powerful political tool. Beyond the lush descriptions of New Orleans, Cable offered a fiction of principle and moral gravity. In an 1882 commencement speech at the University of Mississippi, he explicitly called for an activist southern literature, one that aimed to reform and purify the present, even if it meant criticizing aspects of the southern past. This was no simple task. It required southern authors to display the "courage" to be "iconoclasts in our own homes."[67] Blind fealty to a bygone society would do little good, Cable insisted. A frank accounting of the region's past, by southerners and for southerners, was vital. In this way, literature could be an agent of political and social change.

In his fiction, Cable practiced what he preached, mixing a hefty dose of politics with his southern pastoral. The key to Cable's literary politics was an implied equivalency between the events he described and the society in which he lived and wrote. *The Grandissimes*, Cable's most overtly political work, is set in the waning days of French Louisiana, as the residents of New Orleans prepare for the transition to American control. Cable's choice of this particular moment was no coincidence. Much of the drama in *The Grandissimes* revolves around French Creole resistance to the perceived encroachment of American settlers and governance. Cable's French Creoles are haughty, proud, and self-satisfied. Led by the irascible patriarch Agricola Fusilier, they resist all change as a matter of principle, display an unreasonable hostility to any form of innovation, and harbor a deep resentment toward "aliens, intehlopehs, invadehs."[68] Even after the United States takes control, they continue to resist, pining for an irretrievable past, threatening revolution, and doing all they can to undermine good government. The parallels to Cable's contemporary South are striking. French Louisiana's resistance to American governance seems an obvious proxy for postwar southern opposition to Reconstruction. The more obnoxious aspects of French Creole society—its self-satisfaction, its xenophobia, its willful antimodernism—can likewise be read as Cable's critiques of his own time. More generally, Cable warns that blind allegiance to the past (be it a past in which the French controlled Louisiana or a past in which southern whites ruled absolutely) is simply a form of denial, one that will ultimately prove self-destructive. As much as a story about the cession of Louisiana, therefore, *The Grandissimes* is a commentary on the post–Civil War South.[69]

The political centerpiece of *The Grandissimes* is the saga of Bras Coupé. Taking up two full chapters in the heart of the novel, the tale of an African prince who resisted slavery to the death offers a striking indictment of white supremacy. Indeed, when compared to Uncle Remus, another fictional slave who made his literary debut in 1880, Cable's avenging slave rebel is a truly astounding figure.[70] Captured in war and shipped to Louisiana aboard the ill-named ship *Égalité*, Bras Coupé quickly proves himself to be physically, morally, and mentally superior to his captors. Rather than accept his enslavement, Bras Coupé takes to the Louisiana bayou to live as a maroon, "declaring his independence on a slight rise of ground hardly sixty feet in circumference and lifted scarce above the water in the inmost depths of the swamp."[71] However, the inexorable logic of race and slavery would brook no compromise. Bras Coupé's eventual demise is assured. When he is captured, the slave rebel is whipped and tortured before he finally finds freedom in death.

The significance of Bras Coupé to the political agenda of *The Grandissimes* extends beyond the events themselves. As important is the frequency with which the residents of Cable's New Orleans turn to the story.

Illustration of Bras Coupé from George Washington Cable's *The Grandissimes: A Story of Creole Life* (1880). The saga of Bras Coupé is at the heart of the novel's critique of southern race relations. Library of Congress.

Though Bras Coupé's rebellion, *marronnage*, capture, mutilation, and death precede the novel's main storyline by almost a decade, the events are burned into the memories of all who witnessed them. The Bras Coupé story is recalled and retold with stunning frequency in the novel. The tale is guarded and protected, even revered. It is a precious thing, the collective memory that unifies white New Orleans. Cable's Creoles cannot escape Bras Coupé. For all their obsession with heredity, breeding, and honor, it is the story of a black man's resistance to slavery that anchors white identity in the novel. As always, Cable invited his readers to apply this logic to contemporary southern affairs. Just as surely as in the time of Bras Coupé, post-Reconstruction southern whiteness was constructed in opposition to a systematically abused blackness. In the final summation, Cable argued, white supremacy was not an objective fact but a habit of domination.

In order to comment on the illogical and arbitrary nature of the South's racial order, Cable frequently turned to the historical plight of the mixed-race residents of New Orleans. In *Madame Delphine*, his 1881 novella, the ambiguity of racial identity takes center stage. The story turns on the plight of the quadroon Madame Delphine and her octoroon daughter Olive. Because both women possess black blood, the prevailing racial orthodoxy of the era deems them fit concubines for white men but denies them the right to marry across the color line.[72] When the light-skinned Olive falls in love with a white man, and he with her, Madame Delphine is placed in an impossible position. In order to secure her daughter's happiness, Delphine must prove Olive's whiteness. This means, of course, denying her own status as a mother. In an elaborate lie, she claims that Olive was actually the child of a Spanish couple who had died of yellow fever. A suitably whitened Olive is free to marry, while a brokenhearted Delphine dies after confessing her perfidy to a priest. The priest's anguished cry—"Lord, lay not this sin to her charge!"—contains the story's central political statement.[73] Though Madame Delphine repudiates her own flesh and blood and lies in the presence of civil and ecclesiastical authorities, she is not to blame for her actions. The fault rests with a society that would force a mother to such extreme measures. In calling attention to the fictive nature of racial lines, *Madame Delphine* presents a damning indictment of the South's racial caste system.

Though race relations remained Cable's primary political concern throughout the 1880s, he also ventured further afield. In 1881 and 1882, Cable published a number of articles in the *New Orleans Times-Democrat* calling for reform of the state's prisons and asylums. In his 1884 novel *Dr. Sevier*, Cable took up this cause, enumerating the abhorrent conditions that prevailed in the New Orleans prison, which he described as "this resting and refreshing place for vice, this caucus for the projection of future crime, this ghastly burlesque of justice and the protection of society."[74] Cable's 1888 novel *Bonaventure* narrates the trials and tribulations of a francophone teacher employed in an Acadian community on the Bayou Teche. Despite its unassuming subtitle, *A Prose Pastoral of Acadian Louisiana*, *Bonaventure* can be read as a call for increased attention to the woeful condition of schools in the southern interior.[75] In both cases, a political critique of the contemporary South lay just underneath the surface of Cable's fictional treatment of the past.

Even as it conformed to the broader patterns of the local-color genre, therefore, George Washington Cable's work consistently displayed a political edge entirely its own. Carefully woven into the magnolias and the moonlight (or, more appropriately, the *clair de lune*) was an impassioned advocacy of reform. Cable was not troubled by the apparent contradiction between his fiction and his politics. Indeed, he believed that there was no contradiction at all. Though couched in the unthreatening rhetoric of a picturesque southern past, Cable's fiction was as deeply imbued with politics as any of his public lectures or nonfiction writing. As Cable saw it, southern fiction need not blindly support the status quo or idealize the region's past. It could prove a powerful force for change.

Throughout the 1880s, Cable's literary efforts earned him numerous accolades from northern readers. Critics pronounced Cable a "genius in his way," praised him for opening "a new vein in literature," and declared that his was "perhaps the most valuable literary work done in this country at the present day."[76] In the early part of the decade, Cable was compared (often favorably) to Nathaniel Hawthorne, Henry James, William Dean Howells, and Charles Dickens.[77] However, reviews of Cable's fiction and newspaper coverage of his frequent public readings suggest a disjuncture between the fiction Cable set out to write and the way that his audience understood his work. Though Cable laced his fiction with a politics of conscience and reform, readers did not always get the message. Blinded by local color and taken in by the more picturesque and exotic elements of Cable's work, many contemporary readers overlooked the politics entirely. In fact, the apolitical gloss that readers applied to his fiction—and the visions of a romantic and idyllic southern past that his writings, thus misread, helped to conjure—may have actually undercut reform.

To be sure, some reviewers recognized that more than local color was at stake in Cable's fiction. A review in *Century Illustrated Magazine* noted that much of Cable's work seemed to be imbued with "a deep-lying purpose, not only to elevate these lower orders of the community, but even more to humanize and civilize the dominant race which has suffered so deeply from its false relation to its dependents."[78] Other reviewers commented on the obvious parallels between Cable's treatments of the past and the present-day condition of the South. "To all intents and purposes," a particularly astute review of *The Grandissimes* noted, "the book is a study (and a very profound and striking one) of Southern society during the period of reconstruction."[79] Similarly, the *Atlantic Monthly* focused on the contemporary resonances of *The Grandissimes*. The moral and political issues animating the novel, it said, were precisely those questions that had "perplexed the entire body of thoughtful men in the nation ever since the downfall of the Confederacy."[80]

Most northern reviewers, however, missed the political content of Cable's work or chose to treat it as an unfortunate distraction from what they assumed was Cable's true purpose: constructing a romanticized, almost dreamlike, vision of a bygone Louisiana. The words that seem to crop up most frequently in contemporary commentary on Cable—"quaint," "delicate," "charming," "picturesque," "romantic," "pathetic"—suggest the level on which most northerners engaged with his work.[81] A reviewer in *The Nation* found Cable's work to be "enshrouded in the poetic and many-tinted Louisiana haze," while a writer in the *Literary World* gushed that "a recent perusal of Mr. Cable's romances has left something like a delicious perfume floating in my memory."[82] A review of 1888's *Bonaventure* noted the "mythic vagueness" and "dreamy haze" that seemed to surround the book. "When you have finished it," the reviewer mused, "you are not quite sure what the characters have been doing; you are only delightfully conscious of an exceeding pleasure in what you have been reading."[83] Needless to say, this sort of "pleasure" left little room for politics. For many northern readers, the picturesque and colorful aspects of Cable's writing simply overwhelmed his reform agenda.

Other readers emphasized the *local* aspect of Cable's local color, reading Cable's stories solely for the window they provided onto a unique time and place. As mentioned, the political content of Cable's writing relied on an implied proximity between the places and events he described and the time in which he wrote. In emphasizing the ways in which his imagined Louisiana was unusual, distinct, and beyond the American mainstream, therefore, northern readers undercut Cable's reform agenda. A review of *Madame Delphine*, for instance, paid little heed to the plight of the story's mixed-race protagonists or its commentary on the mutability of racial categories. Instead, the reviewer declared himself "possessed by the beauty, the languor, the quaintness, the wholly un-northerly and almost wholly un-American aspects of an early period of that city by the Gulf."[84] A Wilmington, Delaware, newspaper similarly noted that Cable's writing "takes us into a strange world, where the customs, the emotions, and the habitual state of mind are primitive and pagan."[85] One reviewer called *Dr. Sevier* "a perfect picture of that peculiar relic of New Orleans olden times," while a California newspaper praised Cable for capturing "a phase of life on this continent the details and colors of which were fading with the passing years."[86] This approach distanced Cable's fiction from contemporary affairs, denying that the bizarre, wondrous, and foreign New Orleans that Cable described could have anything to say about the late nineteenth-century South. The very thing, in other words, that made Cable's fiction worth reading—his depiction of a long-lost New Orleans—also helped to dull its political edge.

For many reviewers, the dreamy qualities of Cable's fiction—the quaint descriptions and tropical settings that so pleased northern readers—were inseparable from Cable's status as a southerner. A Chicago newspaper, for instance, claimed that Cable's "work is distinctively Southern."[87] A review in *The Nation*, meanwhile, praised the "warmth and color" of Cable's prose before deeming these attributes "properly Southern qualities."[88] Similarly, an essay on southern literature asserted that Cable "has more of the rich, sun-warmed gifts of the South in his nature" than any of his competitors.[89] It is clear, therefore, that Cable's appeal somehow transcended the words on the page. The author's southern birth added to the charm of his fiction; a Cable story was "a tale of Southern life, told in the accents of the South."[90] Cable's southern identity, then, imparted authenticity, at least as far as northern readers were concerned. Significantly, however, it only did so within certain bounds. The reading patterns of northern audiences limited the grounds on which Cable could speak and write authoritatively. Northern readers were delighted to have Cable teach them about the South, provided the picture he offered them was appropriately quaint and picturesque.

This was George Washington Cable's dilemma. As written, Cable's fiction advanced powerful arguments for change; as read, it helped to enshrine an idealized, romantic image of the antebellum South in the national imagination. It may have been that the local-color genre was simply incapable of carrying the political weight that Cable forced on it. The rich sensory tapestries that Cable created had an unintended effect, deflecting attention from the present-day political concerns that he placed at the center of his work. As northern readers devoured Cable's tales of the southern past, they allowed themselves to ignore the continuing challenge of race relations in the post-Reconstruction South. In spite of his best intentions, Cable's politically charged stories of colonial New Orleans did little to counteract the plantation sketches of Joel Chandler Harris or the Old Virginia tales of Thomas Nelson Page. In fact, Cable may have unwittingly done as much to construct an idealized vision of the Old South as either of these contemporaries. Rather than forcing the nation to confront the political challenges of the present-day South, Cable's fiction helped readers elide this reality. Matters like civil rights and black suffrage just did not feel as pressing when wrapped in the dreamy, jasmine-scented haze of a New Orleans afternoon.

## Charles W. Chesnutt:
## The Politics of Uncle Julius's Grapevine

Solely on the basis of his own regional trajectory, it would appear that African American author Charles W. Chesnutt was bound to write himself a prominent place in the late nineteenth-century debate over the nature of the South. Chesnutt was born in Cleveland, Ohio, in 1858 but spent his formative years in the South. Growing up in Fayetteville, North Carolina, Chesnutt experienced the promises and betrayals of Reconstruction at close range. Chesnutt spent his young adulthood teaching at black schools in and around Charlotte, North Carolina, before moving back to the North in 1883.[91] In the second half of the 1880s, when Chesnutt finally set out to gratify his long-held ambition to be a writer, it became clear that matters of region would loom large in his work. Chesnutt's southern upbringing offered a sense of authenticity that the fiction of a Yankee might have lacked, while his northern residence shielded him from the intellectual censorship he undoubtedly would have encountered had he remained in North Carolina. Although Chesnutt's later published works, notably *The Marrow of Tradition* (1901), would drink deeply from the well of the South, it is in the "conjure stories" that he published throughout the 1880s and 1890s (collected and published as *The Conjure Woman* in 1899) that Chesnutt offered some of his most sustained and insightful commentary on the nature of the South and the power of storytelling.

When he took up fiction in earnest, Chesnutt found the times propitious for the brand of literature he proposed to offer. As early as 1880, Chesnutt had noted that "the northern mind" seemed hopelessly fascinated by "the southern Negro."[92] Eight years later, in a letter to George Washington Cable, an important literary mentor, Chesnutt pointed to the "growing demand for literature dealing with the Negro, and for information concerning subjects with which he is any manner connected." Chesnutt speculated that great opportunities existed for "a writer who was connected with these people by ties of blood and still stronger ties of sympathy."[93] He considered himself uniquely qualified to meet this popular demand. Significantly, however, Chesnutt's early stories were published without explicit mention of the author's race. Only in 1899, after the publication of *The Conjure Woman*, did his racial identity become common knowledge among northern readers.[94]

Even so, it is clear that Chesnutt's turn to literature had as much to do with political considerations as with artistic ones.[95] As he told Cable, he felt "impelled" to take up his pen "by a deep and growing interest in the discussion and settlement of the Southern question, and all other questions which affect the happiness of the millions of colored people in this country."[96] In his literary work, Chesnutt sought to harness northern interest in southern affairs, pushing popular thought in a direction more conducive to African American rights. In a letter to Booker T. Washington, Chesnutt noted the power of literature to shape public opinion, declaring that "the medium of fiction offers a golden opportunity to create sympathy throughout the country for our cause." For proof, Chesnutt turned to those he considered his ideological adversaries: "It has been the writings of Harris and Thomas Nelson Page and others of that ilk which have furnished my chief incentive to write something upon the other side of this very vital question." In his attempt to author "the other side," Chesnutt recognized that he was swimming against the tide. By the 1890s, Chesnutt could not offer the first or the only literary sketch of southern black life. He was writing into a field crowded with other, highly troublesome depictions of southern African Americans. Even so, he remained hopeful. "I know I am on the weaker side in point of popular sympathy," he wrote, "but I am on the stronger side in point of justice and morality, and if I can but command the skill and the power to compel attention, I think I will win out in the long run, so far as I am personally concerned, and will help the cause, which is vastly more important."[97]

Like Page and Cable, Chesnutt believed that the medium of literature possessed a distinct political and cultural currency. Chesnutt articulated the core of his literary theory in a speech titled "Literature in Its Relation to Life," delivered before an African American literary association in Washington, DC, in 1899. Fiction, Chesnutt explained, "may be viewed in two aspects—as an expression of life, past and present, and as a force directly affecting the conduct of life, present and future. I might call these the subjective and objective sides of literature—or, more lucidly, the historical; and the dynamic, the forceful, the impelling. History is instructive, and may warn or admonish; but to this quality literature adds the faculty of persuasion, by which men's hearts are reached, the springs of action touched, and the currents of life directed." For Chesnutt, literature does not merely reflect the society that creates it. It carries within it the latent power to shape that society. In its "dynamic . . . forceful . . . impelling" guise, literature represents a potent force for change. It does not support the status quo but challenges it. While analytical writing can only engage with the mind, literature touches an entirely different organ, the heart.

In this way, it does not simply argue but moves. In its historical form, Chesnutt said, literature is merely an "expression of life," depicting a society as it is. As Chesnutt put it somewhat disparagingly, this type of literature may be effectively summed up in the truism "Would you know a nation, read its books."[98] In Chesnutt's hands, however, literature would not reflect the values of a society; it would shape them. It would depict American society not as it was but as it should be. Would you *move* a nation, Chesnutt might have suggested, *write* its books.

On the surface, Chesnutt's decision to write the sort of dialect tales that make up *The Conjure Woman* seems a rather peculiar choice. In the very structure of the tales, Chesnutt paid homage to Thomas Nelson Page and Joel Chandler Harris, his avowed literary nemeses. Chesnutt's conjure tales are set on the old McAdoo plantation in North Carolina, the home of a former slave named Uncle Julius. Like the ex-slave narrators in the work of Page and Harris, Uncle Julius's long life and longer memory allow him access to the plantation's distant past. In this case, Julius tells stories for John and Annie, a northern couple who purchase the plantation sometime after the Civil War. Again like Page and Harris, each conjure tale offers a story-within-a-story, with a framing narration in standard English and an embedded dialect tale. As he attempted to counteract the negative influence of Page and Harris, therefore, Chesnutt invited his readers to recall them with every word he wrote. Contemporary reviewers were quick to notice the parallels when *The Conjure Woman* was published in 1899. The reviewer for the *Outlook* wrote that Chesnutt's handling of dialect was "as soft and smooth" as "Mr. Joel Harris's," while *Current Literature* wrote that Chesnutt plied his trade "with a skill not inferior to that of Joel Chandler Harris [and] Thomas Nelson Page."[99] Though they noted the similarities, these reviewers declined to interrogate them, thereby missing the larger implications of Chesnutt's work. As the references to Page and Harris in his letter to Booker T. Washington suggest, Chesnutt consciously modeled his stories on those of his competitors in order to invite—even demand— comparison. Indeed, the political purposes of *The Conjure Woman* were largely rooted in the book's internal critique of contemporary white supremacist southern fiction.[100]

"The Goophered Grapevine," a short story that appeared in the *Atlantic Monthly* in 1887 and later became the opening tale in the *Conjure Woman*, highlights this pattern of reference and subversion. The story opens with John and Annie's arrival at their new home in North Carolina. John, who narrates the conjure tales, describes the couple's first meeting with Uncle

Julius, a "venerable-looking colored man" they find sitting on an old log and "smacking his lips with great gusto" over a pile of grapes. After John and Annie introduce themselves, Julius asks John if he is "de Norv'n gemman w'at's gwine ter buy de ole vimya'd." John responds in the affirmative, to which Julius replies, with grave seriousness, "'f I 'uz in yo' place, I wouldn' buy dis vimya'd." When pressed, Uncle Julius explains that it is "goophered,—conju'd, bewitch'."[101]

At this point, John describes Uncle Julius's switch into storytelling mode, noting that "as he became more and more absorbed in the narrative, his eyes assumed a dreamy expression, and he seemed to lose sight of his auditors, and to be living over again in monologue his life on the old plantation."[102] Julius explains that "many years befo' de wah," Douglas McAdoo, his former master, covered a part of his plantation with grapevines and made a tidy profit selling scuppernong wine. When some of McAdoo's grapes began to disappear, he suspected his slaves but could not catch the culprit. A desperate McAdoo turned to "Aun' Peggy," a much feared and much respected conjure woman living nearby, who planted "de mos' powerfulles' kin' er goopher" on the grapevines. Word quickly spread among the slaves, and the grape theft stopped immediately.[103] The next year, however, a new slave named Henry ate the cursed grapes. As a result, Henry found himself tied to the life cycle of the grapevines. When the vines grew and blossomed in the spring, so did Henry. When they withered in the fall, so did Henry. This, of course, was inconvenient, but Henry made do. Unfortunately, after a few years of this cycle, an itinerant northerner arrived on the McAdoo farm and advocated a radical new method of grape cultivation. McAdoo went along with him, to the detriment of the vineyard and poor Henry. When the vines all died before the end of the year, Henry went with them—he "des went out sorter like a cannel."[104] Finishing his story and waking from his trance, Uncle Julius reiterates his earlier warnings: "en I tell yer w'at, marster, I wouldn' 'vise you to buy dis yer ole vimya'd, 'caze de goopher's on it yit, en dey ain' no tellin' w'en it's gwine ter crap out."[105]

Thus far, the story would not seem too out of place in a collection by Joel Chandler Harris or Thomas Nelson Page. After John reassumes narrative control, however, Chesnutt's story moves in a markedly new direction. John informs the reader that he bought the vineyard despite Julius's warnings. The grape harvest had been excellent, and the goopher had yet to rear its ugly head. John had also discovered the provenance of Uncle Julius's story. Before John and Annie's arrival, Julius had "derived a respectable revenue from the product of these neglected grapevines."[106] The goopher story had been nothing more than an exceedingly clever attempt to keep John from ruining this arrangement. Lest readers worry about Uncle Julius, however, Chesnutt has John hire him as a coachman, thereby keeping Julius well employed and available to tell future stories.

Other stories in *The Conjure Woman* display a similar logic. In "Po' Sandy," Uncle Julius uses a conjure tale to prevent John from knocking down an old meetinghouse; in "Mars Jeems's Nightmare," a timely story gains employment for Julius's ne'er-do-well grandson; in "The Conjurer's Revenge," Julius wins a new set of clothes.[107] In each case, Julius uses a conjure tale to achieve a desired end. Though John and Annie assume that Julius's tales offer an authentic glimpse of the "simple but intensely human inner life of slavery," Julius's motives are far more complicated.[108] Unlike Thomas Nelson Page's black narrators, who exist simply to tell their stories for the edification of white listeners, Uncle Julius possesses a consciousness that extends beyond the limits of his conjure tales. He is capable of forethought, planning, and misdirection, as evidenced in his assumption of the storytelling "trance." More than this, his stories always serve a distinct present-day purpose. Each conjure tale, full of wonderful fantasy and grim humor, is really an elaborate farce, a smoke screen that Julius uses to obscure and advance a secret agenda. Uncle Julius does not tell stories of the past for their own sake. Indeed, the tales' primary function is to improve their teller's lot in the here and now.

In Charles Chesnutt's conjure tales, storytelling and power are inextricably linked. The ability to tell the story of a place—in this case, of the McAdoo plantation and its environs—is closely connected to real world control over that place. Clearly, Uncle Julius's stories fall into the "dynamic . . . forceful . . . impelling" class of literary production. Despite his feigned ignorance, his mask of absolute transparency, Julius does not use his conjure tales to describe the world as it actually is. Instead, he relies on his tales to shape that world and to advance his place in it. In a vastly unequal power relationship, he consistently turns to the only weapons at his disposal: his knowledge of local history and his ability to tell a story. Stories, then, are not value-neutral, feel-good yarns to be spun around the cabin fire and forgotten soon thereafter. They are, in fact, potent cultural tools, layered with political intention and fraught with social meaning. As such, stories do not exist in a vacuum. Where there is a story, there is a reason for that story.

Through Uncle Julius, Chesnutt called attention to the previously invisible structures of authorship and intent that underlay the writings of his competitors. As he highlighted Julius's mobilization of stories for a very tangible end, Chesnutt reminded readers that other storytellers might be engaged in similar practices. If every story was told for a purpose, and could not be separated from the political goals that had brought it into being, the mantle of unquestionable cultural authority that many northerners unthinkingly bestowed on white southern authors appeared misplaced. If Julius was telling his stories for a purpose, why were Harris and Page telling theirs? What political agenda might underlay these works? These men, Chesnutt insisted, were storytellers just as surely as Uncle Julius. By turning a spotlight on the hidden assumptions that underlay the Remus stories and Page's dialect tales, Chesnutt sought to deny them the explanatory power they required to do their cultural work. Stories of the South, Chesnutt implied, were always more than mere stories.

Together, Harris, Page, Cable, and Chesnutt highlight the importance of local-color fiction for the late nineteenth-century Southern Question. The issues raised in the period's southern fiction—the meaning of the region's past, the question of southern distinctiveness, the relationship between the races—both reflected and influenced larger debates taking place outside the realm of literature. These four authors were well aware of the political significance of southern literature. Each sought to harness its potency, though each did so for distinctly different purposes. In writing fiction, southern authors were not simply telling stories. They were rewriting the place of the South in a post-Reconstruction nation.

# CHAPTER FIVE

# Performing Race, Staging Slavery

On a summer day in 1895, an "infantile black Georgian" stood in the doorway of his parents' small cabin, denying entry to a *New York Times* reporter. "Hi, dar! you brack rascal, git out'n de gemmen's way," the boy's mother scolded. "Doan you see he wanter git inter der cabin tu see yer ol daddy, wat's wukin foah deah life?" Finding her order unheeded, the child's mother "summarily removed" the boy from the doorway. The correspondent entered and sat himself at the table, where "old Joe," the patriarch of the family, was busily "mending a dilapidated pair of trousers" he had procured years before in Atlanta. Though the ensuing conversation has not survived, there appears, at first glance, to be little that is surprising about this exchange. The notion of a journalist interviewing a humble African American family while on assignment in the Deep South is largely unremarkable, as is the reporter's willingness to employ crude dialect and condescending language in describing the scene. One factor, however, made this particular exchange distinctive: it took place not in Georgia but in Brooklyn, New York. The occasion was the opening of an unusual exhibition called *Black America*. On a piece of land borrowed from Buffalo Bill's Wild West show, organizers had re-created a southern plantation, complete with cabins, cotton fields, and 500 black performers (including the family described in the *New York Times*). For a small fee, New Yorkers could visit the grounds, talk with the cast, and imagine themselves transported to the land of cotton. Dixie, it seems, had arrived in Brooklyn.[1]

In terms of its size, scale, and extravagance, *Black America* was largely unique in the history of popular performance in the United States. As an imaginative recreation of southern African American life, however, it was not without precedent. In the years between the fall of the Reconstruction regimes and the rise of Jim Crow, stage depictions of southern blackness were a constant in northern performance culture. At *Black America* and at hundreds of smaller venues, northerners daily witnessed the staging of slavery and race. Such performances took a number of forms. The soaring renditions of slave spirituals presented at a Fisk Jubilee Singers concert stood in stark contrast to the overdrawn stereotypes of the minstrel show, yet both offered northern audiences an opportunity to reflect on the nature of the southern past. At the theater, northerners saw their imagined South come to life.

Despite the frequency with which it addressed issues of race and slavery in the South, late nineteenth-century performance culture is seldom discussed in connection with the nation's retreat from Reconstruction. The oversight seems curious. Though Gilded Age performance culture was marked by a rich diversity of form and a high tolerance for innovation and experimentation, its political message was profoundly conservative. Gilded Age performance sanitized slavery and essentialized race. Peddling nostalgia and capitalizing on popular longing for an idealized southern past, northern theatrical productions reinforced many of the same racial stereotypes used to rationalize black second-class citizenship in the South.[2] Northern audiences seldom witnessed depictions of African American progress and development since emancipation. Instead, popular performances trafficked in romanticized visions of the southern plantation, ignoring the brutality of slavery and denying the possibility of African American advancement.

This chapter analyzes a number of distinct sites at which northern theater-goers encountered images of the South between 1877 and 1895. It opens with a discussion of the Fisk Jubilee Singers, a troupe of African American entertainers whose powerful renditions of slave spirituals offered the most authentic reproduction of the antebellum South to grace the Gilded Age stage. Try as they might, however, the Fisk Jubilee Singers could never entirely escape the shadow of blackface minstrelsy, the most popular cultural form of the nineteenth century and the second type of performance addressed in this chapter. Born in the antebellum period, traditional blackface minstrelsy featured white performers who darkened their faces with burnt cork in order to impersonate southern plantation slaves. In the postwar era, black performers also took to the minstrel stage, often dispensing with the cork but maintaining much of the form's racist content. By the early 1890s, black minstrelsy had evolved into the third cultural form addressed in this chapter: a series of spectacular southern-themed "plantation shows," culminating in 1895's *Black America*. Finally, the chapter analyzes stage performances of *Uncle Tom's Cabin*. Though they were extraordinarily popular, "Tom shows" largely replaced the political fire of Harriet Beecher Stowe's antislavery classic with novelty acts and prepackaged spectacle. Taken together, these four forms of performance—jubilee singing, white and black minstrelsy, plantation shows, and stage performances of *Uncle Tom's Cabin*—testify to the centrality of southern themes in northern performance culture during the 1880s and 1890s.

Performance culture occupied a distinctive place in popular discussions of the Southern Question. With the important exception of the Fisk Jubilee Singers, the performers and troupes discussed in this chapter did not self-consciously set out to redefine the South or to make a statement on contemporary race relations. Though the minstrel stage reproduced a wholly unrealistic vision of slavery and disseminated damaging stereotypes of African Americans, entertainment—not politics—was the primary goal. In contrast to the propaganda of the New South boosters or the proslavery apologia of southern plantation fiction, therefore, the political significance of performance culture was implicit, not overt. This fact, however, should not blind us to the central role that the theater played in the reimagining of the South in the years after Reconstruction. Southern-themed performances endlessly reinforced a standard set of images of the South. Over time, performances became more lavish, but the core tropes and ideas remained largely unchanged. Gilded Age performance culture depicted slavery as a cause for mockery and hilarity, repackaged the antebellum plantation as a site of spectacle and extravaganza, and imagined southern race relations largely in terms of an idealized paternalism. Whatever their intentions, late nineteenth-century performers and promoters played a key role in shaping popular understandings of Dixie.

## The Fisk Jubilee Singers and the Meanings of Authenticity

The Fisk Jubilee Singers arrived in Cincinnati in 1871 carrying the clothes on their back and the hopes of their school on their shoulders. Founded in Nashville, Tennessee, in 1866 under the auspices of the American Missionary Association, Fisk University quickly became a center for African American higher education in the South. Mixing academic study with religious instruction and racial uplift, Fisk was well suited to meet the demand for qualified African American teachers in the Reconstruction South. Unfortunately, noble aspirations do not pay the bills, and Fisk was chronically short of money. By 1870, the situation had become desperate, prompting George L. White, Fisk's white treasurer and director of the university chorus, to offer a bold solution. The vocal talents of White's chorus had earned the university some much-needed income at a series of concerts around Nashville. The success of these ventures led White to propose a northern concert tour. White suspected that a mixture of philanthropy and curiosity would prompt northerners to patronize a troupe of singing freedpeople connected with one of the South's fledgling black educational institutions. White and his small band of singers headed north in October 1871. Though they had no clear itinerary and no winter clothes, they were determined to save Fisk.[3]

Early signs were not propitious. The troupe's first concerts did not showcase the slave spirituals for which the Fisk singers would soon become famous. Instead, White's singers, who had been trained in the "difficult and popular music of the day, composed by our best native and foreign artists," offered a program of standards and patriotic songs. This material failed to capture the northern imagination. Early crowds were small and disinterested, and the troupe barely managed to break even during its first weeks on tour. Only when the group adopted a new name—the Jubilee Singers—and a new repertoire heavier in spirituals did audiences begin to respond. As one of the group's early historians put it, George White soon "found his well-disciplined choir singing the old religious slave songs, his audiences demanding these, and satisfied with little besides, till the cries of the oppressed went echoing all over the North, as some rare heaven-born relic of a bondage past."[4] The Jubilee Singers arrived in New York in early December 1871, where a triumphant concert at Henry Ward Beecher's Plymouth Church in Brooklyn cemented the group's reputation. Over the next year and a half, the Jubilee Singers earned enough money to pay off Fisk's debts, to help purchase twenty-five acres of land for a new campus, and to begin construction on a new academic building, fittingly called Jubilee Hall.

This origins story, a real life Reconstruction-era fairy tale, remained an important part of the Jubilee Singers' legend. By the early 1880s, however, the ill-clad, wide-eyed students of 1871 were a distant memory. After their early success in the North, the Singers spent much of the mid-1870s traveling through Europe. In England, they prayed with the great evangelists Dwight Moody and Ira Sankey, sang for Queen Victoria and members of Parliament, and ate breakfast with Prime Minister William Gladstone and his family.[5] In Germany, they were received by the crown prince and crown princess and sang for the emperor.[6] These trips were also highly profitable. By the end of the decade, Fisk University was on secure economic footing. Jubilee Hall had been completed, and a second building on Fisk's campus, Livingstone Hall, was under construction, largely thanks to the Jubilee Singers.[7] When the Jubilee Singers began to prepare for another northern tour in 1879, therefore, their place in the world of popular entertainment was dramatically different from what it had been eight years earlier. This time, the Jubilee Singers would travel the region as a world-renowned troupe of professional entertainers.

Of course, the source of the Jubilee Singers' popularity had not changed. The troupe continued to specialize in traditional black religious melodies such as "Steal Away to Jesus," "Swing Low Sweet Chariot," "Roll, Jordan, Roll," and "Didn't My Lord Deliver Daniel."[8] For northern audiences, this repertoire turned a Jubilee Singers concert into something of a history lesson. More than mere performers, the Jubilee Singers served as guides to the hidden life and culture of southern slaves. From the safety of their seats in the local church or performance hall, northerners could catch a glimpse of the spiritual life of the slave quarter. The Jubilee Singers, a Massachusetts newspaper wrote, re-created "the music with which American slaves have consoled and amused themselves through the ages of oppression, to which now, thank heaven, they have added the glorious songs of deliverance."[9] Critics lauded the Jubilee Singers for their "pathos and rich harmony," the "sweetness and fervor" of their singing, and the "originality" and "quaintness" of their material.[10] The slave songs frequently brought forth an emotional response from their audience. A New York clergyman described the spirituals as "genuine heart-music, whose rich, wild melodies go to the very fount of tears."[11] A Boston newspaper found that the music "seems to well up from the soul," noting that "men who are never moved by what has been denominated 'artistic music,' of the Italian or German school, listen, with tears, to the music of the Fisk Jubilee Singers."[12] Even President Chester A. Arthur was reported to have "wept like a little child" when the Jubilee Singers performed "Steal Away to Jesus" at the White House.[13]

However, there were always two distinct visions of southern blackness in play at a Fisk Jubilee Singers concert. The spirituals, rooted in an antebellum slave cosmology and a culture of resistance and survival, offered the first. The second vision, less frequently commented on but no less significant, was visible in the singers themselves. Their fame offered the Jubilee Singers a particularly rich opportunity to shape how white northerners

R. W. THOMAS    PATTI J. MALONE.    C. W. PAYNE    F. J. LOUDIN. GEORGE A GIBBONS. MAGGIE E. WILSON. G. E. BARRETT.
MAGGIE S. CAINES    MATTIE L. LAWRENCE    W A BENCHLEY    BELLE F. GIBBONS

Photograph of the Fisk Jubilee Singers, from the 1885 edition of J. B. T. Marsh's
*The Story of the Jubilee Singers*. The troupe's proper attire and respectable appearance
were central to their political message. Frederick Loudin is standing in the center.
Library of Congress.

understood the South and African American culture. The Jubilee Singers'
self-presentation contrasted starkly with the material they performed. The
Singers never played the role of slaves onstage. Formal dress and polished
diction were every bit as central to the Jubilee Singers' message as the
spirituals they performed. Refusing to hide behind a mask of servility or
buffoonery, the singers offered the northern public a vision of educated,
well-traveled, politically engaged, morally upright African American pro-
fessionals. They were the living embodiment of African American potential
and progress. They were respectability and uplift personified, validating
emancipation and Reconstruction by their very existence. Though they
sang the songs of slavery, the Jubilee Singers themselves were absolutely
and unequivocally products of freedom and emancipation. In the context
of a nation slowly backpedaling from its experiments in racial democracy,
this was an important statement indeed.[14]

Their extensive travels and their time in Europe transformed the Jubilee Singers from scared college students into impassioned and deeply

committed reformers who were not afraid to address contemporary racial issues during their performances. Bass singer Frederick Loudin possessed a spectacular voice and a political conscience to match. Loudin joined the Jubilee Singers in 1875, before their second tour of England, and he quickly became the group's spokesman. Throughout their 1879–80 tour, Loudin punctuated most concerts with an impromptu address on race relations. During a Fredonia, New York, concert, Loudin reminded the crowd that "in some portions of the country their people were still oppressed almost as cruelly as in the days of slavery."[15] Toward the end of another performance, Loudin used "the most eloquent and forcible language" to insist that "the country had not been freed from the curse of slavery" and to urge his listeners to continue the struggle to "give all men equality before the law."[16] Manifestations of prejudice in the North sparked some of Loudin's most pointed diatribes. Whenever the Jubilee Singers were denied lodging in a northern hotel—an occurrence that happened with some regularity—Loudin would be sure to let their audiences know about it.[17] Loudin's favorite tactic in such circumstances was to offer invidious comparisons between the first-class treatment that the Jubilee Singers had received in monarchical Europe and the oppression that still reigned in the United States, "where 'all men are born free and equal' . . . (so they say)."[18]

By the 1880s, the Fisk Jubilee Singers regularly delivered a powerful message of reform along with their slave spirituals. Frederick Loudin's impassioned appeals turned every Jubilee Singers' performance into an opportunity for reflection and recommitment to the cause of racial justice. Through word, deed, and carriage, the Fisk Jubilee Singers testified to the progress of the race since emancipation. They had traveled the world and dined with royalty. By their very presence, they demanded that white Americans treat them with respect and fairness. In stark contrast to the slapstick buffoonery of the minstrel stage, the Jubilee Singers used performances of the black past in service of the African American present. Where minstrelsy was a voice for retrogression and reaction, the Jubilee Singers offered a powerful testament to uplift and possibility.

The question is whether northerners got the message. It is undeniable that the Fisk singers exerted a salutary influence on northern race politics throughout the 1870s and 1880s. The Jubilee Singers provided an important alternative performance of southern black life and an antidote to the racial stereotypes common on the minstrel stage and elsewhere. Yet try as they might, the Jubilee Singers were never entirely free to shape their own message. Northern audiences came to Jubilee Singers concerts with a set of racialized expectations that subtly shaped the way that they engaged with the performance. The Jubilee Singers' formulation of race and slavery was only one among many competing for the attention (and dollars) of northern audiences. Even at the height of their popularity, the Jubilee Singers were still entertainers who remained partially captive to the views and experiences of their audience. The meaning of a Fisk Jubilee Singers concert—its larger political, racial, and regional significance—was necessarily the result of a negotiation between audience and performers.

It is here that the depth of the Jubilee Singers' connection with black-face minstrelsy becomes apparent. From the very beginning, minstrelsy was the cultural form that the Jubilee Singers had set themselves most firmly against, but it was also the one to which they were most frequently compared.[19] The American Missionary Association and the trustees of Fisk University were initially reluctant to support George White's plans because they feared that White's chorus would turn Fisk into a minstrel laughingstock.[20] When the Democratic *New York Herald* got word of the Jubilee Singers' performance at Henry Ward Beecher's Plymouth Church, the newspaper's headline read: "Beecher's Negro Minstrels . . . The Great Plymouth Preacher as an End Man . . . A Full Troupe of Real Live Darkies in the Tabernacle of the Lord."[21] Even the Jubilee Singers' supporters found it difficult to avoid referencing blackface minstrelsy. During the Jubilee Singers' first tour, Theodore Cuyler, a Presbyterian clergyman and early supporter, offered a recommendation in the *New York Tribune* couched largely in opposition to minstrelsy: "We have long enough had its coarse caricatures in corked faces; our people can now listen to the genuine soul-music of the slave cabins."[22] In 1880, Cuyler turned to minstrelsy again: "Long enough has the negro been caricatured by clowns in corked faces. Before the memories of slavery and the war die out, the whole nation ought to listen once more to the echoes of those days of struggle in the magnificent voices of the original troupe of 'Jubilee Singers.'"[23]

In fact, the lines between minstrelsy and jubilee singing were always more porous than the Fisk singers would have liked to believe. Inspired by the Fisk singers' early success, legions of imitators began touring the country in the mid-1870s, bearing names like the Louisiana Jubilee Singers, the Original Virginia Colored Jubilee Singers, Perkins' Celebrated Colored Virginia and Texas Jubilee Singers, the North Carolina Jubilee Singers, and the Norfolk Jubilee Singers.[24] Some, such as a troupe from Hampton University in Virginia, were undoubtedly equal to the Fisk singers in talent, conviction, and respectability. Others, such as P. T. Wright's Nashville

Students and Slayton's Jubilee Singers, traded on the Fisk Jubilee Singers' notoriety in order to secure patronage for shows immediately recognizable as minstrelsy.[25] To further blur the lines, many full-fledged minstrel troupes regularly incorporated jubilee singing in their programs.[26] Though the Fisk Jubilee Singers had established themselves as an alternative to minstrelsy, legions of jubilee singing imitators had the effect of narrowing the gap between the cultural forms.

At times, even the Fisk Jubilee Singers were forced to submit to popular pressures, performing music with roots on the minstrel stage rather than in the slave quarter. Many Fisk Jubilee Singers performances included "Suwanee River" (also known as "The Old Folks at Home"), a tune written by white composer Stephen Foster, the most famous minstrel songster of the nineteenth century. It is possible that the Fisk singers' willingness to perform minstrel material had its roots in a self-conscious attempt to repackage and reframe these songs, to transform the music of oppression into evidence of racial progress. Contemporary press coverage, however, suggests that audiences seldom saw matters this way. "Suwanee River" was an audience favorite, a frequent encore request, and the subject of much positive commentary. A Rochester, New York, newspaper noted that "'The Old Folks at Home' always has a new and peculiar significance coming with mournful earnestness from dusky throats, and last evening song and singers were given a round of applause before the first note had been uttered."[27] A reviewer for an Indiana newspaper lauded the "power and pathos" he found in the Jubilee Singers' renditions of the spirituals, and then, without any apparent sense of contradiction, cited "The Old Folks at Home" as one of his two favorite pieces.[28] The Jubilee Singers even performed the song during an 1880 visit to the White House.[29]

The point is not to criticize the Jubilee Singers for their failure to uphold some sort of musical purity; it is, instead, to suggest that such purity was impossible. It may be that many of the northerners in the audience failed, on a fundamental level, to understand the difference between a Stephen Foster tune and a slave spiritual. In any case, few in the audience seem to have found the musical cross-pollination problematic. At least one audience member, however, made her displeasure known. In January 1880, a Worcester, Massachusetts, newspaper reported a "pleasing incident" that had occurred at a Jubilee Singers' concert. "A colored woman advanced in years," the paper reported, was "listening with rapt attention to the religious songs" that made up the majority of the program. But she "was seen to grow uneasy while the singers were giving a hash of plantation music, and when they broke out with 'Dixie,' she bolted down the aisle, cane and umbrella in hand, with a look on her face which indicated great horror." This response elicited great laughter from the audience. In its report, the paper did not see fit to consider the old woman's sense of betrayal at having the religious songs of slavery paired with the "plantation music" of the minstrel stage and the unofficial anthem of the Confederacy. Similarly, the article left the feelings of the Jubilee Singers to the imagination. Though the paper noted that the Singers "took part" in the laughter, one can only speculate as to the true effect that the elderly woman's pain and rage had on the performers.[30]

The specter of minstrelsy made itself felt in other ways. At the heart of the Jubilee Singers' appeal was the presumption of authenticity. Even as they requested material from the minstrel stage, audiences recognized, at a basic level, that the Jubilee Singers were not simply performing slavery. They had lived it. Though the troupe's lineup shifted over time, the majority of the nineteenth-century members of the Fisk Jubilee Singers were, in fact, emancipated slaves. With this in mind, northern commentators allowed themselves to believe that a Fisk Jubilee Singers concert was somehow less a performance than a reflection of the performers' personal histories. "There was never singing more intensely dramatic than this, for there was never singing more sincere," the New York Tribune wrote. "It was not an exhibition of art; it was the expression of real emotion."[31] The New York Times added that "the secret is, the melodies they sing are 'the songs of their captivity.'"[32] A Massachusetts newspaper likewise insisted that "the wild wailing" and "jubilant melodies" of the Jubilee Singers were made all the more enjoyable by a knowledge that the singers "have learned in sorrow what they teach in song."[33] This sense of authenticity served as the bulwark separating the Jubilee Singers from minstrelsy. The Jubilee Singers were the genuine article, former slaves singing the songs of slavery. One went to the minstrel show to see a reproduction of slave culture; one saw the Jubilee Singers to witness the real thing.[34]

However, authenticity could prove a double-edged sword. It was, first of all, easy to make too much of the Jubilee Singers' status as former slaves. Frederick Loudin, for one, was a northerner, born free in Ohio to parents who had never been slaves.[35] For the most part, those Jubilee Singers who had experienced slavery were mere children at the time of their emancipation. By the 1880s, most had spent many more years in freedom than they had in slavery.[36] Beyond this, it is important to note that the northern public's myopic focus on the Jubilee Singers' slave heritage came at a cost to the troupe and their political message. To focus exclusively on those years spent in slavery was to miss other aspects of the Jubilee Singers' histories and identities. Such a view wholly discounted the possibility of growth, change, and development *since* slavery. The singers who traveled the North in the early 1880s were not the same people they had been two decades before. Free, educated, and successful, the Fisk Jubilee Singers were slaves no longer. Northern audiences frequently overlooked this fact, understanding the Jubilee Singers exclusively as former slaves and thus failing to recognize their full political significance. Ironically, the same history of enslavement that gained the Jubilee Singers a hearing in the first place rendered many northerners deaf to the troupe's powerful message of racial progress.

When the Jubilee Singers began to tour the North again after their European hiatus, a number of commentators expressed disappointment. Though they praised the singing and the harmony, they found something missing. "The Fisk University Jubilee Singers are not what they were five years ago, when they first visited this city," a newspaper in Lawrence, Massachusetts, complained. Their concert was "a fine musical entertainment," but the reviewer noted "an absence of the genuine and hearty manner, and peculiar dialect, wont to be given by colored singers, from the plantations and campmeetings of the south, and which charmed and fascinated the people of the north in the years after the war."[37] A paper in Peoria, Illinois, agreed. "They are now a concert troupe, and very good," the paper began, "but they are no longer jubilee singers." Their years of touring had worked a change, the reviewer explained, and not for the better. The reviewer mourned that the Jubilee Singers "smack[ed] of the north, of free schools and equal rights, respectability and order, and not of the southern cane brake, the blood-hounds, the rice swamps, the camp meetings, the pine woods where the torches flash." To truly appreciate the music of slavery, the listener "must see the cotton fields, the presence of the overseer; he must hear in imagination the crack of the whip, the baying hounds, the splash of the dark waters of the river and must, as a solemn undertone, catch the wild refrain, 'Will you let my people go.'"[38] The Fisk Jubilee Singers had once offered northern audiences just such an authentic experience, but after a number of tours abroad and a decade in the spotlight, they had strayed too far from their slave past. The Fisk Jubilee Singers had traveled the world, toured the country, dined with royalty, and saved their university. And yet many northerners wished that they would act more like slaves.

Such complaints are telling. The Fisk Jubilee Singers were authentic;

they were authentically professional, authentically well-traveled, and authentically talented. They were authentic proof that the policies of the Reconstruction era had not been mistaken, and that a continued national commitment to African American rights was both wise and required. This perspective was often ignored, however, as northerners demanded authenticity of a very particular stripe. As the experience of the Fisk Jubilee Singers suggests, performances of race and slavery in the late nineteenth-century North were largely judged with reference to a set of expectations that left little room for African American progress, evolution, or uplift. Try as they might, the Fisk Jubilee Singers never exercised complete control over their performances. Their message of racial uplift coexisted (and often conflicted) with the northern public's avowed desire to witness an authentic portrayal of the slave past. Though few would have mistaken them for a minstrel troupe, the Jubilee Singers were still largely beholden to white expectations regarding southern African Americans. In the end, the late nineteenth-century career of the Fisk Jubilee Singers highlights both the political possibilities of black performance and the ways the racial expectations of northern audiences systematically undercut those possibilities.

## Visions of the South in White and Black Minstrelsy

For much of the nineteenth century, blackface minstrelsy—the nation's first homegrown cultural form and its most popular style of mass entertainment—played a formative role in shaping northern ideas about slavery and the South. Through sectional conflict, Civil War, emancipation, and Reconstruction, white performers in blackface delighted northern audiences with their plantation sketches and their racial caricatures. Offering a fast-moving mix of witty repartee, off-color puns, absurd monologues, outrageous dancing, and tear-jerking ballads, minstrels managed to fill auditoriums, lampoon societal norms, and reinforce white supremacy at the same time. Though minstrelsy primarily appealed to a working-class clientele, the sheer ubiquity of minstrel representations of the South for much of the nineteenth century created a set of stereotypes and expectations that deeply affected ideas about the region at all levels of northern society.[39] Given its wild popularity and its continuous engagement with southern images and themes, it may well be that blackface minstrelsy exerted a greater influence on nineteenth-century northern understandings of the South than any other cultural form.

In its infancy, blackface minstrelsy had been a relatively simple affair.

In the antebellum period, a successful minstrel troupe required only a row of chairs, a handful of performers, a few instruments, and a supply of burnt cork. In the decades after the Civil War, however, the minstrel show underwent a fundamental transformation. The mammoth blackface extravaganzas of the Gilded Age were a far cry from the small-scale affairs that had delighted antebellum audiences. Late nineteenth-century shows frequently featured dozens of performers, elaborate stage sets, and an endless stream of gimmicks and hijinks. Leading companies traveled the nation in their own railroad cars, carrying staging, props, backdrops, and pyrotechnics with them. Minstrel managers battled to provide the grandest, most extravagant production around. The result was an eclectic mix of racial comedy, musical performance, grand dance routines, and a wide array of specialty acts, including clog dancers, contortionists, and female impersonators. Using a language of aggregation perfectly fitted to the temper of the Gilded Age North, an 1882 advertisement for a traveling minstrel troupe promised "2 burlesque prima-donnas, 14 brilliant end-men, 10 genteel song-and-dance men, 12 cabin Banjo-players, 14 shouting Cottonfield Belles, 18 Jolly Comedians, 10 Silver-shoed Cloggists, 20 Comic and Sentimental Vocalists," in addition to "26 celebrated Musicians, 36 in a Military Brass Band, and 100 other features of merit."[40] The ubiquitous adjectives attached to the names of the leading minstrel companies—Mastodon Minstrels, Megatherian Minstrels, Mammoth Minstrels, Gigantic Minstrels—dramatized the newfound obsession with size and grandeur. This was minstrelsy on an industrial scale.[41]

What had not changed was minstrelsy's frequent engagement with southern themes. Though postbellum minstrelsy addressed a much wider spectrum of topical material than had antebellum minstrelsy—from baseball to labor strife to parodies of Gilbert and Sullivan—plantation songs and sketches remained integral to the minstrel program.[42] The thematic content of these southern sketches, moreover, remained remarkably consistent across time. Even as they competed to provide the biggest and boldest minstrel entertainment, white minstrel troupes presented a static, unchanging picture of the South. A few guiding assumptions shaped postbellum white minstrelsy's approach to southern themes. First of all, southern sketches dealt almost exclusively with slavery. Emancipation had little discernible effect on the minstrel presentation of southern black life, which continued to revolve around the cotton field and the slave quarter. When free black characters were presented at all, they could be expected to rue their emancipation and to long for the good old days before the war. Second, blackface minstrels assumed that slavery was just, humane, and even fun. Whips and slave traders had no place on the minstrel stage. Manual labor remained largely invisible, as the antebellum plantation became a site for song and dance rather than uncompensated toil. Finally, white minstrels presented an idealized vision of the master/slave relationship. In both antebellum and Gilded Age minstrelsy, the deep reverence of slaves for their masters domesticated and naturalized the institution. In the process, minstrelsy romanticized white/black relations in the South, encouraging northern passivity and inaction in the face of continuing southern racial strife.

The plantation song and dance routine was the most common type of southern sketch in Gilded Age white minstrelsy. Against a backdrop of generic southern imagery, most often a cotton field, blackface performers sang and danced with abandon, transforming oppression and exploitation into popular entertainment. In the mid-1880s, J. H. Haverly's blackface troupes offered an array of southern-themed dance extravaganzas, including a "MAMMOTH SONG AND DANCE" called "THE COTTON PICKERS," and a "Grand Production of the Monster Song and Dance, entitled 'AWAY DOWN IN DIXIE.'"[43] Billy Emerson's Megatherian Minstrels presented "16 Song & Dance Artists" in a "Great Plantation Sketch entitled SOUTHERN LIFE IN SLAVERY DAYS," while Lew Dockstader's Refined Minstrels introduced a "Genuine old time minstrel feature" called "THE COTTON FIELD," which depicted "the most popular old time melodies, scintillations of darky wit and humor," and "grotesque dances" of the South.[44] Dockstader also produced a number of extended southern sketches featuring dialogue and scene changes along with the obligatory singing and dancing. "Happy Coons in Dixie Land," for instance, offered a glimpse of "Darkey Life, with Scenes, Song and Story in his Cabin, the Field, and his Merry Pastimes after his day's work is done."[45] On one level, the southern content in such sketches merely provided an excuse to introduce the lavish stage spectacles on which latter-day blackface minstrelsy thrived. At the same time, these song and dance routines did important ideological work, turning a landscape of brutal physical compulsion into one defined by amusement and pleasure.

Gilded Age minstrelsy frequently evoked kindly masters, faithful slaves, and the harmonious racial order of the Old South. The aged former slave longing for the "good old days" before emancipation became a minstrel fixture. Songs expressing such sentiments were innumerable, and for the most part, indistinguishable. "Down South Whar de Sugar Cane Grows,"

Scene from a southern sketch performed by Lew Dockstader's Minstrels (ca. 1880s). Though this photograph depicts a levee scene, plantation settings were also quite common. Harry Ransom Center, University of Texas at Austin.

a fairly representative sample of the genre, featured a "poor old darkey" crooning, "Oh it nearly breaks dis heart of mine to think I'll never hear / Ole massa's kind and gentle voice again."[46] In "My Old Savannah Home," a former slave ruefully noted, "Oh, the times ain't what they used to be when Massa had his say."[47] In 1885, James McIntyre and Tom Heath, a white minstrel duo who specialized in southern material, presented "Way down South," a sketch that dramatized the relationship between faithful slave and kindly master. Billed as a "life-like picture of scenes in the South as seen befo' de' war," the piece opened with a former runaway slave's return to the plantation from which he had escaped years before. Dissatisfied with his life in freedom, the prodigal slave begs his master to allow him to take up his former condition of bondage. When the suspicious master finally relents, all the slaves on the plantation—including the voluntarily reenslaved protagonist—are given a holiday, punctuated, somewhat predictably, with a plantation dance.[48] As it dramatically reversed the northward course followed by generations of slave escapees, "Way down South" sent an unmistakable message: African American freedom was impermanent and unnatural; white supremacy was inevitable and beneficial to both races.

Taken as a whole, depictions of the South in postbellum blackface minstrelsy reinforced a nostalgic and idealized image of the southern past. The ideological power of postbellum white minstrelsy lay in its ability to innovate in form—and thereby to continue to draw audiences—while remaining remarkably consistent in content. Thematically speaking, Gilded Age blackface minstrelsy offered little that was new or distinctive with regard to the South. The minstrel stage had presented images of happy slaves and plantation frolics since the antebellum period. For example, Stephen Foster's "Massa's in the Cold, Cold Ground," first published in 1852, foreshadowed the idealized master/slave relationship so frequently dramatized in postbellum minstrelsy.[49] But familiarity possessed its own political significance. With regard to the Southern Question, postwar white minstrelsy functioned not by innovation but by repetition. The minstrel stage offered a set of symbols and images that were instantly recognizable and accessible to northern audiences. Rather than breaking new ground, Gilded Age minstrel troupes endlessly reproduced a standard set of tropes: the faithful slave, the kind master, the cotton field song and dance, the longing for the good old days before the war. Even as they competed to offer the most extravagant spectacle of southern life, minstrel troupes felt little compulsion to present a new or different take on the region. Southern sketches continued to appeal to northern minstrel audiences precisely because they were familiar, even predictable. Minstrel depictions of the South offered a calming vision of stability and continuity to a northern public grappling with the challenges of industrialization and urbanization. At the same time, they reinforced a deeply problematic vision of slavery, denied the significance and justice of emancipation, and questioned the viability of African American citizenship in the postwar United States.

Though white minstrel troupes continued to provide northerners with many of their ideas about the South, traditional blackface companies faced new competition in the postwar period. The increased involvement of African American performers represented the greatest innovation in postbellum minstrelsy. African Americans had appeared on minstrel stages as early as the mid-1850s, but it was not until Reconstruction that black minstrel troupes achieved sustained success and recognition. By the 1880s, the leading black minstrel troupes were traveling the country in personalized railroad cars, playing before capacity crowds, and out-earning many white minstrel troupes. Though white managers led most black troupes, many African American performers, including the comedian Billy Kersands, the songwriter James Bland, and the husband and wife team of Billy and Cordelia McClain, achieved national stardom and substantial salaries for their efforts. At the same time, minstrelsy afforded scores of lesser-known performers an opportunity to make a career in show business. That said, the legacies of black minstrelsy are deeply mixed. Black troupes performed much of the same material as contemporary white minstrel troupes. In order to secure a hearing onstage, African Americans—who often performed without blackface—were forced to cater to audience expectations, reproducing a series of white-authored stereotypes about black people. In so doing, black performers lent credence to the very white supremacist assumptions that so deeply curtailed African American opportunity.[50]

In the battle for minstrel supremacy, managers of black minstrel troupes resorted to many familiar gimmicks. Like its white counterpart, Gilded Age black minstrelsy fetishized scale and spectacle. In language nearly identical to that used to advertise white minstrel companies, managers trumpeted the size of their troupes and the extravagance of their productions. In 1881, a leading minstrel manager announced a "GIGANTIC COLORED MINSTREL CARNIVAL" starring Billy Kersands and featuring 100 black performers. The production was advertised with an imposing broadside, several feet tall, that listed every one of the "GREAT BLACK HUNDRED" by name.[51] A year later, promoters organized an unprecedented "MARRIAGE OF MINSTRELSY" in Chicago. Bringing one troupe from New York and another troupe from San Francisco, audiences were promised "TWO MONSTER SHOWS IN ONE!" and "THE PICK OF THE EARTH'S COLORED TALENT!"[52] Like their white counterparts, black minstrel companies acted under the assumption that quantity equaled quality. In order to secure patronage, managers made common practice of the exaggerated and the extravagant.

But spectacle was only a part of the appeal of black minstrelsy. Arguably more significant was a perceived facility with southern and plantation material. From the beginning, black troupes depicted the South far more frequently and at far greater depth than white troupes. Where postbellum white troupes usually devoted only a small part of a program to southern sketches, black companies made a living reproducing the plantation in the years after Reconstruction.[53] For the most part, the content of these southern sketches varied little from similar acts performed by white minstrels. As in white minstrelsy, plantation sketches most often involved wild dancing and conspicuous merrymaking. An advertisement for Haverly's Genuine Colored Minstrels promised "Plantation Mirth and Melody on a Scale Beyond Parallel! An Inimitable Reproduction of 'Darky' Life in the Cornfield, Canebrake, Barnyard, and on Levee and Flatboat!"[54] A typical Callender's Georgia Minstrels program featured a "Comic Plantation Sketch" called "Brudder Bones' Serenade," a performance by a "Plantation Quartette" known as the "Canebrake Spectres," and "Love in Georgia,"

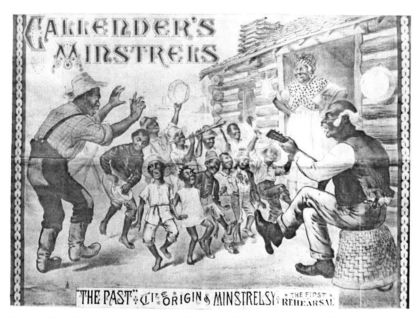

Poster advertising a performance by Callender's Minstrels (ca. 1880s). The poster
makes a claim for the racial and historical authenticity of the troupe's plantation material.
MS Thr 556 (25), Harvard Theatre Collection, Houghton Library, Harvard University.

described as a "Beautiful Plantation Sketch."[55] Denying the compulsory
labor at the heart of the antebellum slave regime, black minstrel troupes
refigured the plantation as a site of mirth, hilarity, and hijinks. Kindly
masters and devoted elderly slaves also made frequent appearances in
black minstrel productions. African American songwriter James Bland's
best-known tune, "Carry Me Back to Old Virginny," offered a former slave's
lament for his long-lost plantation home and the deceased "old massa"
with whom he hoped to be one day reunited "on that bright and golden
shore."[56] On the black minstrel stage, just as surely as the white, slavery
became a benign institution, emancipation became a burden, and white
southerners became the best friends of African Americans.

There was, however, an added layer of complexity when it came to black
minstrel depictions of the South. A firmly held conviction that African
American performers were uniquely suited to the presentation of plantation material shaped both the content of black minstrelsy and the ways
northern audiences responded to black minstrel shows. Simply by virtue
of their race, African American minstrels were thought to impart greater
realism and authenticity to southern material.[57] The fact that the performers were black, and not just wearing blackface, lent an air of believability to

plantation material far beyond that which northern audiences accorded to white performers. Cagey minstrel promoters did all they could to encourage this tendency. In truth, minstrel depictions of slavery and the southern plantation bore little relation to historical reality, no matter who performed them. The racial and regional logic of late nineteenth-century black minstrelsy, however, transformed stereotype into fact. Black performers came to seem authentic in a way that white performers never could. The appeal of black minstrelsy lay in its alleged ability to accurately and realistically re-create the antebellum southern plantation for northern audiences. In this guise, black minstrelsy proved a powerful force in shaping northern conceptions of race and slavery after Reconstruction.

When he purchased Charles Callender's Georgia Minstrels in 1877, J. H. Haverly added a moderately successful black touring company to his already formidable minstrel empire. Renaming the company Haverly's Genuine Colored Minstrels, the promoter used his knack for publicity and showmanship to expand audiences while moving the stage show in a more self-consciously southern direction. By the time he sold the troupe in 1882, Haverly had turned his Genuine Colored Minstrels into a wildly popular and hugely influential theatrical powerhouse.[58] The secret lay in the packaging. In an 1879 advertisement in the *New York Clipper*, the nation's premier entertainment weekly, Haverly insisted on the essential accuracy of his troupe's depictions of the South: "No other Company Shows, nor Can show, with such Conspicuous Fidelity to Nature, the Uproariously Comic and Perennially Amusing and Vivid Phases of Southern Plantation Life as this Remodeled and Improved Company does in its Great Exhibition of THE DARKY AS HE IS AT HOME."[59] Here and elsewhere, Haverly insisted on a linkage between the race of his performers and the realism of his plantation sketches. The fact that the performers in Haverly's Genuine Colored Minstrels were African Americans did not mean that they were, or even that they had been, plantation slaves. However, Haverly used the *racial* authenticity of his performers to make a claim for their *regional* and *historical* authenticity. Because the performers were black, he claimed, audiences could rest assured that the depiction of southern slavery would be truthful and realistic. A Haverly playbill from 1881 promised:

COTTON FIELD PASTIMES, By the Sunny Children of the South.
CANEBRAKE FROLICS, By the little Pickaninnies.
FLATBOAT VARIETIES, By those who have participated in them.
PLANTATION REVELS, BY NATIVES

LEVEE COMICALITIES, By old Mississippi steamboat hands.
CAMP MEETING REFRAINS, By a Corps of Female Jubilee Singers.
Making the air resound with their uproarious Southern
     Absurdities.[60]

Here, Haverly completely effaced the distinction between his performers and the plantation slaves that they depicted during his show. In fact,
Haverly denied that his Genuine Colored Minstrels were performing at
all. Instead, he encouraged his audiences to believe that the performances
they witnessed were authentic reenactments of life on the antebellum
southern plantation.

Northern audiences responded. Reviewers largely accepted Haverly's
fundamental promotional premise: that because his actors and musicians
were African Americans, they were better understood as participants
than performers. A reviewer for the *New York Clipper* praised the Haverly
troupe's realism, noting that "the entertainments are chockfull of novelty,
and depict our colored brothers at their plantation sports and pastimes
with greater fidelity than any 'poor white trash' with corked faces can
ever do."[61] Similarly, the *Baltimore American* insisted that there was a
substantive difference between Haverly's Genuine Colored Minstrels and
traditional white minstrel troupes: "The show is a unique one in every
respect, not only because it is participated in by real darkies, but because
it is a departure from the old stereotyped minstrel performances." The
production, the newspaper continued, was not really a minstrel show at
all. Instead, it offered a true-to-life recreation of a long-lost place and time.
"There is no attempt to burlesque this, that or the other," the paper concluded, "but what its performers try to do, and succeed in wonderfully, is
to give a true idea of the antebellum plantation life with striking realism
and wonderful excellence."[62]

When Charles and Gustave Frohman purchased the Genuine Colored
Minstrels from J. H. Haverly in 1882, they picked up where he had left off.
With their purchase of the revived Georgia Minstrels from Charles Callender a year before, the acquisition of Haverly's troupe put the Frohmans
at the pinnacle of black minstrelsy.[63] They wasted little time. In order to
emphasize the grandeur of their company, now called Callender's Con-
solidated Colored Minstrels, the Frohmans outfitted each performer with
an overcoat, a black suit, two band uniforms, and foul weather gear, each
piece bearing the monogram "C. M." The company even began to travel
in personalized railroad cars bearing the word "Africa" on their side. Ex-

travagance, however, was only the beginning. The Frohmans also sought realism. They furnished the troupe with new staging, new scenery, new props, and new costuming, all of it designed to evoke the antebellum South. The updated show opened, according to one report, with "fifty to sixty performers perched on logs and stumps of trees, and accurately costumed in the clothing of the old-time slave days in the south." A southern cypress tree covered in "long gray moss" and "special scenery . . . prepared at considerable expense" completed the stage picture.[64] The production that followed this elaborate staging undoubtedly reproduced the usual plantation stereotypes then common in both black and white minstrelsy. An 1884 Callender's program, for instance, promised "Field hands," "cotton pickers," "moonlight pastimes," "cottonfield frolics," and "the exciting VIR-GINIA REEL."[65] Yet when combined with the Frohmans' careful attention to the trappings of authentic southernness, these acts could be passed off as a real depiction of life on the old plantation.

The Frohmans' most outrageous piece of promotion was a full-page advertisement, placed in the *New York Clipper* in March 1882, that claimed to recount an actual interview with an unnamed member of the Callender troupe. Though the piece was a fabrication, it offers a prime example of the way black minstrel troupes clung to a discourse of realism even as they perpetuated the most damaging and threadbare of racial stereotypes. Written in thick dialect and filled with proslavery apologia, the "interview" sought to validate the troupe's claims to authenticity through a recitation of an imagined minstrel's life story. The performer introduced himself as a "rale brack Efiopian," descended from an African cannibal chief. He had, he said, spent the best times of his life as a slave in Louisiana, before emancipation "spilt all my fine prospects." With Callender's, however, he felt as if he had never left his plantation home. Though "dar has been a great deal ob talk and abbertising 'bout de plantation scenes and real brack minstrels" circulating in the northern press, only Callender's would present "de genuine plantation darky on de stage." In fact, the show was so lifelike that audiences would be unable to tell the difference between the South and Callender's representation of it: "De old plantation frolics and de cotton-field sports will be pictured so natural dat de audience will tink dey is down in Louisiana wid cotton bales, alligators, canebrakes and cypress swamps all 'round dem." When exposed to "dese trufes of de plantation," he predicted, white audience members would murmur, "I wish de Almighty had painted me brack as dese brack fellers up dere dat am making all dis music."[66]

Of course, it is unlikely that many readers of the *New York Clipper* would have been taken in by the veracity of the "interview." Yet this is not the proper standard by which to judge this cultural artifact. In concocting the advertisement, the Frohman brothers accurately judged the temper of white minstrel patrons. Audiences undoubtedly would have seen through the advertisement's pretense (just as they would have known that they were not actually at a southern plantation while in a northern minstrel theater). The involvement of African American performers, however, allowed promoters access to a discourse of authenticity that proved irresistible to minstrel show patrons. Of course, this much vaunted authenticity only went so far. Their claims to the contrary notwithstanding, black minstrel troupes were largely reiterating stereotypes that had been on display on the minstrel stage for years. Whatever the race of the performers, Gilded Age minstrelsy was grounded in a vision of the South that misrepresented the region's past and present. When couched in a language of authenticity, however, such depictions came to seem dangerously real.

## Authentic Spectacles:
## Plantation Shows and *Black America*

From the purported realism of black minstrelsy, it was a relatively small step to the next development in southern-themed performance. Starting in the early 1890s, a number of extravagant, full-length southern-themed productions—usually called "plantation shows" or "plant shows"—began to compete with traditional minstrelsy. Rather than the variety of unrelated short sketches that made up the minstrel show, plantation shows offered (in theory, at least) a coherent plotline that structured the action. Most were set on the plantation, but some shows featured other stereotypically southern settings, including swamps, steamboat levees, and camp meetings. Plantation shows were quick to incorporate many of the technical and stylistic innovations of Gilded Age minstrelsy. They featured large companies, elaborate staging, and exaggerated promotional techniques. Taking a cue from the success of black minstrel troupes, plantation shows featured predominantly African American casts and maintained a deep rhetorical investment in authenticity and realism even as they reinforced many familiar stereotypes regarding race, slavery, and the South. Though plantation shows are best understood as an evolutionary stage of minstrelsy, promoters consistently claimed to present northern audiences with a true-to-life picture of the South.

In April 1892, the classified section of the *New York Clipper* featured a small advertisement reading "CLEVER COLORED TALENT WANTED QUICK." The posting instructed "Ladies and Gents of experience, refinement and culture in Cake Walking, Shouting, Singing, Plantation Melodies, Quadrilles, Wing, Reel and Buck Dancing" to "Telegraph at once for our Spectacular Production of 'THE SOUTH BEFORE THE WAR.'"[67] A week later, a note in the *Clipper* offered a more thorough explanation:

> J. H. WHALLEN, of Whallen & Martell's Specialty Co., and also proprietor of the Buckingham Theatre, Louisville, Ky., is organizing a colored company for a summer tour. The title of the company will be "The South Before the War," and will be composed of regular Southern negroes, male and female. They will introduce the old plantation songs, jigs, buck dancing, etc., prevailing at that time. A feature will be a real cotton picking scene, showing the darkies picking cotton, while singing their melodies. Chas. Howard, the original Old Black Joe, will lead the cotton pickers, and will also act as stage manager.[68]

The plantation show was born. The brainchild of managers Harry Martell and John Whallen, *The South before the War* offered audiences a full-length southern extravaganza depicting "the pleasant side of slavery."[69] It boasted a large and talented cast drawn from both white and black minstrelsy, and featured a number of elements drawn directly from the minstrel stage, including plantation dances, slapstick comedy, copious malapropisms, and faithful slaves. The production combined these minstrel foundations with a number of other features (notably the "real cotton picking scene" that opened the show) meant to imply authenticity and realism. *The South before the War* was an immediate success. It toured continuously throughout the 1890s and spawned a host of imitators. It also marked an important new development in the history of late nineteenth-century performance culture.[70]

In its presentation and publicity, *The South before the War* was deeply indebted to late nineteenth-century minstrelsy. A promotional booklet produced in the mid-1890s promised that patrons of *The South before the War* would be treated to "a Plethora of Pure Plantation Pastimes," courtesy of the "The Biggest, Greatest, Richest, Grandest and most Unique Colored Co." in the business. The production boasted "Fifty Sugar-rolling, Cotton Stowing, Hilarious, Hallelujah Howling, Genuine Southern Darkies," "Fifty Shouting Ebony Exhorters," "Thirty Dark-Skinned Dextrous Dancers," and "Thirty Wondrous Women Wing Dancers," along with a variety of other attractions.[71] The show itself also featured many well-worn minstrel tropes. It opened with a standard minstrel gambit: the return of the elderly runaway slave to his home plantation, where he was reunited with his family and his former master. The second act, set on a steamboat levee, largely served as a vehicle for lowbrow physical humor, while the third act opened with a religious meeting and closed with a plantation cakewalk. Many of the one-liners ("If a man had a gun, what a great place this camp meeting would be for coon hunting") and scenarios (stolen chickens, a razor fight) that punctuated the production were, likewise, standard minstrel fare.[72] The similarities to mainstream minstrelsy were not lost on the white minstrel duo McIntyre and Heath, who claimed—with ample justification—that the script of *The South before the War* was a thinly veiled reworking of their 1885 sketch "Way down South." Even the name of the slave runaway, "Old Eph," was the same in both productions.[73]

In spite of the obvious influence of minstrelsy, *The South before the War* was presented to the public as an authentic depiction of southern black life. A publicity statement written by managers Harry Martell and John Whallen promised that "those of us who knew the 'Souf befo' the Wah'" and remembered "the happy days, and pleasant nights spent by the darkies in the cottonfields and canebrakes" now had the "opportunity of seeing and living ever again those happy times" thanks to *The South before the War*. The production had no place for "burnt-cork and velvet-brushed inconsistent Ethiopian imitators." Instead, the audience would be treated to "sixty genuine Southern darkies in genuine southern fun making." The stage set, the managers insisted, was as authentic as the performers. The cotton-picking scene took place in a field that was "true to nature, actually 'jes from de Souf,'" while the steamboat landing offered "a piece of perfect realism seldom equaled in scenic effect." Rather than a mere stage production, *The South before the War* was a "truthful portrayal of nature, showing with photographic exactness its people as they were in fact." The result was less an evening's entertainment than a trip through time and space. "From the rising to the falling of the curtain," concluded the publicity statement, "one is transported through the pleasant media of song, dance, music and merriment, in an inimitable manner back to the good old days of the past and The South Before the War."[74]

This statement seems strikingly disconnected from the content of the show it sought to publicize. Where the statement advertised the production's "photographic exactness" and its "perfect realism," the stage production itself was more interested in spectacular dance numbers and cheap

SOUTH BEFORE THE WAR.

UN-PARALLELED.

INCOMPARABLE.

PICKING COTTON.

"The original and only show of its kind on the American stage."
Traveling on its own $12,000 Pullman Palace Car.

Page from a promotional pamphlet for *The South before the War* (ca. 1890s). The image depicts the troupe's purportedly authentic cotton-picking scene. MSS 87, The South Before the War Company Papers, Irving S. Gilmore Music Library, Yale University.

laughs. Any audience member with a brain and a pulse should have been able to tell the difference between the South before the war and *The South before the War*. To establish its credibility, however, the show did not need to reach back to the antebellum South. Instead, it could look to legions of southern-themed shows and to thousands of northern stage performances of race and slavery. By the 1890s, the minstrel South had become so familiar as to seem at least as real as historical reality itself. The production drew its inspiration not from history but from history as refracted and distorted through the lens of minstrelsy. From this perspective, *The South before the War* was completely and utterly authentic.

Contemporary reviewers largely followed Whallen and Martell's lead in emphasizing the realistic aspects of *The South before the War*. The *New York Times* offered a relatively noncommittal review but recommended the performance for "people who like genuine darkey songs and dances and part singing."[75] The *Detroit Free Press* lauded the production's authentic recreation of "old-time plantation pastimes," while the *New York Clipper* noted that "the lovers of the good old Southern pastimes, as indulged in by the colored population of ante-bellum days, found plenty of food for delight in the performance."[76] The *Washington Post* went a step further.

Insisting that "prior to the late war the condition of the Southern dark[e]y, aside from the mere fact of servitude, was not one of extreme misery," the *Post* declared that "the scenes of plantation days" offered "highly realistic pictures" which "introduce[d] the darkey in his favorite pastimes."[77] A *Boston Globe* reviewer even got the idea that many members of the company in *The South before the War* were "actual field hands from the cotton belt."[78] This claim was not only false but also one that Whallen and Martell had never made themselves. Though they undoubtedly recognized that *The South before the War* was, at a fundamental level, entertainment, these reviewers displayed a remarkable willingness to echo Whallen and Martell's language of authenticity. Though they were seldom able to articulate precisely why they felt this way, reviewers were curiously invested in the notion that *The South before the War* represented something more—more authentic, more realistic, more accurate—than mere minstrelsy.

Emulation would prove the sincerest form of flattery. The immediate success of *The South before the War* spawned hosts of imitators. The first, an 1893 production called *Slavery Days*, promised "a series of startling and novel surprises" but largely recycled the premise and attractions of *The South before the War*.[79] Even so, the *New York Clipper* praised the production's "original and realistic plantation cotton picking scene showing a real cotton field as it was in slavery days, with the darkies in the field singing and picking the cotton."[80] The next year, *The Old South*, *On the Mississippi*, and *In Old Virginia* joined the ranks of the touring plantation shows.[81] This encroachment prompted Whallen and Martell to take action. In early 1895, they published an open letter in the *New York Clipper* urging "PIRATES OF ORIGINAL IDEAS" to cease and desist. They claimed an exclusive right to the name "SOUTH BEFORE THE WAR," as well as related titles including "OLD SOUTH," "SOUTH BEFORE AND AFTER THE WAR," and "SLAVERY DAYS," and promised to prosecute any manager or theater that infringed on their territory.[82]

Copyright and copycats aside, Whallen and Martell largely missed the point. When it first appeared, *The South before the War* was certainly a new departure in northern performance culture, but it was not out of keeping with previous trends. *The South before the War* was, in fact, a perfectly logical evolutionary development. Stage depictions of slavery and the South had a long history in northern popular culture. Once the involvement of African American performers allowed managers to claim that their southern sketches were authentic, it was only a matter of time before someone took the next step. *The South before the War* may have been the first company to base an entire production on a claim of authentic southernness, but it would not be the last. In the battle for audience patronage, promises of authenticity and realism had become every bit as significant as size and spectacle.

*Black America*, an 1895 southern-themed spectacular, marked the culmination of these trends. The production grew from an unlikely partnership between Billy McClain, a black minstrel show standout and member of the cast of *The South before the War*, and Nate Salsbury, a white Union army veteran and the manager of Buffalo Bill's Wild West.[83] The pair made a formidable duo. McClain provided artistic vision, musical know-how, and contacts in the minstrel world; Salsbury offered a white public face, substantial economic clout, and a keen sense of promotion and showmanship. Together, they produced an event unique in the annals of American popular culture, transforming Ambrose Park in Brooklyn into a southern plantation, complete with slave cabins, farm animals, cotton fields in bloom, gins and presses, and hundreds of African American performers. After a month and half in New York, the production moved up the coast to Boston's Huntington Avenue Circus Grounds. For a small fee, *Black America* allowed curious Yankees to experience "the lovable bright side of the true Southern Negro presented in a series of animated scenes of rural simplicity in Dixie."[84] Though the *Black America* company put on two stage shows a day, the production's real innovation occurred offstage. With the price of admission, visitors purchased not only a seat at one of the performances but also the right to walk the grounds, tour the cabins, speak to the performers, and experience plantation life in the sunny South. Though Salsbury and McClain claimed to have re-created an authentic plantation village on the fairgrounds, they had, in fact, created the most elaborate performance of race and slavery that the nation had ever seen.[85]

The *Black America* stage show was actually something of a throwback, owing more to traditional minstrelsy than to the plantation shows. The program offered a variety of acts, some only tangentially related to the South, and made no attempt to provide an overarching narrative framework. The production opened with "a Novel and Fascinating Concert by Freedmen of the South." The *Black America* chorus sang a number of traditional southern spirituals, including "Roll, Jordan, Roll" and "Stand on the Walls of Zion," but the majority of the material came from the minstrel stage, including tunes by Stephen Foster and James Bland. The stage show also presented a "Real Old Virginia Promenade and Cake Walk" and

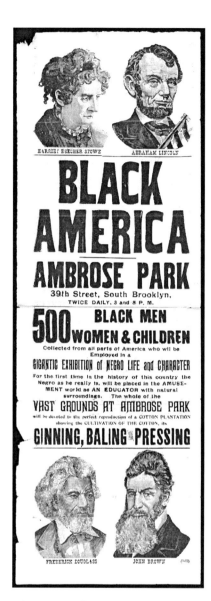

Advertisement for *Black America* promising a depiction of "the Negro as he really is" (1895) (left). The list of attractions on the back of the broadside (right), however, suggests the minstrel roots of the production. Yale Collection of American Literature, Beinecke Rare Book and Manuscript Library, Yale University.

a display of "the Leading Buck and Wing Dancers of Dixie."[86] When a "watermelon cart hitched to a tiny ox and mule" was driven onto the stage partway through the performance, audiences delighted in the scramble that ensued as performers broke ranks and raced for the fruit.[87] In a truly bizarre twist, the performance closed with the raising of portraits of John Brown, Frederick Douglass, Harriet Beecher Stowe, Ulysses S. Grant, William Tecumseh Sherman, and Abraham Lincoln at the back of the stage.[88] What three abolitionists, a pair of Union generals, and the "Great Emancipator" would have thought of *Black America* remains an open question.

From the beginning, however, the stage production was of secondary importance. *Black America* offered something more. Advertisements promised "real living scenes in the life of the real Southern negro, amidst real cotton fields and in real cabins."[89] Consciously setting itself apart from minstrelsy and plantation shows, *Black America* aimed not only to entertain but also to immerse visitors in the southern plantation. There were any number of sites at which northerners could witness a representation of the South, but only at *Black America* could they walk among the cabins, touch the cotton bolls, and interact with the performers.[90] As the *New York Times* described it, "The cabins scattered over the grounds are exact reproductions of the old slave cabins in the South, and the work in the cotton fields that they perform is as it was when the negroes were chattels and not free men."[91] The *Boston Globe* was equally impressed when *Black America* arrived in New England: "There are real cabins, a real cotton gin and press, real cotton field with cotton growing, real levees with steamboat landing and southern palms and foliage, merging into the scenic effects, and other real features of southern life."[92] Northern visitors truly felt transported to another time and place. The result, the *New York Tribune* wrote, was "as different from any plantation scenes in a play as the World's Fair was from a country fair in Skowhegan."[93]

This obsession with reality carried over to the cast of *Black America*, which, Nate Salsbury insisted, was exclusively made up of genuine black southerners. One advertisement promised "500 real negroes from the South (none from the North), as they are in THEIR OWN PLANTATION LIFE."[94] In an interview with a Boston newspaper, Salsbury reiterated that "all these negroes came from the South, mostly from Virginia, North and South Carolina. They are not show people," he continued, "but are the genuinely southern negro in all his types." Salsbury even claimed to have turned away a number of talented black performers simply because they were northerners; as he put it, "I will not have anything but a southern negro in the company."[95] Commentators in Boston and New York were quick to pick up on this fact. "The combination comprises over 500 darkies from the various slave States, selected with great care for their peculiar fitness as types of their race," the *New York Tribune* insisted.[96] Another paper noted that the performers were "brought direct from the fields and plantations of the South, and put before the Northern people, presenting animated scenes of rural simplicity in Dixie, among which they were born and brought up."[97] The *Boston Globe* affirmed that the performers "are genuine darkies, and southern darkies at that."[98] Unlike minstrelsy and the plantation shows, which could only mimic southern black life, *Black America* strove to re-create it.

Upon scrutiny, Salsbury's claim that the production's cast was made up of a collection of southern theatrical neophytes does not stand up. In fact, Billy McClain had combed the ranks of the nation's black performers to fill the enormous cast with singers, dancers, impersonators, instrumentalists, and comedians. By one estimate, *Black America* employed sixty-three black jubilee quartets.[99] The true nature of the production appears to have been common knowledge among black performers themselves. In an interview published in the *Chicago Tribune* during the run of *Black America*, an unnamed African American musician offhandedly noted that the production was providing work for a "good many" of the East Coast's "colored stage people."[100] Though it is conceivable that all of these performers were southerners (depending on how loosely one defines the term), it is clear that Salsbury's claim to have imported the whole cast directly from the plantations of the South was an intentional misstatement.

And yet the fact that Salsbury felt compelled to repeatedly make such a claim merits consideration, as does the remarkable credulity with which the northern press treated his account of the performers' origins. "One of the chief charms of the exhibition is its naturalness," a New York newspaper wrote. "'Black America' produces the genuine article," a style of southern black life that "cannot be imitated even by the blacks of the North, much less by the negro delineators of modern minstrelsy."[101] Northern reviewers frequently claimed that the cast of *Black America* was not performing at all. "The people who take part in 'Black America' are not actors," one visitor declared. "They are the natural production of a section of the United States, and all they are called upon to do in the giving of 'Black America' is to act naturally." Since Nate Salsbury had claimed that any performer "attempting affectation will be instantly discharged," audiences would be sure to "see before them no imitations, nothing out of what is real."[102] For some, *Black America* even turned into a kind of educational experience. The *New York Tribune* noted that the visitors to the show were of a higher social class than those who generally attended minstrel performances, a fact it attributed to the event's pedagogical function. "Many of the best known citizens of New-York and Brooklyn have been to the exhibition not only once, but two or three times," the *Tribune* noted.[103] Perhaps for this reason, *Black America* was deemed appropriate for children. After estimating that 90 percent of a crowd of 7,000 was made up of "little folks," the *Boston Globe* expressed its approval, explaining that the show "has an artistic and educative value far above its qualifications as a means of passing a pleasant hour."[104]

Clever promotion aside, *Black America* was a minstrel show, plain and simple. Whatever they had done before they joined *Black America*, the cast spent the summer of 1895 performing black southernness. The language of authenticity was a mere marketing ploy (albeit a very effective one). At the *Black America* grounds, visitors were encouraged to believe that they were experiencing real life rather than watching a performance. Minstrelsy and plantation shows might emphasize their realism, but *Black America* claimed to be something else entirely. For northern visitors, *Black America* seemed to offer an opportunity to observe southern African Americans in their natural environment, free from the artificiality and confines of the theater. In fact, Salsbury and McClain had simply turned the entire fairgrounds into a minstrel stage. Performers played their assigned roles in the village just as surely as they played them onstage. Northern visitors had little interest in interacting with experienced African American stage performers. Instead, they longed to engage with "the true southern darkey" as the minstrel stage had long depicted him—natural, uneducated, deferent, unselfconscious, and hilarious.[105] The cast of *Black America* obliged them. The production would not be the final word in the evolution of minstrelsy, and African Americans would take the form in important new directions in the years after 1895. *Black America* was, however, a fitting capstone to two decades' worth of minstrel promotion and practice. For its boosters and its patrons alike, *Black America* became something more than a minstrel or plantation show. It did not pretend to be an authentic representation of black life in the South. Rather, it was able to deny that it was a representation at all.

The complicity of black performers in the spread of a false and dangerous set of images of the South raises important and troubling questions.

How did minstrel performers understand their role in shaping popular perceptions of the South? How did they feel about the pictures of blackness that they helped to perpetuate on the minstrel stage? What went through Billy Kersands's mind when he delighted audiences (and upheld crude racial stereotypes) by cramming billiard balls or a saucer and teacup inside his unusually large mouth?[106] Or songwriter James Bland's when he penned another song condoning slavery and idealizing "ole massa"? Or Billy McClain's, when he surveyed the field at *Black America* and saw the results of his handiwork: an idealized and wholly unrealistic depiction of the southern plantation that was accepted as truth by thousands of visitors every day? Since giving an honest answer to these questions during their careers would have jeopardized these black minstrels' ability to make a living, historians may never know for sure. Nonetheless, a couple of comments are in order.

First of all, to expect black performers to have been more selective in their employment is to vastly overestimate the options available to them in the late nineteenth-century United States. For most black performers, the choice was stark: minstrelsy or an occupation outside of show business. Black performers were captive to public demand, and the northern public was clear in its love for the minstrel show. As W. C. Handy, famed African American bluesman and one-time minstrel, explained in his memoirs, minstrelsy was the only option for an aspiring black musician in the late nineteenth century. "All the best talent of that generation came down the same drain," he wrote. "The composers, the singers, the musicians, the speakers, the stage performers—the minstrel shows got them all."[107] Minstrel stars earned high wages, top billing, public acclaim, and their choice of companies. Rank-and-file cast members were more likely to find themselves underemployed, underappreciated, underpaid, and constantly on the road. For many black performers in the late nineteenth century, however, eking out an existence in minstrelsy proved better than any of the available alternatives.[108]

Given these realities, it is not surprising that one can find numerous examples of covert resistance embedded in black minstrel performances.[109] Though James Bland's song "Tell the Children Good-bye" does not directly address slavery, its opening lines—"I've packed up my satchel / and I soon will have to leave you, / Tell all de children goodbye"—strongly conjure the memory of the slave market.[110] The plantation that Bland evokes in this song is one scarred by generations of forced partings and tearful goodbyes. As such, it offers an important corrective to the idealized visions of slavery far more common in minstrel music. Another striking example of this sort of resistance occurred in September 1895. When the *Black America* stage show returned to New York after its Boston stint (this time sans plantation village), a *New York Tribune* critic noticed a peculiar tendency in the choral singing. He found the choir's renditions of minstrel tunes such as "The Old Folks at Home" and "Massa's in the Cold, Cold Ground" disappointing, their performances marked by a conspicuous lack of feeling and "a disregard of fluency and homogeneity of tone." Other songs—notably the Union army anthem "John Brown's Body"—seemed to bring out the singers' best.[111] It was, he reflected, like watching two different choruses. Though the *Tribune* reviewer expressed puzzlement over this phenomenon, the explanation seems rather obvious. The *Black America* choir was expressing a musical preference for one type of song over the other and, in so doing, making a clear political statement. No matter how frequently such incidents occurred, however, one still faces the fact that thousands of African Americans chose to take to the minstrel stage in the late nineteenth century, voluntarily recapitulating (and thereby affirming) damaging white-authored stereotypes.

In the end, it may be that black minstrel performers simply did not feel that they had cause to be ashamed. Though African American elites freely expressed their disdain for minstrelsy, the African American masses seem to have felt otherwise, and popular black minstrel troupes played to African American audiences as well as white ones.[112] In 1891, a long-time minstrel performer named Ike Simond (alias "Old Slack") published a memoir of his years in the minstrel business. The book is filled with Simond's encounters with minstrel royalty (including Billy Kersands, James Bland, and J. H. Haverly) and betrays a somewhat exaggerated sense of its author's place in the history of his chosen art form. More than this, Simond's memoir bespeaks deep pride and a sense that his twenty-five years in the minstrel business were well-spent.[113] W. C. Handy was also cheerful about his years on the minstrel circuit. Minstrelsy "had taken me from Cuba to California, from Canada to Mexico," he wrote. "It had taught me a way of life I still consider the only one for me."[114]

There are, after all, a variety of yardsticks by which to judge black minstrelsy. Though they were forced to work within the confines of minstrelsy, late nineteenth-century African American performers were able to make a space in which to present their gifts to the public. Minstrel depictions of the South may have had more to do with northern racism than with southern reality, but the talent that filled auditoriums was real. Many black performers got their start on the minstrel stage, and from minstrel roots would grow powerful African American musical forms including jazz and ragtime. After the turn of the century, a new cadre of African American performers and composers, notably Bert Williams and George Walker, began to transform minstrelsy. In their hands, popular performance emerged as subversive force capable of challenging many of the stereotypes and misrepresentations that an earlier generation of minstrel performers had helped to construct and perpetuate.[115] Along with a candid admission of the limitations and liabilities that the minstrel form imposed, therefore, it is important to remember the ways African American performers were able to make the minstrel stage their own.

## Spectacle and Politics in Gilded Age "Tom Shows"

When it was published in 1852, Harriet Beecher Stowe's abolitionist novel *Uncle Tom's Cabin* quickly became the most inflammatory, explosive, and politically significant literary text of the antebellum period. Adapted to the stage shortly thereafter, *Uncle Tom's Cabin*'s moral fervor, emotional power, and iconic characters soon made it a theatrical institution. Throughout the 1850s, northern audiences thrilled to dramatic reenactments of Eliza's escape across the Ohio River, Uncle Tom's tender relationship with Little Eva, and Tom's brutal death at the hands of Simon Legree. Antebellum productions of *Uncle Tom's Cabin* largely fell into two categories. Most followed George Aiken's 1852 dramatic adaptation, which was faithful to the novel's plot and to its author's abolitionist intentions.[116] Some productions, however, explicitly sought to discredit and undercut Stowe's antislavery message. Minstrel shows and southern propagandists both offered proslavery dramatic adaptations of *Uncle Tom's Cabin* in the years before the Civil War.[117] Regardless, the political content of the play remained its defining characteristic in the antebellum period. Love it or loathe it, *Uncle Tom's Cabin* made a powerful political statement on the stage as surely as on the page.

By the 1880s, however, a curious thing had happened. Stage productions of *Uncle Tom's Cabin* remained popular, but the political edge had largely evaporated. In place of politics, postbellum productions of *Uncle Tom's Cabin* came to emphasize display and spectacle. Much like postwar minstrelsy, "Tom shows" competed to offer the largest cast, the most sumptuous scenery, and the oddest novelties. Where antebellum audiences had mourned for Tom and cursed Legree, Gilded Age crowds cheered for trained Siberian bloodhounds and spectacular plantation dance routines. At the postwar Tom show, in fact, the story of *Uncle Tom's Cabin* largely disappeared, becoming little more than a vehicle for stage trickery and ostentatious display. In the process, the political content that had once defined the production became increasingly peripheral.[118] The movement from the abolitionism of *Uncle Tom's Cabin* to the empty spectacle of the Gilded Age Tom show offers an interesting chapter in the cultural history of the postbellum United States. More than this, it provides a unique perspective on the nation's declining commitment to African American rights and a prime example of the role that popular culture played in this transition.

It has been estimated that there were nearly 500 *Uncle Tom's Cabin* companies on tour in the 1890s, meaning that Tom shows were a fairly regular occurrence in any major city or town of the North.[119] Residents of Detroit who missed Jay Rial's company in early October 1881, for instance, only needed to wait one week for Henry Jarrett's version of *Uncle Tom's Cabin* to roll into town.[120] During the 1893 theatrical season, San Francisco theater-goers could have seen four different traveling Tom shows.[121] Given this extraordinarily crowded marketplace, it was incumbent on each *Uncle Tom's Cabin* company to do more than simply entertain. Since each production was judged not on its own merits but in relation to what had come before, Tom shows were under constant pressure to update, expand, and innovate. The familiarity of the *Uncle Tom's Cabin* story to most audience members made it exceedingly difficult for companies to offer much that was new when it came to the plot, the script, or the characters. Tom shows therefore maintained the familiar storyline while resorting to a variety of strategies designed to provide audiences with a show worth their time and money.

As in contemporary minstrelsy, size sold. Promoters trumpeted the expanse and expense of their productions in the hopes of attracting audiences. In 1895, one Tom show—aptly dubbed Stowe and Co.—proclaimed itself the "LARGEST AND BEST IN THE WORLD," boasting that it required "3 special cars to transport this, the World's Great 'U.T.C.'"[122] Anthony & Ellis' Mammoth Uncle Tom's Cabin Company also declared itself the "Largest and Best" Tom show on the road, though its "30 Artists" actually made the show relatively small.[123] E. O. Rogers's company promised fifty performers, Edwin F. Davis's Uncle Tom's Cabin Co. featured fifty-one, while a production of the Ideal Uncle Tom's Cabin company boasted a cast of eighty.[124] Even grander was C. H. Smith's Double Mammoth Uncle

Tom's Cabin Company, which lived up to its name with a cast numbering 100.[125] Clearly, Tom shows were not immune to the supersized logic of Gilded Age popular theater. Though a production may have featured only a dozen speaking roles, companies filled out their cast lists and padded their choruses in order to be able to claim to be the biggest and the most spectacular Tom show around.

This emphasis on scale led to one of the most peculiar developments in the Tom show: the "double company." Such companies featured two actors playing one role during a single performance of *Uncle Tom's Cabin*. Most often, this honor was reserved for Topsy and Lawyer Marks. In Stowe's novel, Topsy the slave girl was a humorous though ultimately redemptive character, while Marks was a scheming slave trader. In the play, both were transformed into lowbrow comic figures. Since both characters were traditional audience favorites, Tom show promoters seem to have assumed that two would be better than one. By the early 1880s, any Tom show worth its salt was able to boast "2 TOPSYS AND 2 MARKS."[126] An 1881 Boston production advertised "the two great Topsys—Kate Partington and Minnie Foster."[127] A Detroit newspaper announced the imminent arrival of an Uncle Tom company with the headline: "We've Another Uncle Tom's Cabin Snap—A Double Headed One, Too."[128]

No Tom show was complete without its traveling menagerie. A centerpiece of the *Uncle Tom's Cabin* stage show was the slave mother Eliza's daring dash to freedom across the frozen Ohio River. To add interest and realism to this scene, Tom shows employed trained dogs to chase the fugitive across the stage. In typical fashion, companies competed to offer the largest and the most exotic canine contingent. A thrilling chase scene featuring a pack of "IMPORTED, TRAINED, NEGRO-HUNTING SIBERIAN BLOODHOUNDS" quickly became an expected part of a production.[129] Individual Tom show dogs even won a degree of fame. A particularly impressive hound named Sultan was reportedly a favorite of ex-president Ulysses S. Grant and the object of a $3,000 standing offer from Buffalo Bill Cody.[130] Donkeys, generally associated with the character Marks, were also central to many Tom shows. Jay Rial's Ideal Uncle Tom's Cabin Company featured "the celebrated trick donkey, 'Jerry,'" while Anthony & Ellis' Famous Ideal Double Company traveled with "'KNOX,' the smallest donkey on the stage."[131] Miniature ponies, usually the property of Little Eva, often rounded out a Tom show's animal contingent. By 1892, when an announcement for an upcoming Tom show in the *New York Clipper* blithely noted that "the usual amount of dogs, ponies, donkeys, etc. will be carried," animals were as much a part of stage productions of *Uncle Tom's Cabin* as Tom, Little Eva, or Simon Legree.[132]

Many *Uncle Tom's Cabin* companies went to even more elaborate lengths to attract patronage. Magnificent stage pictures (or tableaux) often punctuated performances. The death of Little Eva was transformed into a spectacular set piece, featuring hosts of angels and a graceful ascension into heaven. In 1882, Anthony & Ellis's Company presented the "Grand Transformation—The beautiful Gates Ajar—Eva in Heaven—Magnificent Allegorical Tableaux."[133] The Stetson *Uncle Tom's Cabin* company used special lighting for its depiction of "EVA'S ASCENT TO THE GOLDEN REALMS."[134] Other productions turned to less celestial topics in their search for spectacle. Peck and Fursman's company offered a reenactment of "the exciting historical race between the Mississippi River steamers ROBERT E. LEE and NATCHEZ," featuring "two complete practical working models of these famous boats." The "explosion scene," the company insisted, "will be without exception the most complete piece of stage craft ever accomplished."[135] Perhaps the most bizarre Tom show spectacle occurred during a production that featured the black Australian boxer Peter Jackson in the role of Uncle Tom. Though critics praised Jackson's theatrical skills, audiences were more interested in his pugilistic ones; a three-round boxing exhibition proved the highlight of each performance.[136]

Given the Tom show's wholehearted embrace of spectacle, it is unsurprising that grand plantation scenes were staged with some frequency. The first interracial production of *Uncle Tom's Cabin*, featuring black minstrel star Sam Lucas, opened in 1880.[137] From this point forward, Tom shows provided an important source of work for black performers. Their involvement, in turn, encouraged productions of *Uncle Tom's Cabin* to present elaborate plantation scenes, featuring cotton picking, jubilee singing, and slave dancing. Salter and Martin's Uncle Tom's Cabin Company promised "Cotton Fields and Plantation Scenes Portraying the Habits of the Southern Negroes with effect."[138] An 1885 Tom show had its own "plantation festival," complete with a forty-person jubilee chorus.[139] An 1886 performance, meanwhile, took place entirely outside, on a lawn "transformed into a plantation, with fields of cotton, slaves at work, houses, and cabins and other distinguishing features of the land of Dixie."[140] As they turned even Simon Legree's plantation—depicted in Stowe's text as a hellish factory in the fields—into another opportunity for lavish spectacle and display, Gilded Age Tom shows proved just how unmoored they had become from the text on which they were ostensibly based.

By the 1890s, *Uncle Tom's Cabin* was little more than a vehicle for a series of outrageous theatrical novelties. Ironically, the familiarity of the story—*Uncle Tom's Cabin* was, after all, the bestselling novel of the century—meant that productions could largely ignore the plot. Northern audiences did not come to the theater to see what happened to Uncle Tom and Little Eva; they knew how the story ended long before they arrived. They came, instead, to see how a particular production of *Uncle Tom's Cabin* would distinguish itself from all those that had come before. How fabulous was Eva's ascension to heaven? How spectacular was the plantation dancing? How tight was the jubilee harmony? How breathtaking was Eliza's dash across the ice? How ferocious were the dogs? How hilarious was Topsy? How many Topsies were there? In the midst of the carnival of excess that was a Gilded Age Tom show, the story itself largely disappeared. Indeed, one did not go to a Tom show to see *Uncle Tom's Cabin*. One went to a Tom show to see the pageantry, spectacle, and one-upmanship that invariably came with a production of *Uncle Tom's Cabin*.

This fact had serious political consequences. Though slavery itself was dead by the 1880s and 1890s, its memory was not. Depictions of the peculiar institution were alive and well on the northern stage. In this context, *Uncle Tom's Cabin* might have offered a powerful voice for racial justice in the South and in the nation. In stark contrast to the happy slaves and idealized race relations presented on the minstrel stage, Stowe's novel depicted a brutal, dehumanizing labor regime that poisoned all those who came in contact with it. Even in the Gilded Age, a stage production of *Uncle Tom's Cabin* that remained true to the spirit of Stowe's original text could have offered a powerful corrective to the misrepresentations rampant in postbellum minstrelsy. At best, such a production might have offered a shining example of the political potency of popular art and rejuvenated northern interest in racial democracy. At the very least, it could have offered a self-conscious alternative to the nearly hegemonic power of the minstrel stage.

Rather than a counterpoint to minstrelsy, however, Tom shows offered a complement to it. Both cultural forms achieved significant popularity largely by peddling idealized and unrealistic images of the southern past. Less than thirty years after the close of the Civil War, northern theatrical promoters proved willing to sacrifice history on the altar of entertainment. In spite of the best effort of groups like the Fisk Jubilee Singers, Gilded Age performance culture largely whitewashed the violence of slavery, idealized southern race relations, and denied the significance of emancipation and Reconstruction. In so doing, it rationalized northern inaction in the face

This advertisement for Stetson's Big Double Uncle Tom's Cabin Co. makes plain the connections between Tom shows and minstrelsy (ca. 1880s or 1890s). Harry Birdoff Collection, Harriet Beecher Stowe Center, Hartford, Connecticut.

of southern racial strife and denied the possibility of African American equality. Performance culture, of course, was only one site at which the nature of the South was debated and contested in the years after 1877. In the context of the continuing assault on African American civil and political rights, however, one should not overlook the significance of the stories of the South presented on the northern stage. Through sheer repetition and familiarity, the thoroughly unreconstructed visions of the southern past presented in northern performance culture were deeply woven into the region's consciousness. As white northerners considered their response to the Jim Crow regime put in place after 1890, they carried this cultural baggage with them.

# PART III
# Destruction, 1890–1915

# CHAPTER SIX

# Jim Crow Nation

In February 1900, in the midst of a Senate debate over suffrage in the territory of Hawaii, South Carolina's Benjamin Tillman took the floor. Recalling his state's 1895 disfranchisement of African American voters, "Pitchfork Ben" affirmed his support for a restricted suffrage in Hawaii before using the issue of nonwhite voting to transition to more familiar rhetorical ground. With his usual flair, Tillman began to rail against northern snobbery. He chastised the region for its studied unwillingness to recognize the severity of the South's racial crisis and the wisdom of its chosen remedies: political disfranchisement, physical segregation, and, when necessary, racial violence and spectacle lynching. "You have been sneering at us a long time, and I don't like it," he thundered. "I'm getting tired of these taunts and sneers. . . . You won't let us alone." Tillman's charge spoke volumes about the mindset of the white supremacist South at the dawn of the twentieth century. But so did a tart retort offered by Senator John C. Spooner of Wisconsin: "The Senator won't let us let him alone."[1]

Between 1890 and 1910, white supremacist southerners worked a revolution in southern race politics.[2] Into the 1880s, African Americans across the South continued to vote, to serve in public office, and to enjoy unfettered access to the region's conveyances and conveniences. In addition, a homegrown, self-conscious, and highly successful African American elite offered a powerful testament to the possibility of black uplift and racial self-improvement.[3] By 1890, these circumstances had grown intolerable to many in the white South, who set out to secure white supremacy, limit black opportunity, and destroy what remained of the Reconstruction amendments in one fell swoop. Over the next two decades, white southerners established an adaptable and flexible system of oppression and control that would maintain white supremacy almost inviolate until the mid-twentieth century. Through the systematic revision of southern state constitutions and the careful deployment of such antidemocratic means as the Grandfather Clause and the white primary, white southerners turned the region's electoral politics lily white.[4] The rise of spatial segregation and the definition of certain spaces as "white" and others as "colored" built the reality of white supremacy into the very landscape of the region.[5] The lynchings and race riots that convulsed the South after 1890 bespoke a single truth: black bodies, corporeal just as surely as political, had no rights that the southern white man was bound to respect.[6] Jim Crow segregation, disfranchisement, and systematic racial violence were neither natural nor inevitable. They were, instead, the result of a planned and coordinated attack on African American civil and political rights.

And yet Senator Spooner had a point. For a people that only wanted to be "let alone" to solve their race problem, white southerners spent an inordinate amount of time and energy keeping themselves in the forefront of the national conversation. For all the system's violence and injustice, the birth of Jim Crow occurred in a remarkably forthright and open manner. Building on the foundations laid by New South boosters, authors of plantation fiction, and minstrel show promoters, turn-of-the-century white supremacists harnessed the political power of stories. The architects of Jim Crow waged two concurrent campaigns in the 1890s and 1900s. The first was a determined and vicious push for political domination that produced disfranchisement, segregation, and spectacle lynching. The second campaign was waged not with grandfather clauses, nooses, and "whites only" placards but with words. It was a sustained public relations barrage, a storytelling offensive that aimed to explain and naturalize racial murder and political domination. In their overtures to the nation, white southerners presided over a bit of rhetorical alchemy, making the unnatural seem natural, the discriminatory seem charitable, and the hard work of white supremacy appear inevitable and barely conscious. The white South did not deserve the scorn of the nation, the literary emissaries of Jim Crow informed northern audiences, but its sympathy. Disfranchisement, segregation, and lynching were not tools of dominance but reflexive acts of self-defense. The white South was innocent, even praiseworthy. This campaign of explanation went hand-in-hand with the campaign for domination. To secure white supremacy at home, the white South needed to justify it to the rest of the nation.

Throughout the turn-of-the-century years, missionaries of Jim Crow sought to do just that. White southern treatments of the "negro question" or the "race problem" were common fare in northern journals and news-papers.[7] Major presses based in New York and Boston published scores of books advocating disfranchisement, explaining segregation, and defending racial violence. Southern speakers spread the gospel of white supremacy throughout Yankeedom, at chautauquas and city halls, in churches and on town greens.[8] Atlanta journalist John Temple Graves—"that silvern-tongued orator from Dixie"—seemed to spend more time above the Mason-Dixon line than below it, offering dozens of well-attended and well-reported speeches on African American degeneracy, the inevitability of race conflict, and the need for a physical separation of the races.[9] An actor-turned-preacher-turned-novelist-turned-demagogue named Thomas Dixon Jr. opened a window onto the mind of the white supremacist South in his wildly popular novels *The Leopard's Spots* and *The Clansman*.[10] When Ben Tillman was not decrying northern insensitivity in the Senate, he was happily taking "Yankee money" for a nearly endless string of speaking engagements.[11] Disfranchisement, segregation, and lynching were not carried out on tiptoes. Jim Crow arrived amid trumpets and fanfare.

Recognizing the political significance of this white supremacist appeal, turn-of-the-century African American activists offered their own stories of the South. It is no coincidence that some of the era's most significant black-authored texts (including Ida B. Wells's antilynching pamphlets, Booker T. Washington's *Up from Slavery*, W. E. B. Du Bois's Atlanta University stud-ies, and Charles Chesnutt's *The Marrow of Tradition*) were largely medi-tations on the character of the South. The battle over the race question was also, on a fundamental level, a conflict over the nature of the region. While southern white supremacists offered northern audiences tales of degraded black criminals and terrorized white victims, African American commentators drew a picture of black progress and white brutality. Black activists denied that Jim Crow was a matter of self-defense. Instead, they argued that white actions constituted a bald-faced seizure of power and a calculated denial of hard-earned political and civil rights. In a desperate attempt to defend black lives and livelihoods, African Americans presented the nation with their own vision of affairs in Dixie.

Throughout the formative years of Jim Crow, white supremacists and African Americans waged a literary war for the soul of the South. Though segregation, disfranchisement, and lynching were largely southern phe-nomena, discussion of the race question pervaded the culture of the na-tion at large. Northerners seeking to understand affairs in the South faced a choice between two starkly divergent visions of the region. Were the architects of Jim Crow acting out of self-defense or self-aggrandizement? Were southern African Americans a race of dangerous criminals or a systematically abused minority? Did southern whites possess an inherent racial expertise or just a cynical desire to dominate? Would federal defense of African American rights constitute a return to the sectional hostilities of Reconstruction or a much needed intervention on behalf of a beleaguered population? In this context, Ben Tillman and his white supremacist ilk could not afford to let the nation alone; neither could their African American adversaries. The battle to control southern race politics during the formative years of Jim Crow was waged largely in the cultural spaces of the North.

In the end, the outcome of this contest must be judged in terms of the nation's actions (or lack thereof). Apart from a pair of abortive attempts to rekindle federal involvement in southern racial affairs—the 1890 Lodge Federal Elections Bill would have allowed oversight of some southern elections, while the 1901 Crumpacker Bill would have reduced southern congressional representation on the basis of African American disfranchisement—the nation did little to stop the rise of Jim Crow.[12] This was not a function of ignorance or a lack of awareness. Given the remarkable transparency with which the destruction of African American civil rights was carried out in the South, northern nonaction can only be understood as a conscious decision. By the end of the first decade of the twentieth century, the white South had successfully embroiled the nation in its racial politics. If white northerners did not precisely laud segregation or rush to overturn the Fifteenth Amendment (as some radical white southerners encouraged), they also did little to turn back the tide of white supremacy. To fail to recognize the extent to which the nation at large engaged with and participated in the destruction of African American rights is to give the North a pass on one of the more unsavory aspects of American history. Jim Crow was not born fully formed and insuperable. Northerners watched at every step. For the most part, they did nothing. White southerners built Jim Crow, but they did it on a national stage. By the end of the first decade of the twentieth century, the new birth of freedom heralded by Reconstruction was but a distant memory. In its place stood Jim Crow Nation.

### From the Southern Question to the Negro Problem

In the 1890s, the white supremacist South invented a crisis. They called it the Negro Problem. In order to explain their unprecedented attacks on

African American citizenship, southern white supremacists told the nation a horror story. They insisted that the South was under siege. Three decades after emancipation, they said, African Americans had proven themselves incapable of advancement, unworthy of the ballot, and indifferent to laws, thrift, and education. They had become a danger to the well-being, even the continued survival, of southern whites. The inferiority of a race had become the torment of a region. Gone were the days of faithful slaves and cordial relations between the races. The region now lived, in the words of Georgia Methodist bishop Atticus Haygood, under a "black shadow."[13] The race question was all-encompassing, the color line written in blood. A dangerous beast had been unleashed during Reconstruction, and the white South was fighting for its life.[14]

Within the South, stories of black deviance and degeneracy proved remarkably effective in consolidating white opinion, papering over economic divisions within the white community, and securing the ascendancy of the Democratic Party.[15] Nationally, sordid tales of black violence and white victimhood became a powerful tool in shaping popular opinion. As a story broadcast to the nation at large, the Negro Problem allowed southern white supremacists to turn a concerted effort to undermine racial democracy into an unthinking reaction to a regional emergency. Jim Crow was the result of a series of conscious acts and deliberate steps. Disfranchisement necessitated the amending of state constitutions; segregation demanded the reordering of urban space; spectacle lynching required mob coordination and planning. To hear Jim Crow propagandists tell it, however, southern white supremacy was essentially *defensive*. Proximity to an inferior race constituted a clear and present danger to the white South. By this logic, segregation, disfranchisement, and lynching were not part of a malicious plan to secure political and economic control. They were the desperate responses of a people whose very survival was at stake.

When stripped to its bare essentials, much of the so-called Negro Problem was actually reducible to a single, glaring truth: there were black people in the South. If Dixie remained a region apart in the 1890s, southern whites insisted, this distinctiveness had little to do with the lingering hatreds of the Civil War or with any sort of innate difference between northern and southern whites. Instead, it was the region's sizable black population that set the South off from the national mainstream. The fact that two distinct, antagonistic races lived in the South was, John Temple Graves told a Chautauqua, New York, audience, "a problem of safety, of domestic tranquility, of national unity, the greatest problem facing the people of this transcendent age."[16] Jim Crow propagandists argued that the very presence of African Americans constituted a direct assault on southern whiteness. Southern whites did not curtail black civil and political rights out of malice or greed. They were simply reacting to a racial crisis that threatened everything they held dear.

To explain segregation and disfranchisement, white supremacists offered a timeless maxim: two distinct races could not coexist for any extended period of time. In his 1889 book *An Appeal to Pharaoh*, Carlyle McKinley put the matter in terms a child (or a northerner) could understand: "Birds and beasts, fishes, reptiles and insects—nay, the very trees of the forest, and flowers and weeds of the field—group themselves together, 'after their kind,' in obedience to the edict that was pronounced at creation. Man is no exception to the universal rule."[17] In framing the matter as a racial question rather than a political one, white supremacist storytellers denied their own agency in the restriction of African American civil and political rights. White southerners insisted that they were simply responding to biological imperatives. In his 1894 text *The Ills of the South*, Mississippi educator Charles Otken wrote that "history has no record of two races as unlike as the Anglo-Saxon and the African, living together in harmony under like conditions."[18] Racial friction, in this telling, was inevitable. Before the Civil War, the civilizing and uplifting influence of slavery had allowed the races to maintain a relatively peaceful coexistence, but with these restraints removed, nature must take over. The forced proximity of the two races in the South amounted to a racial time bomb. Segregation promised the only solution.

Such issues were no mere abstractions. The specter of interracial sex and the destruction of the white race seemed to underlay every instance of black/white contact. The central theme of the postwar era, Alabama senator John Morgan argued in the Boston-based *Arena*, was the "constant but futile effort on the part of the negro race and their political masters to force them, by political pressure and by acts of Congress, upon the white race as equals and associates in their domestic relations." This "invasion," Morgan prophesied, "shall not cease until the races become homogenous through complete admixture."[19] Needless to say, white southerners would stand for no such thing. "The colour line must be drawn firmly, unflinchingly— without deviation or interruption of any kind whatever," Tulane University professor William Benjamin Smith declared. "The moment the bar of absolute separation is thrown down in the South, that moment the bloom of her spirit is blighted forever, the promise of her destiny is annulled, the proud fabric of her future slips into dust and ashes."[20] As they set about drawing a strict color line through the public spaces of the South, white southerners argued that they were only acting out of self-defense.

Southern white supremacists applied a similar logic to the political realm, perfecting a tale of an electorate corrupted and contaminated by hordes of ignorant black voters. Disfranchisement was not a perversion of democracy, they insisted, but an attempt to purify the body politic. In an 1890 article in the *Arena*, South Carolina senator and former governor Wade Hampton postulated that "the prosperity and the perpetuity of government depend most on the homogeneity of its people." As such, "no greater crime against civilization, humanity, constitutional rights and Christianity was ever perpetrated under the guise of philanthropy" than the enfranchisement of African Americans during Reconstruction.[21] By their very presence in the South's towns and cities, black men and women imperiled the safety of public space; as voters, they had the same polluting effect on the political realm. In a speech delivered in Boston in 1899, former Georgia governor William J. Northen insisted that the black vote had produced nothing except "division and hate and blood and carnage." Black voters, Northen said, saw the ballot as a weapon, a means to "dominate the white people of the South." African American enfranchisement, he concluded, was "responsible for most of the blood that has been spilt, the outrages that have been perpetrated, and the sorrows that have come to the whites and negroes of the South."[22] Such a dangerous and unnatural state of affairs demanded immediate action.

By 1908, every ex-Confederate state had taken steps to limit African American suffrage. Though the mechanisms of disfranchisement varied by state, southern white supremacists were remarkably forthright about their intentions and their tactics. They were also quick to celebrate their successes. In 1900, Walter Hawley, a southern-born reporter for the *New York Sun*, cheered that "a permanent and peaceful ending of an unbearable condition has now been accomplished in South Carolina, Mississippi, and Louisiana, where ignorant and half-savage blacks have by legal means been deprived of the right to vote." Hawley gleefully anticipated that "in the coming national election less than 500,000 negroes living in Southern States will cast ballots that will count in that contest, and within ten years probably not more than half that number will possess or attempt to exercise the right of suffrage."[23] On Capitol Hill, Ben Tillman was equally candid. "We took the government away. We stuffed ballot boxes. We are not ashamed of it," he told the Senate. "We called a constitutional convention

*Collier's Weekly* depiction of the Wilmington Race Riot, November 26, 1898. Intentionally or not, the illustrator re-created the southern white supremacist version of events in Wilmington. Library of Congress.

and we eliminated all the colored people we could."[24] These were not the words of a population that had stolen the vote. They were the exultations of a class that had emerged victorious from a struggle for its political life.

The Wilmington massacre of 1898 offers a prime example of how Jim Crow propagandists rationalized the violence of turn-of-the-century white supremacist politics.[25] On November 8, 1898, a mob of armed white men took to the streets of Wilmington, North Carolina, and disbanded the local government in an organized, calculated perversion of democracy. Wilmington had been the site of a thriving black community and an important source of African American political power in the Old North State. When the dust settled, dozens of African Americans lay dead, hundreds more had fled the city forever, and a white supremacist government had been installed in place of the city's duly elected biracial regime. Shortly thereafter, North Carolina's white supremacist Democrats amended the state constitution to disfranchise black voters. Even in an era marked by savage racial violence and paramilitary politics, the Wilmington massacre was notable for its brutality and the unabashedly self-serving motivations of its perpetrators.

In the weeks that followed the massacre, however, the white storytellers of Wilmington went to work. By the time they finished, the Wilmington massacre had been transformed from a racially motivated coup d'état into a praiseworthy exercise in white political resistance. The propagandists of white supremacy told a familiar tale of incompetent local government, black political malfeasance, and white self-defense. According to A. J. McKelway, who rushed defenses of white Wilmingtonians to two major northern journals in the immediate aftermath of the riot, the elevation of African Americans to public office had spawned a black crime spree, with "burglaries, highway robberies, or incendiary fires of almost nightly occurrence."[26] The "reputable citizens" of Wilmington told *Collier's Weekly* correspondent Charles Francis Bourke that "white women found it unsafe to walk through the streets in daytime without an escort."[27] The riot, in this telling, was a wholly justifiable response to outrageous circumstances. The illustration that *Collier's* printed along with its article on the coup—featuring two armed black men and, conspicuously, no sign of white violence or provocation—helped to advance this reading of events in Wilmington. McKelway went so far as to praise the white men of Wilmington for the calm and measured manner with which they overthrew the city government. Such "patience and self-restraint," he concluded, have "no parallel in the history of popular government."[28] Thanks to the skillful manipulation of white supremacist storytellers, events in Wilmington took on another character entirely. Democracy was turned into black domination, violent perpetrators became innocent victims, and racial massacre was recast as justifiable self-defense. Such was the explanatory power of the Negro Problem.

The most familiar manifestation of the larger Negro Problem discourse was the figure of the black rapist. White southerners conjured up a rape epidemic during the 1890s, using it to justify segregation, disfranchisement, and, most frequently, lynching. The specter of black-on-white rape proved remarkably effective in marshaling white (and white supremacist) unity in the South, but it was no less significant in securing northern complicity in Jim Crow.[29] The literature of the Negro Problem was saturated with lurid descriptions of black-on-white sexual assault. White supremacists claimed that a generation removed from the enforced civilization of slavery, African American men were rapidly degenerating. They had come to pose an ever present threat to the safety of southern white women. Tales of white female victimhood proved to be the South's most effective rhetorical weapon. Visions of the fearsome black ravisher lurking in the dark constituted an almost unimpeachable argument in favor of white supremacy, licensing systematic barbarism and unbelievable acts of cruelty.

White supremacist commentators vied to offer the most blood-curdling depictions of black rapists and brutalized white women. Charles H. Smith took a break from his day job spinning folksy wisdom in newspaper columns under the alias Bill Arp to ask northern readers of the *Forum* to consider the black monster "who would whet his knife and lie in wait for a little school-girl twelve years old, and after he had seized and gagged and ravished her, cut her throat and drag her to a ditch and tumble her in."[30] In a speech before the American Academy of Political and Social Science, North Carolinian George T. Winston offered more of the same: "The black brute is lurking in the dark, a monstrous beast, crazed with lust. His ferocity is almost demoniacal. A mad bull or a tiger could scarcely be more brutal."[31] Speaking in Boston, former Georgia governor William J. Northen forced his audience to imagine that the white South's terror was its own:

> Let it be your daughter, sitting at tea with husband and little children, happily enjoying an evening meal. A bloody murderer stealthily approaches, and with the blow of a fiend, buries an axe to the eye in the husband's head; he fells him; beat his brains till they spread in sickening horror over the floor. . . . See him then as he confronts, in all the appalling horror of fiendish glare, with uplifted axe, the trembling form of the wife—your daughter (can you imagine)[,] curses as only a demon from hell can swear; jerks her down—your daughter, (can you imagine), and rolls her in the warm blood of the only one she had hoped to defend her from such awful, awful, awful cruelty and shame! Hear her piteous cries as she writhes for two long, long hours in the embrace of a villain, and then see her as she falls at her father's gate—your gate (can you imagine), half clad and in a death swoon, to tell her horrible, sickening, disgusting, loathsome story?

Northen's refrain—"can you imagine"—brought the white supremacist message to the very hearts, homes, and hearths of the North. "What would you do?" Northen challenged his audience. "What would your neighbors do? What would a mob in Massachusetts do?"[32] Southern whites were not monsters, Northen insisted. They were average men and women put in extraordinary circumstances. Put in a similar situation, even the most sanctimonious Yankee would act the same way.

Southern white women proved willing and able to plead their own case.[33] Writing in the *Independent* in 1899, Corra Harris promised to provide northern readers with a "Southern Woman's View" of the race question. "In this section of Georgia, which is not far from Palmetto, no white girl, however young, or woman, however old, would be safe alone on the public highway," Harris wrote. "The farmers do not dare to leave their wives and daughters at home while they are in the fields."[34] Northern men would be slower to criticize southern lynchings, Harris charged, if their own wives and daughters lived in such mortal danger. Women's rights advocate and future senator Rebecca Latimer Felton was no quivering southern belle, but she knew how to mobilize one for political gain. Playing to an audience on both sides of the Mason-Dixon line, Felton scolded and cajoled the manhood of the South into a righteous defense of its beleaguered womanhood, famously asserting that "if it requires lynching to protect woman's dearest possession from ravaging, drunken human beasts, then I say lynch a thousand negroes a week if it is necessary."[35]

The black rapist and the cowering white victim functioned as gendered metaphors that gave structure to the entire discourse of the Negro Problem. The narrative of the bloodthirsty black rapist and the innocent white victim perfectly mirrored the white South's larger explanation of its racial troubles. White supremacists insisted that the entire South was under siege, locked in mortal combat with a bloodthirsty inferior. Southern womanhood came to stand in for all those things that the white South valued: political sovereignty, personal honor, upright decorum, the purity of the blood line. The fears that animated the white South's rape complex— violation, contamination, destruction—were precisely those that white supremacists argued underlay *every* interaction with black southerners. The ballot box and the streetcar risked the same defilement as the rape victim. In an attempt to depict its plight, to make the crisis that engulfed it readily understandable to a northern audience, the white South could not have found a better proxy than its own ever-threatened womanhood.

Having explained its crisis to the nation, the white supremacist South demanded the time and space to reconfigure its racial order free from outside interference. This meant, first of all, a renunciation of federal interventionism. "The solution must be left to time and to the sound judgment of the

Southern people, who have the trouble before them every day," Mississippi senator James Z. George wrote in the *Independent*. "So far the difficulties have been greatly augmented by the (probably well intended tho unwise) interference of people who know little of the situation."[36] Mississippi governor John Marshall Stone agreed, adding that "external interference cannot possibly promote the solution of this Southern problem or lessen its tension, and that at last it must be left in the hands of the communities immediately and directly concerned in its settlement and adjustment."[37] In the context of the South's great crisis, northerners owed it to their southern brethren to refrain from any action that could worsen the predicament. As agrarian reformer and Populist leader Tom Watson put it in an 1892 article in the *Arena*, "the Northern leader who really desires to see a better state of things in the South, puts his finger on the hands of the clock and forces them backward every time he intermeddles with the question."[38]

Northern criticism of southern racial affairs was frequently figured as an assault on the safety and security of the white South. A number of commentators made a direct link between northern support for African American rights and episodes of black-on-white violence in the South. Bishop Atticus Haygood hypothesized that "if papers and men, remote from them, said as much to the negro concerning the enormity of rape as they say to the white people concerning the enormity of lynching, raping would become less common."[39] Corra Harris criticized northern commentators who put their "sympathies wholly on the side of these brutes, passing with a word over their crimes to bitter denunciation of our avengers." Such actions had dire effects, Harris insisted. "When you men of the North condemn your brethren here in the usual wholesale manner the negro takes it for granted you are on his side."[40] The result, invariably, was an increase in sexual assault. According to the logic of the Negro Problem, the failure to support the white South amounted to an attack on white womanhood. When the editor of the *Boston Transcript* criticized Rebecca Latimer Felton for her "lynch a thousand negroes a week" comment, Felton shot back a fiery response. "We owe much of our race troubles in the South to the maudlin sympathy for the negro, and the unmitigated hate for Southern people, indulged in by such journals," Felton wrote. "Pliable ignorance on the part of the negro and malignity on the part of the Boston Transcript has made, perhaps, many unfortunate, but criminal victims for the lyncher's rope all over the South."[41]

As a story about life in the turn-of-the-century South, the Negro Problem naturalized an unprecedented reign of legislative manipulation, social apartheid, and physical terror. It allowed southern white supremacists to cast themselves as beleaguered victims, and to turn a campaign of racial oppression into a desperate struggle for survival. The discourse of the Negro Problem functioned as a sort of cultural inoculation against federal intervention. In mass-market magazines, popular books, and well-publicized speeches, white southerners self-consciously cultivated a crisis atmosphere in order to secure the nation's compliance during the formative years of Jim Crow. If the situation in the South was truly as critical as Jim Crow apologists insisted it was, northerners had no choice but to fall in line. As it excused and explained the actions of the white South—no matter how unjust or bloody they became—the Negro Problem helped to secure the nation's acquiescence in the systematic destruction of African American civil and political rights.

## Black Counternarratives in the Era of Jim Crow

The white supremacist discourse of the Negro Problem brought forth an impassioned response from African American activists. On the ground in the South, African Americans employed a variety of strategies to contest racial oppression even after the passage of disfranchisement statutes made traditional political activity nearly impossible.[42] At the same time, a cadre of black activists based largely in the North struggled against white supremacy in the realm of culture. Understanding that southern segregation, disfranchisement, and lynching required northern acquiescence, black activists sought to counteract the stories that rationalized the white supremacist reign of terror. As long as the propagandists of Jim Crow enjoyed a monopoly on the ear and the conscience of the nation, black civil and political rights would remain insecure. The future of the race largely depended on the success with which African Americans made their case to the nation. To halt the march of Jim Crow, black activists would need to do some storytelling of their own.[43]

Of course, even breaking into the national conversation was a challenge for black storytellers. In her 1892 text *A Voice from the South*, black feminist Anna Julia Cooper complained of the difficulty that African Americans, particularly women, had in making themselves heard amid the chorus of voices addressing the race question. Black people were the "great *silent* factor" in the "American commonwealth," Cooper wrote.[44] Though they were "the most talked about of all the forces in this diversified civilization," they were seldom allowed to speak for themselves, instead remaining "the dumb skeleton in the closet provoking ceaseless harangues . . . but little understood and seldom consulted."[45] Cooper elaborated on these themes in a 1902 speech, "The Ethics of the Negro Question." She complained that the tales of white southern alarmists enjoyed such wide currency that most white northerners seemed inclined to accept them as true and to ignore all evidence to the contrary. As a result, the African American point of view on the race question remained largely unheard. When a black person attempted "to speak out an intelligible utterance," Cooper complained, whites heard only the echoes of their own "preconceived notions." The effect, she said, was something like a "phonograph" that "talks back what is talked into" it.[46] Until African Americans rectified this narrative inequality, their civil and political rights were in grave danger.

The construction of a more positive vision of racial character was a central task facing African American activists in the turn-of-the-century years. Where Jim Crow propagandists emphasized degeneracy and criminality, African American storytellers accentuated capability and achievement. Cooper's close associate Frances Ellen Watkins Harper undertook precisely this sort of project in her 1892 novel *Iola Leroy*.[47] The novel's political significance is tied to the racial awakening of its mixed-race title character. Raised free and white, Iola Leroy is forced to confront the reality of the color line when an uncle's betrayal reveals her black blood. From this point forward, Leroy devotes her life to African American advancement. Given popular preoccupations with black ignorance, violence, and criminality, Harper's title character—pious, educated, committed, eloquent, and, significantly, female—marked an important new departure. The novel's political message, however, runs deeper than this. Though Leroy might easily pass for white (indeed, she had unknowingly done so as a child), she consistently refuses to do so. Once her mixed-race heritage is revealed to her, Leroy consciously *chooses* blackness. The character's act of self-definition allowed Harper to recast the meaning of race in the United States. The novel's affirmation of blackness as a positive good undercut the most basic logic of the Negro Problem discourse.[48]

Catalogs of black achievement offered a simple but effective way to strike a blow against white supremacy. These texts frequently consisted of little more than lists of black accomplishments or biographies of notable African Americans. In context, however, such work carried a powerful racial message.[49] "The Progress of the Afro-American since Emancipation," black historian I. Garland Penn's contribution to an 1893 pamphlet protesting the treatment of African Americans at the World's Columbian Exposition, listed black attainments in education, the professions, literature, journalism, religion, business, art, and music. The piece even included a table of black property ownership by state and a partial list of patents granted to African American inventors since the war.[50] Shortly after the turn of the century, journalist Pauline Hopkins published a twelve-part series called "Famous Men of the Negro Race" in the *Colored American Magazine*, following it with another called "Famous Women of the Negro Race."[51] In 1903, poet Paul Laurence Dunbar authored a piece on "Representative American Negroes" that lauded the successes of a pantheon of significant African Americans, including scholars W. E. B. Du Bois and Kelly Miller, politicians George White and Robert Smalls, and educators William H. Councill and Booker T. Washington.[52] Such unapologetic celebrations of black ability offered a corrective to a culture obsessed with black inferiority and degeneracy.

Though narratives of African American achievement were quite common in the post-Reconstruction era, few black leaders proved as adept at telling these stories as Booker T. Washington. For nearly a decade after his triumphant speech at the 1895 Atlanta exposition, "The Wizard of Tuskegee" stood unchallenged as the race's most influential spokesperson and the South's most significant emissary of black progress.[53] Offering a steady stream of rags-to-riches tales and southern success stories, Washington's relentless optimism provided a stark contrast to the dire prophecies and predictions of white supremacist naysayers. In speeches and articles in the popular press, Washington depicted the graduates of the Tuskegee Institute as living embodiments of racial capability, whose training and skills served as a powerful rebuke to white supremacy.[54] Of course, Booker T. Washington was his own best argument. Though he peppered his articles and speeches with anecdotes from his past, it was in his 1901 classic *Up from Slavery* that Washington most clearly offered his own history—his rise from a Virginia slave cabin to the pinnacle of fame and influence—as a response to white supremacy. When he described his accomplishments at Tuskegee or reminded readers of his connections with leading politicians, financiers, and philanthropists, Washington was, in fact, arguing for the potential of black America. In *Up from Slavery*, Washington sought to fashion himself into something more than a race leader. He became a symbol and a testament to possibility. He was the living, breathing contradiction to all the foul charges levied by southern white supremacists. In the era of the Negro Problem, Booker T. Washington offered himself as a *solution*.[55]

Emphasizing progress and achievement was not the only strategy that African American agitators employed in their attacks on white supremacy. Black activists also worked to shift the nation's focus from the alleged misdeeds of African Americans to the unchecked violence and brutality of white southerners. This alternative conceptualization of southern affairs recalled images of the Bloody South popularized during the reign of the Ku Klux Klan. Black activists claimed that the Klan spirit was alive and well in the turn-of-the-century South. Jim Crow, they argued, was a reflection of white race hatred, not black degeneracy. African American commentators affirmed that there was a dangerous, unpredictable, antidemocratic racial entity in the South. They insisted, however, that the guilty race was *white*, not black.

After the threat of a lynching made her an unwilling expatriate to the North, journalist Ida B. Wells devoted herself to a single goal: opening the eyes of the nation to the true state of affairs in the South. Wells's antilynching pamphlets, notably *Southern Horrors* (1892) and *A Red Record* (1895), describe dozens of extralegal executions carried out for crimes ranging from well-poisoning to wife-beating to stealing hogs to being "saucy."[56] While they spun tales of black deviance for northern audiences, white supremacists willingly countenanced mass murder, forced castration, and burning alive. In the South, Wells argued, "the rule of the mob is absolute."[57] The pertinent issue, Wells insisted, was not black crime, but the seemingly inexhaustible bloodlust of white southerners. Wells's antilynching pamphlets do not make for easy reading; they were not meant to. Wells hoped that her parade of gut-wrenching southern outrages would shock the North into action. She would force the nation to gaze on the foul deeds of the South until "public opinion shall demand a cessation of the reign of barbarism, lynch law, and stake burning."[58] When "a demand goes up from fearless and persistent reformers from press and pulpit, from industrial and moral associations that this shall be so from Maine to Texas and from ocean to ocean," Wells promised, black lives in the South might finally be secure.[59]

If anyone could match the blistering rhetorical fury of Ida B. Wells, it was Bishop Henry McNeal Turner. Since the Civil War, Turner had been a tireless critic of southern white violence and race hatred. By the 1890s, he had lost all hope in a future for African Americans in the United States, becoming the nation's most vocal and influential advocate for repatriation to Africa.[60] "Other American Negroes may sing My country, 'tis of thee, Sweet land of liberty, Of thee we sing," Turner told a race convention in

1893. "But here is one Negro, whose tongue grows palsied, whenever he is invited to put music to these lines."[61] Convinced that white America was constitutionally incapable of justice, righteousness, or good faith, Turner urged black Americans to look to Africa. Though he never espoused compulsory colonization, each new explosion of southern brutality seemed to validate Turner's notion that God's plan for the race lay across the ocean. "If you desire to know what I really think of this and all other lynching bees," he wrote in the aftermath of a quadruple lynching in Palmetto, Georgia, "I can tell you in a few words: I believe it is the negative voice of God speaking to the nation and thundering in the ears of the negro to wake up."[62] Turner argued that a nation of lynchers deserved the scorn of the civilized world. Rather than begging southern white murderers for rights and respect, African Americans should "return to the land of our ancestors, and establish our own nation, civilization, laws, customs, style of manufacture."[63] Free from the tyranny of whites and resettled in their ancestral homeland, African Americans would write themselves a new history.

In making a claim on the nation's sympathy, turn-of-the-century African American activists authored their own stories of the South. Some emphasized the noteworthy accomplishments of a race unjustly maligned, while others sought to expose the horrific misdeeds of southern white supremacy. At the same time, black activists worked to call attention to the lies, falsehoods, fabrications, and fictions with which southern white supremacists defended their actions. They attempted to prove that white tales of black deviance and degeneracy were nothing but a smokescreen, a narrative meant to obscure a concerted white supremacist assault on African American citizenship. Simply acknowledging the structures of storytelling that underlay southern white supremacy—particularly the so-called Negro Problem—could prove an important political strategy. By pointing out the constructed and essentially fictive nature of much white supremacist discourse, black agitators hoped to make visible the all-important cultural work of Jim Crow. The Negro Problem, black commentators insisted, was not a sociological fact or a matter of evolutionary biology. It was just a story.

In 1895, Frederick Douglass, the aging black abolitionist and tireless advocate for African American rights, published an article titled "Why Is the Negro Lynched?" in the *A.M.E. Church Review*. Rather than lynching itself, Douglass's last published work focused on the "so-called, but mis-called 'Negro Problem.'"[64] With bitter sarcasm, Douglass marveled at the rapidity with which the South's black population had turned into a race of rampaging beasts and hardened criminals—that is, if one took the white South's word for it. Though the practice of lynching was abhorrent, Douglass argued, the rhetorical constructions that justified it may have been even more damaging. By casting it as a "Negro Problem" (that is, a problem with African Americans) southern whites blamed lynching's victims and excused, even celebrated, their own conduct. The discourse of the Negro Problem turned murderers into heroes and victims into criminals. "The marvel is that this old trick of misnaming things, so often displayed by Southern politicians, should have worked so well for the bad cause in which it is now employed," Douglass wrote. The "American people have fallen in with the bad idea that this is a Negro problem."[65] As long as the white South was thus allowed to justify its brutality, black lives would be expendable and black rights nonexistent. "Words are things," Douglass warned, and must be taken seriously.[66]

A number of black commentators took aim at the bugbear of the black rapist, the white supremacist South's preferred excuse for lynching and mob violence. Ida B. Wells attacked the "thread bare lie" of black-on-white rape in her antilynching pamphlets.[67] She recognized that the rape complex had proven remarkably effective in securing northern complicity in the face of southern racial violence. "Humanity abhors the assailant of womanhood, and this charge upon the Negro at once placed him beyond the pale of human sympathy," she wrote. "With such unanimity, earnestness and apparent candor was this charge made and reiterated that the world has accepted the story that the Negro is a monster which the Southern white man has painted him."[68] In an article in the *North American Review*, journalist and activist Mary Church Terrell wrote that "the North frequently sympathizes with the Southern mob because it has been led to believe that the negro's diabolical assaults upon white women are the chief cause of lynching."[69] She insisted, however, that this explanation failed to accord with the facts. "It is a great mistake to suppose that rape is the real cause of lynching in the South," Terrell wrote.[70] The black rapist was a figment of the white supremacist imagination, a devilishly effective story concocted by those who sought to "misrepresent and maliciously to slander a race already resting under burdens greater than it can bear."[71]

In his 1901 novel *The Marrow of Tradition*, Charles Chesnutt powerfully dramatized the fictive nature of the black rapist construction.[72] In Chesnutt's retelling of the 1898 Wilmington coup, the murder (and alleged rape) of the spinster Polly Ochiltree serves as a call-to-arms for white supremacy. Encouraged by a trio of scheming politicians who urge them to rally to the defense of a victimized white womanhood, townspeople in Chesnutt's fictional "Wellington" prepare to lynch a mild-mannered black butler named Sandy Campbell. There is only one problem: Sandy Campbell is innocent. A debauched white aristocrat named Tom Delamere, possessing a talent for minstrelsy and a paucity of scruples, had blacked his face and passed himself off as Campbell in order to steal money to pay his gambling debts. During the robbery, Delamere had killed Mrs. Ochiltree. In *The Marrow of Tradition*, therefore, the would-be rapist and murderer is *white*. The black criminal is merely the construction of a white man who uses the figure as a means to achieve his own malicious ends. From here, it was only a small logical step to Chesnutt's larger argument. The diabolical and dangerous black rapist, he argued, was an elaborate fiction constructed in the hopes of furthering a white supremacist agenda. White southerners had built themselves a bogeyman and used him to rationalize segregation, disfranchisement, and lynching. If most white supremacists did not go as far as Tom Delamere—that is, blacking up and embodying the role of the deviant and dangerous black man—the difference was a matter of degree, not of kind.[73]

Although black commentators insisted that the discourse of the Negro Problem was merely a white supremacist fairytale, they could not deny its real-world consequences. Jim Crow propaganda rationalized disfranchisement, explained segregation, and normalized unbelievable acts of white cruelty. Southern white supremacists expertly manipulated northern public opinion, distorting affairs in the South and robbing African Americans of the sympathy they deserved and the national support they needed. Even as they derided it as a fiction, therefore, turn-of-the-century African Americans recognized that they lived in a world shaped by the Negro Problem. The "unasked question" with which black scholar and activist W. E. B. Du Bois opened his classic *The Souls of Black Folk*—"How does it feel to be a problem?"—reflects a deep awareness of this predicament.[74] The fact that the Negro Problem was a story, a fictive construction that said more about white fears than black reality, did not make its burden any lighter or its effects any less real. Both personally and politically, the discourse of the Negro Problem presented a formidable obstacle to African American advancement and equality.

## The Race Experts

At 8:00 P.M. on May 8, 1900, an esteemed collection of southern white men came together in Montgomery, Alabama, for the inaugural meeting of the Southern Society for the Promotion of the Study of Race Conditions and Problems in the South. The object of the society, according to its constitution, was to provide a forum for "the expression of the varied and even antagonistic convictions of representative Southern men on the problems growing out of the race conditions obtaining in the South." Believing that "frank and full discussion" of the race problem would advance the "education of the public mind," the members of the society committed themselves to a program of correspondence and publication, culminating in the Montgomery conference.[75] Though the society's constitution espoused no purpose beyond the frank and open exchange of ideas, the very structure of the organization established definite parameters within which this discussion could take place. "As Southern men," the constitution read, "we feel that any real solution of our race problem can be best approached by the people of the South themselves, and under the leadership of those forces which represent the dominant influences of our own section."[76] To this end, the constitution stipulated that "Southern men of every creed and political party shall be eligible to membership in the society."[77] The Southern Society, then, was just that: a *southern* society. The race problem, members reasoned, was primarily a southern concern. As such, its solution needed to emanate from the white South. Believing that "much of true progress in connection with our racial difficulties has been embarrassed by the fact that the leadership of Southern opinion has been too largely attempted merely from the North," society members simply chose to exclude nonsoutherners.[78] Aside from a few northerners "asked to be present as our guests," the Southern Society might as well have hung a sign: No Yankees Allowed.[79]

The 1900 Montgomery Conference anticipated one of the central tenets animating southern white supremacy after the turn of the century. Though the discourse of the Negro Problem remained a powerful tool in the South's storytelling arsenal, white supremacists began to supplement this tale with another: a vision of the white southerner as race expert. White supremacists laid claim to an innate racial knowledge, and, by extension, a particular ability to manage the South's black population. This new story reflected changing political realities in the South. By 1902, Georgia was the only ex-Confederate state whose electorate remained even nominally biracial. The white South had survived the firestorm of the 1890s and, by its own estimation, had its race problem well in hand. Securing northern consent, however, remained a challenge. The race-expert discourse smoothed Jim Crow's rough edges and papered over its unsightly spots. It naturalized white supremacist acts of domination and helped to deflect any critiques that emanated from outside of the South. Once cast as necessary evils, segregation and disfranchisement now came to be celebrated as positive goods. Jim Crow must be reasonable, rational, and responsible. It was, after all, the handiwork of the nation's race experts.

The race-expert narrative turned southernness into a credential. On the basis of a knowledge rooted in years of experience and lifelong proximity to African Americans, white supremacists insisted on their own ability to speak authoritatively on racial matters. "The South claims the possession of knowledge superior to that of the North with regard to the negro's wants, character, and condition," a Tuscaloosa, Alabama, resident named Walter Guild explained in the *Arena* in 1900. "The Southerner is 'on the ground' with generations of experience and with every facility for accurate information."[80] North Carolina senator Furnifold Simmons professed a "more or less intimate acquaintance with the character and adaptation and capabilities of the negro," while Ben Tillman "claimed by birth, education, long residence in the south, and opportunity for and constant application to the study of the topic, to be peculiarly fitted to discuss this gravest problem before the nation."[81] A deep knowledge of African American character was a part of a southern upbringing, these storytellers insisted. Race knowledge was an organic outgrowth of the South's rich soil. "I am a Southern woman, thirty-five years of age, married, and the mother of one child," a contributor to the *Independent* wrote. "I know the negro from tradition and experience."[82]

Such claims were hardly value neutral. Since the white South could claim to "know the negro," it followed that white southerners should have the exclusive right to control the region's racial affairs. "What is called 'race prejudice' is not race prejudice at all, but is race knowledge," Mississippi representative John Sharp Williams explained to the northern readership of *Metropolitan Magazine* in 1907. "If I were to call our race feeling anything etymologically, I would call it a 'post-judice' and not a 'pre-judice.'"[83] The language of expertise rationalized the violence of lynching, the illegality of disfranchisement, and the arbitrary injustice of segregation. White southerners were not cruel, unjust, or oppressive, they simply knew better than the rest of the nation. Thomas Nelson Page opened a 1907 *McClure's* article with the statement that "there are some things so well understood by those who know the negroes, as to appear to them almost truisms." Among them, Page cited racial degeneracy, the derogatory impact of "outside influences" on black-white relations in the South, the negative effects of political involvement on black conduct, and African Americans' overriding desire to cohabitate with white women.[84] Page's framing—in which a failure to accept the truth of African American inferiority signified a complete lack of racial knowledge—perfectly encapsulated the political logic of the race-expert discourse.

Southern racial storytellers frequently offered their personal histories as proof of their transcendent racial knowledge. Hearkening back to the by-gone days of slavery, white southerners reminisced about doting mammies and faithful slaves. Alabaman Hilary A. Herbert told the Montgomery convention about an ancient slave named Uncle Peter, whose kindliness and religiosity offered Herbert some hope for a positive solution to the Negro Problem.[85] Joel Chandler Harris opened a three-part *Saturday Evening Review* series on "The Negro as the South Sees Him," with a lengthy treatment of the "Old-Time Darky."[86] George T. Winston fondly recalled time spent with his father's slaves. "There is a marvelous attraction between a white child and a Negro," he explained. "I have eaten many a meal with my father's slaves in their cabins, always treated with consideration, respect and affection, but not greater than I myself felt for the master and mistress of the humble cabin."[87] Slaveholding, in this narrative, constituted a form of expertise. A personal history with favorite slaves allowed white southerners to speak authoritatively on racial matters more generally.

With few exceptions, white southerners eschewed the burgeoning fields of eugenics and race science.[88] Southern race experts were unlikely to compile tables of European races or to debate the relative merits of different classes of immigrants. Mississippian Alfred Holt Stone offered the American Sociological Society a rather blunt assessment of the worth of much of this research in a 1907 speech in Madison, Wisconsin. "We have wasted an infinite amount of time in interminable controversies over the relative superiority and inferiority of different races," Stone offered. "Such discussions have a certain value when conducted by scientific men in a purely scientific spirit. But for the purpose of explaining or establishing any fixed principle of race relations they are little better than worthless."[89] Rather than measuring skulls and studying genetic histories, white southerners grounded their authority in a different sort of knowledge, one born of experience and heritage. In explaining his credentials in the opening pages of his 1905 text *The Color Line*, William Benjamin Smith of Tulane University turned to his southernness rather than his academic training. "The present writer professes neither authority nor special fitness to speak for the South," Smith explained, but the facts of race issue are "so transparent and so easily understood of any one here in the midst that he cannot believe he commits any sensible error in his statement of the case."[90] This sort of knowledge could not be measured in a laboratory, read in a book, or learned in school. It was the in-born possession of the white South.

The logical corollary to white southern racial expertise was a conviction that northerners were incapable of understanding the idiosyncrasies of southern race relations. "It is hardly possible for any one, no matter how great his intellect or resplendent his genius, to reach a correct conclusion without understanding the conditions that surround the subject," Alabama governor Joseph F. Johnston said at the Montgomery conference. "And yet many who never set foot in the South are ready to solve this question without study or reflection."[91] Northerners might pick up a book or make a journey through the South, but they could never know the region's black population in the way that native whites did. The Mason-Dixon line became an intellectual boundary, neatly separating those who were authorized to speak on the race problem from those who were not.

Since Yankees failed to understand the race question, the North's pet theories—notions like African American citizenship and voting rights— must be equally fatuous. "Reasoning from abstract philanthropy at the distance of a thousand miles," John Temple Graves told a Chicago audience, the North "cherishes a fixed faith in the unity of race and the equality of man."[92] From such a distance, democracy and equality might have their appeal. Those who were on the ground in the South had no such illusions. "The distant mountain is picturesque; it is only those who are struggling up its side that see the danger of the precipices they walk besides, the chasm that yawns, or the boulder that has slain," a southern woman named Ellen Barret Ligon wrote in *Good Housekeeping*. "Negro equality is a theory; negro outrages and insults resulting from the inculcation of the doctrine of equality are hideous facts."[93] William Benjamin Smith was equally dismissive of the northern point of view. "The testimony of the North and of Europe is hardly more relevant than would be that of the Martians," Smith wrote. "Their treatment of the subject is merely academic and sentimental. They have generous ethical ideas, respectable but well-worn and overworked maxims, high humanitarian principles" but "the practical problem never confronts them in its unrelieved difficulties and dangers." He concluded that "Southern hearts are not less benevolent than Northern, but Southern eyes are of necessity in this matter wide open, while most others are shut."[94] African American citizenship might seem reasonable to those safely ensconced in their northern homes. To those on the ground in the South, black inferiority was an undeniable fact.

At its heart, the question was an epistemological one. Jim Crow propagandists insisted that their own racial knowledge, rooted in firsthand experience, was of a purer, higher, and truer stripe than northern racial thought. "I apprehend that the purposes of this discussion will best be served by excluding from consideration every form of expression save a plain statement of facts," Alfred Moore Waddell, one of the leaders of the 1898 Wilmington coup, told the Montgomery conference. "I am here not to philosophize, or to discuss abstractions, but to tell what I know from observation and experience."[95] This, Waddell insisted, was the only standpoint from which to tackle the race question. Thomas Nelson Page admitted that "the attitude of the Northerners toward the negro is often based on a sentiment which does the highest honor to its possessors," but he suggested that "sentiment" was dangerous unless "informed by knowledge."[96] Writing in the *Independent*, Georgian Corra Harris warned that "you cannot judge these people sitting on a divan in New York, looking at them through stained-glass windows of poetic sentimentality."[97] Northerners might offer theories, sentiments, and abstractions, but they lacked the firsthand experience of white southerners. As such, they should leave racial affairs to those equipped to understand them.

Though he was comparatively moderate on the race issue, Bishop Atticus Haygood of Georgia was dismissive of much northern opinion on racial matters. In a memorable article written for the *Methodist Review*, Haygood described a meeting with a young northerner who proposed, on the basis of a six-week trip through the South, to write the definitive study of southern race relations. "His childlike unconsciousness of his ample ignorance of the subjects involved in his proposed solution was almost beautiful," Haygood wrote. "It was certainly incomparable, and imitable only by men from his section, whose provincialism accounts largely for its egotism." Haygood found the young man's conceit to be typical of northerners, who displayed a marked "incapacity to be just when writing, speaking, or thinking of Southern white people."[98] Their approach to the race question was colored by this distrust. Though Haygood urged his fellow white southerners to display justice and Christian charity in their dealings with the region's black population, he was certain that ill-conceived northern criticism did little to improve southern race relations. The solution to the race question must come from the South.

Thomas Dixon Jr.'s 1902 novel *The Leopard's Spots* offers a striking sketch of northern racial ignorance in the figure of Miss Susan Walker, a Boston philanthropist who appears in the novel only long enough to get the worst of an encounter with John Durham, a preacher whose southern chivalry does not extend to meddlesome Yankees. In the wake of the Civil War, Miss Walker arrives in the fictional North Carolina town of Hambright, prepared to devote her "life and fortune" to the "education and the elevation of the Negro race."[99] In typical northern fashion, however, Miss Walker's philanthropy combines an inflated sense of self-worth with an almost total lack of firsthand experience with black people. Her half-baked plans, Durham fears, will only exacerbate southern racial strife. "In the settlement of this Negro question you are an insolent interloper," he thunders. "You're worse; you are a [willful], spoiled child of rich and powerful parents playing with matches in a powder-mill."[100] Durham, the white southerner, plays the role of the hardened realist, fearful for the future of the South and entirely pessimistic regarding the possibility of African American improvement. Miss Walker is the flighty northern idealist, an impulsive philanthropist whose previous good works include the construction of a "home for homeless cats" in Boston.[101] White southern knowledge must triumph over northern theories, Dixon insisted. In the midst of a racial crisis, the South could little afford to indulge in sentiment and philanthropy.

Of course, there were some caveats to the logic of white southern race expertise. As Andrew Sledd and John Spencer Bassett, a pair of outspoken southern racial moderates, discovered, white skin and a southern birth did not excuse the expression of heterodox sentiments.[102] By the same token, some northerners, including statistician Walter Willcox and African American journalist William Hannibal Thomas, were accorded great respect in southern white supremacist circles precisely because they came down on the right side of the race question in spite of their nativity.[103] These exceptions serve as a reminder that white southern racial expertise was never an objective fact or a hard and fast rule. It was, instead, a story that white southerners told in order to invalidate the arguments of those with whom they disagreed. The power of the race-expert discourse lay in its ability to cut off conversation on the race question even before it started. Southerners possessed knowledge, northerners had theories; white supremacy was rooted in fact, support for African American civil and political rights was mere sentimentalism. In insisting that their own race knowledge was of a higher type than northern race knowledge, white supremacist southerners preemptively justified their actions and denied the possibility of engaged, intelligent support for African American rights. In the process, they turned a campaign of terror, discrimination, and vote suppression into a rational, reasonable response to larger racial truths.

It is no coincidence that turn-of-the-century white supremacist writings frequently invoked the memory of Reconstruction. White southerners found in the immediate postwar period ample evidence for their claims to a monopoly on race knowledge. The evils of Reconstruction, white supremacist storytellers insisted, flowed directly from wrongheaded northern intervention in southern racial policy. Reconstruction offered the ultimate example of the dangers that outside involvement in southern affairs posed to the welfare of the region. In the late 1860s, northern radicals and demagogues had nearly destroyed the South. Little more than three decades later, as southern white supremacists took steps to limit black political participation and overturn what remained of the constitutional legacies of Reconstruction, they set out to ensure that the nation would not make the same mistake again.[104]

"What, then, is this thing which we call 'Reconstruction'?" Mississippian Alfred Holt Stone asked in his 1908 book *Studies in the American Race Problem*. "In the South it is that period of misery which covered the decade or more between 1865 and 1875 or 1880, and measured the time during which the control of their domestic affairs was lost and regained by Southern white men."[105] Stone cast Reconstruction as an unparalleled crisis of authority. The "misery" of the period was directly related to the failure of southern white men to control the region's domestic (that is, racial) affairs. Thomas Nelson Page argued that the rebuilding of the postwar South had "called for the widest knowledge and the broadest wisdom," attributes that he assumed were the exclusive purview of white southerners. "Unhappily," Page concluded, "both knowledge and wisdom appeared to have been resolutely banished in the treatment of the subject."[106] White southern accounts of Reconstruction carefully juxtaposed northern abstraction and idealism with white southern knowledge and realism. Flying by the seat of their collective pants as they ruled the South from afar, northern Republicans had overturned the South's racial order and imperiled the region's very existence.

When they were feeling charitable, white southern commentators argued that the northern architects of Reconstruction simply had not known any better. Joel Chandler Harris believed that any injustice suffered by African Americans since the war had "been almost entirely due to the unwise and unnecessary crusade inaugurated . . . by the politicians of the North, who neither knew nor cared anything for the situation at the South."[107] Other southern storytellers cited more sinister motives. Mississippi's James K. Vardaman was not one to mince words. "The crime of all crimes," he claimed, "was committed when, in the agonizing spasm of infuriated men, just after the Civil War, the North expressed its hatred of the white people of the South in the amendments to the Constitution which vested the negro with all the rights and privileges of citizenship."[108] Whether they chalked it up to ignorance or malice, however, two points were particularly salient. First, Jim Crow propagandists cast Reconstruction as the darkest, most dangerous moment in U.S. history. Second, they uniformly agreed that northern control of southern race relations was a defining characteristic of the period. This reading of Reconstruction vindicated the conduct of the white supremacist South and presented a powerful argument against further federal interventionism.

Such thinking led southern white supremacists to resurrect a familiar figure. Clifton R. Breckinridge of Arkansas used his speech at the Southern Society meeting in Montgomery to critique the "locusts of Egypt," the "professional patriot, the mountebank, the harpy, the carpet-bagger."[109] At the same conference, Alabama congressman Hilary Herbert insisted that "it was the carpet-bagger that drew the color line."[110] Virginian Myrta Lockett Avary offered a similar treatment in her 1906 memoir. "The carpet-bagger was the all-important figure in Dixie after the war. He was lord of our domain; he bred discord between races, kept up war between sections, created riots and published the tale of them, laying all blame on whites."[111] The carpetbagger stereotype proved every bit as well-suited to the political needs of the early twentieth century as to the 1860s and 1870s. To raise the specter of the carpetbagger was to none-too-subtly remind northern readers of the sordid history of northern involvement in the racial affairs of the South.

Thomas Nelson Page and Joel Chandler Harris each published Reconstruction-themed novels around the turn of the twentieth century. Both Page's *Red Rock* (1898) and Harris's *Gabriel Tolliver* (1902) took scheming, conniving carpetbaggers as their central villains. In Harris's novel, the arrival of the carpetbagger Gilbert Hotchkiss signals the onset of Radical Reconstruction in Shady Dale, Georgia. An abolitionist and philanthropist, Hotchkiss sees in Reconstruction an opportunity to put his theories to the test. After doing all he can to promote a "spirit of incendiarism among the negroes," however, the "ill-informed emissary of race hatred and sectional prejudice" is summarily shot by one of his black constituents.[112] If Harris at least accorded his carpetbag villain the benefit of a sincere (though misguided) belief in racial equality, Page's Jonadeb Leech proves to be a bloodsucker every bit as odious as his namesake. Leech has no particular regard for black rights or citizenship, but he finds in the Reconstruction of the South a perfect opportunity for self-aggrandizement. Leech is the embodiment of corrupt carpetbagger rule, the "vampire, sucking the life-blood of the people; the harpy, battering on the writhing body of the prostrate State."[113] The carpetbaggers might be gone, but the lessons they taught retained their salience.

As they remembered Reconstruction, turn-of-the-century white southerners were actually speaking about their own place and time. As a southern historian by the name of Woodrow Wilson put it in a 1901 article in the *Atlantic Monthly*, "Reconstruction is still a revolutionary matter. Those who delve in it find it like a banked fire, still hot and fiery within, for all it has lain under the ashes for a whole generation; and a thing to take fire from."[114] In the mind of the white supremacist South, Reconstruction meant two things: racial chaos and northern control. Juxtaposing their own adept handling of the Negro Problem in the 1890s with the North's abortive attempts to legislate impossibilities in the 1860s, white supremacists could conclude that history had borne out their status as the proper arbiters of southern racial norms. Only white southerners, with their innate expertise and their hard-won experience, possessed the credentials necessary to address the race question. Northerners might imagine the black man, but they could never know him. Reconstruction was the white South's historical silver bullet, the era that seemed, once and for all, to prove the essential righteousness of the South's claims to racial expertise. As such, a white supremacist rewriting of Reconstruction proved an indispensable corollary to the rise of Jim Crow.

Viewed from a slightly different angle, however, the race-expert discourse—particularly southern engagement with the memory of Reconstruction—appears as much a reflection of political weakness as strength. The sheer preponderance of writing about Reconstruction in the formative years of Jim Crow highlights a real fear on the part of southern whites. After all, why continue to drag out the carcass of Reconstruction if the issues involved were no longer salient? Indeed, implicit in the race-expert framework was white southerners' uncertainty that the days of federal involvement in southern racial affairs were over. The fact that the federal government *did not* intervene during this period should not be construed as evidence that it *could not* have intervened. As southern white supremacists sought to overturn the democratic structures erected during Reconstruction, they had to keep one eye on the North and the possibility of renewed intervention. This fact accounts for the shrill tone of much white supremacist propaganda. Jim Crow apologists were forced to insist on their own status as race experts precisely because their control of the South was not absolute. Until the nation admitted the essential righteousness of the white supremacist cause, empty assertions of white southern racial expertise would have to suffice.

## History, Social Science, and the Struggle against Jim Crow

African Americans proved less than willing to accept southern whites' self-appointment as race experts. They recognized that the language of racial expertise had its roots in the political needs of white supremacy, not in any sort of true knowledge. White supremacist southerners' claims to "know the negro" were, in fact, little more than a form of intellectual minstrelsy. That the architects of Jim Crow would claim to speak for the South's black population seemed the height of hypocrisy. Black activists forcefully responded to the discourse of white southern expertise, advancing their own competing claims of knowledge and racial understanding. The last decade of the nineteenth century and the first decade of the twentieth witnessed a proliferation of African American historical scholarship and research in the social sciences. Individually and collectively, African Americans delved into the race's past and systematically explored its present condition, offering a vision of racial progress and possibility that stood in stark contrast to the vision put forward by the white South's race experts.

The late nineteenth and early twentieth centuries marked a high point in the publication of African American "race histories"—sweeping, synthetic overviews of black history deeply imbued with the rhetoric of uplift, potential, and progress.[115] These histories varied widely in style, coverage, and quality. Taken as a genre, however, they represent an important front in the cultural battle against white supremacy. African American race histories were not dispassionate, scientific studies of the sort that the turn-of-the-century American historical profession was increasingly coming to idealize.[116] Scholarly objectivity was not the goal of race history during the Jim Crow era. This was scholarship with a purpose. African American race histories explicitly aimed to instill racial pride in their readers. They taught valuable moral lessons, provided models for black youth, and refuted the lies and misrepresentations of white supremacist race experts. Most of all, turn-of-the-century race histories affirmed that African Americans *had* a history worth keeping. As they insisted on the relevance of the race's past, they pointed the way to a brighter future.

African American race histories tended to be ambitious in their scope, with most opening in Africa before following the Middle Passage to America. Some authors, including Congregationalist pastor Peter Thomas Stanford, derided Africa as "a land of ignorance and darkness."[117] However, since a central concern of the race history was the establishment of a praiseworthy ancestry for black Americans, most authors worked hard to glorify the race's distant past. "Historical records prove the Negro as ancient as the most ancient races," wrote Edward Austin Johnson in *A School History of the Negro Race in America*. "*The pyramids of Egypt*, the great temples on the Nile, were either built by Negroes or people closely related to them." Modern-day African Americans, he concluded, were the "descendants of a race of people once the most powerful on earth, the race of the Pharaohs."[118] In a pamphlet called *A Primer of Facts Pertaining to the Early Greatness of the African Race*, journalist and novelist Pauline Hopkins extolled the virtues of the ancient Egyptian and Ethiopian civilizations, praising their "wisdom and literature" and their "great advancement in science and the mechanical arts."[119] This glorious lineage formed the inheritance of the race, the gift of Africa to the civilization of the modern United States.

Of course, race histories also grappled with topics more directly related to the turn-of-the-century Southern Question, notably slavery and Reconstruction.[120] In *The Tragedy of the American Negro*, Peter Thomas Stanford decried "the hideous traffic in human flesh and blood" and the ideology that supported it, one that classed "a man with a coloured skin with the beasts of the field."[121] The darkness and degradation of slavery, however, served a crucial purpose in the narrative arc of many African American race histories.[122] Slavery provided an ideal foil, a built-in contrast that highlighted the race's impressive growth since emancipation. In their 1897 text *The Progress of a Race*, H. F. Kletzing and W. H. Crogman reminded readers of the pitiful state of the South's slave population on the eve of the Civil War: "Look at the colored race of that time, grossly ignorant, destitute of clothing, without homes, without name, persecuted, forced to bear much on account of the prejudices against color." Less than forty years later, "this despised race" had made "progress such as history nowhere else records."[123] The temporal proximity of slavery threw the development of the race into bold relief. If slavery represented the darkest hour in African American history, it was also the baseline from which subsequent progress could be measured.

Reconstruction offered a more vexing historical riddle. Though the race histories uniformly lauded emancipation, a number were rather critical of federal policy in the immediate postwar period. In *The Story of the Negro*, published in 1909, Booker T. Washington recalled that "all through the days of Reconstruction I had a feeling that there was something in the situation" that was "unstable and could not last." Suffrage, Washington wrote, had come too quickly. "It did not seem possible that a people who yesterday were slaves could be transformed within a few days into citizens capable of making laws for the government of the State or the government of the Nation."[124] Kletzing and Crogman found it "natural" that the freedpeople should have made some "mistakes." But, the authors were quick to add, "they made less mistakes than the bummers who came south for plunder during reconstruction times, and with the false promise of 'forty acres and a mule,' led the unlettered race into a season of idleness and vain hopes."[125] Rather than defending black conduct during Reconstruction, Kletzing and Crogman passed the blame. As always, the carpetbagger proved a handy scapegoat.

Other race histories were more willing to take a stand for the wisdom and righteousness of the Reconstruction enterprise. Peter Thomas Stanford pinned the blame for the period's unrest squarely on the white South. Reconstruction, he wrote, offered a glimpse of "the white man of the south in the character of a demon, who was determined to remand the coloured man as nearly as possible to his former condition."[126] Throughout the South, Stanford continued, "a reign of terror existed, and in a short time several thousand murders were committed, and plunder and slaughter were effected the like of which has not been seen in any civilized country."[127] William Albert Sinclair was even more forthright. Dubbing Reconstruction "an era that tried men's souls," Sinclair began by praising the "self-mastery and self-restraint" of congressional Radical Republicans. Such laudable virtues, he declared, had been conspicuously lacking among white southerners, who were "wrought into a frenzy" of racial violence and hatred. Bringing the question back to the memory battles of the turn-of-the-century era, Sinclair noted that "the violent Southern leaders trace their grievances back to the events of the Reconstruction era," making "many misleading and mischievous declarations about the 'damnable crime' committed on the white people of the South by giving the negro the ballot." Sinclair noted, however, that these same white supremacist ideologues "omit absolutely all reference to the causes and conditions which made negro suffrage a possibility"—that is, a white supremacist reign of terror that turned the South into a "charnel-house and chamber of horrors."[128]

Though a strident defense of Reconstruction was a profoundly important political gesture in the context of a sustained southern attack on the Fourteenth and Fifteenth Amendments, such detailed analysis of particular historical moments was not the fundamental purpose of turn-of-the-century race histories. On the whole, the texts were less interested in the events of the past than they were in constructing a larger argument about racial change over time. History was interesting, in other words, not because it showed where African Americans had been but because it highlighted how far the race had come. It is not surprising, therefore, that "progress" was a word mobilized with remarkable frequency in the Jim Crow–era histories.[129] Edward Johnson's *A School History of the Negro Race in America*, which included chapters titled "Progress since Freedom," "Religious Progress," "Educational Progress," and "Financial Progress," was largely typical of the genre.[130] For his part, G. F. Richings claimed that he did not seek to create a "'literary' work" in his race history but merely "aimed to set forth a few facts, which are incontrovertible evidences of the progress made by colored people."[131] In a particularly evocative metaphor, H. F. Kletzing and W. H. Crogman imagined African American history as a "long column of America's dark sons moving steadily and surely up the hill of progress, removing one by one the obstacles impeding the onward step and spirit of advancement of the age."[132] Progress was the central theme of the African American race history, the genre's most powerful response to the misrepresentations of southern white supremacy.

African American intellectuals understood that the telling of race histories was a deeply political act, directly connected to the struggle over Jim Crow. African American race histories offered a self-conscious corrective to a culture obsessed with black inferiority and degeneracy. It is no coincidence that the qualities black historians chose to emphasize—progress, potential, and achievement—were precisely the racial characteristics that southern white supremacists denied and that segregation and disfranchisement sought to strangle. Race historians were not writing history for history's sake. They were writing for the present and the future. Establishing a valuable racial past was essential to making an argument for rights and privileges in the era of Jim Crow.

The publications of the American Negro Academy and the Atlanta University Conferences for the Study of the Negro Problem offer a logical counterpoint to the cultural work of the turn-of-the-century race histories. To an even greater degree than the race historians, the members of the American Negro Academy and the editors of the Atlanta University studies (notably W. E. B. Du Bois) evinced a deep-rooted belief in the power of knowledge—calm, rational, and scientific—to improve the nation's racial situation. In the light of increased racial knowledge and self-understanding, they argued, the logic of white supremacy would begin to crumble. Combining scholarship and politics, turn-of-the-century African American intellectuals struck back against Jim Crow.[133]

The American Negro Academy, founded in 1897, was a self-consciously exclusive organization, with membership limited to the race's intellectual, artistic, and scientific elite.[134] Recognizing that African Americans faced a "persistent, relentless" white supremacist campaign "to thwart the Negro at every step of his upward struggles," the academy published "broad and scholarly" papers on a variety of race-related topics between 1897 and 1924.[135] These "Occasional Papers" served at least two distinct purposes. First, academy members hoped that their work would, in the words of academy founder Alexander Crummell, "bring forth, stimulate, and uplift all the latent genius, garnered up, in the by-places and sequestered corners of this neglected Race."[136] Through "the agency of the cultured men" of the race, the academy hoped to promote the spread of civilization and the "scientific processes of literature, art, and philosophy" among the masses.[137] Second, the occasional papers—in which the best minds of the race carefully unpacked the most pressing social and political problems facing the nation—can be read as the American Negro Academy's standing challenge to white supremacy. Refusing to stoop to the level of demagoguery, academy members treated their topics with scientific care and exactitude. The work of the American Negro Academy was to collect, preserve, and share racial knowledge, the key to a brighter future.

"It is only thus," Crummell wrote, that "we can nullify and break down the conspiracy which would fain limit and narrow the range of Negro talent in this caste-tainted country."[138]

It is fitting that Kelly Miller and W. E. B. Du Bois authored the first and second occasional papers that the American Negro Academy published. Perhaps more than any of their contemporaries, black or white, Miller and Du Bois had each earned the mantle of "race expert." Miller, professor of sociology and mathematics at Howard University, published widely on the race question at the turn of the century. With rare exceptions, Miller eschewed incendiary rhetoric, preferring to engage white supremacy on intellectual grounds. Miller's contribution to the occasional papers—a copiously footnoted, point-by-point evisceration of statistician Frederick Hoffman's antiblack text *Race Traits and Tendencies of the American Negro*—provides a case in point.[139] In his frequent publications in the popular press, Miller maintained this scholarly posture. A 1902 article published in the *Arena* applied a number of significant "sociological maxims" to the contemporary race question.[140] For a 1904 piece in *New England Magazine*, Miller analyzed census data and population patterns to disprove common misapprehensions regarding southern African Americans.[141] In 1905, he offered the readers of *National Magazine* a detailed analysis of the oft-discussed white supremacist fear of "social equality." Miller concluded that because it was "not amenable to the formulas of logic," "impatient of fact," and "intolerant of argument and demonstration," the concept deserved the scorn of serious thinkers.[142] In his writings on the race question, Miller urged the nation to stick to the facts. The race problem, like any other scientific riddle, would respond only to patient research and honest investigation. Wild abstractions, fantastic theories, and nightmarish worst-case scenarios had no place in the conversation.

By the time he took over control of the Atlanta University studies in 1897, W. E. B. Du Bois was the author of numerous books and articles on the race question. Barely thirty years old, Du Bois was already one of the most respected African American intellectuals in the country. Under Du Bois's leadership, which lasted until 1914, the annual sociological conferences at Atlanta University offered some of the most significant explorations of black life produced in the era of Jim Crow.[143] Motivating the conferences was a "conviction that a careful study of the condition and needs of the Negro population" would prove helpful not just for its inherent scientific worth but also for its use in the settlement of the race question.[144] The topics addressed—self-help, business, higher education, common schooling, the church, crime, health—were crucial to a proper understanding of black life in the southern United States. They were, however, subjects about which the nation, including the black community, actually knew very little. "We must no longer guess at their condition, we must know it," Du Bois wrote in the introduction to one of the studies. "We must not experiment blindly and wildly, trusting to our proverbial good luck, but like rational, civilized, philanthropic men, spend time and money in finding what can be done before we attempt to do it." [145] To solve the race problem, black intellectuals needed first to understand the true state of the race.

Despite their protestations of objectivity, the Atlanta studies did not forgo agitation entirely. The 1901 study of common schools concluded with a call for increased federal funding for African American education, while the 1904 conference on black criminality criticized southern state governments for their role in the maintenance of an unjust penal system.[146] In a larger sense, however, data collection and the transmission of race knowledge were, by their very nature, deeply political acts in the midst of the turn-of-the-century battle over white supremacy. The cultural work of southern white supremacists carefully erased *real* southern African Americans, replacing them with a composite figure drawn from the deepest and darkest of white nightmares. In such a context, the Atlanta studies—which used advanced sociological methods to give voice to the lived experience of the masses of the nation's black population, free of the controlling and confining narratives of southern white supremacy—constituted a radical refutation of the rhetorical logic of Jim Crow. Seeking to establish a firm intellectual foundation on which to base plans for the future, the Atlanta University studies evinced a belief in the transformative power of social science. If white supremacist stories threatened the future of the race, African American intellectuals crafted a response out of cold, hard, scientific facts.

## Jim Crow's Manifest Destiny

During the first decade of the twentieth century, Jim Crow propagandists began to look to the future. Even as they endlessly recycled tales of racial expertise in the hopes of staving off federal interventionism, southern storytellers allowed themselves to imagine a nation united under the banner of southern-style white supremacy. White southerners demanded that Yankees respect their racial point of view and affirm the South's permanent right to establish and police its color line, but they sought something more than mere approval. Jim Crow possessed a distinct missionary impulse. The ultimate security for white supremacy did not reside in a northern disavowal of interventionism but in the replication of southern race politics in the North. At the dawn of the twentieth century, southern storytellers urged the nation to embrace its latent white supremacy and to join the South in a glorious Anglo-Saxon alliance. Race, they argued, must eventually trump region.

White southerners had long made it a mantra that the northern commitment to African Americans was merely a function of ignorance and distance. Given adequate exposure, white southerners predicted, northern race policies would creep ever closer to those established in the South. "Put yourself, men of Illinois, in the place of the people you perhaps condemn," John Temple Graves told the students of the University of Chicago. "Suppose that by the steady drift of emigration the negro had come from the South to be a majority in every congressional district, in every legislative precinct, and in every municipal ward of Illinois." Under such circumstances, would not "the streets of Springfield and Chicago, and the woods and prairies of Illinois" quickly be "filled with eager white men asking how the South suppressed the negro vote?"[147] While it was only the South that struggled with its black menace, William Benjamin Smith wrote, northerners could afford to ignore the crisis. But "let the Blacks turn their faces northward in great numbers, let them begin to swarm by myriads, and derange the labour conditions, and drag down the scale of wages, and oust the Whites from their places," and "philanthropy will be thrown to the winds, and the arm of the government at Washington will not be strong enough or long enough to guard these wards of the nation from violence and persecution and outrage."[148]

White supremacists combed northern newspapers, legislation, and jurisprudence for manifestations of northern discrimination, seeming to find a certain glee in the slippages they found in the North's mask of racial democracy. Southern white supremacists seldom missed an opportunity to remind northerners just how vacuous their claims to the moral high ground were. "There is not a state in the Union, from Massachusetts to California, which . . . does not to-day, somewhere within its borders, in some way discriminate against the Negro race," Alfred Holt Stone wrote. "We are fundamentally alike in our attitude toward the Negro."[149] En route to a July 1903 debate with Senator Joseph Burton of Kansas, Ben Tillman stopped in Chicago to discuss lynching. Rather than focusing on the

South, however, Tillman hit the assembled northerners with a quartet of racial incidents that had recently taken place in their own backyard. "Did I read of the trouble at Danville?" Tillman asked. "And did you read of the Evansville (Ind.) affair, of the Peoria (Ill.) difficulty, and of the Belleville (Ill.) unpleasantness? A problem of the South? It seems to me the problem of the United States."[150] John Temple Graves was equally blunt in a 1903 speech in the same city. "Race prejudice has no sectional lines. It is held in no geographical boundaries . . . all our splendid platitudes are wrecked on this stern fact. All our brave philanthropies beat out their beautiful lives on this inexorable truth."[151]

Jim Crow propagandists asked the North to consider its own racial history, specifically its historic oppression of Native Americans and Chinese immigrants, before criticizing the South. "The race instinct is now slumbering," but "it is not extinct," William Benjamin Smith wrote. "Of this fact our treatment of the Chinese has already furnished a striking illustration." In 1882, a unified American whiteness had "hurled back the Chinaman into the ocean and barred our ports unyieldingly against him."[152] Such actions, Jim Crow propagandists insisted, grew from the same deeply ingrained race consciousness that motivated southern disfranchisement and segregation. Georgia's Rebecca Latimer Felton reminded northerners that a belief in racial purity had led the "Puritan Yankee and the English Cavalier" to push the American Indian "over the back wall of the Continent." The same consideration had produced the "Exclusion Act that keeps the American door closed to China because yellow is not the color to suit."[153] And yet, Felton mused, northerners had the audacity and impertinence to protest when southern whites sought to strip the ballot from black voters. For her part, Felton could "see nothing in [a black voter's] African antecedents, which would have commended him to the rights of citizenship, above the red Indian or yellow Chinaman."[154] Felton was confident, however, that the inexorable march of history would lead toward white supremacy. The "pendulum which swung forward towards social and political equality in the North and West, in the years following the close of the civil war," Felton predicted, was now swinging "with equal force towards white supremacy in the control and management of the colored race."[155] Once the North came to fully embrace the heritage it shared with the white South—a race history of aggressive, violent, xenophobic, Anglo-Saxon dominance—a glorious national future would be assured.

The rise of an American overseas empire after 1898 similarly played into white supremacist hands. Though many white southerners resolutely opposed the U.S. occupation of the Philippines and Puerto Rico, the influx of millions of nonwhite people into the American body politic seemed to present the nation at large with much the same problem that white southerners insisted they had been facing for years.[156] In making laws for the territory of Hawaii, historian and sociologist Jerome Dowd noted, the federal government "carefully provided for white supremacy by an educational qualification for suffrage that excludes the semi-civilized natives. No sane man," he continued, "would think of placing Manila under the control of a government of the Philippine Islands based upon universal suffrage. Yet the problem in the South and the problem in the Philippines and in Hawaii differ only in degree."[157] Having implemented a restricted suffrage in its imperial possessions, Dowd asked the nation to recognize the wisdom of the white South's attempts to impose a similarly limited suffrage at home. Senator Ben Tillman was a vocal critic of American expansionism, but he was quick to recognize that the nation's newfound imperial ambitions made for excellent white supremacist propaganda. How, Tillman asked in a *North American Review* article, could the "Party of Lincoln" critique southern race relations while denying self-sovereignty to Puerto Ricans and Filipinos? The South had "inherited" its race problem and was, therefore, only trying to bring it to a satisfactory conclusion. Northern Republicans, by contrast, sought "to incorporate nine millions more of brown men" for the express purpose of domination. The North, Tillman concluded, now "has a bloody shirt of its own."[158] On another occasion, Tillman sarcastically asked whether the federal government planned to provide colonized Filipinos with "forty acres and a mule."[159]

The dream of a nation united in white supremacy is at the heart of *The Clansman* (1905), Thomas Dixon Jr.'s second Reconstruction novel. Though Ben Cameron, Confederate veteran and the founder of the Ku Klux Klan, receives top billing, the awakening of Austin Stoneman, the Radical Republican architect of Reconstruction and a thinly veiled caricature of Thaddeus Stevens, is central to the novel's racial politics. *The Clansman* opens in Washington, DC, where Stoneman almost single-handedly presides over Radical Reconstruction. When illness forces Stoneman to head for the warmer climes of South Carolina for rest and recuperation, he remains unswerving in his support for black equality. However, late in the novel, when Stoneman discovers that black soldiers are preparing to execute his son Phil, he begins to see the light. At this point, Stoneman must put his faith in white supremacy and the Ku Klux Klan. A coordinated Klan assault frees Phil Stoneman and ends black Republican rule in South

In this illustration from Thomas Dixon Jr.'s *The Clansman: An Historical Romance of the Ku Klux Klan* (1905), Radical Republican leader Austin Stoneman "hurl[s] the everlasting curse of a nation" on the white South. By the novel's end, Stoneman embraces the logic of southern white supremacy. Library of Congress.

Carolina in a single spasm of racial violence. In his last line of the novel, Austin Stoneman announces his conversion: "The Klan!—The Klan! No? Yes! It's true—glory to God, they've saved my boy!—Phil—Phil!"[160]

In his journey from naive egalitarianism to a hard-won understanding of the inevitability of racial conflict, Austin Stoneman can be read as a proxy for the North at large. When confronted with the realities of African American deviance and degeneracy, Dixon insisted, even the most radical Yankee would come to embrace the tenets of white supremacy. The novel deploys a predictable sort of regional arithmetic. When exposed to the South's race problem firsthand, northerners—first Stoneman's children, then the great Radical himself—come to recognize the wisdom and necessity of southern-style white supremacy. In *The Clansman*, Dixon rewrote the history of the 1860s and 1870s to better fit the needs of the turn-of-the-century regime of segregation, disfranchisement, and lynching. Rather than attempting to force its race politics on the South, Dixon's North (in the person of Stoneman) learns to embrace southern racial thought. Racial equality was an illusion; white supremacy was a fact. The white South had been right all along.

"The problem of the Twentieth Century," W. E. B. Du Bois insisted in *The Souls of Black Folk*, "is the problem of the color-line."[161] Left without comment in Du Bois's famous formulation was the status of another significant line: the Mason-Dixon. For their part, southern white supremacists hoped that the twentieth century would witness the elision of sectionalism, at least as far as race was concerned. They imagined a unified Anglo-Saxon nation committed to the perpetuation of white supremacy at home and abroad. Even as they warned against northern interference in their racial affairs, southern white supremacists posited an essential kinship with the white people of the North. This connection, rooted in the essential, immutable truth of racial conflict, would prove more enduring than passing disagreements over Jim Crow. As an imperial North pondered overseas control, as it watched its black population grow, it would begin to understand the significance of white supremacy, aligning itself with the heroic measures of the white South. White supremacy was not a southern delusion. It was a fundamental truth, a matter of blood and heritage. As the twentieth century got underway, radical white supremacists allowed themselves to imagine a new era, a new order, a new nation—Jim Crow nation.[162]

In a sense, however, this dream had already come true. The retreat from Reconstruction was a national affair. The entire United States bore the responsibility for the rise of Jim Crow. White supremacist storytellers proved remarkably successful in shaping the popular conversation on race after 1890. Tales of a dangerous and debased black population garnered northern sympathy, while assurances of white southern racial expertise rationalized unprecedented attacks on black civil and political rights. By the end of the twentieth century's first decade, southern white supremacists had stripped black voters of the ballot in all eleven states of the former Confederacy and had drawn the color line through the public spaces of the South. In the process, they had lynched and murdered with impunity. These occurrences were no secret. The betrayal of racial democracy played itself out on a national stage. Northerners were privy to every bloody detail. Jim Crow may have made its home in the South, but it was the nation's shame.

# Epilogue

This book began with the death of the Confederate nation. It ends with *The Birth of a Nation*. In 1915, as white supremacist southerners put the finishing touches on the machinery of Jim Crow segregation, northerners flocked to theaters to see D. W. Griffith's epic cinematic retelling of *The Clansman*, Thomas Dixon Jr.'s novel of Reconstruction. *The Birth of a Nation* was a phenomenon. Tickets sold for an astronomical two dollars in some cities, yet northerners descended on theaters in record numbers. As they did, they opened their minds and hearts to the message of the white supremacist South. The film transported northern viewers to the contested ground of postwar South Carolina, allowing them—indeed, forcing them—to gaze on Reconstruction with white southern eyes. Northern audiences hissed at the conniving Radical Republican leader Austin Stoneman. They cheered the lynching of the black rapist Gus. They thrilled to the triumphant ride of the Ku Klux Klan and exalted in the overthrow of black political supremacy. They may have even shed a tear at the pair of North/South marriages that close the film. *The Birth of a Nation* turned Reconstruction into a morality play, a struggle between the forces of light and darkness for control of the South and the soul of the nation. Griffith's tale of a brave and virile white South throwing off the tyrannical yoke of Reconstruction was more than a movie. It was the psyche of the white South on the silver screen, a vision of the region's historical self-understanding presented to an eager nation.[1]

African Americans were quick to recognize the political dangers that *The Birth of a Nation* posed. The National Association for the Advancement of Colored People (NAACP), founded in 1909, launched a nationwide protest against the film. "'The Birth of a Nation' is an indefensible libel upon a race," wrote a contributor to the *Crisis*, the NAACP's magazine.

"'The Birth of a Nation' is not history; it is travesty. It is not realism; it is an abomination."[2] The organization used all the means at its disposal to battle the deleterious influences of Griffith's film. They filed injunctions, encouraged the film's censorship, organized pickets, and on at least one occasion, disrupted a screening with eggs and stink bombs.[3] The NAACP campaign met with some success. A number of localities refused to screen *The Birth of a Nation*, and a few of the film's most offensive scenes were excised. Even so, the protests could not derail the *Birth of a Nation* juggernaut. Northern audiences spoke with their dollars. In one New York theater, the film ran for an entire year.[4]

*The Birth of a Nation* did not offer the final word on the nature of southern identity or the place of African Americans within the region's body politic. Such questions would linger well into the twentieth century, to the civil rights movement and beyond. The film does, however, serve as a logical endpoint for this book. *The Birth of a Nation* presented a resounding answer to the question that has structured this study: *What is the South?* Ben Cameron, the film's dashing protagonist and the leader of the Ku Klux Klan, offers an idealized embodiment of southern manhood and a symbol of the region's rebirth. D. W. Griffith's South is brave, heroic, and virtuous. White southerners suffer grievous wrongs during Reconstruction, but a reunified nation is born from their suffering. Above all, Griffith's South is thoroughly committed to the righteousness of white supremacy and prepared to defend it to the end. For enraptured northern moviegoers, this vision proved irresistible.

As significant was the film's stylized portrayal of postwar sectional rapprochement. *The Birth of a Nation* dramatizes a literal and metaphorical reunion between the sections, opening with scenes of North/South fraternity and culminating in double marriage. In the middle, of course, one finds the horrific (but temporary) strife of Reconstruction. In the film, Ben Cameron and the riders of the Ku Klux Klan are not merely defenders of the antebellum status quo, they are also agents of sectional reunion. The battle against Reconstruction is a necessary precondition for reunion, a ritual that allows the restoration of sectional harmony. The internal logic of the film makes reunion an inevitability. Eventually, viewers recognize, the film's northern characters will cease their dalliance with racial equality and return to their natural alliance with the white South. The forces of white supremacy and sectional reconciliation must triumph in the end. When they do, the North/South reunion, already consecrated in bloodshed, has only to be solemnized in marriage.

Movie still from D. W. Griffith's *The Birth of a Nation* (1915). Ben Cameron and the Ku Klux Klan exact revenge on Gus, the deviant black criminal. As it dramatized the retreat from Reconstruction and the triumph of white supremacy, *The Birth of a Nation* capped fifty years of southern storytelling. Photographs and Prints Division, Schomburg Center for Research in Black Culture, The New York Public Library, Astor, Lenox, and Tilden Foundations.

In contrast to *The Birth of a Nation*'s telescoped path to reunion, the real-life retreat from Reconstruction proved contingent, complicated, and endlessly contested. Rather than a reunion of two estranged regions, the postbellum decades witnessed the construction of a new South and a new nation. Though many of the stories of the South discussed in this book (including *The Birth of a Nation*) imaginatively engaged with the southern past, this fact should not blind us to the essential novelty of the larger processes described. From travel writers to New South boosters, from local-color fiction to the literature of the Negro Problem, northerners and southerners endlessly debated the nature of the South and its place in the postwar United States. In the five decades after 1865, this intellectual work laid the groundwork for the betrayal of Reconstruction and the rise of Jim Crow. In articles, speeches, sermons, fiction, travelogues, popular theater, and visual culture, the nation reimagined Dixie. Fifty years' worth of southern stories redefined the very meaning of the region.

An overreliance on the idea of "reunion" has blinded historians to these deeper trends in the postwar sectional relationship. For all its value, the reunion model ultimately falls short because it fails to grapple fully with shifting notions of the South in the Reconstruction and post-Reconstruction decades. The postwar sectional relationship was not a return to anything. It was starkly and distinctly new. Indeed, the reunion framework elides the most consequential question of all: Reunion with *what South*? The South that "reunited" with the rest of the nation in the wake of Reconstruction was, in fact, a completely novel creation, the result of decades of imaginative work, debate, and negotiation. On a fundamental level, therefore, the retreat from Reconstruction was a product of intellectual processes as well as political ones. Between 1865 and 1915, northerners and southerners rewrote the South. Their stories helped to inscribe white supremacy at the heart of the postwar United States.

# Notes

ABBREVIATIONS

AMAA      American Missionary Association Archives, 1828–1969 (microfilm),
          Amistad Research Center, Tulane University, New Orleans, LA
AMSC      American Minstrel Show Collection, 1823–1947, Houghton Library,
          Harvard University, Cambridge, MA
AWTP      Albion W. Tourgée Papers, 1801–1924 (microfilm), Lamont Library,
          Harvard University, Cambridge, MA
BRTD-NYPL Billy Rose Theatre Division, New York Public Library, New York, NY
BRTP      Benjamin Ryan Tillman Papers, Clemson University Special
          Collections, Clemson, SC
CWCC      Charles W. Chesnutt Collection, Fisk University Special Collections,
          Nashville, TN
DCS       Dumont Collection Songsters (microfilm), Library of Congress,
          Washington, DC
FBR       Records of the Bureau of Refugees, Freedmen, and Abandoned
          Lands (microfilm), National Archives, Washington, DC
FJSC      Fisk Jubilee Singers Collection, Fisk University Special Collections,
          Nashville, TN
GWCP      George Washington Cable Papers, 1871–1947, Louisiana Research
          Collection, Howard-Tilton Memorial Library, Tulane University,
          New Orleans, LA
HBSC      Harriet Beecher Stowe Center, Hartford, CT
HMTP      Henry McNeal Turner Papers, 1835–1916, Moorland-Springarn
          Research Center, Howard University, Washington, DC
HWGP      Henry Woodfin Grady Papers, 1828–1971, Manuscripts, Archives,
          and Rare Books Library, Emory University, Atlanta, GA
IBWP      Ida B. Wells Papers, 1884–1976, University of Chicago, Chicago, IL
JCHP      Joel Chandler Harris Papers, 1848–1908, Manuscripts, Archives,
          and Rare Books Library, Emory University, Atlanta, GA
KMFP      Kelly Miller Family Papers, 1894–1989, Manuscripts, Archives, and
          Rare Books Library, Emory University, Atlanta, GA

| MSC | Minstrel Show Collection, 1831–1959, Harry Ransom Center, University of Texas, Austin, TX |
| RLFP | Rebecca Latimer Felton Papers, Hargrett Rare Book and Manuscript Library, University of Georgia, Athens, GA |
| SBWCP | *South before the War* Company Papers, Irving S. Gilmore Music Library, Yale University, New Haven, CT |
| SDC | Sam DeVincent Collection of Illustrated American Sheet Music, ca. 1790–1987, Smithsonian Archives Center, Washington, DC |
| TNPC-V | Thomas Nelson Page Collection, 1836–1952, Small Special Collections Library, University of Virginia, Charlottesville, VA |
| TNPP-D | Thomas Nelson Page Papers, 1739–1927, David M. Rubinstein Rare Book and Manuscript Library, Duke University, Durham, NC |
| WCBA | Warshaw Collection of Business Americana, ca. 1724–1977, Smithsonian Archives Center, Washington, DC |
| YU | Yale University, Beinecke Rare Book and Manuscript Library, New Haven, CT |

## INTRODUCTION

1. Morison, *Oxford History of the American People*, 707.

2. In a collection of historiographical essays on Reconstruction, Thomas Brown has quantified the shift toward a long view of Reconstruction, finding "more than three dozen works with titles that bracket dates beginning during the war or at its end and extending beyond 1890, most often to 1900 or to the years just before or after World War I." Brown, *Reconstructions*, 7.

3. Ayers, "What We Talk About When We Talk About the South," 66–74; Edwards, "Southern History as U.S. History," 533–35; Cobb, *Away down South*, esp. 1–9.

4. See, for instance, Buck, *Road to Reunion*; and Taylor, *Cavalier and Yankee*.

5. Phillips, "Central Theme"; Potter, "Enigma"; Woodward, *Burden of Southern History*, 187–212; Degler, "Thesis, Antithesis, Synthesis"; Conkin, "Hot, Humid, and Sad."

6. Smiley, "Quest for the Central Theme," 307. Smiley provides a helpful introduction to much of the literature on southern identity. See also Edwards, "Southern History as U.S. History"; and Cobb, *Away down South*.

7. For older accounts that take an interregional perspective, see Taylor, *Cavalier and Yankee*; Woodward, *American Counterpoint*; and Kirby, *Media-Made Dixie*.

8. Edwards, "Southern History as U.S. History," 535.

9. Susan-Mary Grant, *North over South*; McIntyre, *Souvenirs of the Old South*.

10. Ring, *Problem South*.

11. Cox, *Dreaming of Dixie*.

12. Greeson, *Our South*; Duck, *Nation's Region*; McPherson, *Reconstructing Dixie*.

13. Lassiter and Crespino, *Myth of Southern Exceptionalism*.

14. Michael O'Brien has argued that the idea of the distinctive South "has secured such a hold on the American mind that it is a postulate, to which the facts of Ameri-

can society must be bent, and no longer a deduction." O'Brien, *Idea of the American South*, xiv. See also Cobb, *Away down South*, 8; and Greeson, *Our South*, 1.

15. Calhoun, *Conceiving a New Republic*.

16. Blum, *Reforging the White Republic*.

17. Heather Cox Richardson, *Death of Reconstruction*.

18. Blight, *Race and Reunion*; Silber, *Romance of Reunion*.

19. In this, I align myself with the work of Natalie J. Ring and Caroline E. Janney. By focusing on the ways the South remained a "problem" in twentieth-century American life, Ring offers a significant critique of the "reunion" framework. Ring, *Problem South*. In her study of Civil War memory, Janney draws a helpful distinction between reunion and reconciliation, arguing that war wounds went deeper than the literature of reunion would suggest. Janney, *Remembering the Civil War*.

20. Silber and Blight consciously structure their analyses around "reunion." Other works discussed here, notably Blum and Heather Cox Richardson, are also indebted to the reunion model, if less explicitly. Silber, *Romance of Reunion*; Blight, *Race and Reunion*; Blum, *Reforging the White Republic*; Richardson, *Death of Reconstruction*.

CHAPTER 1

1. Townsend, *Campaigns of a Non-combatant*, 330.

2. On Gardner, see Katz, *Witness to an Era*, esp. 80–87. See also Trachtenberg, *Reading American Photographs*, 71–118.

3. For an analysis of the political and cultural significance of Civil War ruins, see Nelson, *Ruin Nation*.

4. Sidney Andrews, *South since the War*, 1.

5. On Barnard, see Davis, *George N. Barnard*, esp. 77–105.

6. On northern images of the antebellum South, see Taylor, *Cavalier and Yankee*; Susan-Mary Grant, *North over South*; Greeson, *Our South*; and McIntyre, *Souvenirs of the Old South*, 11–38.

7. See Gambill, *Conservative Ordeal*.

8. Dennett, *South as It Is*, vii.

9. Ibid., vii.

10. Trowbridge, *South*, iii.

11. Schurz, *Report on the Condition of the South*, 2.

12. Reid, *After the War*, 340.

13. Hamilton, *Wool Gathering*, 198; Dennett, *South as It Is*, 34–35.

14. Sidney Andrews, *South since the War*, 233.

15. Ibid., 201.

16. Benjamin Truman, "Cities of Georgia," *New York Times*, 3 December 1865, 3.

17. Reid, *After the War*, 390.

18. Sidney Andrews, *South since the War*, 16–17.

19. Ibid., 20.

20. Reid, *After the War*, 175.

21. Trowbridge, *South*, 510.

22. For a related discussion of northern travelers and the southern landscape, see McIntyre, *Souvenirs of the Old South*, 68–97.

23. Reid, *After the War*, 390.

24. "Observer" [Carl Schurz], "The Sea Islands and Free Labor," *Boston Daily Advertiser*, 31 July 1865, 2.

25. Reid, *After the War*, 135.

26. Sidney Andrews, *South since the War*, 29.

27. Trowbridge, *South*, 143.

28. Dennett, *South as It Is*, 58–59.

29. I am influenced here by Edward Said's notion that knowledge collection formed a vital part of European imperialism. Said, *Orientalism*, 31–48.

30. Sidney Andrews, *South since the War*, 37.

31. Trowbridge, *South*, 70–71.

32. Benjamin Truman, "The South as It Is," *New York Times*, 31 October 1865, 1.

33. Dennett, *South as It Is*, 278–79; Trowbridge, *South*, 160. See also Silber, *Romance of Reunion*, 26–28.

34. "Observer" [Carl Schurz], "The 'Unconquered' Class," *Boston Daily Advertiser*, 8 August 1865, 2; Sidney Andrews, *South since the War*, 13.

35. Reid, *After the War*, 46.

36. Henry McNeal Turner, "Army Correspondence," *Christian Recorder*, 25 February 1865, 29.

37. Henry McNeal Turner, "Army Correspondence," *Christian Recorder*, 27 May 1865, 83.

38. Trowbridge, *South*, 130–31.

39. Hamilton, *Wool Gathering*, 209–10.

40. Reid, *After the War*, 348.

41. Sidney Andrews, *South since the War*, 15.

42. Reid, *After the War*, 59.

43. Ibid., 16.

44. Henry McNeal Turner, "Army Correspondence," *Christian Recorder*, 25 February 1865, 29.

45. Schurz, *Report on the Condition of the South*, 42.

46. Trowbridge, *South*, 220.

47. Hamilton, *Wool Gathering*, 249.

48. Heather Cox Richardson has placed the attempt to transform southern freedmen into northern-style free laborers at the heart of northern Republican plans for Reconstruction. Heather Cox Richardson, *Death of Reconstruction*, 6–40.

49. Schurz, *Report on the Condition of the South*, 16.

50. Reid, *After the War*, 344.

51. Sidney Andrews, *South since the War*, 25.

52. Trowbridge, *South*, 369.

53. Dennett, *South as It Is*, 53.

54. Ibid., 84.

55. Sidney Andrews, *South since the War*, 224.

56. Dennett, *South as It Is*, 357.

57. Trowbridge, *South*, 143.

58. Historian Richard N. Current has used the term "northernization" to describe the northern desire to remake the South in its own image throughout much of American history. Current, *Northernizing the South*. See also Powell, "American Land Company."

59. Item 686, reel 4, AWTP. On Tourgée, see Elliott, *Color-Blind Justice*.

60. On the role of the South in the construction of antebellum northern identity, see Susan-Mary Grant, *North over South*; and Greeson, *Our South*.

61. See Lawson, *Patriot Fires*.

62. On the centrality of free labor to the postwar northern Republican worldview, see Heather Cox Richardson, *Death of Reconstruction*, 6–40. The classic study of the free labor ideology remains Foner, *Free Soil, Free Labor, Free Men*.

63. "The Two Races in the South and the Labor Question," *New York Times*, 16 November 1865, 4.

64. " . . . Negro Will Not Work," *Chicago Tribune*, 22 May 1865, 2.

65. Schurz, "*For the Great Empire of Liberty, Forward!*" 13.

66. On the transition to free labor in the postwar South, see Foner, *Reconstruction*, 124–75; Saville, *Work of Reconstruction*; O'Donovan, *Becoming Free in the Cotton South*; and Rodrigue, *Reconstruction in the Cane Fields*.

67. Child, *Freedmen's Book*, 269–76, Yale Collection of American Literature, YU.

68. Morris, *Freedmen's Schools and Textbooks*, 13.

69. Ibid., 85.

70. Brown, *John Freeman and His Family*, 10.

71. On the AMA, see Joe Richardson, *Christian Reconstruction*. On religion and Reconstruction more generally, see Blum, *Reforging the White Republic*, 51–86; Stowell, *Rebuilding Zion*; and Blum and Poole, *Vale of Tears*.

72. *Nineteenth Annual Report of the American Missionary Association*, 11–12.

73. William T. Eustis Jr., "Religious Reconstruction in the South," *Home Missionary*, October 1865, 136–37.

74. On northerners and southern gender roles, see Silber, *Romance of Reunion*, 13–38.

75. De Forest, *Miss Ravenel's Conversion*, xviii–xix.

76. Ibid., 464. See also Silber, *Romance of Reunion*, 110–11.

77. "Transition—North and South," *Chicago Tribune*, 29 May 1865, 2; "The Present Spirit of the South," *New York Times*, 3 May 1865, 4.

78. "The Return Home," *Harper's Weekly*, 20 May 1865, 320.

79. Blassingame and McKivigan, *Frederick Douglass Papers*, 4.

80. Ibid., 15–16.

81. On racial conditions and black activism in the Reconstruction-era North, see Quigley, *Second Founding*, 15–26; Schwalm, *Emancipation's Diaspora*; Masur, *Example for All the Land*; and Kantrowitz, *More than Freedom*.

82. Foner, *Reconstruction*, 222–24.

83. Quigley, *Second Founding*, 3–14.

84. *Proceedings of the National Convention of Colored Men*, 34.

85. Ibid., 41–42.

86. Garnet, *Memorial Discourse*, 85–86.

87. William Howard Day, "Oration," in *Celebration by the Colored People's Educational Monument Association*, 11.

88. Ibid., 15.

89. Ibid., 14.

90. Foster, *Brighter Coming Day*, 218.

91. "A Southward Movement," *Boston Herald*, 3 May 1865, 4.

92. "Mohamed and the Mountain," *National Freedman*, 15 September 1865, 272.

93. For northern planters, see Powell, *New Masters*.

94. Dennett, *South as It Is*, 2.

95. For information on missionary schoolteachers in the South, see Jones, *Soldiers of Light and Love*; and Butchart, *Schooling the Freedpeople*, 78–119.

96. Henry Ward Beecher, "Our Time, Its Special Danger, and Its Great Need," *Independent*, 6 April 1865, 1.

97. Joe Richardson, *Christian Reconstruction*.

98. On religion and the Civil War, see Stout, *Upon the Altar of the Nation*. See also Noll, *Civil War as a Theological Crisis*; and Rable, *God's Almost Chosen Peoples*.

99. "The Country: Its Condition and Prospects," *American Missionary*, July 1865, 154.

100. "Annual Report of the New York National Freedman's Relief Association," *National Freedman*, June 1866, 169.

101. Document 45614, Louisiana Reel 1, AMAA.

102. Document 19332, Georgia Reel 1, AMAA.

103. Document 19371, Georgia Reel 1, AMAA.

104. "Northern Men and Southern Plantations," *Hartford Daily Courant*, 9 January 1866, 2.

105. "The New System," *Harper's Weekly*, 15 July 1865, 434.

106. Morgan, *Yazoo*, 25.

107. "The South in Adversity," *New York Tribune*, 23 June 1865, 4; "Emigration to the Southern States," *New York Times*, 18 August 1865, 4.

108. "What the South Wants," *New York Times*, 3 March 1866, 4.

109. Knox, *Camp-Fire and Cotton-Field*, 501–2.

110. Ibid., 524.

111. "Our Maps of the Southern States," *Harper's Weekly*, 6 January 1866, 3.

112. Powell, *New Masters*, 28, 39.

113. "The Rights of Colored Men and Women," *Christian Recorder*, 7 January 1865, 1.

114. Junius, "Brooklyn Correspondence," *Christian Recorder*, 18 March 1865, 42.

115. "Colored Men of Enterprise, Read This," *Christian Recorder*, 29 April 1865, 66.

116. Tourgée, *Fool's Errand*, 20.

117. Powell, *New Masters*, 151.

118. Butchart, *Schooling the Freedpeople*, 80.

119. Document 71780, Mississippi Reel 1, AMAA.

120. Document 45661–62, Louisiana Reel 1, AMAA.

121. Document 45694, Louisiana Reel 1, AMAA.

122. On the Freedmen's Bureau, see Cimbala, *Under the Guardianship of the Nation*; and Foner, *Reconstruction*, 153–70.

123. "Report of Br. Majr. Gn. Davis Tillson," reel 32, Publication Number M799, Records of the Assistant Commissioners for the State of Georgia, FBR.

124. For Warren's description of the armed men, see Mortimer A. Warren to H. R. Pease, 30 November 1865, reel 3, Publication Number M1026, Records of Superintendents of Education, Louisiana, FBR.

125. This document is numbered multiple times. Document 45651–56, Louisiana Reel 1, AMAA.

126. On Turner's early emigrationism, see Campbell, *Middle Passages*, 107–9.

127. Henry McNeal Turner, "Army Correspondence," *Christian Recorder*, 25 March 1865, 45.

128. Redkey, *Respect Black*, 13.

129. "Letter from Henry M. Turner," *Christian Recorder*, 24 November 1866, 185.

130. Foner, *Reconstruction*, 196–97, 225–26.

131. Ibid., 228–80. For an overview of Radical personnel and policy, see Benedict, *Compromise of Principle*, esp. 21–58.

132. U.S. Congress, *Congressional Globe*, 39th Cong., 1st sess., 1866, 2883.

133. Ibid., 39th Cong., 1st Session, 1865, 91.

134. Palmer and Ochoa, *Selected Papers of Thaddeus Stevens*, 45.

135. Ibid., 23.

136. U.S. Congress, *Congressional Globe*, 39th Cong., 1st sess., 1866, 1309.

137. Ibid., 39th Cong., 1st sess., 1866, 341.

138. Ibid., 39th Cong., 1st Sess., 1866, 296.

139. Ibid., 39th Cong., 2nd Sess., Appendix, 1867, 78.

140. Ibid., 39th Cong., 2nd Sess., 1866, 116, 118.

CHAPTER 2

1. Both had actually been in existence before 1868. The Ku Klux Klan was founded in 1866; the term *carpetbagger* was coined in 1867. It was not until early 1868, however, that either received sustained national attention. See Tunnell, "Creating the 'Propaganda of History,'" 792–800; and Trelease, *White Terror*, 3–6, 109–10. Most nineteenth-century Americans hyphenated the term "carpet-bagger." This usage has since gone out of fashion. I follow the newer spelling—"carpetbagger"—but retain the hyphen when it appears in a quotation. The treatment of "Ku Klux Klan" varied widely. "Ku-Klux Klan," "Ku-Klux-Klan," and "Kuklux Klan" were all common. For consistency's sake, I use "Ku Klux Klan," except of course when other spellings appear in quotations.

2. Trelease, *White Terror*. See also Foner, *Reconstruction*, 342–43.

3. See Current, "Carpetbaggers Reconsidered"; and Current, *Those Terrible Carpetbaggers*. I follow the general outlines of Current's "non-valuational" definition of *carpetbagger*, first offered in 1964: "White northerners who went south after the beginning of the Civil War and, sooner or later, became active in politics as Republi-

cans." Current, "Carpetbaggers Reconsidered," 144. Though some individual carpet-baggers were undoubtedly as corrupt as they were painted by nineteenth-century southern propagandists and remembered in twentieth-century popular memory, this chapter, like Richard Current in his work, will proceed on the assumption that most were not actually that terrible. It should also be noted that the term *carpetbagger* was applied almost exclusively to men and seldom to African Americans. Black and female migrants to the South were certainly not spared the opprobrium of their white southern neighbors, but the term *carpetbagger* was rarely applied to either group.

4. On the early history of the term, see Tunnell, "Creating the 'Propaganda of History,'" 792–800.

5. Bascom, *Carpet-bagger in Tennessee*, 4–5.

6. *Works of Charles Sumner*, 537.

7. William Lloyd Garrison, "The Impending Crisis," *Independent*, 13 August 1868, 1.

8. *Springfield Daily Republican*, 7 October 1868, 5.

9. "Pebbles," *Independent*, 9 July 1868, 3.

10. *New York Tribune*, 17 August 1868, 4.

11. "Butler in Gloucester," *New York Tribune*, 10 August 1868, 2.

12. "Carpet-baggers," *Harper's Weekly*, 3 October 1868, 627.

13. "Carpet-Baggers," *Chicago Tribune*, 5 September 1868, 2.

14. "The Apostolic Title," *Zion's Herald*, 20 August 1868, 3.

15. "Nasby," *Hartford Daily Courant*, 9 June 1869, 1.

16. Kerr, *Smoked Glass*, 244.

17. "Appreciation of Art in North Carolina," *Harper's Weekly*, 31 October 1868, 695.

18. The term is Richard Current's. I use it throughout this chapter to refer to the stereotypical, disparaging vision of northern migrants. See Current, *Those Terrible Carpetbaggers*.

19. Lester and Wilson, *Ku Klux Klan*, 53.

20. On the founding and evolution of the Ku Klux Klan, see Trelease, *White Terror*, 3–27.

21. "The Kuklux Klan: The Rebel Organization in Tennessee," *New York Times*, 20 January 1868, 2.

22. "Tennessee," *Chicago Tribune*, 5 February 1868, 2.

23. "A Deed of the Kuklux-Klan," *Chicago Tribune*, 10 April 1868, 2. On the Ashburn murder, see Link, *Atlanta*, 93–105.

24. "A New Raw-Head-Bloody-Bones: The 'Ku-Klux-Klan,'" *New York World*, 7 April 1868, 4.

25. "Washington," *New York World*, 10 April 1868, 3. On Klan denial among both Democrats and Republicans, see Parsons, "Klan Skepticism."

26. *Masked Lady of the White House*, 30.

27. Ibid., 33.

28. "Tennessee," *New York Times*, 27 March 1868, 2. The "water trick" was quite common in northern reporting, if not necessarily in practice. See Stearns, *Black Men of the South*, 422.

29. "The Ku-Klux Klan," *Chicago Tribune*, 11 September 1868, 2.

30. Buell, *Buell's Ku-Klux-Klan Songster*, 9–11.

31. *Nation's Peril*, 38, 50.

32. *Horrible Disclosures*, 38.

33. Ibid., 48, 41. On the role of sexual violence in the Reconstruction South, see Rosen, *Terror in the Heart of Freedom*.

34. "Ku-Klux in North Carolina," *New York Tribune*, 31 August 1870, 2.

35. Frank Bellew, "Visit of the Ku-Klux," *Harper's Weekly*, 24 February 1872, 160.

36. Stearns, *Black Man of the South*, 425.

37. Pierson, *Letter to Charles Sumner*, 19.

38. *Oaths, Signs, Ceremonies, and Objects*, 12.

39. "Ku-Kluxism," *Harper's Weekly*, 19 December 1868, 813.

40. "The Crisis of Our Civilization," *Independent*, 22 October 1868, 4.

41. Douglass's treatment of the Ku Klux Klan accords with his larger attempts to shape the memory of the Civil War. See Blight, *Frederick Douglass' Civil War*, 219–39.

42. "The Reign of Terror South," *New National Era*, 2 February 1870, 2.

43. "Another Murder," *New National Era*, 28 July 1870, 2.

44. "The New Insurrection Begun," *New National Era*, 30 March 1871, 2.

45. "The Ku-Klux Reign of Terror," *New National Era*, 5 October 1871, 3.

46. Albion W. Tourgée, "Some of the Outrages," *New York Tribune*, 24 May 1870, 2.

47. U.S. Congress, *Congressional Globe*, 42nd Cong., 1st Sess., 1871, 451.

48. On the theatrical and performative aspects of the Klan, see Parsons, "Midnight Rangers."

49. See Lester and Wilson, *Ku Klux Klan*, 55; "The Ku Klux Klan," *Christian Recorder*, 7 November 1868, 126; and *Boston Daily Advertiser*, 13 April 1868, 1.

50. Trelease, *White Terror*, 61.

51. *Oaths, Signs, Ceremonies, and Objects*, 25–26.

52. "K: K: K:; Mysterious Orders of the Tennessee Rebel Banditti," *Chicago Tribune*, 14 March 1868, 2.

53. Stevenson, *Ku Klux Klan*, 9–10.

54. "The Ku-Klux Proclamation," *New York World*, 19 October 1871, 4.

55. "KUKLUX KLAN: Twenty Persons Arrested in Memphis," *New York Times*, 8 April 1868, 1.

56. "THE KUKLUX KLAN: The Memphis Division Ferreted Out," *Chicago Tribune*, 10 April 1868, 2.

57. *Oaths, Signs, Ceremonies, and Objects*, 15.

58. *Horrible Disclosures*, 35. Mark C. Carnes has argued that secret ritual played a central role in nineteenth-century masculine culture and homosocial relations. The popularity of rituals—particularly initiation ceremonies—across the nation might explain the eagerness with which northern commentators approached this particular aspect of the Klan. Carnes, *Secret Ritual and Manhood in Victorian America*.

59. *Horrible Disclosures*, 70–74. Quote on 74.

60. Ibid., 79.

61. Ibid., 80.

62. *Terrible Mysteries of the Ku Klux Klan*, 20–21.

63. Ibid., 56.

64. Trelease, *White Terror*, 383–98.

65. On racial violence, memory, and narration, see Williams, *They Left Great Marks on Me*.

66. *Testimony Taken by the Joint Select Committee*, vol. 5, *South Carolina*, 1408.

67. Ibid., vol. 2, *North Carolina*, 32.

68. Ibid., vol. 11, *Mississippi*, 484.

69. Ibid., vol. 3, *South Carolina*, 577.

70. Ibid., 428.

71. Ibid., 381.

72. Ibid., vol. 2, *North Carolina*, 167.

73. Ibid., 103.

74. Ibid., vol. 12, *Mississippi*, 889.

75. Ibid., vol. 10, *Alabama*, 1719.

76. Ibid., vol. 9, *Alabama*, 1017.

77. Ibid., vol. 3, *South Carolina*, 386–87.

78. Ibid., vol. 9, *Alabama*, 675.

79. Ibid., vol. 3, *South Carolina*, 525.

80. "The Ku-Klux Reports to Congress," *Frank Leslie's Illustrated Newspaper*, 9 March 1872, 402.

81. *Report of the Joint Select Committee*, 99.

82. Ibid., 99, 98.

83. Ibid., 99.

84. McKee, *Enforcement of the Fourteenth Amendment*, 6.

85. *Report of the Joint Select Committee*, 289.

86. Ibid., 294.

87. Ibid., 522.

88. Ibid., 448.

89. For the election of 1872 and the Liberal Republican campaign, see Foner, *Reconstruction*, 499–511; Calhoun, *Conceiving a New Republic*, 33–46; and Slap, *Doom of Reconstruction*.

90. As Mark Wahlgren Summers has noted, such "southern tours" often resulted in a skewed vision of southern affairs, overly sympathetic to the plight of the white South and needlessly critical of Reconstruction. Summers, *Press Gang*, 191–206.

91. Lurton Dunham Ingersoll, *Life of Horace Greeley*, 525.

92. "The Curse of the Carpet-baggers," *New York Tribune*, 2 August 1872, 4.

93. "The Carpet-Baggers, the Organs, and Mr. Greeley," *Springfield Daily Republican*, 27 September 1872, 4.

94. "Louisiana," *Chicago Tribune*, 12 February 1872, 4.

95. "The Voice of Oberlin: Speech of Ex-President Mahan," *Cincinnati Commercial*, 22 August 1872, 2.

96. Gath, "The South," *Chicago Tribune*, 4 October 1872, 4.

97. "Carpet-bag Rule," *Chicago Tribune*, 2 August 1872, 4.

98. "Carpet-bag Despotism," *Chicago Tribune*, 26 August 1872, 4.

99. "The Carpet-Baggers Vindicated," *Hartford Daily Courant*, 15 October 1872, 2.

100. Gerrit Smith, *Extracts from a Speech of Hon. Gerrit Smith*, 2; "The Carpet-bag Governments," *Independent*, 24 October 1872, 4.

101. "Alabama: What an Alabamian Thinks of the State of Affairs in the South," *New York Times*, 13 August 1872, 2.

102. "Carpet-Baggers," *New York Times*, 4 September 1872, 4.

103. "Who Are the Carpet-Baggers?" *Boston Daily Globe*, 6 September 1872, 4.

104. Bartlett, *Dictionary of Americanisms*, 100–102.

105. Ibid., 341.

106. On King and *The Great South*, see Greeson, *Our South*, 241–51. See also James S. Pike, *Prostrate State*.

107. King, *Great South*, 96.

108. Thomas Wentworth Higginson, "Who Is Responsible for the Carpet-Baggers?" *Independent*, 12 February 1874, 1.

109. "The People of the South," *Christian Union*, 22 April 1874, 311.

110. "The Southern Saint Bartholomew," *Hartford Daily Courant*, 3 September 1874, 2.

111. J. Sella Martin, "Unification," *New York Tribune*, 24 September 1873, 4.

112. "Troubles in Arkansas," *Christian Recorder*, 23 July 1874, 8.

113. "The South," *Hartford Daily Courant*, 20 December 1876, 2.

114. Quoted in "Condition of the South," *New York Times*, 8 December 1874, 5.

115. "Carpet-Baggers," *Chicago Inter-Ocean*, 20 June 1876, 4.

116. Jennie Eggleston Zimmerman, "The First of the Carpetbaggers," *Christian Union*, 17 March 1875, 220–21, quote on 221.

117. "Come to Stay," *Harper's Bazaar*, 17 June 1876, 395.

118. "The Outrages Again—Their Cause and Their Cure," *Springfield Daily Republican*, 11 January 1875, 4.

119. See Gillette, *Retreat from Reconstruction*, 76–185. Carole Emberton persuasively argues for the inextricable link between politics and violence in the Reconstruction South. Emberton, *Beyond Redemption*. For an overview of Reconstruction-era violence, see Rable, *But There Was No Peace*. For the response of the national Republican Party to these events, see Calhoun, *Conceiving a New Republic*, 47–89.

120. Quoted in Gillette, *Retreat from Reconstruction*, 157.

121. Rable, *But There Was No Peace*, 122–86. See also Emberton, *Beyond Redemption*, 168–205.

122. Morton, *South*, n.p.

123. Eugene Lawrence, "The Same Old Pirate Afloat Again," *Harper's Weekly*, 19 September 1874, 778.

124. Eugene Lawrence, "The Ku-Klux and the Colored Voters," *Harper's Weekly*, 24 June 1876, 510; Eugene Lawrence, "Northern Settlers and the Ku-Klux," *Harper's Weekly*, 1 July 1876, 534; Eugene Lawrence, "The Ku-Klux Democracy," 15 July 1876, 575.

125. Redkey, *Respect Black*, 38.

126. "Veni Vidi," "Another Chapter of Blood at Vicksburg," *Christian Recorder*, 22 July 1875, 1.

127. Historian William Gillette has concluded that "Grant's southern policy was a study in incongruity; a curious, confusing, changeable mix of boldness and timidity, decision and indecision, activity and passivity, as he shifted between reinforcement and retrenchment, coercion and conciliation." Gillette, *Retreat from Reconstruction*, 166–67. See also Calhoun, *Conceiving a New Republic*, 47–89; Waugh, *U.S. Grant*, 103–54; and Simpson, *Reconstruction Presidents*, 163–96.

128. In the introduction to his book, Nordhoff insisted that "I sought only for facts, and did not care what side they favored." Nordhoff, *Cotton States*, 9.

129. Ibid., 16.

130. Ibid., 32, 57, 75.

131. Ibid., 11–12.

132. Ibid., 17.

133. "Louisiana," *Christian Union*, 23 September 1874, 230.

134. D. W. B., "Washington," *Independent*, 26 November 1874, 15.

135. "The Republican Party on Trial," *New York Times*, 25 January 1875, 4.

136. *Proceedings of the Republican National Convention*, 27.

137. "Condition of the South," *New York Times*, 28 October 1874, 1.

138. D. W. B., "Things at Washington," *Independent*, 21 January 1875, 14.

139. On Hayes's southern policy, see Simpson, *Reconstruction Presidents*, 199–228; and Calhoun, *Conceiving a New Republic*, 137–68.

140. "Reconstruction Just Finished," *Boston Daily Globe*, 23 April 1877, 4.

141. "The Twin Sores," *Chicago Daily Tribune*, 11 April 1877, 1.

142. "President Hayes and the Colored People," *Christian Recorder*, 19 April 1877, 1.

143. "A Carpet-Bag Exodus," *New York Tribune*, 2 April 1877, 4.

144. "The Southern Question," *Harper's Weekly*, 14 April 1877, 282.

145. Langston, *Other Phase of Reconstruction*, 14.

146. "The New Policy Train," *Frank Leslie's Illustrated Newspaper*, 21 April 1877, 128.

147. "Obituary," *Chicago Daily Tribune*, 23 April 1877, 4.

148. On the writing of *A Fool's Errand*, see Elliott, *Color-Blind Justice*, 169–70.

149. Item 2428, reel 18, AWTP.

150. Tourgée, *Fool's Errand*, 161. See also Elliott, *Color-Blind Justice*, 170–82.

151. Tourgée, *Invisible Empire*, 386.

152. On the memory of the KKK, see Lowery, "Reconstructing the Reign of Terror."

CHAPTER 3

1. "'The New South.' By Hon. Henry Grady. First Article," *New York Ledger*, 21 December 1889, Bound Volume 8, HWGP.

2. On the New South ideology, see Gaston, *New South Creed*; Doyle, *New Men, New Cities, New South*; Link, *Atlanta*, 136–56; Ayers, *Promise of the New South*, 20–21; and Woodward, *Origins of the New South*, 142–74.

3. "The New South," *Raleigh News and Observer*, 1 April 1883, 2.

4. "The New South," *Atlanta Constitution*, 4 March 1882, 4, reprinted from *Mobile Register*.

5. Henry Watterson, "The Reunited Union," *North American Review*, January 1885, 25.

6. Walter H. Page, "Study of an Old Southern Borough," *Atlantic Monthly*, May 1881, 648.

7. Harris, *Life of Henry Grady*, 88.

8. Wilbur Fisk Tillett, "The White Man of the New South," *Century Illustrated Magazine*, March 1887, 769.

9. "The New South," *St. Louis Globe-Democrat*, 4 January 1881, 4.

10. "What the Papers Say," *Atlanta Constitution*, 16 October 1881, 2, reprinted from *Galveston News*.

11. "Plain Talk from a Southern Educator," *Hartford Daily Courant*, 3 February 1882, 2; "A Great Mill in the South," *Atlanta Constitution*, 11 February 1882, 3.

12. Hoke Smith, "The Resources and Development of the South," *North American Review*, August 1894, 129.

13. "A Louisiana Editor on the South," *New Orleans Daily Picayune*, 18 September 1887, 11.

14. Harris, *Life of Henry Grady*, 11.

15. Advertisement, *Chicago Daily Inter-Ocean*, 29 November 1890, 4.

16. *Excursion Guide of the Virginia Midland Railway*, 29. On the built environment of the New South, see Hillyer, "Designing Dixie."

17. *Price and Descriptive List. Sinclair's Real Estate Agency. Orlando, Orange County, Florida. 1885* (Orlando, FL: Mahlon Gore, 1885), 4, box 2, folder 2, Florida Subseries, WCBA.

18. *Sheffield, Ala. The Iron Manufacturing Center of the South. On the Tennessee River. Its Wonderful Resources, Advantages, and Prospects. Issued by the Sheffield Land, Iron, and Coal Co.* (New York: South Publishing, 1888), 12, box 1, folder 9, Alabama Subseries, WCBA.

19. Ibid., 7, 9.

20. "A Reply to a Criticism," *Manufacturers' Record*, 15 March 1884, 119.

21. "The South's Brilliant Future," *Manufacturers' Record*, 17 March 1888, 11.

22. "Construction Department," *Manufacturers' Record*, 8 March 1884, 92.

23. Ibid., 8 March 1884, 92.

24. Ibid., 10 May 1884, 350.

25. Ibid., 15 August 1885, 10.

26. Ibid., 13 March 1886, 154; ibid., 12 June 1886, 614.

27. "'The New South.' By Hon. Henry Grady. First Article," *New York Ledger*, 21 December 1889, Bound Volume 8, HWGP.

28. "New South: Its Industrial Progress in 1887 Reviewed," *New Orleans Daily Picayune*, 24 December 1887, 1.

29. Historian Paul Gaston has criticized New South boosters for a fundamental misunderstanding of the industrial process. Sure that their vast stores of raw materials would necessarily lead to wealth, the boosters indulged in wild flights of fancy and undue optimism, thereby hindering the very growth on which they counted. Gaston, *New South Creed*, 205–7.

30. Hillyard, *New South*, 4.

31. Ibid., 407–18.

32. On Atlanta, see Link, *Atlanta*; and Doyle, *New Men, New Cities, New South*, esp. 16–58.

33. "The Development of an Alabama Town," *Manufacturers' Record*, 29 August 1885, 72.

34. "A Thriving North Carolina Town," *Manufacturers' Record*, 17 April 1886, 292; "A Prosperous Town in a Prosperous State," *Manufacturers' Record*, 3 May 1884, 316; "The Development of an Alabama Town," *Manufacturers' Record*, 29 August 1885, 72.

35. Kimball, *International Cotton Exhibition*, 149.

36. For a fuller treatment of the 1881 Exposition, see Prince, "Rebel Yell for Yankee Doodle." Tera Hunter's analysis of the 1881 Atlanta washerwomen's strike provides an important counterpoint to the Exposition's message of prosperity and progress. Hunter, *To 'Joy My Freedom*, 74–97. See also Link, *Atlanta*, 146–48; and Doyle, *New Men, New Cities, New South*, 152–58.

37. "Interviewing the Interviewer," *Atlanta Constitution*, 11 October 1881, 2.

38. "J. A. D.," "The New South—Attractions of Alabama and Mississippi," *Frank Leslie's Illustrated Newspaper*, 15 March 1890, 136. On northern tourism and investment in the New South, see Hillyer, "Designing Dixie," 1–32.

39. Ayers, *Promise of the New South*, 12.

40. For the political and cultural significance of northern tourism in the South, see McIntyre, *Souvenirs of the Old South*.

41. *Summer Resorts and Points of Interest*.

42. *Scenic Attractions and Summer Resorts*.

43. *A Handbook of the South*, 12.

44. See McIntyre, *Souvenirs of the Old South*, 99–136.

45. Engelhardt, *Richmond, Virginia and the New South*, 14, 31.

46. *Florida, Cuba, and Jamaica* (n.p., n.p., 1896), 13, 27, box 1, folder 3, Florida Subseries, WCBA.

47. *Dream of "Ellen N."*

48. Ernest Ingersoll, *To the Shenandoah and Beyond*.

49. Graves, *Winter Resorts*.

50. "Immigration to the South," *Manufacturers' Record*, 25 August 1888, 11.

51. *Something of Interest to All: The Southland* (n.p., n.p., 1893), 7, YU.

52. "The New South or the Old," *Louisville Courier-Journal*, 1 July 1889, 4.

53. Engelhardt, *Richmond, Virginia and the New South*, 1.

54. *Southern Homes! Illustrated Pamphlet of Iberia Parish, Louisiana* (New Iberia, LA: New Iberia Enterprise Steam Print, 1890), 18, YU.

55. *Facts about Tallapoosa*, n.p.

56. James H. Foss, *Florida Facts* (Boston: Winship, Daniels & Co., ca. 1888), box 1, folder 3, Florida Subseries, WCBA.

57. Harrison, *How to Get Rich*; Robertson, *Road to Wealth*.

58. Harrison, *How to Get Rich*, 5–6.

59. "The New South Abounding in Resources and Bright in Promise," *Daily Arkansas Gazette*, 12 October 1883, 3.

60. "A Suggestion to Southern Towns," *Manufacturers' Record*, 7 May 1887, 8.

61. "Another Step Forward," *Manufacturers' Record*, 1 March 1884, 63.

62. Harris, *Life of Henry Grady*, 137.

63. Nathaniel Southgate Shaler, "The Economic Future of the New South," *Arena*, August 1890, 258.

64. "The New South or the Old," *Louisville Courier-Journal*, 1 July 1889, 4.

65. "'The New South.' By Hon. Henry W. Grady. Second Article," *New York Ledger*, n.d. [December 1889], Bound Volume 8, HWGP.

66. Blair, *Prosperity of the South*, 5.

67. Ibid., 6.

68. Charley Dudley Warner, "The South Revisited," *Harper's New Monthly Magazine*, March 1887, 634.

69. Field, *Blood Is Thicker than Water*, 14.

70. Henry W. Grady to Hon. Daniel S. Lamont, 15 July 1887, box 1, folder 2, HWGP.

71. Contemporary travel writing on Appalachia and the mountain South offers a helpful contrast to the optimism of New South boosters and their northern allies. See McIntyre, *Souvenirs of the Old South*, 39–67; and Silber, *Romance of Reunion*, 124–58.

72. Field, *Blood Is Thicker than Water*, 151.

73. E. S. Nadal, "A Trip South," *Christian Union*, 7 January 1886, 8.

74. "The Future of the New South," *New Orleans Daily Picayune*, 23 April 1888, 2.

75. Layton, *Pilgrimage South*, 36.

76. "Cartoons and Comments," *Puck*, 10 December 1884, 226.

77. Rebecca Harding Davis, "Here and There in the South. I—Old and New," *Harper's New Monthly Magazine*, July 1887, 238.

78. Ibid., 238.

79. Rebecca Harding Davis, "Here and There in the South. II—In Mobile," *Harper's New Monthly Magazine*, August 1887, 438.

80. Rebecca Harding Davis, "Here and There in the South. III—Along the Gulf," *Harper's New Monthly Magazine*, September 1887, 601.

81. Rebecca Harding Davis, "Here and There in the South. V—In Attakapas," *Harper's New Monthly Magazine*, November 1887, 925.

82. "A Brand New South," *New Orleans Daily Picayune*, 7 October 1887, 4, reprinted from *New York Herald*.

83. "A Great Mill in the South," *Atlanta Daily Constitution*, 11 February 1882, 3, reprinted from *Philadelphia Press*.

84. "Mr. Gould's Views about the South," *Manufacturers' Record*, 29 March 1884, 175; Edmonds, *South's Redemption*, 5.

85. Henry E. Bowen, "The New South," *Independent*, 15 March 1883, 3–4.

86. "The New North," *Atlanta Constitution*, 2 June 1890, 4.

87. Henry Watterson, "The 'Solid South,'" *North American Review*, January 1879, 47.

88. "Bourbon Sherman and the New South," *New Mississippian*, 29 September 1885, 2.

89. Quoted in *Milwaukee Sentinel*, 8 January 1887, 4.

90. "The Four Rips; or, Twenty Years behind the Age," *Puck*, 16 September 1885, 40–41.

91. William Link adeptly explores the relationship between race politics and New South ideology. Link, *Atlanta*, esp. 136–56. See also Williamson, *Crucible of Race*, 117–51; and Woodward, *Strange Career of Jim Crow*, 31–67.

92. Harris, *Life of Henry Grady*, 100.

93. Bingham, *New South*, 12.

94. Ibid., 14.

95. Edmonds, *South's Redemption*, 55–56.

96. Edmonds, quoted in Gaston, *New South Creed*, 126.

97. Hoke Smith, "The Resources and Development of the South," *North American Review*, August 1894, 131.

98. Edward Atkinson, "The Solid South?," *International Review*, March 1881, 200.

99. Natalie Ring's evocation of "the problem South" offers an important counterpoint to the optimism that many northern New South boosters expressed. See Ring, *Problem South*, esp. 18–57.

100. "New South," *Atlanta Constitution*, 17 March 1885, 8.

101. "The New South," *Christian Union*, 5 February 1885, 3.

102. Schurz, *New South*, 29.

103. Edward Atkinson to Gen. J. C. Armstrong, 2 November 1880, box 17, Letterbook 11, Edward Atkinson Papers, Massachusetts Historical Society, Boston.

104. McClure, *South*, 104.

105. Kelley, *Old South and the New*, 161–62.

106. Charley Dudley Warner, "The South Revisited," *Harper's New Monthly Magazine*, March 1887, 638.

107. "The New South," *Los Angeles Times*, 15 August 1883, 2.

108. Thomas Nast, "The Queen of Industry; or, The New South," *Harper's Weekly*, 14 January 1882, 17.

109. McClure, *South*, 223.

110. Ibid., 225–26.

111. Charles Dudley Warner, "Impressions of the South," *Harper's New Monthly Magazine*, September 1885, 549–50.

112. Lauren Dunlap, "The South and Southern Questions," *International Review*, August 1882, 182.

113. George W. Cable, "The Freedmen's Case in Equity," *Century Illustrated Magazine*, January 1885, 409.

114. Ibid., 411.

115. Ibid., 409.

116. Henry W. Grady, "In Plain Black and White," *Century Illustrated Magazine*, April 1885, 916.

117. "Mr. Grady's New South," *New York Freeman*, 29 January 1887, 2.

118. *Richmond Planet*, 11 October 1890, 2.

119. "The New South Racket," *New York Freeman*, 22 January 1887, 2.

120. "The Southern Negro," *Washington Bee*, 6 August 1887, 2.

121. Redkey, *Respect Black*, 54.

122. "Our Civil Rights," reprinted from *Christian Recorder*, box 106-2, folder 15, HMTP.

123. Fortune, *Black and White*, 56.

124. Ibid., 11.

125. Ibid., 14.

126. See Norrell, *Up from History*, 121–28.

127. Harlan, *Booker T. Washington Papers*, 583.

128. Ibid., 584.

129. Ibid., 585.

130. Ibid., 587.

CHAPTER 4

1. Wardlaw, *Southern Literature*, 7. Wardlaw's dismissal notwithstanding, the work of historian Michael O'Brien highlights the impressive intellectual and literary accomplishments of the Old South. See O'Brien, *Conjectures of Order*.

2. Wardlaw, *Southern Literature*, 6.

3. Ibid., 13.

4. Richard W. Gilder, "The Nationalizing of Southern Literature. Part II.—After the War," *Christian Advocate*, 10 July 1890, 3.

5. Ibid., 4.

6. Albion W. Tourgée, "The South as a Field for Fiction," *Forum*, December 1888, 406–7.

7. Ibid., 408, 405.

8. This moment occurs in the story "How Mr. Rabbit Was Too Sharp for Mr. Fox." After his curiosity and temper allow Brer Fox to catch him, Brer Rabbit outsmarts his adversary by begging the Fox not to throw him in the Brier Patch. Brer Fox does, and Brer Rabbit, having been born and raised in the briers, escapes without injury. Harris, *Uncle Remus*, 31.

9. Ibid., 94.

10. For Harris's biography, see Bickley, *Joel Chandler Harris*.

11. Eric Sundquist provides an important take on the conflicting, contentious, and often confusing race politics of *Uncle Remus*. Sundquist, *To Wake the Nations*, 337–47. See also MacKethan, *Dream of Arcady*, 61–85. Robert Bone goes so far as to suggest that Joel Chandler Harris displayed "schizoid tendencies," reasoning that "only a split personality can account for an author who juxtaposes such antithetical images of Negro life as Uncle Remus and Brer Rabbit!" Bone, *Down Home*, 27.

12. Harris, *Uncle Remus*, 3.

13. See Baer, *Sources and Analogues*.

14. On slave tales, see Levine, *Black Culture and Black Consciousness*, 81–135.

15. On the "faithful slave," see Blight, *Race and Reunion*, 284–91; and McElya, *Clinging to Mammy*.

16. On race and race-making in Uncle Remus, see Hale, *Making Whiteness*, 54–60.

17. See the tales "The Awful Fate of Mr. Wolf" and "The End of Mr. Bear." Harris, *Uncle Remus*, 63–67, 119–23, quote on 120.

18. Harris, *Uncle Remus*, 5, 6.

19. *Pittsburgh Telegraph*, n.d., n.p., ser. 4, box 23, Scrapbook, JCHP.

20. Harris, *Uncle Remus*, 3.

21. Ibid., 4–10.

22. "Uncle Remus," *New York Herald*, n.d., n.p., ser. 4, box 23, Scrapbook, JCHP.

23. "Negro Folk Lore," *New York Times*, n.d., n.p., ser. 4, box 23, Scrapbook, JCHP.

24. "Uncle Remus," *New York Evening Post*, n.d., n.p., ser. 4, box 23, Scrapbook, JCHP.

25. "A Home Genius: Joel Chandler Harris and the Literary Circle," unknown newspaper, n.d., n.p., ser. 4, box 23, Scrapbook, JCHP.

26. Mrs. Mary Bayard Clarke, "Literary Gossip," Unknown Newspaper, n.d., n.p., ser. 4, box 23, Scrapbook, JCHP.

27. Unknown newspaper, n.d., n.p., ser. 4, box 23, Scrapbook, JCHP.

28. "Books in New York," *Republican*, n.d., n.p., ser. 4, box 23, Scrapbook, JCHP.

29. *Appleton's Journal*, n.d., n.p., ser. 4, box 23, Scrapbook, JCHP.

30. *New York Times*, n.d., n.p., clipping, box 17, TNPP-D.

31. *Boston Commonwealth*, n.d., n.p., ser. 4, box 23, Scrapbook, JCHP.

32. *Hartford Times Commercial*, n.d., n.p., ser. 4, box 23, Scrapbook, JCHP.

33. *Chicago Interior*, n.d., n.p., ser. 4, box 23, Scrapbook, JCHP.

34. *Eclectic Magazine*, n.d., n.p., ser. 4, box 23, Scrapbook, JCHP.

35. "Uncle Remus," *New York Commercial Advertiser*, n.d., n.p., ser. 4, box 23, Scrapbook, JCHP.

36. *Hartford Times-Commercial*, n.d., n.p., ser. 4, box 23, Scrapbook, JCHP.

37. *Davenport Gazette*, n.d., n.p., ser. 4, box 23, Scrapbook, JCHP.

38. Advertisement issued by Charles Scribner's Sons, box 17, TNPP-D.

39. Joel Chandler Harris to Thomas Nelson Page, 31 December 1885, box 1, TNPP-D.

40. Page, *Old South*, 43.

41. Ibid., 167.

42. Page, *Red Rock*, viii. David Blight has analyzed the role that Page's plantation tales played in fostering sectional reunion. Blight, *Race and Reunion*, 222–27. From a more literary perspective, see Hobson, *Tell about the South*, 129–57; and MacKethan, *Dream of Arcady*, 36–60.

43. "Recollections and Reflections" (unpublished memoir), box 17, TNPP-D.

44. All of these stories were collected in Page, *In Ole Virginia*. Trent Watts offers a reading of "Marse Chan" that emphasizes images of home and manhood. Watts, *One Homogenous People*, 44–58.

45. See Hobson, *Tell about the South*.

46. Page, *Old South*, 259.

47. "The South as a Field for Literature, 1888," box 32, TNPC-V.

48. Page, *Old South*, 57.

49. Ibid., 50.

50. "The South as a Field for Literature, 1888," box 32, TNPC-V.

51. Page, *Old South*, 258.

52. Page, *Negro*, 15.

53. Page, *Old South*, 268.

54. "New South at Close Range, 1892," box 31, TNPC-V.

55. Page, *Old South*, 266; untitled speech, box 33, TNPC-V.

56. Page, *Old South*, 255.

57. Ibid., 253.

58. Page, *Necessity*, 4.

59. Ibid., 3.

60. "The South as a Field for Literature, 1888," box 32, TNPC-V.

61. Page, *Old South*, 269.

62. "The South as a Field for Literature, 1888," box 32, TNPC-V.

63. "My Politics" (unpublished manuscript), 1, box 104, folder 6, GWCP.

64. "My Politics," 6–13, box 104, folder 6, GWCP.

65. On Cable's race politics, see Williamson, *Crucible of Race*, 93–100; and Hale, *Making Whiteness*, 44–51.

66. Jennifer Rae Greeson argues that Cable's vision of New Orleans is significantly more global and cosmopolitan than it might initially appear. Greeson, *Our South*, 261–68.

67. Arlin Turner, *Negro Question*, 44.

68. Cable, *Grandissimes*, 194.

69. Greeson argues that "Cable's Creole stories are investigations of the modern Reconstruction project writ large." Greeson, *Our South*, 263.

70. The Bras Coupé story is narrated in chapters 28 and 29 of Cable, *Grandissimes*, 219–52.

71. Ibid., 236.

72. As Grace Hale has noted, the figure of the light-skinned black woman was also central to Cable's arguments against segregation in his nonfiction writing. Hale, *Making Whiteness*, 44–46.

73. Cable, *Madame Delphine*, 125.

74. Cable, *Dr. Sevier*, 216.

75. Cable, *Bonaventure*.

76. "Cable's 'Old Creole Days,'" *Scribner's Monthly*, July 1879, 473; *Advance*, 20 March 1884, Scrapbook, GWCP; *Dial*, December 1884, Scrapbook, GWCP.

77. Assorted Clippings, Scrapbook, GWCP.

78. "George W. Cable," *Century Illustrated Magazine*, February 1882, 605.

79. "Cable's *Grandissimes*," *Scribner's Monthly Magazine*, November 1880, 160.

80. Arlin Turner, *Critical Essays on George Washington Cable*, 14.

81. Assorted clippings, Scrapbook, GWCP.

82. Arlin Turner, *Critical Essays on George Washington Cable*, 20, 69.

83. "*Bonaventure*," *Critic*, 26 May 1888, Scrapbook, GWCP.

84. Arlin Turner, *Critical Essays on George Washington Cable*, 27.

85. "Mr. Cable's Readings—The Impression Made Last Night by the Novelist," *Wilmington Morning News*, 10 February 1886, Scrapbook, GWCP.

86. B. O. Aylesworth, "Literary Department," *Christian Examiner*, 15 October 1884, Scrapbook, GWCP; *Morning Call* (San Francisco), Scrapbook, GWCP.

87. *Dial* (Chicago), December 1884, Scrapbook, GWCP.

88. Arlin Turner, *Critical Essays on George Washington Cable*, 24.

89. President Merrill E. Gates, "The New South and American Literature," *Rutgers College Targum*, Scrapbook, GWCP.

90. "Mr. Cable's Second Reading," *Boston Daily Advertiser*, 17 February 1886, Scrapbook, GWCP.

91. For Chesnutt's early biography, see William Andrews, *Literary Career of Charles W. Chesnutt*, 1–38. See also Williamson, *Crucible of Race*, 61–66.

92. Brodhead, *Journals of Charles W. Chesnutt*, 125.

93. Charles W. Chesnutt to George Washington Cable, 4 March 1889, box 1, CWCC.

94. William Andrews, *Literary Career of Charles W. Chesnutt*, 36–37.

95. Literary critic Paul Petrie argues that "as thoroughly as any other figure in American literature, Charles W. Chesnutt's writing career proceeded from a prior commitment to a particular set of social and political goals." Petrie, *Conscience and Purpose*, 109–48, quote on 109.

96. Charles W. Chesnutt to George Washington Cable, 4 March 1889, box 1, CWCC.

97. Charles W. Chesnutt to Booker T. Washington, 5 November 1901, box 2, CWCC.

98. Charles W. Chesnutt, "Literature in Its Relation to Life," box 11, CWCC.

99. "Novels and Tales," *Outlook*, 15 April 1899, 884; *Current Literature*, October 1900, 416.

100. Literary critic Eric Sundquist argues that Chesnutt is intentionally "signifying" on Harris—that what appears to be repetition and recapitulation is, in fact, deconstruction and subversion. Sundquist, *To Wake the Nations*, 323–47. Lucinda MacKethan argues that the familiarity of the dialect form allowed Chesnutt to critique the works of Page and Harris, "exposing the artificiality of the white South's supposedly idyllic Arcadia." MacKethan, *Dream of Arcady*, 86–96, quote on 96. See also William Andrews, *Literary Career of Charles W. Chesnutt*, 39–73; and McWilliams, *Charles W. Chesnutt and the Fictions of Race*, 76–99.

101. Chesnutt, *Conjure Woman*, 34–35.

102. Ibid., 35.

103. Ibid., 35–36.

104. Ibid., 42.

105. Ibid., 43.

106. Ibid., 43.

107. Each of these stories appears in Chesnutt, *Conjure Woman*, 44–81.

108. The quote is from "Dave's Neckliss," another of Chesnutt's conjure tales. Chesnutt, *Conjure Woman*, 124.

CHAPTER 5

1. "Wild Negro Chants and Dances," *New York Times*, 25 May 1895, 9.

2. A number of scholars have noted the role that nostalgia and a reaction against modernity played in shaping ideas about the South. Cox, *Dreaming of Dixie*; Silber,

*Romance of Reunion*, 93–123; Hale, *Making Whiteness*, 51–67; McPherson, *Reconstructing Dixie*, 1–38.

3. The early history of the Fisk Jubilee Singers has been recounted in a number of places. See Anderson, *"Tell Them We Are Singing for Jesus,"* 26–56; Ward, *Dark Midnight When I Rise*, 127–78; and Eric Bernard Grant, "'Message in Our Music,'" 4–49. For a contemporary account of the Jubilee Singers' early years, see Gustavus D. Pike, *Jubilee Singers*.

4. Gustavus D. Pike, *Jubilee Singers*, 47.

5. Marsh, *Story of the Jubilee Singers*, 48–74.

6. Ibid., 91–92.

7. E. M. Cravath, "Fisk University's Great Necessity" (introductory note), in ibid., n.p.

8. Various programs, Jubilee Singers Programs, 1880s–1890s, FJSC.

9. *Melrose Journal*, 6 December 1879, Scrapbooks, 1879–81, FJSC.

10. "The Jubilee Concert and Social," unknown newspaper, n.d., Scrapbooks, 1879–81, FJSC; *Boston Journal*, 13 October 1879, Scrapbooks, 1879–81, FJSC; *Somerville Journal*, 22 November 1879, Scrapbooks, 1879–81, FJSC.

11. Rev. Theo. L. Cuyler, "Fisk University Jubilee Singers," *New York Evangelist*, 11 March 1880, Scrapbooks, 1879–81, FJSC.

12. *Boston Daily Traveller*, 15 January 1880, Scrapbooks, 1879–81, FJSC.

13. "The Jubilee Singers," *Chicago Daily Tribune*, 21 February 1882, 2.

14. On the discourse of respectability in the African American community, see Gilmore, *Gender and Jim Crow*, 1–30.

15. Unknown newspaper, n.d., Scrapbooks, 1879–81, FJSC.

16. *Daily Evening Traveller*, 17 November 1879, Scrapbooks, 1879–81, FJSC.

17. See, for example, "Refused by the Troy Hotels," *New York Times*, 24 December 1885, 1.

18. "F. J. Loudin's Letter," unknown newspaper, n.d., Scrapbooks, 1879–81, FJSC.

19. Cultural critic Paul Gilroy has put the work of the Fisk Jubilee Singers in conversation with blackface minstrelsy. Gilroy notes that "black people singing slave songs as mass entertainment set new public standards of authenticity for black cultural expression. The legitimacy of these new cultural forms was established precisely through their distance from the racial codes of minstrelsy." Gilroy, *Black Atlantic*, 90. See also Eric Bernard Grant, "Message in Our Music," 20–23.

20. Ibid., 6–12.

21. Ibid., 33.

22. Marsh, *Story of the Jubilee Singers*, 31.

23. Rev. Theo. L. Cuyler, "Fisk University Jubilee Singers," *New York Evangelist*, 11 March 1880, Scrapbooks, 1879–81, FJSC.

24. Jubilee Singers, Playbills 1888–1891, folder 455, AMSC; "Other Jubilee Companies," ser. 3.3, box 72, folder C, SDC.

25. On P. T. Wright's Nashville Students, see Abbott and Seroff, *Out of Sight*, 170–77; advertisement, *New York Clipper*, 19 November 1892, 597. For Slayton's Jubilee Singers, see "Other Jubilee Companies," ser. 3.3, box 72, folder C, SDC.

26. For a discussion of spirituals and the minstrel stage, see Toll, *Blacking Up*, 235–44.

27. *Rochester Democrat and Chronicle*, 11 February 1881, Scrapbooks, 1879–81, FJSC.

28. Unknown newspaper, 12 June 1880, Scrapbooks, 1879–81, FJSC.

29. "At the White House," unknown newspaper, 13 March 1880, Scrapbooks, 1879–81, FJSC.

30. *Daily Sun* (Worcester, MA), 10 January 1880, Scrapbooks, 1879–81, FJSC.

31. Quoted in concert program, 1880, Jubilee Singers Programs, 1880s–1890s, FJSC.

32. Ibid.

33. *Melrose (MA) Journal*, 6 December 1879, Scrapbooks, 1879–81, FJSC.

34. On authenticity and imitation in nineteenth-century culture, see Orvell, *Real Thing*.

35. Marsh, *Story of the Jubilee Singers*, 112–15.

36. It is difficult to know the precise ages of many of the early Jubilee Singers. My claims here are drawn from brief biographical sketches compiled by Toni Anderson. See Anderson, *"Tell Them We Are Singing for Jesus,"* 217–21.

37. *Daily American* (Lawrence, MA), 22 October 1879, Scrapbooks, 1879–81, FJSC.

38. "The Fisk Jubilee Singers," *Peoria Journal*, 29 May 1881, Scrapbooks, 1879–81, FJSC.

39. Many historians have noted that blackface minstrelsy was central to the formulation of both whiteness and blackness in the antebellum period. See Lott, *Love and Theft*; Roediger, *Wages of Whiteness*, 115–32; and Saxton, *Rise and Fall of the White Republic*, 165–82. As William J. Mahar points out, the blackface mask also allowed performers to address an array of issues often unrelated to race. See Mahar, "Ethiopian Skits and Sketches," 163–75.

40. Advertisement, *New York Clipper*, 23 September 1882, 441.

41. Historians have analyzed antebellum blackface minstrelsy with much greater frequency and in much greater depth than postbellum blackface minstrelsy. Robert Toll's description of these changes remains the best available. Toll, *Blacking Up*, 134–55.

42. Toll has argued that postbellum white minstrels almost entirely dispensed with plantation material. Though he is correct to note that white minstrels shifted their focus to a broader range of topics, his claim that southern themes completely disappeared is an overstatement. Toll, *Blacking Up*, 160–87.

43. Haverly's United Mastodon Minstrels (and related companies), folder 429, AMSC.

44. Emerson's Minstrels, folder 362, AMSC; Dockstader's Minstrels, folder 350, AMSC.

45. Dockstader's Minstrels, ser. 1, box 6, folder 15, MSC.

46. "Down South Whar de Sugar Cane Grows," *Woodson & Allen's Carry Me Back to Old Virginia Songster* (New York: New York Popular Publishing, 1881), 4, vol. 9, item 91, DCS.

47. "My Old Savannah Home," *Johnson & Cooper's Sunny South Songster* (New York: New York Popular Publishing, 1880), 13, vol. 13, item 133, DCS.

48. Hyde & Beyman's Operatic Spectacular Minstrels, folder 443, AMSC.

49. *Minstrel Songs Old and New* (Boston: Oliver Ditson, 1882), 15–17, ser. 3.1, box 70, folder GG, SDC.

50. See Toll, *Blacking Up*, 195–270.

51. Haverly's United Mastodon Minstrels (and related companies), folder 429, AMSC.

52. Advertisement, *New York Clipper*, 23 September 1882, 444.

53. Toll, *Blacking Up*, 205–6.

54. Advertisement, *New York Clipper*, 7 August 1880, 160.

55. Callender's Minstrels, ser. 1, box 44, folder 4, MSC.

56. James Bland, "Carry Me Back to Old Virginny," ser. 3.8, box 123, folder H, SDC.

57. The issue of authenticity is central to the study of African American performance in the late nineteenth and early twentieth centuries. See Krasner, *Resistance, Parody, and Double Consciousness*, 15–40; Sotiropoulos, *Staging Race*, 81–122; Taylor and Austen, *Darkest America*, 25–80; Chude-Sokei, *Last "Darky,"* 17–45; and Webb, "Authentic Possibilities," 63–82.

58. On Haverly, see Toll, *Blacking Up*, 205–9.

59. Advertisement, *New York Clipper*, 6 September 1879, 192.

60. Haverly's United Mastodon Minstrels (and related companies), folder 429, AMSC.

61. "City Summary," *New York Clipper*, 24 July 1880, 142.

62. Advertisement, *New York Clipper*, 20 September 1879, 208.

63. Toll, *Blacking Up*, 209–11.

64. "Negro Minstrelsy," *New York Clipper*, 18 March 1882, 858.

65. Callender's Georgia Minstrels, folder 295, AMSC.

66. Advertisement, *New York Clipper*, 4 March 1882, 836.

67. Advertisement, *New York Clipper*, 16 April 1892, 95.

68. "Variety & Minstrelsy," *New York Clipper*, 23 April 1892, 101.

69. "World Players," *New York Clipper*, 14 May 1892, 148.

70. On plantation shows and *The South before the War*, see Abbott and Seroff, *Out of Sight*, 360–73. For a treatment of *The South before the War* that explores the production's use of traditional African American cultural forms, see Webb, "Authentic Possibilities," 65–73.

71. *Harry Martell's South before the War Co.* (promotional brochure), box 1, folder 1, SBWCP.

72. Complete script, box 1, folder 2, SBWCP.

73. Abbott and Seroff, *Out of Sight*, 366–67.

74. Publicity statement, box 1, folder 1, SBWCP.

75. "Colored Folks at the Bijou," *New York Times*, 20 November 1894, 5.

76. "The Stage," *Detroit Free Press*, 29 May 1892, 13; "New York City," *New York Clipper*, 21 January 1893, 738.

77. "The Old-Time Plantation at Kernan's Lyceum Theater," *Washington Post*, 26 February 1893, 14.

78. "Plays and Players," *Boston Daily Globe*, 15 December 1895, 18.

79. Advertisement, *New York Clipper*, 10 June 1893, 227.

80. "World Players," *New York Clipper*, 10 June 1893, 217.

81. Advertisement, *New York Clipper*, 18 August 1894, 383; "Maryland," *New York Clipper*, 15 September 1894, 436; advertisement, *New York Clipper*, 24 November 1894, 612.

82. Advertisement, *New York Clipper*, 12 January 1895, 725.

83. On Billy McClain, see Reed, *Hot from Harlem*, 42–51; and Fletcher, *100 Years of the Negro in Show Business*, 91–102. On Nate Salsbury and *Buffalo Bill's Wild West*, see Kasson, *Buffalo Bill's Wild West*; and Warren, *Buffalo Bill's America*.

84. Black America, folder 250, AMSC.

85. On the intellectual genealogy and cultural significance of *Black America*, see Carico, "Free Plantation," 128–220.

86. Black America, folder 250, AMSC.

87. Unknown newspaper, July 1895, Scrapbook, BRTD-NYPL.

88. "WILD NEGRO CHANTS AND DANCES," *New York Times*, 25 May 1895, 9. For a detailed description of the *Black America* stage show written by an associate of Salsbury, see "Nate Salsbury's 'Black America,'" Nathan Salsbury Essays [ca. 1890–1965], Nathan Salsbury Collection, YU.

89. Advertisement, *New York Clipper*, 8 June 1895, 223.

90. This aspect of *Black America* might be fruitfully compared to late nineteenth-century ethnological exhibits, notably the human displays at the 1893 World's Columbian Exposition in Chicago. See Hinsley, "World as Marketplace," 344–65; and Rydell, "'Darkest Africa,'" 135–55.

91. "Scenes in 'Black America,'" *New York Times*, 26 May 1895, 16.

92. "Summer Theatres," *Boston Daily Globe*, 14 July 1895, 18.

93. "'Darkies' as They Were in 'Dixie,'" *New York Tribune*, 19 May 1895, 14.

94. Advertisement, *New York Tribune*, 4 June 1895, 11.

95. "An American Manipulator," *Boston Transcript*, July 1895, Scrapbook, BRTD-NYPL.

96. "'Darkies' as They Were in 'Dixie,'" *New York Tribune*, 19 May 1895, 14.

97. "Grand Opera House," unknown newspaper, n.d., Scrapbook, BRTD-NYPL.

98. "Darkies in the 'Profesh,'" *Boston Daily Globe*, 28 July 1895, 21.

99. Fletcher, *100 Years of the Negro in Show Business*, 94.

100. "Bright for the Black Professional," *Chicago Tribune*, 4 August 1895, 42.

101. "Grand Opera House," unknown newspaper, n.d., Scrapbook, BRTD-NYPL.

102. "Black America," unknown newspaper, n.d., Scrapbook, BRTD-NYPL.

103. "Charms of Black America," *New York Tribune*, 30 June 1895, 10.

104. "Music and Drama," *Boston Daily Globe*, 25 July 1895, 8.

105. "Grand Opera House," unknown newspaper, n.d., Scrapbook, BRTD-NYPL.

106. Kersands was well-known for this routine. Toll, *Blacking Up*, 254–57.

107. Handy, *Father of the Blues*, 36.

108. For a candid assessment of the opportunities and travails of black minstrelsy, see Toll, *Blacking Up*, 218–29.

109. Thomas Riis emphasizes the extent to which black minstrel "tricksters" were able to "show the white minstrel audience what they wanted them to see." Riis, *Just before Jazz*, 6–7. David Krasner offers a helpful guide for reading such resistance

in African American theater. Krasner, *Resistance, Parody, and Double Consciousness*, 5–14. Barbara Webb argues against Krasner's "progressive" narrative of African American artistic maturation but still concludes that at sites like *Black America*, "black performers created possibilities for something called African American performance." Webb, "Authentic Possibilities," 63, 65.

110. *American Minstrel Songster*, n.p.

111. "Black America Again," *New York Tribune*, 26 September 1895, 6.

112. Karen Sotiropoulos emphasizes the esteem that African American performers were accorded in the black community. In cities like New York, performers played an important role in cultivating a vibrant black political and artistic life. Sotiropoulos, *Staging Race*, 42–80. See also Riis, *Just before Jazz*, 29–48.

113. Simond, *Old Slack's Reminiscence*.

114. Handy, *Father of the Blues*, 72–73.

115. Lynn Abbott and Doug Seroff offer an overview of this transition in Abbot and Serroff, *Ragged but Right*. See also Brundage, *Beyond Blackface*; Sotiropoulos, *Staging Race*; and Chude-Sokei, *Last "Darky."*

116. See Gossett, *Uncle Tom's Cabin and American Culture*, 260–83. For all things related to *Uncle Tom's Cabin*, the *Uncle Tom's Cabin and American Culture* website at the University of Virginia (http://utc.iath.virginia.edu/) is an extraordinary resource.

117. On the relation between antebellum minstrelsy and *Uncle Tom's Cabin*, see Meer, *Uncle Tom Mania*, 19–72.

118. David S. Reynolds offers a helpful overview of these developments. Reynolds, *Mightier than the Sword*, 177–200. See also Gossett, *Uncle Tom's Cabin and American Culture*, 367–87.

119. Gossett, *Uncle Tom's Cabin and American Culture*, 370. See also Reynolds, *Mightier than the Sword*, 177–78.

120. "Amusements," *Detroit Free Press*, 12 October 1881, 6.

121. "'Uncle Tom's Cabin' Galore," *San Francisco Chronicle*, 11 February 1893, 10.

122. Advertisement, *New York Clipper*, 24 August 1895, 397.

123. Advertisement, *Chicago Daily Tribune*, 27 February 1880, 7.

124. "World Players," *New York Clipper*, 9 July 1892, 279; "World Players," *New York Clipper*, 22 December 1894, 668; advertisement, *Hartford Courant*, 8 April 1880, 1.

125. "The Summer Stage," *Boston Daily Globe*, 4 June 1882, 4.

126. Newspaper clipping, unknown newspaper, Uncle Tom's Cabin Collection, HBSC.

127. "The Drama," *Boston Daily Globe*, 1 May 1881, 9.

128. "The Stage," *Detroit Free Press*, 23 April 1882, 15.

129. Commemorative card, Anthony & Ellis' Famous Ideal Uncle Tom's Cabin, 1882, Uncle Tom's Cabin Collection, HBSC.

130. "Entertainments," *Hartford Daily Courant*, 12 September 1881, 2; "The Summer Stage," *Boston Daily Globe*, 4 June 1882, 4.

131. Advertisement, *Los Angeles Times*, 27 May 1882, 2; advertisement, *Hartford Daily Courant*, 8 September 1882, 1.

132. "World Players," *New York Clipper*, 9 July 1892, 279.

133. Commemorative card, Anthony & Ellis' Famous Ideal Uncle Tom's Cabin, 1882, Uncle Tom's Cabin Collection, HBSC.

134. Advertisement, New York Clipper, 15 October 1892, 516.

135. Clipping, *New York Clipper*, Harry Birdoff Collection, HBSC.

136. "Peter Jackson in 'Uncle Tom's Cabin' at Harris," *Washington Post*, 4 March 1894, 14; "Uncle Tom's Cabin," *Boston Daily Globe*, 1 May 1894, 4.

137. Advertisement, *Hartford Courant*, 8 April 1880, 1.

138. Advertisement, Ed. R. Salter and Al. W. Martin Uncle Tom's Cabin Co., 1896, Harry Birdoff Collection, HBSC.

139. "The Summer Stage," *Boston Daily Globe*, 14 June 1885, 10.

140. "Summer Amusements," *Boston Daily Globe*, 8 August 1886, 10.

CHAPTER 6

1. "Race Question Discussed," *New York Tribune*, 27 February 1900, 2.

2. In this chapter, the term *white supremacist* is used to describe those white southerners who actively promoted the policies of Jim Crow on a national stage. It refers, in other words, to the small group of southerners who publicly advocated white supremacy, rather than the much larger group who passively accepted the tenets of white supremacy. For a detailed account of the diversity of southern racial thought in the turn-of-the-century period, see Williamson, *Crucible of Race*, esp. 79–139.

3. Gilmore, *Gender and Jim Crow*, esp. 1–31.

4. For an overview of disfranchisement, see Perman, *Struggle for Mastery*.

5. Hale, *Making Whiteness*, 121–98. See also Dailey, Gilmore, and Simon, *Jumpin' Jim Crow*, 3–6.

6. On southern lynching, see Brundage, *Lynching in the New South*; for spectacle lynching as a tool of white supremacy, see Hale, *Making Whiteness*, 199–240; and Wood, *Lynching and Spectacle*.

7. As Natalie Ring notes, discussion of the race problem was not limited to southern white supremacists. Ring's discussion of the ways in which "social scientists and self-proclaimed experts"—many of them northerners—grappled with the race question offers an important complement to my own discussion. Ring, *Problem South*, 175–215, quote on 179. See also Frederickson, *Black Image in the White Mind*, 256–82.

8. Joel Williamson is one of the few historians to explore the white supremacist South's appeal to the North during the formative years of Jim Crow. Williamson, *Crucible of Race*, 330–40.

9. "The Laurels of Demosthenes," *Saturday Evening Post*, 19 September 1908, 17. Vertical File, "John Temple Graves," Hargrett Manuscript and Rare Book Library, University of Georgia, Athens. On Graves, see Williamson, *Crucible of Race*, 214–15.

10. On Dixon, see Gillespie and Hall, *Thomas Dixon Jr.*; Williamson, *Crucible of Race*, 140–79; and Gilmore, *Gender and Jim Crow*, 66–70.

11. Clipping, unknown newspaper, ser. 5, box 2, Scrapbook 11, BRTP. For an analysis of Tillman's northern tours, see Kantrowitz, *Ben Tillman*, 281–86.

12. On the Lodge Bill, see Calhoun, *Conceiving a New Republic*, 226–59; and Perman, *Struggle for Mastery*, 38–43. On the Crumpacker Bill, see Perman, *Struggle for Mastery*, 224–31.

13. Atticus Haygood, "The Black Shadow in the South," *Forum*, October 1893, 167.

14. Williamson roots these images in a widely shared white southern worldview (termed "Radicalism") tied to a perceived lack of white male control during the 1890s and early 1900s. Williamson, *Crucible of Race*, 111–39.

15. See Gilmore, *Gender and Jim Crow*, 91–118; Kantrowitz, *Ben Tillman*, 156–97; Feimster, *Southern Horrors*, 62–86, 125–57; Godshalk, *Veiled Visions*, 35–56; Watts, *One Homogenous People*, 1–40; and Dailey, *Before Jim Crow*, 103–31.

16. "Suggests a Negro State," *Washington Post*, 13 August 1893, 6.

17. McKinley, *Appeal to Pharaoh*, 62.

18. Otken, *Ills of the South*, 248.

19. John T. Morgan, "The Race Question in the United States," *Arena*, September 1890, 386.

20. William Benjamin Smith, *Color Line*, 8–9.

21. Wade Hampton, "The Race Problem," *Arena*, July 1890, 132, 135.

22. Northen, *Negro at the South*, 16, 15.

23. Walter L. Hawley, "Passing of the Race Problem," *Arena*, November 1900, 23.

24. James Creelman, "A Defender of the Senate," *Pearson's Magazine*, June 1906, 627.

25. See Prather, *We Have Taken a City*; Cecelski and Tyson, *Democracy Betrayed*; and Gilmore, *Gender and Jim Crow*, 105–18.

26. A. J. McKelway, "The Race Problem in the South," *Outlook*, 31 December 1898, 114. As Glenda Gilmore has shown, this crime wave existed only in the white supremacist imagination. Gilmore, *Gender and Jim Crow*, 82–89.

27. Charles Francis Bourke, "The Committee of Twenty-Five," *Collier's Weekly*, 26 November 1898, 5.

28. A. J. McKelway, "The Cause of the Troubles in North Carolina," *Independent*, 24 November 1898, 1490. Stephen Kantrowitz has argued that the duality that McKelway invokes—violence and self-restraint—was at the heart of white southern masculinity in the late nineteenth century. Kantrowitz, "The Two Faces of Domination in North Carolina, 1800–1898," in Cecelski and Tyson, *Democracy Betrayed*, 95–112.

29. Joel Williamson placed the "Black Beast Rapist" at the heart of his analysis of turn-of-the-century racial radicalism. Williamson, *Crucible of Race*, 115–19. Gilmore has recast this figure as the "incubus," a mythological figure who has intercourse with women while they sleep. Glenda Elizabeth Gilmore, "Murder, Memory, and the Flight of the Incubus," in Cecelski and Tyson, *Democracy Betrayed*, 73–94. See also Feimster, *Southern Horrors*, 62–87; Wood, *Lynching and Spectacle*, 19–44; and Jacquelyn Hall, "'Mind That Burns," 328–49.

30. Charles H. Smith, "Have American Negroes Too Much Liberty?," *Forum*, October 1893, 182.

31. George T. Winston, "The Relation of the Whites to the Negroes," *Annals of the American Academy of Political and Social Science*, July 1901, 108.

32. Northen, *Negro at the South*, 14. On Northen's later campaign to limit lynching in Georgia, see David F. Godshalk, "William J. Northen's Public and Personal Struggles against Lynching," in Dailey, Gilmore, and Simon, *Jumpin' Jim Crow*, 140–61.

33. As Crystal Feimster notes, southern white women were some of the primary authors of the black rapist myth. Feimster, *Southern Horrors*, 125–41.

34. Mrs. L. H. Harris [Corra Harris], "A Southern Woman's View," *Independent*, 18 May 1899, 1354.

35. "Protect the Women," *Boston Globe*, 16 November 1898, 12. On Felton, see Williamson, *Crucible of Race*, 124–30; Feimster, *Southern Horrors*; and LeeAnn Whites, "Love, Hate, Rape, Lynching: Rebecca Latimer Felton and the Gender Politics of Racial Violence," in Cecelski and Tyson, *Democracy Betrayed*, 143–62.

36. James Z. George, "The Negro Problem as It Exists in the South," *Independent*, 4 December 1890, 1.

37. John Marshall Stone, "The Suppression of Lawlessness in the South," *North American Review*, April 1894, 501.

38. Thomas E. Watson, "The Negro Question in the South," *Arena*, October 1892, 544.

39. Atticus Haygood, "The Black Shadow in the South," *Forum*, October 1893, 173.

40. Mrs. L. H. Harris [Corra Harris], "A Southern Woman's View," *Independent*, 18 May 1899, 1355.

41. "Mrs. Felton's Reply," *Macon Telegraph*, 20 August 1897, n.p., box 16, folder 6, RLFP.

42. A number of historians have focused on the ways southern African Americans continued to act politically even after disfranchisement. See Ortiz, *Emancipation Betrayed*; Hunter, *To 'Joy My Freedom*; and Hahn, *Nation under Our Feet*, 364–465.

43. Historian Shawn Leigh Alexander offers an extraordinarily helpful study of black civil rights agitation in the turn-of-the-century decades. Alexander, *Army of Lions*.

44. Cooper, *Voice from the South*, 178.

45. Ibid., 179.

46. "The Ethics of the Negro Question." box 23-4, folder 32, Anna J. Cooper Papers, Moorland-Springarn Research Center, Howard University, Washington, DC.

47. For a reading of Frances Ellen Watkins Harper and *Iola Leroy* in the context of turn-of-the-century black feminism, see Carby, *Reconstructing Womanhood*, 62–94.

48. Harper, *Iola Leroy*.

49. On the meanings of progress in postbellum black culture, see Blight, *Race and Reunion*, 300–337.

50. Penn, "Progress of the Afro-American," 44–64.

51. Both series are reprinted in their entirety in Dworkin, *Daughter of the Revolution*, 9–198.

52. *Negro Problem*, 187–209.

53. On Washington's ideology and politics, see Norrell, *Up from History*. For African American challenges to Washington's leadership, see Alexander, *Army of Lions*, 177–219.

54. In a 1900 article in *Century Illustrated Magazine*, Washington told the story of William, a Tuskegee graduate whose hard work and honesty had helped his former employer see the error his white supremacist ways. Booker T. Washington, "Signs of Progress among the Negroes," *Century Illustrated Magazine*, January 1900, 472–73.

55. Washington, *Up from Slavery*, esp. 179–93.

56. Ida B. Wells, "A Red Record," in Royster, *Southern Horrors*, 106–17. For background on Wells's antilynching career, see Giddings, *Ida*, 156–432; Bederman, *Manliness and Civilization*, 45–76; and Feimster, *Southern Horrors*, esp. 87–124.

57. "Lynch Law in All Its Phases: Address at Tremont Temple, Feb. 13, 1893," box 8, folder 8, IBWP.

58. "The Reign of Mob Law: Iola's Opinion of Doings in the Southern Field," *New York Age*, 18 February 1893, box 8, folder 8, IBWP.

59. "Lynch Law in All Its Phases. Address at Tremont Temple, Feb. 13, 1893," box 8, folder 8, IBWP.

60. See Campbell, *Middle Passages*, 103–35; and Angell, *Bishop Henry McNeal Turner*, 215–37.

61. "Speech before the National Council of Colored Men, Cincinnati Ohio, Nov. 28, 1893," box 106-1, folder 21, HMTP.

62. Statement on the Lynching at Palmetto, GA, box 106-1, folder 22, HMTP.

63. Henry McNeal Turner, "American Negro," 196.

64. Douglass, *Why Is the Negro Lynched?*, 30–31.

65. Ibid., 32.

66. Ibid., 30.

67. Wells, "Southern Horrors," in Royster, *Southern Horrors*, 52.

68. Wells, "A Red Record," in Royster, *Southern Horrors*, 78.

69. Mary Church Terrell, "Lynching from a Negro's Point of View," *North American Review*, June 1904, 854–55.

70. Ibid., 853–54.

71. Ibid., 857.

72. Literary critic Ryan Simmons describes *The Marrow of Tradition* as Chesnutt's attempt to counter the white South's "untruthful literature" with his own "truthful literature." Simmons, *Chesnutt and Realism*, 87–112. Quote on 87.

73. Chesnutt, *Marrow of Tradition*, 175–95.

74. Du Bois, *Souls of Black Folk*, 37.

75. *Race Problems of the South*, 5. On the Montgomery conference, see Williamson, *Crucible of Race*, 416–17. For a contemporary African American critique of the conference, see Mebane, *"Negro Problem."*

76. *Race Problems of the South*, 7.

77. Ibid., 9.

78. Ibid., 10.

79. Ibid., 11. In fact, at least four northerners were invited to speak at the 1900 Montgomery conference: Walter Willcox, a Cornell University statistician and expert on black criminality; Hollis Burke Frisell, northern-born principal of the Hampton Institute in Virginia; Herbert Welsh, a native of Philadelphia and an expert on Indian

affairs; and W. Bourke Cockran, a New York Democrat who used his speech to advocate repeal of the Fifteenth Amendment. Of the four, only Welsh offered sentiments that in any way challenged the white supremacist consensus.

80. Walter Guild, "A Plea from the South," *Arena*, November 1900, 40.

81. Furnifold Simmons, "The Political Future of the Southern Negro," *Independent*, 28 June 1906, 1525; clipping, unknown newspaper, ser. 5, box 2, Scrapbook 11, BRTP.

82. "The Negro Problem: How It Appeals to a Southern White Woman," *Independent*, 18 September 1902, 2224.

83. John Sharp Williams, "The Negro and the South," *Metropolitan Magazine*, November 1907, 138.

84. Thomas Nelson Page, "The Great American Question," *McClure's Magazine*, March 1907, 565.

85. *Race Problems of the South*, 32.

86. Joel Chandler Harris, "The Negro as the South Sees Him. I—The Old-Time Darky," *Saturday Evening Review*, 2 January 1904, 1–2, 23.

87. George T. Winston, "The Relation of the Whites to the Negroes," *Annals of the American Academy of Political and Social Science*, July 1901, 106.

88. For a discussion of eugenics in the South, see Larson, *Sex, Race, and Science*.

89. Stone, *Studies in the American Race Problem*, 214. On Stone, see Hollandsworth, *Portrait of a Scientific Racist*.

90. William Benjamin Smith, *Color Line*, 4.

91. *Race Problems of the South*, 21.

92. Graves, "Problem of the Races," 9.

93. Ellen Barret Ligon, "The White Woman and the Negro," *Good Housekeeping*, November 1903, 427–28.

94. William Benjamin Smith, *Color Line*, 23–24.

95. *Race Problems of the South*, 39, 43.

96. Thomas Nelson Page, "The Great American Question," *McClure's Magazine*, March 1907, 566.

97. Mrs. L. H. Harris [Corra Harris], "A Southern Woman's View," *Independent*, 18 May 1899, 1354.

98. Typescript, "The Negro Problem: God Takes His Time—Man Must," box 1, folder 3, Atticus G. Haygood Family Papers, Manuscripts, Archives, and Rare Books Library, Emory University, Atlanta, GA.

99. Dixon, *Leopard's Spots*, 44.

100. Ibid., 47.

101. Ibid., 49.

102. See Williamson, *Crucible of Race*, 259–67.

103. On Willcox, see Williamson, *Crucible of Race*, 123. On Thomas, see John David Smith, *Black Judas*.

104. On the memory of Reconstruction, see Baker, *What Reconstruction Meant*. See also Hale, *Making Whiteness*, 75–84.

105. Stone, *Studies in the American Race Problem*, 265.

106. Page, *Negro*, 35.

107. Joel Chandler Harris, "The Negro of To-Day: His Prospects and His Discouragements," *Saturday Evening Post*, 30 January 1904, 3.

108. James K. Vardaman, "Governor Vardaman on the Negro," *Current Opinion*, March 1904, 271.

109. *Race Problems of the South*, 172.

110. Ibid., 35.

111. Avary, *Dixie after the War*, 325.

112. Harris, *Gabriel Tolliver*, 182, 176.

113. Page, *Red Rock*, 564.

114. Woodrow Wilson, "The Reconstruction of the Southern States," *Atlantic Monthly*, January 1901, 1.

115. Laurie F. Maffly-Kipp has argued that turn-of-the-century race histories need to be understood as part of a much longer trajectory of African American historical thought. See Maffly-Kipp, *Setting Down the Sacred Past*, esp. 201–33. See also Stephen Hall, *Faithful Account of the Race*, esp. 151–87. For a more general account of African American memory in the age of Jim Crow, see Brundage, *Southern Past*, 138–82.

116. Novick, *That Noble Dream*, 47–85.

117. Stanford, *Tragedy of the Negro in America*, 13.

118. Johnson, *School History of the Negro Race*, 9.

119. Quoted in Dworkin, *Daughter of the Revolution*, 341.

120. On African American historians and slavery, see John David Smith, *New Creed*, 197–238.

121. Stanford, *Tragedy of the Negro in America*, 32.

122. Maffly-Kipp argues that for turn-of-the-century race historians, emancipation served "as the axis around which the rest of history turned." Maffly-Kipp, *Setting Down the Sacred Past*, 212.

123. Kletzing and Crogman, *Progress of a Race*, 141.

124. Washington, *Story of the Negro*, 28.

125. Kletzing and Crogman, *Progress of a Race*, 188.

126. Stanford, *Tragedy of the Negro*, 99.

127. Ibid., 101.

128. Sinclair, *Aftermath of Slavery*, 38–40, 97.

129. On race histories and the rhetoric of progress, see Blight, *Race and Reunion*, 332–34.

130. Johnson, *School History*, 142–66.

131. Richings, *Evidences of Progress among Colored People*, 436.

132. Kletzing and Crogman, *Progress of a Race*, 607.

133. On the rise and professionalization of turn-of-the-century social science, see Ross, *Origins of American Social Science*. See also Ring, *Problem South*, 175–215.

134. See Moss, *American Negro Academy*.

135. "Announcement," in W. E. Burghardt Du Bois, "American Negro Academy Occasional Papers, No. 2: The Conservation of Races," 4, reprinted in *American Negro Academy Occasional Papers*.

136. Alexander Crummell, "The American Negro Academy Occasional Papers, No. 3: 'Civilization the Primal Need of the Race' and 'The Attitude of the American Mind toward the Negro Intellect,'" 7, reprinted in *American Negro Academy Occasional Papers*.

137. Ibid., 3–4.

138. Ibid., 7.

139. Kelly Miller, "The American Negro Academy, Occasional Papers, No. 1: A Review of Hoffman's Race Traits and Tendencies of the American Negro," reprinted in *American Negro Academy Occasional Papers*.

140. Kelly Miller, "The Anglo-Saxon and the African," *Arena*, December 1902, 575, box 29, folder 6, KMFP.

141. Kelly Miller, "Darkest America," *New England Magazine*, March 1904, esp. 16–18, box 29, folder 10, KMFP.

142. Kelly Miller, "Social Equality," *National Magazine*, February 1905, 524, box 29, folder 16, KMFP.

143. See Lewis, *W. E. B. Du Bois*, 211–37.

144. W. E. B. Du Bois, ed., "The Negro Common School," 1, reprinted in *Atlanta University Publications*, vol. 1.

145. Ibid., 1.

146. Ibid. 118; W. E. B. Du Bois, ed., "Some Notes on Negro Crime, Particularly in Georgia," 65–66, reprinted in *Atlanta University Publications*, vol. 2.

147. Graves, "Problem of the Races," 12–13.

148. William Benjamin Smith, *Color Line*, 178.

149. Stone, *Studies in the American Race Problem*, 13.

150. "Tillman on Lynchings," *New York Times*, 27 July 1903, 2.

151. Graves, "Problem of the Races," 18–19.

152. William Benjamin Smith, *Color Line*, 25–26.

153. "The Inheritance of the Anglo-Saxon," box 16, folder 6, RLFP.

154. "The Race Problem in the United States," box 16, folder 4, RLFP.

155. Untitled manuscript, box 13, folder 4, RLFP.

156. For the connections between imperialism and southern white supremacy, see Ring, *Problem South*, 18–57; Love, *Race over Empire*, esp. 159–95; Greeson, *Our South*, 227–90; Stecopoulos, *Reconstructing the World*; and Schmidt, *Sitting in Darkness*.

157. Jerome Dowd, "Paths of Hope for the Negro," *Century Illustrated Magazine*, December 1900, 280.

158. Ben Tillman, "Causes of Southern Opposition to Imperialism," *North American Review*, October 1900, 444, 446.

159. Clipping, ser. 5, box 2, Scrapbook 11, BRTP.

160. Dixon, *Clansman*, 373. For northern responses to Dixon's work, see Okuda, "Nation Is Born."

161. Du Bois, *Souls of Black Folk*, 34.

162. On northern race and racism in the twentieth century, see Sugrue, *Sweet Land*. See also Matthew D. Lassiter, "De Jure/De Facto Segregation: The Long Shadow of a National Myth," in Lassiter and Crespino, *Myth of Southern Exceptionalism*, 25–48.

1. For background on the film, see Chadwick, *Reel Civil War*, 96–150; Rogin, "'Sword Became a Flashing Vision'"; and Cripps, *Slow Fade to Black*, 41–69.

2. "Miscegenation," *Crisis*, February 1916, 175.

3. On the protests, see Chadwick, *Reel Civil War*, 124–26. Cripps, *Slow Fade to Black*, 51–69; and Sullivan, *Lift Every Voice*, 48–50. As Davarian L. Baldwin notes, *The Birth of a Nation* also led to the creation of a number of African American "race films." Baldwin, *Chicago's New Negroes*, 121–54.

4. On reviews and popularity, see Chadwick, *Reel Civil War*, 130–35.

# Bibliography

ARCHIVAL MATERIALS

Athens, Georgia
  University of Georgia, Hargrett Rare Book and Manuscript Library
    Rebecca Latimer Felton Papers
    John Temple Graves Vertical File
Atlanta, Georgia
  Emory University, Manuscripts, Archives, and Rare Books Library
    Henry Woodfin Grady Papers, 1828–1971
    Joel Chandler Harris Papers, 1848–1908
    Atticus G. Haygood Family Papers, 1861–1952
    Kelly Miller Family Papers, 1894–1989
Austin, Texas
  University of Texas, Harry Ransom Center
    Minstrel Show Collection, 1831–1959
Boston, Massachusetts
  Massachusetts Historical Society
    Edward Atkinson Papers
Cambridge, Massachusetts
  Harvard University
    Houghton Library
      American Minstrel Show Collection, 1823–1947
    Lamont Library
      Albion W. Tourgée Papers, 1801–1924 (microfilm)
Charlottesville, Virginia
  University of Virginia, Small Special Collections Library
    Thomas Nelson Page Collection, 1836–1952
Chicago, Illinois
  University of Chicago
    Ida B. Wells Papers, 1884–1976

Clemson, South Carolina
  Clemson University Special Collections
    Benjamin Ryan Tillman Papers
Durham, North Carolina
  Duke University, David M. Rubinstein Rare Book and Manuscript Library
    Thomas Nelson Page Papers, 1739–1927
Hartford, Connecticut
  Harriet Beecher Stowe Center
    Harry Birdoff Collection
    Uncle Tom's Cabin Collection
Nashville, Tennessee
  Fisk University Special Collections
    Charles W. Chesnutt Collection
    Fisk Jubilee Singers Collection
New Haven, Connecticut
  Yale University, Beinecke Rare Book and Manuscript Library
    Nathan Salsbury Papers
    Yale Collection of American Literature
  Yale University, Irving S. Gilmore Music Library
    South before the War Company Papers
New Orleans, Louisiana
  Tulane University, Amistad Research Center
    American Missionary Association Archives, 1828–1969 (microfilm)
  Tulane University, Louisiana Research Collection, Howard-Tilton
      Memorial Library
    George Washington Cable Papers, 1871–1947
New York, New York
  New York Public Library, Billy Lee Rose Theatre Division
Washington, D.C.
  Howard University, Moorland-Springarn Research Center
    Anna J. Cooper Papers, 1881–1958
    Henry McNeal Turner Papers, 1835–1916
  Library of Congress, Performing Arts Reading Room
    Dumont Collection Songsters (microfilm)
  National Archives
    Records of the Bureau of Refugees, Freedmen, and Abandoned Lands
      (microfilm)
  Smithsonian Archives Center
    Sam DeVincent Collection of Illustrated American Sheet Music,
      ca. 1790–1987
    Warshaw Collection of Business Americana, ca. 1724–1977

## NEWSPAPERS AND PERIODICALS

American Missionary

Annals of the American Academy of
  Political and Social Science

Arena

Atlanta Constitution

Atlantic Monthly

Boston Daily Advertiser

Boston Daily Globe

Boston Herald

Century Illustrated Magazine

Chicago Inter-Ocean

Chicago Tribune

Christian Advocate

Christian Recorder

Christian Union

Cincinnati Commercial

Collier's Weekly

The Crisis

Current Literature

Current Opinion

Daily Arkansas Gazette

Detroit Free Press

Forum

Good Housekeeping

Harper's New Monthly Magazine

Harper's Weekly

Hartford Daily Courant

The Home Missionary

Independent

Los Angeles Times

Louisville Courier-Journal

Manufacturers' Record

McClure's

Metropolitan Magazine

National Freedman

New Mississippian

New National Era

New Orleans Daily Picayune

New York Clipper

New York Freeman

New York Times

New York Tribune

New York World

North American Review

Outlook

Pearson's Magazine

Puck

Raleigh News and Observer

Richmond Planet

San Francisco Chronicle

Saturday Evening Post

Scribner's Monthly

Springfield Daily Republican

St. Louis Globe-Democrat

Washington Post

Zion's Herald

## GOVERNMENT DOCUMENTS

U.S. Congress. *Congressional Globe.* 1865–67.

*Report of the Joint Select Committee to Inquire into the Condition of Affairs in the Late Insurrectionary States, Made to the Two Houses of Congress, February 19, 1872.* Washington, DC: Government Printing Office, 1872.

*Testimony Taken by the Joint Select Committee to Inquire into the Condition of Affairs in the Late Insurrectionary States.* 12 vols. Washington, DC: Government Printing Office, 1872.

*The American Minstrel Songster.* Philadelphia: J. W. Pepper, 1881.

*The American Negro Academy Occasional Papers, 1–22.* New York: Arno, 1969.

Andrews, Sidney. *The South since the War.* Boston: Ticknor and Fields, 1866.

*Atlanta University Publications.* 2 vols. New York: Octagon, 1968.

Avary, Myrta Lockett. *Dixie after the War: An Exposition of Social Conditions Existing in the South, in the Twelve Years Succeeding the Fall of Richmond.* New York: Doubleday, Page, 1906.

Bartlett, John Russell. *Dictionary of Americanisms: A Glossary of Words and Phrases Usually Regarded as Peculiar to the United States.* 4th ed. Boston: Little, Brown, 1877.

Bascom, Dick. *The Carpet-bagger in Tennessee.* N.p.: n.p.,1869.

Bingham, Robert. *The New South. An Address by Maj. Robert Bingham, of Bingham School, N.C., in the Interest of National Aid to Education. Delivered February 15th, 1884, in Washington, D.C.* N.p.: n.p., 1884.

Blair, Lewis Harvie. *The Prosperity of the South Dependent upon the Elevation of the Negro.* Richmond, VA: Everett Waddey, 1889.

Blassingame, John W., and John R. McKivigan, eds. *The Frederick Douglass Papers.* Ser. 1, vol. 4. New Haven, CT: Yale University Press, 1991.

Brodhead, Richard, ed. *The Journals of Charles W. Chesnutt.* Durham, NC: Duke University Press, 1993.

Brown, Helen L. *John Freeman and His Family.* 1864. Reprint, New York: AMS, 1980.

Buell, E. C. *Buell's Ku-Klux-Klan Songster.* New York: Dick and Fitzgerald, 1868.

Cable, George W. *Bonaventure: A Prose Pastoral of Louisiana.* 1888. Reprint, New York: International Association of Newspapers and Authors, 1901.

———. *Dr. Sevier.* 1884. Reprint, New York: Charles Scribner's Sons, 1918.

———. *The Grandissimes: A Story of Creole Life.* New York: Charles Scribner's Sons, 1880.

———. *Madame Delphine.* New York: Charles Scribner's Sons, 1881.

*Celebration by the Colored People's Educational Monument Association in Memory of Abraham Lincoln, on the Fourth of July, 1865.* Washington, DC: McGill & Witherow, 1865.

Chesnutt, Charles W. *The Conjure Woman and Other Conjure Tales.* Edited by Richard H. Brodhead. 1899. Reprint, Durham, NC: Duke University Press, 1993.

———. *The Marrow of Tradition.* 1901. Reprint, New York: Penguin, 1993.

Child, Lydia Maria. *The Freedmen's Book.* Boston: Ticknor & Fields, 1865.

Cooper, Anna Julia. *A Voice from the South.* 1892. Reprint, New York: Oxford University Press, 1988.

De Forest, John W. *Miss Ravenel's Conversion from Secession to Loyalty.* Edited by Gary Scharnhorst. 1867. Reprint, New York: Penguin, 2000.

Dennett, John. *The South as It Is: 1865–1866.* Edited by Henry M. Christman. 1866. Reprint, Baton Rouge: Louisiana State University Press, 1995.

Dixon, Thomas, Jr. *The Clansman: An Historical Romance of the Ku Klux Klan.* New York: Doubleday, Page, 1905.

————. *The Leopard's Spots: A Romance of the White Man's Burden, 1865–1900*. 1902. Reprint, New York: A. Wessels, 1908.

Douglass, Frederick. *Why Is the Negro Lynched? Reprinted by Permission from "The A.M.E. Church Review" for Memorial Distribution*. Bridgewater, UK: John Whitby and Sons, 1895.

*The Dream of "Ellen N." An Illustrated Descriptive and Historic Narrative of Southern Travels. Issued under the Auspices of the Louisville and Nashville Railroad Passenger Department*. Cincinnati: John F. C. Mullen, 1886.

Du Bois, W. E. B. *The Souls of Black Folk*. Edited by David W. Blight and Robert Gooding Williams. 1903. Reprint, New York: Bedford/St. Martin's, 1997.

Dworkin, Ira, ed. *Daughter of the Revolution: The Major Nonfiction Works of Pauline E. Hopkins*. New Brunswick, NJ: Rutgers University Press, 2007.

Edmonds, Richard Hathaway. *The South's Redemption: From Poverty to Prosperity*. Baltimore: Manufacturers' Record, 1890.

Engelhardt, George W. *Richmond, Virginia and the New South*. Richmond: Wm. Ellis Jones, n.d.

*The Excursion Guide of the Virginia Midland Railway: The Short-Line Through-Car Route between the North and South*. New York: Aldine, 1882.

*Facts about Tallapoosa, Haralson County, Georgia, the New Manufacturing City*. N.p.: n.p., n.d.

Field, Henry M. *Blood Is Thicker than Water: A Few Days among our Southern Brethren*. New York: George Munro, 1886.

Fortune, T. Thomas. *Black and White: Land, Labor, and Politics in the South*. 1884. Reprint, New York: Washington Square, 2007.

Foster, Frances Smith, ed. *A Brighter Coming Day: A Frances Ellen Watkins Harper Reader*. New York: Feminist Press, 1990.

Garnet, Henry Highland. *A Memorial Discourse; by Rev. Henry Highland Garnet, Delivered in the Hall of the House of Representatives, Washington City, D.C., on Sabbath, February 12, 1865*. With an introduction by James McCune Smith, M.D. Philadelphia: Joseph M. Wilson, 1865.

Graves, John Temple. "The Problem of the Races." In *The Possibilities of the Negro in Symposium*. 1904. Reprint, New York: Negro Universities Press, 1969.

————. *The Winter Resorts of Florida, South Georgia, Louisiana, Texas, California, Mexico and Cuba. Containing a Brief Description of Points of Interest to the Tourist, Invalid, Immigrant or Sportsman, and How to Reach Them*. New York: C. G. Crawford, 1883.

Hamilton, Gail. *Wool Gathering*. Boston: James R. Osgood, 1867.

*A Handbook of the South*. Chicago: Poole Bros., 1890.

Handy, W. C. *Father of the Blues*. 1941. Reprint, New York: Collier, 1970.

Harlan, Louis, ed. *The Booker T. Washington Papers*. Vol. 3, *1889–95*. Urbana: University of Illinois Press, 1974.

Harper, Frances E. W. *Iola Leroy*. 1892. Reprint, Boston: Beacon, 1987.

Harris, Joel Chandler. *Gabriel Tolliver: A Story of Reconstruction*. 1902. Reprint, Ridgewood, NJ: Gregg, 1967.

————. *Uncle Remus: His Songs and His Sayings. The Folk-Lore of the Old Plantation.* New York: D. Appleton, 1881.

Harris, Joel Chandler, ed. *The Life of Henry Grady: Speeches and Writings.* New York: Cassell, 1890.

Harrison, William H., Jr. *How to Get Rich in the South: Telling What to Do, How to Do It, and the Profits to be Realized.* Chicago: W. H. Harrison, 1888.

Hillyard, M. B. *The New South.* Baltimore: Manufacturers' Record, 1887.

*Horrible Disclosures. A Full and Authentic Exposé of the Ku-Klux Klan. From Original Documents of the Order and Other Official Sources.* Cincinnati: Padrick, 1868.

Ingersoll, Ernest. *To the Shenandoah and Beyond: The Chronicle of a Leisurely Journey through the Uplands of Virginia and Tennessee, Sketching Their Scenery, Noting Their Legends, Portraying Social and Material Progress, and Explaining Routes of Travel.* New York: Leve & Alden, 1885.

Ingersoll, Lurton Dunham, ed. *The Life of Horace Greeley.* New York: Union, 1873.

Johnson, Edward Austin. *A School History of the Negro Race in America from 1619 to 1890, with a Short Introduction as to the Origin of the Race.* Rev. ed. Chicago: W. B. Conkey, 1895.

Kelley, William D. *The Old South and the New.* New York: G. P. Putnam's Sons, 1888.

Kerr, Orpheus. *Smoked Glass.* New York: G. W. Carleton, 1868.

Kimball, Hannibal I. *International Cotton Exhibition 1881: Report of the Director General.* New York: D. Appleton, 1882.

King, Edward. *The Great South.* Hartford, CT: American Publishing, 1875.

Kletzing, H. F., and W. H. Crogman. *Progress of a Race; or, The Remarkable Advancement of the American Negro from the Bondage of Slavery, Ignorance and Poverty to the Freedom of Citizenship, Intelligence, Affluence, Honor and Trust.* 1897. Reprint, New York: Johnson Reprint, 1970.

Knox, Thomas Wallace. *Camp-Fire and Cotton-Field: Southern Adventure in Time of War.* New York: Blelock, 1865.

Langston, John Mercer. *The Other Phase of Reconstruction. Speech of Hon. John Mercer Langston, Delivered at Congregational Tabernacle, Jersey City, New Jersey, April 17, 1877.* Washington, DC: Gibson Brothers, 1877.

Layton, I. Register. *A Pilgrimage South, Under the Auspices of Mary Commandery, No. 36.* Philadelphia: McCalla & Stavely, 1885.

Lester, J. C., and D. L. Wilson. *Ku Klux Klan: Its Origin, Growth, and Disbandment.* 1884. Reprint, New York: AMS, 1971.

Marsh, J. B. T. *The Story of the Jubilee Singers; With Their Songs.* Rev. ed. New York: S. W. Green's Son, 1883.

*The Masked Lady of the White House; or, The Ku-Klux-Klan.* Philadelphia: C. W. Alexander, 1868.

McClure, Alexander K. *The South: Its Industrial, Financial, and Political Condition.* Philadelphia: J. B. Lippincott, 1886.

McKee, George. *Enforcement of the Fourteenth Amendment. Speech of Hon. George S. McKee, of Mississippi, Delivered in the House of Representatives, April 3, 1871.* Washington, F. & J. Rives and G. A. Bailey, 1871.

McKinley, Carlyle. *An Appeal to Pharaoh: The Negro Problem and Its Radical Solution*. New York: Fords, Howard & Hulbert, 1889.

Mebane, George Allen. *"The Negro Problem" as Seen and Discussed by Southern White Men in Conference, at Montgomery, Alabama*. New York: Alliance, 1900.

Morgan, Albert T. *Yazoo; or, On the Picket Line of Freedom in the South: A Personal Narrative*. Washington, D.C.: Published by the Author, 1884.

Morris, Robert C., ed. *Freedmen's Schools and Textbooks*. Vol. 2, *The Freedman's Spelling Book, The Freedman's Second Reader, The Freedman's Third Reader*. 1865. Reprint, New York: AMS, 1980.

Morton, Oliver P. *The South: The Political Situation—Speech of Senator Morton on Louisiana Affairs*. N.p.: n.p., 1874.

*The Nation's Peril. Twelve Years' Experience in the South. Then and Now. The Ku Klux Klan. A Complete Exposition of the Order: Its Purpose, Plans, Operations, Social and Political Significance*. New York: Published by the Friends of the Compiler, 1872.

*The Negro Problem: A Series of Articles by Representative American Negroes of To-day*. New York: James Pott, 1903.

*The Nineteenth Annual Report of the American Missionary Association*. New York: American Missionary Association, 1865.

Nordhoff, Charles. *The Cotton States in the Spring and Summer of 1875*. New York: D. Appleton, 1876.

Northen, William J. *The Negro at the South: Address by W. J. Northen (Ex-Governor of Georgia) before the Congregational Club, Boston, Mass., May 22, 1899*. Atlanta: Franklin, 1899.

*The Oaths, Signs, Ceremonies, and Objects of the Ku-Klux-Klan. A Full Exposé by a Late Member*. Cleveland: n.p.,1868.

Otken, Charles. *The Ills of the South; or, Related Causes Hostile to the General Prosperity of the Southern People*. New York: Putnam's Sons, 1894.

Page, Thomas Nelson. *Necessity for a History of the South, Delivered before the Grand Camp of Confederate Veterans of the State of Virginia, at Its Annual Meeting in the City of Roanoke, June 22, 1892*. Roanoke, VA: Hammond's, 1892.

———. *The Negro: The Southerner's Problem*. New York: Charles Scribner's Sons, 1904.

———. *The Old South: Essays Social and Political*. New York: Charles Scribner's Sons, 1892.

———. *In Ole Virginia; or, Marse Chan and Other Stories*. 1887. Reprint. Nashville, TN: J. S. Sanders, 1991.

———. *Red Rock: A Chronicle of Reconstruction*. New York: Charles Scribner's Sons, 1898.

Palmer, Beverly Wilson, and Holly Byers Ochoa, eds. *The Selected Papers of Thaddeus Stevens*. Vol. 2, *April 1865–August 1868*. Pittsburgh, PA: University of Pittsburgh Press, 1998.

Penn, I. Garland. "The Progress of the Afro-American since Emancipation." In *The Reason Why the Colored American Is Not in the World's Columbian Exposition*.

Edited by Robert Rydell, 44–64. 1893. Reprint, Urbana: University of Illinois Press, 1999.

Pierson, H. W. *A Letter to Hon. Charles Sumner, with "Statements" of Outrages upon Freedmen in Georgia, and an Account of My Expulsion from Andersonville, GA, by the Ku-Klux Klan.* Washington, DC: Chronicle, 1870.

Pike, Gustavus D. *The Jubilee Singers and Their Campaign for Twenty Thousand Dollars.* Boston: Lee and Shepard, 1873.

Pike, James S. *The Prostrate State: South Carolina under Negro Government.* New York: Appleton, 1873.

*Proceedings of the National Convention of Colored Men.* Boston: J. S. Rock and Geo. L. Ruffin, 1864. Reprinted in *Minutes of the Proceedings of the National Negro Conventions, 1830-1864.* Edited by Howard Holman Bell. New York: Arno, 1969.

*Proceedings of the Republican National Convention, Held at Cincinnati, Ohio, Wednesday, Thursday, and Friday, June 14, 15, and 16, 1876.* Concord, NH: Republican Press Association, 1876.

*Race Problems of the South. Report of the Proceedings of the First Annual Conference Held under the Auspices of the Southern Society for the Promotion of the Study of Race Conditions and Problems in the South.* Richmond: B. F. Johnson, 1900.

Redkey, Edwin S., ed. *Respect Black: The Writings and Speeches of Henry McNeal Turner.* New York: Arno, 1971.

Reid, Whitelaw. *After the War: A Tour of the Southern States.* Edited by C. Vann Woodward. 1866. Reprint, New York: Harper Torchbooks, 1965.

Richings, G. F. *Evidences of Progress among Colored People.* 3rd ed. 1896. Reprint, Philadelphia: George S. Ferguson, 1897.

Robertson, E. C. *The Road to Wealth Leads through the South: Solid Facts from Settlers along the Line.* Cincinnati: E. C. Robertson, 1894.

Royster, Jacquelyn Jones, ed. *Southern Horrors and Other Writings: The Anti-Lynching Campaign of Ida B. Wells, 1892-1900.* New York: Bedford/St. Martins, 1997.

*The Scenic Attractions and Summer Resorts along the Railways of the Virginia, Tennessee, and Georgia Air Line.* New York: Aldine, 1883.

Schurz, Carl. *"For the Great Empire of Liberty, Forward!"* New York: John A. Gray & Green, 1864.

———. *The New South.* New York: American News, 1885.

———. *Report on the Condition of the South.* 1865. Reprint, New York: Arno, 1969.

Simond, Ike. *Old Slack's Reminiscence and Pocket History of the Colored Profession from 1865 to 1891.* 1891. Reprint, Bowling Green, OH: Bowling Green University Popular Press, 1974.

Sinclair, William Albert. *The Aftermath of Slavery: A Study of the Condition and Environment of the America Negro.* Boston: Small, Maynard, 1905.

Smith, Gerrit. *Extract from a Speech of Hon. Gerrit Smith, to His Neighbors, in Peterboro, New York, June 22, 1872.* N.p.: n.p., 1872.

Smith, William Benjamin. *The Color Line: A Brief in Behalf of the Unborn.* New York: McClure, Phillips, 1905.

Stanford, Peter Thomas. *The Tragedy of the Negro in America: A Condensed History of the Enslavement, Sufferings, Emancipation, Present Condition and Progress of the Negro Race in the United States of America.* Boston: Charles A. Wasto, 1897.

Stearns, Charles. *The Black Man of the South and the Rebels.* New York: American News, 1872.

Stevenson, Job E. *Ku Klux Klan. Speech of Hon. Job E. Stevenson, of Ohio, Delivered in the House of Representatives, April 4, 1871.* Washington, DC: F. & J. Rives & Geo. A. Bailey, 1871.

Stone, Alfred Holt. *Studies in the American Race Problem.* New York: Doubleday, Page, 1908.

*Summer Resorts and Points of Interest in Virginia, Western North Carolina, and North Georgia.* New York: C. G. Crawford, 1884.

*The Terrible Mysteries of the Ku Klux Klan: A Full Expose of the Forms, Objects, and "Dens" of the Secret Order; with a Complete Description of Their Initiation. From the Confession of a Member.* New York: n.p., 1868.

Tourgée, Albion W. *A Fool's Errand: By One of the Fools.* New York: Fords, Howard, & Hulbert, 1880.

———. *The Invisible Empire.* New York: Fords, Howard, & Hulbert, 1880.

Townsend, George Alfred. *Campaigns of a Non-combatant, and His Romaunt Abroad during the War.* New York: Blelock, 1866.

Trowbridge, John T. *The South: A Tour of Its Battlefields and Ruined Cities.* Hartford, CT: L. Stebbins, 1866.

Turner, Arlin, ed. *Critical Essays on George Washington Cable.* Boston: G. K. Hall, 1980.

———. *The Negro Question: A Selection of Writings on Civil Rights in the South by George Washington Cable.* New York: Doubleday Anchor, 1958.

Turner, Henry McNeal. "The American Negro and His Fatherland." In *Africa and the American Negro.* 1895. Reprint, Miami, FL: Mnemosyne, 1969.

Wardlaw, J. B., Jr. *Southern Literature—Its Status and Outlook: An Address Delivered before the Ladies' Memorial Association of Montgomery County, Virginia at the Montgomery White Sulphur Springs, July 10, 1880.* Macon, GA: J. W. Burke, 1880.

Washington, Booker T. *The Story of the Negro: The Rise of the Race from Slavery.* Vol. 2. New York: Doubleday, Page, 1909.

———. *Up from Slavery by Booker T. Washington with Related Documents.* Edited by W. Fitzhugh Brundage. 1901. Reprint, New York: Bedford/St. Martin's, 2003.

*The Works of Charles Sumner.* Vol. 12. Boston: Lee and Shepard, 1877.


SECONDARY SOURCES

Abbott, Lynn, and Doug Seroff. *Out of Sight: The Rise of African American Popular Music, 1889–1895.* Jackson: University Press of Mississippi, 2003.

———. *Ragged but Right: Black Traveling Shows, "Coon Songs," and the Dark Pathway to Blues and Jazz.* Jackson: University Press of Mississippi, 2007.

Alexander, Shawn Leigh. *An Army of Lions: The Civil Rights Struggle before the NAACP*. Philadelphia: University of Pennsylvania Press, 2011.

Anderson, Toni P. *"Tell Them We Are Singing for Jesus": The Original Fisk Jubilee Singers and Christian Reconstruction, 1871–1878*. Macon, GA: Mercer University Press, 2010.

Andrews, William L. *The Literary Career of Charles W. Chesnutt*. Baton Rouge: Louisiana State University Press, 1980.

Angell, Stephen Ward. *Bishop Henry McNeal Turner and African-American Religion in the South*. Knoxville: University of Tennessee Press, 1992.

Ayers, Edward. *The Promise of the New South: Life after Reconstruction*. New York: Oxford University Press, 1992.

———. "What We Talk About When We Talk About the South." In Edward Ayers et al., *All Over the Map: Rethinking American Regions*, 66–74. Baltimore: Johns Hopkins University Press, 1996.

Baer, Florence E. *Sources and Analogues of the Uncle Remus Tales*. Helsinki, Finland: Academia Scientiarum Fennica, 1980.

Baker, Bruce. *What Reconstruction Meant: Historical Memory in the American South*. Charlottesville: University of Virginia Press, 2007.

Baldwin, Davarian L. *Chicago's New Negroes: Modernity, the Great Migration, and Black Urban Life*. Chapel Hill: University of North Carolina Press, 2007.

Bederman, Gail. *Manliness and Civilization: A Cultural History of Gender and Race in the United States, 1880–1917*. Chicago: University of Chicago Press, 1996.

Benedict, Michael Les. *A Compromise of Principle: Congressional Republicans and Reconstruction, 1863–1869*. New York: Norton, 1974.

Bickley, R. Bruce, Jr. *Joel Chandler Harris*. Boston: Twayne, 1978.

Blight, David W. *Frederick Douglass' Civil War: Keeping Faith in Jubilee*. Baton Rouge: Louisiana State University Press, 1989.

———. *Race and Reunion: The Civil War in American Memory*. Cambridge, MA: Harvard University Press, 2001.

Blum, Edward J. *Reforging the White Republic: Race, Religion, and American Nationalism, 1865–1898*. Baton Rouge: Louisiana State University Press, 2005.

Blum, Edward J., and W. Scott Poole, eds. *Vale of Tears: New Essays on Religion and Reconstruction*. Macon, GA: Mercer University Press, 2005.

Bone, Robert. *Down Home: A History of Afro-American Short Fiction from Its Beginnings to the End of the Harlem Renaissance*. New York: G. P. Putnam's Sons, 1975.

Brown, Thomas J., ed. *Reconstructions: New Perspectives on the Postbellum United States*. New York: Oxford University Press, 2006.

Brundage, W. Fitzhugh. *Lynching in the New South: Georgia and Virginia, 1880–1930*. Urbana: University of Illinois Press, 1993.

———. *The Southern Past: A Clash of Race and Memory*. Cambridge, MA: Harvard University Press, 2005.

Brundage, W. Fitzhugh, ed. *Beyond Blackface: African Americans and the Creation of American Popular Culture, 1890–1930*. Chapel Hill: University of North Carolina Press, 2011.

Buck, Paul. *The Road to Reunion, 1865–1900.* Boston: Little, Brown, 1937.

Butchart, Ronald E. *Schooling the Freedpeople: Teaching, Learning, and the Struggle for Black Freedom, 1861–1876.* Chapel Hill: University of North Carolina Press, 2010.

Calhoun, Charles W. *Conceiving a New Republic: The Republican Party and the Southern Question, 1869–1900.* Lawrence: University Press of Kansas, 2006.

Campbell, James T. *Middle Passages: African American Journeys to Africa, 1787–2005.* New York: Penguin, 2006.

Carby, Hazel. *Reconstructing Womanhood: The Emergence of the Afro-American Woman Novelist.* New York: Oxford University Press, 1988.

Carico, Aaron Yeats. "The Free Plantation: Slavery's Institution in America, 1865–1910." Ph.D. diss., Yale University, 2012.

Carnes, Mark C. *Secret Ritual and Manhood in Victorian America.* New Haven, CT: Yale University Press, 1991.

Cecelski, David S., and Timothy B. Tyson, eds. *Democracy Betrayed: The Wilmington Race Riot of 1898 and Its Legacy.* Chapel Hill: University of North Carolina Press, 1998.

Chadwick, Bruce. *The Reel Civil War: Mythmaking in American Film.* New York: Vintage, 2002.

Chude-Sokei, Louis. *The Last "Darky": Bert Williams, Black-on-Black Minstrelsy, and the African Diaspora.* Durham, NC: Duke University Press, 2006.

Cimbala, Paul. *Under the Guardianship of the Nation: The Freedmen's Bureau and the Reconstruction of Georgia, 1865–1870.* Athens: University of Georgia Press, 1997.

Cobb, James C. *Away down South: A History of Southern Identity.* New York: Oxford University Press, 2005.

Conkin, Paul K. "Hot, Humid, and Sad." *Journal of Southern History* 64, no. 1 (February 1998): 3–22.

Cox, Karen L. *Dreaming of Dixie: How the South Was Created in American Popular Culture.* Chapel Hill: University of North Carolina Press, 2011.

Cripps, Thomas. *Slow Fade to Black: The Negro in American Film, 1900–1942.* 1977. Reprint, New York: Oxford University Press, 1993.

Current, Richard N. "Carpetbaggers Reconsidered." In *A Festschrift for Frederick B. Artz,* edited by David H. Pinkney and Theodore Ropp, 139–80. Durham, NC: Duke University Press, 1964.

———. *Northernizing the South.* Athens: University of Georgia Press, 1983.

———. *Those Terrible Carpetbaggers: A Reinterpretation.* New York: Oxford, 1988.

Dailey, Jane. *Before Jim Crow: The Politics of Race in Postemancipation Virginia.* Chapel Hill: University of North Carolina Press, 2000.

Dailey, Jane, Glenda Elizabeth Gilmore, and Bryant Simon, eds. *Jumpin' Jim Crow: Southern Politics from Civil War to Civil Rights.* Princeton, NJ: Princeton University Press, 2000.

Davis, Keith F. *George N. Barnard: Photographer of Sherman's Campaign.* Kansas City, MO: Hallmark Cards, 1990.

Degler, Carl N. "Thesis, Antithesis, Synthesis: The South, the North, and the Nation." *Journal of Southern History* 53, no. 1 (February 1987): 3–18.

Doyle, Don H. *New Men, New Cities, New South: Atlanta, Nashville, Charleston, Mobile, 1860–1910.* Chapel Hill: University of North Carolina Press, 1990.

Duck, Leigh Anne. *The Nation's Region: Southern Modernism, Segregation, and U.S. Nationalism.* Athens: University of Georgia Press, 2009.

Edwards, Laura F. "Southern History as U.S. History." *Journal of Southern History* 75, no. 3 (August 2009): 533–35.

Elliott, Mark. *Color-Blind Justice: Albion Tourgée and the Quest for Racial Equality from the Civil War to "Plessy v. Ferguson."* New York: Oxford University Press, 2006.

Emberton, Carole. *Beyond Redemption: Race, Violence, and the American South after the Civil War.* Chicago: University of Chicago Press, 2013.

Feimster, Crystal N. *Southern Horrors: Women and the Politics of Rape and Lynching.* Cambridge, MA: Harvard University Press, 2009.

Fletcher, Tom. *100 Years of the Negro in Show Business.* New York: DaCapo, 1954.

Foner, Eric. *Free Soil, Free Labor, Free Men: The Ideology of the Republican Party before the Civil War.* New York: Oxford University Press, 1970.

———. *Reconstruction: America's Unfinished Revolution, 1863–1877.* New York: Harper & Row, 1988.

Frederickson, George. *The Black Image in the White Mind: The Debate on Afro-American Character and Destiny, 1817–1914.* 1971. Reprint, Middletown, CT: Wesleyan University Press, 1987.

Gambill, Edward L. *Conservative Ordeal: Northern Democrats and Reconstruction, 1865–1868.* Ames: Iowa State University Press, 1981.

Gaston, Paul. *The New South Creed: A Study in Southern Mythmaking.* New York: Alfred A. Knopf, 1970.

Giddings, Paula J. *Ida, a Sword among Lions: Ida B. Wells and the Campaign against Lynching.* New York: Amistad, 2008.

Gillespie, Michele K., and Randal L. Hall, eds. *Thomas Dixon Jr. and the Birth of Modern America.* Baton Rouge: Louisiana State University Press, 2006.

Gillette, William. *Retreat from Reconstruction, 1869–1879.* Baton Rouge: Louisiana State University Press, 1979.

Gilmore, Glenda Elizabeth. *Gender and Jim Crow: Women and the Politics of White Supremacy in North Carolina, 1896–1920.* Chapel Hill: University of North Carolina Press, 1996.

Gilroy, Paul. *The Black Atlantic: Modernity and Double Consciousness.* Cambridge, MA: Harvard University Press, 1993.

Godshalk, David. *Veiled Visions: The 1906 Atlanta Race Riot and the Reshaping of American Race Relations.* Chapel Hill: University of North Carolina Press, 2005.

Gossett, Thomas F. *Uncle Tom's Cabin and American Culture.* Dallas: Southern Methodist University Press, 1985.

Grant, Eric Bernard. "'Message in Our Music': Spirituals and the Cultural Politics of Race and Nation, 1871 to 1945." Ph.D. diss., Yale University, 2005.

Grant, Susan-Mary. *North over South: Northern Nationalism and American Identity in the Antebellum Era.* Lawrence: University of Kansas Press, 2000.

Greeson, Jennifer Rae. *Our South: Geographic Fantasy and the Rise of National Literature*. Cambridge, MA: Harvard University Press, 2010.

Hahn, Steven. *A Nation under Our Feet: Black Political Struggles in the Rural South from Slavery to the Great Migration*. Cambridge, MA: Harvard University Press, 2003.

Hale, Grace Elizabeth. *Making Whiteness: The Culture of Segregation in the South, 1890–1940*. New York: Vintage, 1999.

Hall, Jacquelyn Dowd. "'The Mind That Burns in Each Body': Women, Rape, and Racial Violence." In *Powers of Desire: The Politics of Sexuality*, edited by Ann Snitow, Christine Stansell, and Sharon Thompson, 328–49. New York: Monthly Review Press, 1983.

Hall, Stephen G. *A Faithful Account of the Race: African-American Historical Writing in Nineteenth-Century America*. Chapel Hill: University of North Carolina Press, 2009.

Hillyer, Reiko Margarita. "Designing Dixie: Landscape, Tourism, and Memory in the New South, 1870–1917." Ph.D. diss., Columbia University, 2007.

Hinsley, Curtis M. "The World as Marketplace: Commodification of the Exotic at the World's Columbian Exposition, Chicago, 1893." In *Exhibiting Cultures: The Poetics and Politics of Museum Display*, edited by Ivan Karp and Steven D. Lavine, 344–65. Washington, DC: Smithsonian Institution Press, 1991.

Hobson, Fred. *Tell about the South: The Southern Rage to Explain*. Baton Rouge: Louisiana State University Press, 1983.

Hollandsworth, James G., Jr. *Portrait of a Scientific Racist: Alfred Holt Stone of Mississippi*. Baton Rouge: Louisiana State University Press, 2008.

Hunter, Tera W. *To 'Joy My Freedom: Southern Black Women's Lives and Labors after the Civil War*. Cambridge, MA: Harvard University Press, 1997.

Janney, Caroline E. *Remembering the Civil War: Reunion and the Limits of Reconciliation*. Chapel Hill: University of North Carolina Press, 2013.

Jones, Jacqueline. *Soldiers of Light and Love: Northern Teachers and Georgia Blacks, 1865–1873*. 1980. Reprint, Athens: University of Georgia Press, 2004.

Kantrowitz, Stephen. *Ben Tillman and the Reconstruction of White Supremacy*. Chapel Hill: University of North Carolina Press, 2000.

———. *More than Freedom: Fighting for Black Citizenship in a White Republic, 1829–1889*. New York: Penguin, 2012.

Kasson, Joy S. *Buffalo Bill's Wild West: Celebrity, Memory, and Popular History*. New York: Hill and Wang, 2000.

Katz, D. Mark. *Witness to an Era: The Life and Photographs of Alexander Gardner*. New York: Viking, 1991.

Kirby, Jack Temple. *Media-Made Dixie: The South in the American Imagination*. Baton Rouge: Louisiana State University Press, 1978.

Krasner, David. *Resistance, Parody, and Double Consciousness in African American Theatre, 1895–1910*. New York: Palgrave McMillan, 1997.

Larson, Edward J. *Sex, Race, and Science: Eugenics in the Deep South*. Baltimore: Johns Hopkins University Press, 1995.

Lassiter, Matthew D., and Joseph Crespino, eds. *The Myth of Southern Exceptionalism*. New York: Oxford University Press, 2010.

Lawson, Melinda. *Patriot Fires: Forging a New American Nationalism in the Civil War North*. Lawrence: University Press of Kansas, 2002.

Levine, Lawrence W. *Black Culture and Black Consciousness: Afro-American Folk Thought from Slavery to Freedom*. New York: Oxford University Press, 1977.

Lewis, David Levering. *W. E. B. Du Bois: Biography of a Race, 1868–1919*. New York: Henry Holt, 1993.

Link, William A. *Atlanta, Cradle of the New South: Race and Remembering in the Civil War's Aftermath*. Chapel Hill: University of North Carolina Press, 2013.

Lott, Eric. *Love and Theft: Blackface Minstrelsy and the American Working Class*. New York: Oxford University Press, 1993

Love, Eric T. L. *Race over Empire: Racism and U.S. Imperialism, 1865–1900*. Chapel Hill: University of North Carolina Press, 2004.

Lowery, J. Vincent. "Reconstructing the Reign of Terror: Popular Memories of the Ku Klux Klan, 1877–1921." Ph.D. diss., University of Mississippi, 2008.

MacKethan, Lucinda Hardwick. *The Dream of Arcady: Place and Time in Southern Literature*. Baton Rouge: Louisiana State University Press, 1980.

Maffly-Kipp, Laurie F. *Setting Down the Sacred Past: African-American Race Histories*. Cambridge, MA: Harvard University Press, 2010.

Mahar, William J. "Ethiopian Skits and Sketches: The Contents and Contexts of Blackface Minstrelsy, 1840–1890." In *Inside the Minstrel Mask: Readings in Nineteenth-Century Blackface Minstrelsy*, edited by Annemarie Bean, James V. Hatch, and Brooks McNamara, 163–75. Hanover, NH: University Press of New England, 1996.

Masur, Kate. *An Example for All the Land: Emancipation and the Struggle over Equality in Washington, D.C.* Chapel Hill: University of North Carolina Press, 2010.

McElya, Micki. *Clinging to Mammy: The Faithful Slave in Twentieth-Century America*. Cambridge, MA: Harvard University Press, 2007.

McIntyre, Rebecca Cawood. *Souvenirs of the Old South: Northern Tourism and Southern Mythology*. Gainesville: University Press of Florida, 2011.

McPherson, Tara. *Reconstructing Dixie: Race, Gender, and Nostalgia in the Imagined South*. Durham, NC: Duke University Press, 2003.

McWilliams, Dean. *Charles W. Chesnutt and the Fictions of Race*. Athens: University of Georgia Press, 2002.

Meer, Sarah. *Uncle Tom Mania: Slavery, Minstrelsy, and Transatlantic Culture in the 1850s*. Athens: University of Georgia Press, 2005.

Morison, Samuel Eliot. *Oxford History of the American People*. New York: Oxford University Press, 1965.

Moss, Alfred A., Jr. *The American Negro Academy: Voice of the Talented Tenth*. Baton Rouge: Louisiana State University Press, 1981.

Noll, Mark A. *The Civil War as a Theological Crisis*. Chapel Hill: University of North Carolina Press, 2006.

Novick, Peter. *That Noble Dream: The "Objectivity Question" and the American Historical Profession*. New York: Cambridge University Press, 1988.

Nelson, Megan Kate. *Ruin Nation: Destruction and the American Civil War*. Athens: University of Georgia Press, 2012.

Norrell, Robert. *Up from History: The Life of Booker T. Washington*. Cambridge, MA: Harvard University Press, 2009.

O'Brien, Michael. *Conjectures of Order: Intellectual Life and the American South, 1810–1860*. 2 vols. Chapel Hill: University of North Carolina Press, 2003.

———. *The Idea of the American South, 1920–1941*. Baltimore, MD: Johns Hopkins University Press, 1979.

O'Donovan, Susan Eva. *Becoming Free in the Cotton South*. Cambridge, MA: Harvard University Press, 2007.

Okuda, Akiyo Ito. "'A Nation Is Born': Thomas Dixon's Vision of White Nationhood and His Northern Supporters." *Journal of American Culture* 32, no. 3 (September 2009): 214–31.

Ortiz, Paul. *Emancipation Betrayed: The Hidden History of Black Organizing and White Violence in Florida from Reconstruction to the Bloody Election of 1920*. Berkeley: University of California Press, 2005.

Orvell, Miles. *The Real Thing: Imitation and Authenticity in American Culture, 1880–1940*. Chapel Hill: University of North Carolina Press, 1989.

Parsons, Elaine Frantz. "Klan Skepticism and Denial in Reconstruction-Era Public Discourse." *Journal of Southern History* 77, no. 1 (February 2011): 53–90.

———. "Midnight Rangers: Costume and Performance in the Reconstruction-Era Ku Klux Klan." *Journal of American History* 92, no. 3 (December 2005): 811–36.

Perman, Michael. *Struggle for Mastery: Disfranchisement in the South, 1888–1908*. Chapel Hill: University of North Carolina Press, 2000.

Petrie, Paul R. *Conscience and Purpose: Fiction and Social Consciousness in Howells, Jewett, Chesnutt, and Cather*. Tuscaloosa: University of Alabama Press, 2005.

Phillips, Ulrich B. "The Central Theme of Southern History." *American Historical Review* 34, no. 1 (October 1928): 30–43.

Potter, David M. "The Enigma of the South." In *The South and the Sectional Conflict*, 3–16. Baton Rouge: Louisiana State University Press, 1968.

Powell, Lawrence N. "The American Land Company and Agency: John A. Andrew and the Northernization of the South." *Civil War History* 21, no. 4 (December 1975): 293–308.

———. *New Masters: Northern Planters during the Civil War and Reconstruction*. 1980. Reprint, New York, Fordham University Press, 1998.

Prather, H. Leon. *We Have Taken a City: The Wilmington Racial Massacre and Coup of 1898*. Madison, NJ: Farleigh Dickinson University Press, 1984.

Prince, K. Stephen. "A Rebel Yell for Yankee Doodle: Selling the New South at the 1881 Atlanta International Cotton Exposition." *Georgia Historical Quarterly* 92, no. 3 (Fall 2008): 340–71.

Quigley, David. *Second Founding: New York City, Reconstruction, and the Making of American Democracy*. New York: Hill and Wang, 2004.

Rable, George C. *But There Was No Peace: The Role of Violence in the Politics of Reconstruction*. Athens: University of Georgia Press, 1984.

————. *God's Almost Chosen Peoples: A Religious History of the American Civil War*. Chapel Hill: University of North Carolina Press, 2010.

Reed, Bill. *Hot from Harlem: Twelve African American Entertainers, 1890–1960*. Jefferson, NC: McFarland, 2010.

Reynolds, David S. *Mightier than the Sword: "Uncle Tom's Cabin" and the Battle for America*. New York: W. W. Norton, 2011.

Richardson, Heather Cox. *The Death of Reconstruction: Race, Labor, and Politics in the Post–Civil War North, 1865–1901*. Cambridge, MA: Harvard University Press, 2001.

Richardson, Joe M. *Christian Reconstruction: The American Missionary Association and Southern Blacks, 1861–1890*. Athens: University of Georgia Press, 1986.

Riis, Thomas. *Just before Jazz: Black Musical Theater in New York, 1890–1915*. Washington, DC: Smithsonian Institution Press, 1989.

Ring, Natalie J. *The Problem South: Region, Empire, and the New Liberal State, 1880–1930*. Athens: University of Georgia Press, 2012.

Rodrigue, John C. *Reconstruction in the Cane Fields: From Slavery to Free Labor in Louisiana's Sugar Parishes, 1862–1882*. Baton Rouge: Louisiana State University Press, 2001.

Roediger, David. *The Wages of Whiteness: Race and the Making of the American Working Class*. 1991. Reprint, New York: Verso, 2007.

Rogin, Michael. "'The Sword Became a Flashing Vision': D. W. Griffith's *The Birth of a Nation*." *Representations*, no. 9 (Winter 1985): 150–95.

Rosen, Hannah. *Terror in the Heart of Freedom: Citizenship, Sexual Violence, and the Meaning of Race in the Postemancipation South*. Chapel Hill: University of North Carolina Press, 2008.

Ross, Dorothy. *The Origins of American Social Science*. New York: Cambridge University Press, 1992.

Rydell, Robert W. "'Darkest Africa': African Shows at America's World's Fairs, 1893–1940." In *Africans on Stage: Studies in Ethnological Show Business*, edited by Bernth Lindfors, 135–55. Bloomington: Indiana University Press, 1999.

Said, Edward W. *Orientalism*. 1978. Reprint, New York: Vintage, 1994.

Saville, Julie. *The Work of Reconstruction: From Slave to Wage Laborer in South Carolina, 1860–1870*. New York: Cambridge University Press, 1994.

Saxton, Alexander. *The Rise and Fall of the White Republic: Class Politics and Mass Culture in Nineteenth-Century America*. New York: Verso, 1991.

Schmidt, Peter. *Sitting in Darkness: New South Fiction, Education, and the Rise of Jim Crow Colonialism, 1865–1920*. Jackson: University of Mississippi Press, 2008.

Schwalm, Leslie. *Emancipation's Diaspora: Race and Reconstruction in the Upper Midwest*. Chapel Hill: University of North Carolina Press, 2009.

Silber, Nina. *The Romance of Reunion: Northerners and the South*. Chapel Hill: University of North Carolina Press, 1993.

Simmons, Ryan. *Chesnutt and Realism: A Study of the Novels*. Tuscaloosa: University of Alabama Press, 2006.

Simpson, Brooks. *The Reconstruction Presidents*. Lawrence: University Press of
Kansas, 1998.

Slap, Andrew L. *The Doom of Reconstruction: Liberal Republicans in the Civil War
Era*. New York: Fordham University Press, 2006.

Smiley, David L. "The Quest for the Central Theme in Southern History." *South
Atlantic Quarterly* 71, no. 3 (Summer 1972): 307–25.

Smith, John David. *Black Judas: William Hannibal Thomas and the American
Negro*. Athens: University of Georgia Press, 2000.

———. *A New Creed for the Old South: Proslavery Ideology and Historiography*.
Westport, CT: Greenwood, 1985.

Sotiropoulos, Karen. *Staging Race: Black Performers in Turn of the Century
America*. Cambridge, MA: Harvard University Press, 2006.

Stecopoulos, Harilaos. *Reconstructing the World: Southern Fictions and U.S.
Imperialisms, 1898–1976*. Ithaca, NY: Cornell University Press, 2008.

Stout, Harry. *Upon the Altar of the Nation: A Moral History of the Civil War*.
New York: Viking, 2006.

Stowell, Daniel. *Rebuilding Zion: The Religious Reconstruction of the South,
1863–1877*. New York: Oxford University Press, 1998.

Sugrue, Thomas J. *Sweet Land of Liberty: The Forgotten Struggle for Civil Rights
in the North*. New York: Random House, 2008.

Sullivan, Patricia. *Lift Every Voice: The NAACP and the Making of the Civil Rights
Movement*. New York: New Press, 2009.

Summers, Mark Wahlgren. *The Press Gang: Newspapers and Politics, 1865–1878*.
Chapel Hill: University of North Carolina Press, 1996.

Sundquist, Eric. *To Wake the Nations: Race in the Making of American Literature*.
Cambridge, MA: Harvard University Press, 1993.

Taylor, William R. *Cavalier and Yankee: The Old South and American National
Character*. 1957. Reprint, New York: Oxford University Press, 1993.

Taylor, Yuval, and Jake Austen. *Darkest America: Black Minstrelsy from Slavery to
Hip-Hop*. New York: W. W. Norton, 2012.

Toll, Robert. *Blacking Up: The Minstrel Show in Nineteenth-Century America*.
New York: Oxford University Press, 1974.

Trelease, Allen W. *White Terror: The Ku Klux Conspiracy and Southern
Reconstruction*. 1971. Reprint, Baton Rouge: Louisiana State University Press,
1999.

Tunnell, Ted. "Creating 'The Propaganda of History': Southern Editors and the
Origins of Carpetbagger and Scalawag." *Journal of Southern History* 72, no. 4
(November 2006): 789–822.

Trachtenberg, Alan. *Reading American Photographs: Images as History, Mathew
Brady to Walker Evans*. New York: Hill and Wang, 1989.

Ward, Andrew. *Dark Midnight When I Rise: The Story of the Fisk Jubilee Singers*.
2000. Reprint, New York: Amistad, 2001.

Warren, Louis S. *Buffalo Bill's America: William Cody and the Wild West Show*.
New York: Alfred A. Knopf, 2005.

Watts, Trent A. *One Homogenous People: Narratives of White Southern Identity, 1890–1920*. Knoxville: University of Tennessee Press, 2010.

Waugh, Joan. *U. S. Grant: American Hero, American Myth*. Chapel Hill: University of North Carolina Press, 2009.

Webb, Barbara L. "Authentic Possibilities: Plantation Performance of the 1890s." *Theatre Journal* 56, no. 1 (March 2004): 63–82.

Williams, Kidada E. *They Left Great Marks on Me: African American Testimonies of Racial Violence from Emancipation to World War I*. New York: New York University Press, 2012.

Williamson, Joel. *The Crucible of Race: Black-White Relations in the American South since Emancipation*. New York: Oxford, 1984.

Wood, Amy Louise. *Lynching and Spectacle: Witnessing Racial Violence in America, 1890–1940*. Chapel Hill: University of North Carolina Press, 2009.

Woodward, C. Vann. *American Counterpoint: Slavery and Racism in the North/South Dialogue*. Boston: Little, Brown, 1971.

———. *The Burden of Southern History*. 1960. Reprint, Baton Rouge: Louisiana State University Press, 1968.

———. *Origins of the New South*. 1951. Reprint, Baton Rouge: Louisiana State University Press, 1971.

———. *The Strange Career of Jim Crow*. 1955. Reprint, New York: Oxford University Press, 1974.

# Acknowledgments

This book, like all others, has its own story. In its various iterations, it has been part of my life for almost a decade. At Yale University, David Blight believed in the book and its author from the very beginning. David encouraged me to ask big questions and offered a sterling example of committed, passionate, and engaged scholarship. This project began in Glenda Gilmore's research seminar and has benefited from her counsel ever since. Glenda helped me untangle many a confused argument, guided me in the mysterious ways of academia, and continually encouraged a kid from Connecticut who wanted to become a southern historian. Matthew Frye Jacobson opened the wonders of cultural history to a first-year graduate student and then helped me learn to write it. Other faculty members at Yale, notably Robert Stepto, Beverly Gage, Jean-Christophe Agnew, Harry Stout, and Jon Butler, also offered guidance and support.

Since the fall of 2010, I have had the good fortune to work in the history department at the University of South Florida. All of my colleagues have been warm and supportive since day one, but special thanks are due to John Belohlavek, Giovanna Benadusi, Barbara Berglund, Michael Decker, David Johnson, Bill Murray, Fraser Ottanelli, and Phil Levy. Thanks also go to Maura Barrios, Tami Davis, Judy Drawdy, Jennifer Dukes-Knight, and Theresa Lewis, without whom I'd be totally lost. I owe a debt of gratitude to my students at USF, particularly those who have enrolled in my graduate seminars and my Theory of History sections. Though they may not know it, their questions and comments have had a definite impact on my thinking and my argumentation.

Generous funding from a number of sources helped me complete this project. My thanks to the Humanities Institute and the College of Arts and Sciences at the University of South Florida; the Graduate School of Arts and Sciences and the Beinecke Library at Yale University; the Manuscript, Archives, and Rare Book Library at Emory University; and the Gilder Lehrman Center for the Study of Slavery, Resistance, and Abolition. Without the assistance of librarians and archivists from Massachusetts to Louisiana, this would have been a much different (and vastly inferior) book. Though I cannot mention them all individually, I am forever grateful for the guidance, time, and labor so graciously offered by the staff at each repository I visited.

In the late stages of this project, Justin Fewless, Rachel Gilbert, Caitlin Verboon, and Ben Weber saved my neck with some crucial research assistance.

Many thanks to those scholars who have taken the time to discuss my research with me at conferences and other sites, including William Blair, Fitzhugh Brundage, James Cobb, Gregory Downs, Laura Edwards, William Link, Kate Masur, Elaine Frantz Parsons, Jason Phillips, and John David Smith. I would also like to acknowledge panel chairs, commentators, and fellow presenters at annual meetings of the American Historical Association, the Organization of American Historians, the Society of Civil War Historians, the Southern Historical Association, and the Popular Culture Association/American Culture Association. Portions of this work appeared in the *Journal of the Civil War Era*, the *Georgia Historical Quarterly*, and *Storytelling, History, and the Postmodern South*, edited by Jason Phillips. Thanks to the editors and anonymous referees at each of these venues. Finally, I would be remiss if I did not acknowledge Gary Kornblith and Carol Lasser, whose courses at Oberlin College deserve much of the credit (or blame) for getting me into this line of work in the first place.

While working with the University of North Carolina Press, I have had the good fortune to have not one but two wonderful editors. David Perry was an early champion of this project and guided me through the writing and revision process. After Mark Simpson-Vos took over, he expertly moved the project to completion. Thanks are also due to Paula Wald and Alex Martin, who turned a pile of manuscript pages into a book, and Caitlin Bell-Butterfield, who happily answered all my questions, no matter how asinine. I appreciate all the work done by the members of the editorial and production teams at UNC Press. I am also deeply grateful to the manuscript's two anonymous reviewers, who offered extraordinarily detailed and helpful feedback at a number of points. This is a better book because of their hard work.

I have been privileged to spend the past ten years of my life with some of the best friends imaginable. I am certain that I would not have survived graduate school without Carlos Aramayo, Caitlin Casey, Chris Covert, Lisa Covert, Alison Greene, David Huyssen, Eden Knudsen, Grace Leslie, Malcolm McLean, Robin Morris, Dan Peterson, Brenda Santos, Dana Schaffer, Dave Schuller, Jason Ward, and Kirsten Weld. A special thanks to Sam Schaffer, who has been a supporter of this work since our first graduate school seminar and has always been willing to read a draft or eviscerate my notes. Sari Altschuler, Gena Camoosa, Brian Connolly, Scott Ferguson, Darcie Fontaine, Julie Langford, Amy Rust, Adam Schwartz, Michael Spangler, James Turner, Aaron Walker, and the Friday Happy Hour crew have helped to make Tampa my home. An unexpected perk of my research for this book has been the opportunity to spend some time with Anne Fenton, Ciciley Hoffman, Harriet Hurworth, Emily Guder, Jason Guder, Anne Neff, Claire Pettry, Sarah Wallace, and James Weinberger.

My parents, Ken and Jane Prince, have been my biggest supporters throughout this process. I would not be where I am today without their love and encouragement, and I am deeply grateful for everything they have done for me. In the years since I started this project, my sister, Allison Prince, has grown from a little kid into one of my best friends. I enjoy every second we spend together. Though none of my grandparents will ever see this book in print, they are all alive in my memories. Lee and Ann Irwin defy all the negative parent-in-law stereotypes. Their warmth and love have made Lexington, Kentucky, a second home. A multitude of thanks to Jeff Prince and Zig Kantorosinski, who have been unwaveringly hospitable hosts during my many, many, many trips to Washington, DC. The sleeping quarters are nice and the food is wonderful, but the conversation is the best thing of all.

Though I've dedicated this book to Julia Irwin, that honor somehow feels insufficient. For all of the time and energy that she's poured into this book, Julia should probably be listed as a coauthor. Julia is my rock, my muse, my biggest fan, and my partner in crime. Most of all, she's my best friend. Her scholarship and work ethic are inspiring—having a brilliant and talented historian in the house certainly has its advantages. But it is her love and companionship that have made my life wonderful. The time that we spend together is, simply put, the best time I spend. I meant every word I said on that gorgeous April afternoon in 2007. I can't wait to see where we go from here.

# Index

Aesop, 141

African American activists: and definition of South, 5, 209; and white northerners, 11; on Yankeefication of South, 36–39; on Reconstruction, 37, 39; on slavery, 37–38; and black radical tradition, 132; and lynchings, 219, 222, 223–24; counternarratives in Jim Crow era, 219–25, 235–41, 278 (n. 42); and race histories, 235–39, 281 (nn. 115, 122); and race films, 283 (n. 3)

African American rights: declining commitment to, 8, 200; and disfranchisement, 11, 207–15, 219, 225, 227, 243, 246, 278 (n. 42); and Reconstruction, 31; in North, 36–39, 218; and suffrage, 37, 52, 76, 88–89, 207, 213; and Black Codes, 47; and New South, 123–24, 125, 134; and Chesnutt, 161

African Americans: views of carpetbaggers, 10; transition from slavery to freedom, 18, 20, 46; travel writers on, 27–29; on Yankeefication, 36–39; and northern migration to South, 44–45; emigration to Africa, 47; as southern legislators, 53; and deception of carpetbaggers, 54, 81, 82; and Ku Klux Klan, 58, 59, 60, 63, 64, 72, 74–75, 85; and northern interven-

tionism, 88; and New South, 111–12, 122, 123–24, 128, 130, 131, 132, 133; stereotypes of, 111–12, 144, 168; folklore of, 139, 140, 141, 142, 143, 144; in Harris's *Uncle Remus*, 142, 143–44; and Chesnutt's literature, 160, 161; and *Black America*, 166–67; and black uplift, 207, 220. *See also* Freedpeople; Race relations; Slaves and slavery

Aiken, George, 199

Alston, James H., 74

*A.M.E. Church Review*, 223–24

American Academy of Political and Social Science, 216

American Colonization Society, 47, 168

American Home Missionary Society, 33

American Land Company and Agency, 44

*American Missionary*, 41

American Missionary Association (AMA): and Reconstruction, 33, 41, 42, 45–47; and Fisk Jubilee Singers, 168, 173

American Negro Academy, 239–40

American Sociological Society, 228

Ames, Adelbert, 86, 87

Anderson, Toni, 272 (n. 36)

Andrew, John A., 44

Andrews, Sidney, 16–17, 20, 22–23, 25–26, 27, 29

men's Case in Equity," 129–30; and Grady, 130–31; *Old Creole Days*, 135, 153; and race relations, 138, 152, 153, 155–56, 159, 165; and white supremacy, 152, 154, 155; dialect used by, 153; *Madame Delphine*, 153, 155–56, 158; *The Grandissimes*, 153–55, 157; *Bonaventure*, 156, 158; *Dr. Sevier*, 156, 158; and Chesnutt, 160–61

Calhoun, Charles W., 8

Callender, Charles, 182, 184, 185, 186

Capitalism: and New South, 10, 98, 100–101, 109, 110, 114–16; and northern migration to South, 43; and Radical Reconstruction, 50

Carnegie, Andrew, 120

Carnes, Mark C., 259 (n. 58)

Carpetbaggers: as symbol of Reconstruction period, 10, 40, 53, 54–58, 61, 79, 80, 89, 92–93, 233–34, 237; and Republican Party, 10, 53, 54, 55, 57–58, 81, 83, 84, 86–89, 92, 257–58 (n. 3); Democratic Party on, 54, 75, 77, 80; physical descriptions of, 54–55; emergent critique of, 55, 57, 58, 61, 80–89, 258 (n. 18); Liberal Republicans on, 77, 78; as term, 79–80, 83, 257 (n. 1), 258 (n. 3); Radical Republicans on, 81–82; federal government associated with, 86–91; close of era, 90, 93; and New South, 110, 125

Cass, Lewis, 56

*Century Illustrated Magazine*, 129, 136, 157, 279 (n. 54)

Chamberlain, Daniel, 86, 91

Charleston, South Carolina, 16–17, 20

Chesnutt, Charles W.: southern literature of, 11, 137, 138; and race relations, 138; *The Conjure Woman*, 160, 162–65, 270 (n. 108); *The Marrow of Tradition*, 160, 209, 224–25, 279 (n. 72); and Cable, 160–61; political goals of, 160–62, 164, 165, 270 (n. 95); "Literature in Its Relation to Life," 161–62; dialect used by, 162, 163, 270 (n. 100); "The Goophered Grapevine," 162–64; "The Conjurer's Revenge," 164; "Mars Jeems's Nightmare," 164; "Po' Sandy," 164; "Dave's Neckliss," 270 (n. 108)

*Chicago Inter-Ocean*, 82

*Chicago Tribune*: and travel writers, 20; on labor, 32; on Reconstruction, 34, 89; on carpetbaggers, 56, 78, 91; on Ku Klux Klan, 59, 60, 69; on *Black America*, 195

Child, Lydia Maria: *The Freedmen's Book*, 32

Childers, John, 74

*Christian Recorder*, 20, 44, 47, 82, 85, 89

*Christian Union*, 81, 82–83, 87, 118, 126

Churton, Henry. *See* Tourgée, Albion

*Cincinnati Commercial*, 78

*Cincinnati Gazette*, 20

Citizenship: and Radical Republicans, 51, 52; and minstrelsy, 181; and white supremacist southerners, 210–11, 223, 229, 233. *See also* African American rights

Civil rights movement, 248

Civil War: casualties of, 1; effects on South, 1, 2, 15–18, 21–22, 97, 98; and sectional identity, 5, 8; and fall of Richmond, 15–16; and righteousness of northern cause, 19; surrender at Appomattox, 20; and American Missionary Association, 41; and Stowe's *Uncle Tom's Cabin*, 145, 149

Civil War memory, 8, 253 (n. 19), 259 (n. 41)

Clanton, Alabama, 108

Class, 4, 20, 26–27, 32, 34, 177, 198

Clay, Henry, 56

Cleveland, Frances Folsom, 117

Cleveland, Grover, 101, 117–18

Cockran, W. Bourke, 280 (n. 79)

Cody, Buffalo Bill, 201

Coleman, William, 73

Colfax Massacre, 84

Eugenics, 228
Eustis, William T., Jr.: "Religious Reconstruction of the South," 33
Euzelian literary society, 99

Fayetteville, North Carolina, 108
Federal government: and Radical Reconstruction, 49–50, 51; and political violence in South, 69, 72, 84; carpetbaggers associated with, 86–91; and white supremacist southerners, 217–18; and education funding, 241
Feimster, Crystal, 278 (n. 33)
Felton, Rebecca Latimer, 3, 217, 218, 243
Field, Henry M., 117, 118
Fifteenth Amendment, 52, 73, 88, 210, 238, 280 (n. 79)
"The First of the Carpetbaggers," 82–83
Fiske, William, 46
Fisk Jubilee Singers: and southern African American experience, 11; and slave spirituals, 167, 169, 170, 172, 174; and minstrelsy, 167, 173–75, 177, 271 (n. 19); and Fisk University fund-raising, 168–70, 173; European tours of, 169–70, 171, 172, 176; self-presentation of, 170–72, 203; authenticity of, 175–77, 271 (n. 19); ages of, 272 (n. 36)
Fisk University, 168–70, 173
Florida, 90
*Florida Facts* (pamphlet), 113
Fortune, T. Thomas, 132, 133
*Forum*, 136, 216
Foss, James, 113
Foster, Minnie, 201
Foster, Stephen, 174, 181, 192
Fourteenth Amendment, 51, 52, 73, 88, 238
Fowler, Charlotte, 74
*Frank Leslie's Illustrated Newspaper*, 76, 91, 110
Freedmen's Bureau, 46
*The Freedmen's Spelling Book*, 32–33

Freedpeople: slaves transformed into, 18, 20; as northern-style free laborers, 27–29, 32–33, 254 (n. 48); literature for instruction of, 32–33; education of, 32–33, 42, 44, 45, 46, 63; and racial violence, 46; enfranchisement of, 52; and carpetbaggers, 55, 82, 88–89; and Ku Klux Klan, 60, 63
Frisell, Hollis Burke, 279 (n. 79)
Frohman, Charles, 185, 186, 187
Frohman, Gustave, 185, 186, 187

Gardner, Alexander, 15–16
Garnet, Henry Highland, 37–39
Garrison, William Lloyd, 55
Gaston, Paul, 263 (n. 29)
Gender roles, 33–34, 217
General Southern Land Agency, 44
Geography: and southern identity, 4
George, James Z., 218
Georgia, 226–27
Gilded Age: relationship to Reconstruction, 3; relationship between labor and capital in, 8, 101; performance culture of, 11, 167, 168; and New South, 101, 110–11; and minstrelsy, 178, 179–80, 187; and Stowe's *Uncle Tom's Cabin*, 199, 200, 202, 203
Gilder, Richard Watson, 136
Gillette, William, 262 (n. 127)
Gilmore, Glenda, 277 (nn. 26, 29)
Gilroy, Paul, 271 (n. 19)
Gladstone, William, 169
*Good Housekeeping*, 229
Gould, Jay, 120
Grady, Henry W.: role in post–Civil War South, 3; and New South program, 10, 97–98, 102–3, 104, 116, 126, 133; on hard work, 100; on quantification of growth, 106; on industrial growth, 115; and Cleveland's visit to Atlanta, 117–18; on white supremacy, 123; and Cable, 130–31
Grandfather Clause, 208

baggers associated with, 55; and
Fisk Jubilee Singers, 171; and Negro
Problem, 211

Racial egalitarianism: and Reconstruction, 2, 19, 51; late nineteenth-
century abandonment of, 6, 8; lack
of commitment to, 19; and Cable,
152

Racial identity: and Cable, 155–56, 158,
269 (n. 72); and Chesnutt, 160

Racial ideology: and travel writers,
27–28

Racial violence: and Jim Crow, 11, 208;
in North, 37; and freedpeople, 46;
and hostility of white southerners,
47–48, 53, 84; defense of, 209; and
African American counternarratives,
222

Radical Republicans: and Reconstruction, 18, 48–51; and Ku Klux Klan,
59–60, 67; and carpetbaggers, 81–82

Reconstruction: retreat from, 2, 4,
5–6, 8, 9, 10, 81–84, 89, 125, 167,
246, 249, 250; and racial egalitarianism, 2, 19, 51; relationship to Gilded
Age, 3; failed promise of, 8, 82, 98,
210; historiography of, 9; cultural
approach to, 10; northern optimism
concerning, 10, 19, 32, 34–35, 39,
43, 45, 48–49; debates on, 10, 53,
68, 83–84; challenge of, 17, 52–53,
67–68; Radical Reconstruction, 18,
48–51, 52; and Republican Party,
18–19, 30, 34, 54, 84, 89, 254 (n. 48);
purpose of, 19, 53; political work of
travel writers, 22, 25, 30; African
Americans as allies of, 28; Yankeefication of South as ideal of, 31–40;
and education, 32, 40; and free labor
ideology, 32–33; and religion, 33, 41,
42; African American activists on,
37, 39; and hostility of white southerners, 39, 45, 46–48; and northern
migration to South, 39–48, 49,
55–58, 258 (n. 18); Johnson's policies

on, 47; characterization of, 53, 57;
northern sentiments regarding, 54,
83–84, 92–93; Democratic Party on,
75; and election of 1872, 75, 77–79;
and Liberal Republicans, 77; Grant's
policies on, 86, 87, 88, 262 (n. 127);
delegitimization of, 89; memory of,
91–93, 232–35; and New South, 123,
124–25, 129, 132; and race histories,
237–38; and "southern tours," 260
(n. 90). See also Carpetbaggers; Ku
Klux Klan

Reconstruction Acts of 1867, 40, 51, 52

Red Shirts, 53, 84

Regional determinism, 5

Regional identity: as social and cultural construction, 5; and exceptionalism, 6–7, 8, 252–53 (n. 14); and
regional chauvinism, 39, 56. See also
North; South

Reid, Whitelaw, 20, 22, 23, 24–25, 26,
27, 28

Religion: and Reconstruction, 33, 41,
42

Republican Party: and declining
commitment to African American
rights, 8; and carpetbaggers, 10, 53,
54, 55, 57–58, 81, 83, 84, 86–89, 92,
257–58 (n. 3); Radical Republicans,
18, 48–51, 52; and Reconstruction,
18–19, 30, 34, 54, 84, 89, 254 (n. 48);
on Ku Klux Klan, 65–66, 72, 73,
75–77; Liberal Republicans, 77–79;
and noninterventionism policy, 83,
86; and white supremacy, 85; and
views of white southerners, 121

Rial, Jay, 200, 201

Richardson, Heather Cox, 8, 253
(n. 20), 254 (n. 48)

Richings, G. F., 238

Richmond, Virginia, 15–16, 17

*Richmond Planet*, 131

Riis, Thomas, 274 (n. 109)

Ring, Natalie J., 7, 253 (n. 19), 266
(n. 99), 276 (n. 7)

Robertson, Eugene Cook: *The Road to Wealth Leads through the South*, 114

Rock, John S., 37

Rogers, E. O., 200

Said, Edward, 254 (n. 29)

*St. Louis Globe-Democrat*, 100

Salsbury, Nate, 192, 194–96

Sankey, Ira, 169

*Saturday Evening Review*, 228

Scalawags, 53, 86

Schurz, Carl, 20–21, 24, 26, 28, 32, 126

Scott, Robert K., 73

Scott, Walter, 27

Sectional identity, 5, 6, 8, 31, 35–36

Sectional relationship: reunion as model for, 8, 9, 98, 101, 120, 121, 122, 125, 132, 133, 136, 248, 250, 253 (nn. 19, 20), 268 (n. 42); creation of new relationship, 9; evolution of, 10; and assumptions of travel writing, 29–30; and Yankeefication, 39; and carpetbaggers, 91; and New South, 98–99, 101, 109, 115, 118, 119–29, 132, 133–34; and southern literature, 136, 147, 268 (n. 42); and Jim Crow, 208, 241–46

Segregation: transparency of, 11; in North, 37, 38; and Cable, 152, 269 (n. 72); and Fisk Jubilee Singers, 172; and white supremacist southerners, 208, 246, 247; and Negro Problem, 211, 212, 225; and figure of black rapist, 215–16; and African American activists, 219; and race-expert discourse, 227

Seward, William, 66

Shaler, Nathaniel Southgate, 115

Sherman, William Tecumseh, 16, 194

Sickles, Daniel E., 56

Silber, Nina, 8–9, 253 (n. 20)

Simmons, Furnifold, 227

Simmons, Ryan, 279 (n. 72)

Simond, Ike, 198

Sinclair, William Albert, 237–38

*Slavery Days* (plantation show), 191

Slaves and slavery: effects of emancipation on, 1, 2; minstrelsy's idealization of, 11, 168, 177, 178–81, 183, 184–85, 197–98; South defined by slaveholding aristocracy, 17; travel writers on, 30; African American activists on, 37–38; white southerners demoralized by, 66; and Harris's *Uncle Remus*, 139–40, 144–45; and Thomas Nelson Page's plantation fiction, 146, 147–52, 159, 162; and Cable's *The Grandissimes*, 154–55; and Chesnutt's *The Conjure Woman*, 162, 163, 164; and southern-themed performance culture, 167, 168; and Fisk Jubilee Singers, 170–71, 172, 173, 175–76, 203; and plantation shows, 187–92; and Stowe's *Uncle Tom's Cabin*, 199, 203; and Negro Problem, 212; and race-expert narrative, 228; and race histories, 236–37

Slayton's Jubilee Singers, 174

Sledd, Andrew, 231

Smalls, Robert, 221

Smiley, David, 6–7, 252 (n. 6)

Smith, C. H., 200–201

Smith, Charles H., 216

Smith, Gerrit, 78

Smith, Herbert H., 141

Smith, Hoke, 101, 125

Smith, William Benjamin, 212–13, 229–30, 242, 243

Snow, Holofornes, 63

Sotiropoulos, Karen, 275 (n. 112)

South: effects of Civil War on, 1, 2, 15–18, 21–22, 97, 98; competing definitions of, 1, 2–5, 19, 21; and popular culture, 1–3, 4, 7; shifting definitions of, 6; travel writers reporting on, 20–21; Yankeefication of, 31–40; biracial conventions for state constitutions, 52; violence associated with, 62, 63, 65, 66, 67–68, 70, 72, 75, 83, 84–85, 261 (n. 119); Douglass on, 66–67; and noninterventionism policy, 83; values of Old South, 100, 102, 121, 134, 135, 146; race riots in, 208, 214–15. *See also* New South; Sectional relationship; White southerners

*The South before the War* (plantation show), 188–92

South Carolina, 84, 85, 86, 89, 90, 91, 247

Southern exceptionalism, 6–7, 8, 252–53 (n. 14)

Southern identity: reconstruction of, 1, 3, 9; North constructing postwar identity, 4, 7, 10, 19, 31–36; historical literature on, 6–9, 252 (n. 6); and southern-themed performance culture, 10, 11; and southern literature, 150; and civil rights movement, 248

Southern literature: and white southerners, 11, 136–37, 145, 150–51; and "local color," 135–36, 152, 156, 157, 158, 159, 165; Wardlaw on, 135, 267 (n. 1); and southern apologia, 147; political significance of, 165. *See also* Plantation fiction; *and specific writers*

Southern Question: in postbellum period, 3; storytellers involved in, 3, 6; changes in control of, 4–5, 10; debate on, 8, 9, 10, 93; and print culture, 9; and New South, 99, 120, 121, 125, 134; and southern literature, 137, 165; Chesnutt on, 161; and southern-themed performance culture, 168; and minstrelsy, 181; and race histories, 236

Southern Society for the Promotion of the Study of Race Conditions and Problems in the South, 226–27, 233

Southern-themed performance culture: and southern identity, 10, 11; and Fisk Jubilee Singers, 11, 167, 168–77; and *Black America*, 166–67, 192–96, 197, 198, 274 (n. 90), 275 (n. 109); and nostalgia, 167, 270 (n. 2); stage performances of *Uncle Tom's Cabin*, 168, 199–203; and authenticity, 187, 188, 189–92, 194–96; and plantation shows, 187–92, 196. *See also* Minstrelsy

Spooner, John C., 207, 208

*Springfield Daily Republican*, 83

*Springfield Republican*, 78

Stanford, Peter Thomas, 236, 237

Stanton, Edwin, 61

Stearns, Charles, 65

Stephens, Alexander, 47

Stevens, Thaddeus, 49

Stevenson, Job, 69

Stone, Alfred Holt, 228–29, 232, 242

Stone, John Marshall, 218

Stowe, Harriet Beecher: *Uncle Tom's Cabin*, 144–45, 149, 168, 199–203; and *Black America*, 194

*Summer Resorts and Points of Interest in Virginia, North Carolina, and North Georgia*, 111

Summers, Mark Wahlgren, 260 (n. 90)

Sumner, Charles, 48, 55, 66

Sundquist, Eric, 267 (n. 11), 270 (n. 100)

Surratt, Jane, 74

Swearingen Manufacturing Company, 106

Terrell, Mary Church, 224

*The Terrible Mysteries of the Ku Klux Klan*, 70, 71–72

Thirteenth Amendment, 37–38

Thomas, William Hannibal, 231

Thompson, Edward, 63

Tillett, Wilbur Fisk, 100

Tillman, Benjamin, 207, 209, 210, 213–14, 227, 242–43, 244

Tillson, Davis, 46

Toll, Robert, 272 (nn. 41, 42)

*To the Shenandoah and Beyond*, 112

Tourgée, Albion, 3, 31, 45, 67, 91–93, 136, 137

Tourism: and regional identity, 7; and New South, 98, 110–13, 115, 116, 118–19, 134, 265 (n. 71)

of, 25–26, 28–29; on potential of
African Americans as free laborers,
28; hostility of, 39, 45, 46–48, 52–53,
58, 60, 61, 67; stereotypes of, 56,
150; Ku Klux Klan as representative
of, 65–67, 68, 76; violence of, 85;
and New South, 98–100, 101, 127;
Republican Party's views of, 121; as
race experts, 226–35. *See also* White
southern women; White supremacist
southerners

White southern women: rebelliousness
of, 20, 26; fear of African American
men, 215, 216, 217, 218, 278 (n. 33)

White supremacist southerners: and
Jim Crow, 207–10, 241–46, 276 (n. 2);
and African American disfranchisement, 207–15, 219, 225, 227, 243,
246; and segregation, 208, 246, 247;
and Negro Problem, 208–19, 220,
221, 223–24, 225, 226, 234, 249;
and figure of black rapist, 215–17,
218, 224–25; and Montgomery Conference, 226–27; on Reconstruction,
232–33

White supremacy: and definition of
South, 5; minstrelsy's naturaliza-
tion of, 11, 177, 180, 182; opposition
to Reconstruction, 19, 84, 250; in
North, 36; and Freedmen's Bureau,
46; and Ku Klux Klan, 53, 58, 84;
and violence, 85; and New South,
123–25; and Cable, 152, 154, 155; and
Chesnutt, 162; passive acceptance of,
276 (n. 2)

Willcox, Walter, 231, 279 (n. 79)

Williams, Bert, 199
Williams, John Sharp, 227
Williamson, Joel, 276 (n. 8), 277
(nn. 14, 29)
Wilmington massacre of 1898, 214–15,
224–25, 230, 277 (n. 26)
Wilson, Henry, 49, 55
Wilson, Woodrow, 234
Winston, George T., 216, 228
Women: National Women's Rights
Convention, 38; and Ku Klux Klan,
63; washerwomen's strike, 264
(n. 36). *See also* Gender roles; White
southern women
Woodward, C. Vann, 6
World Cotton Centennial Exposition, 118
World's Columbian Exposition, Chicago,
220–21, 274 (n. 90)
Wright, P. T., 173–74

Xulkuk, Nal K., 68

Yankeefication: and labor, 31–33; and
Reconstruction, 31–40; and education, 32–33, 40, 41–42; and religion,
33, 41, 42; and gender roles, 33–34;
northern optimism concerning,
34–35, 39; and homogenization of
sectional identity, 35–36; African
Americans on, 36–39; and northern migration to South, 39–48, 49;
failure of, 47; Radical Yankeefication,
48–51; and New South, 115
Yankee schoolmarms, 53

*Zion's Herald*, 56

CPSIA information can be obtained at www.ICGtesting.com
Printed in the USA
LVOW08s2009071215

465738LV00004B/7/P